MOTIVATION

John P. Houston

University of California, Los Angeles

WITHDRAWN

MOTIVATION

Macmillan Publishing Company
NEW YORK

Collier Macmillan Publishers
LONDON

Macmillan Publishing Company
866 Third Avenue, New York, New York 10022

Collier Macmillan Canada, Inc.

Library of Congress Cataloging in Publication Data
Houston, John P.
    Motivation.

    Bibliography: p.
    Includes index.
    1. Motivation (Psychology) I. Title.
BF503.H68   1985   153.8   84-7899
ISBN 0-02-357150-0

Printing: 1   2   3   4   5   6   7   8   Year: 5   6   7   8   9   0   1   2   3

ISBN 0-02-357150-0

PREFACE

When it comes to writing a textbook, it all boils down to what you have to say and how you say it. I tried to keep those two simple factors in mind while writing this book. Motivation is a varied and fascinating subject. But the topic can be pretty dreary for the undergraduate when the course text covers too much, doesn't include enough, or says poorly what it does say. There is nothing magical or even remotely exotic in my approach. Quite simply, I've tried to provide balanced coverage in an interesting, readable fashion.

My approach is eclectic; this text is not idiosyncratic. The coverage is broad-based and comprehensive without being suffocating. I've included classic material and newer developments without dwelling on dead issues or succumbing to the allure of transitory fads. The text includes what I believe to be the best, the most important, and the most enduring material in the field. Both animal and human research are discussed and efforts have been made to relate the two.

The fascinating thing about motivation is that any given piece of behavior may be looked at, or examined, from so many legitimate perspectives. None of these points of view tells the whole story but each has something to add. For example, suppose we want to understand why a girl hits her younger brother when he steals a piece of cake from her plate. We can study this behavior on a number of levels.

We can, for instance, wonder about what aspects of the nervous system are involved. We can try to determine if the aggression is innate or acquired. The child may have learned to be aggressive. We may pursue the idea that the child has simply modelled her behavior after those around her. Finally we might pursue the possibility that the girl's social environment has contributed to the aggressive behavior, such as might be the case if the child lived in very crowded, uncomfortable circumstances.

In short, motivation is many faceted; it can be understood from a number of equally legitimate points of view. To truly understand motivation one must become familiar with all of these approaches. Accordingly, this text reviews the major approaches to motivation. A quick glance at the detailed table of contents will indicate that coverage begins with the biological approach (Chapters 1–4), moves through the learning approach (Chapters 5–7), and ends with a consideration of the cognitive and social material (Chapters 8–11). This progression represents movement through the levels of study beginning with basic physiological information and concluding with more molar social considerations.

I am confident students will find the book to be easily read and easily understood. I base this confidence upon the success of my introductory text and my learning and memory text. Both of these have been judged to be simply and clearly written.

Fairly complicated source material has been reworked into a form that easily is grasped by the reader. One of my fears is that the student will ask, "What's that got to do with anything?" Accordingly, I've tried to keep the overall focus and structure of the text clearly visible as we move from topic to topic. Transitions are emphasized so that the student will know exactly where we have been and where we are going.

I would like to thank the following for their valuable, essential assistance in preparing this textbook:

Amy D. Bertelson, Washington University
Robert A. Hicks, San Jose State University
John R. Hovancik, Seton Hall University
Virgil C. Nylander, University of Wisconsin–River Falls
Roderick Wong, University of British Columbia

J.P.H.

CONTENTS

SECTION 3   *Learning, Drives, and Incentives*

Cognitive Approaches   **SECTION 4**

CHAPTER 8   *Cognitive Consistency and Expectancy Value Theory*   221

Introduction to
Motivation

CHAPTER 1

$\downarrow$

Definitions, Approaches, and the Plan of the Book

UNREQUITED LOVE: AN EXAMPLE

The study of motivation is complex and diverse because, when we really think about it, we find that our motives, or the determinants of our actions, are complex and diverse. Consider the following example of motivated behavior. A young man attends a social gathering and is immediately struck, almost stunned, by the breathtaking poise and beauty of a particular young woman. The young man screws up his courage and makes his move; he approaches the young woman with what he hopes is an irresistible ironic grin. It appears to work; she approaches him with a smile. His hopes soar, but then they are dashed as she brushes past him to welcome with a hug some large stranger who is immediately loathed by the young man. If those near the young man had been listening, they might have heard him mutter, "Halibut face," as he blushed and sulked away. Much later that evening the young man and several of his rowdy acquaintances are picked up by the local police as he is about to heave a second rock through the front window of the local market. The question is why did he throw the rock; what were his motives?

It is at this point that the difficulty of the task facing the psychologist who is interested in motivation becomes clear. Is it tempting, on the face of it, to conclude that our subject was just taking out his frustration and anger on that huge, clean, inviting, plate glass window. And there may very well be some truth in this interpretation; people are often driven to hostile and aggressive acts by a sense of frustration. But to leave it at that, to conclude that we had successfully identified the cause of his action, would be to seriously oversimplify the situation.

For instance, the rock-throwing incident might have had nothing at all to do with the earlier social rejection. It might have had more to do with that rowdy bunch of friends. Our subject may have thrown the rock to impress them or to gain their acceptance. Or he might have thrown the rock to end a long spell of boredom; it was a novel and exciting thing to do. And before we were certain that we understood the causes of this piece of antisocial behavior we would have to consider possible physical or biological determinates, such as neural disease, hormonal imbalance, or genetic defects. Similarly, we would have to consider the possibility that, in this particular individual, antisocial activities had been rewarded. The behavior may have been learned at some time in the past.

So you can see that any given bit of behavior can have many different causes or determinants. It is this very complexity that intrigues the motivation psychologist, and it is this diversity which the motivation psychologist is determined to unravel and comprehend.

Multiple Causes Clearly the situation is complicated by the fact that behavior can be, and in all likelihood is, multiply determined. Behavior can be determined by the intricate interplay of many different factors. For example, the rock may have been thrown because the thrower was angry, frustrated, trying to impress his friends, drawn irresistibly by that smooth expanse of expensive plate glass, seeking excitement on a boring night, wanting to be caught and punished, and/or growing a brain tumor.

This book describes what psychologists have learned about the fact that there may be many interacting causes or determinants of any given segment of behavior. The results of their studies are not all in; there may be more questions than answers in this field, but progress is being made, and the study of motivation is alive and vital.

Multiple Effects Just as one piece of behavior can have multiple interacting causes so too can one causal factor lead to different kinds of behavior. Two points should be noted here. First, a given causal factor does not always lead to identical behavior in different individuals. For example, being rejected by a desirable person might lead one individual to throw a rock whereas another person might be prompted to crawl under one. Still other individuals might laugh at themselves, or not be affected at all. In other words, the principles of motivation are not going to be simple. A given factor or event does not always lead to the same behavior in all individuals. Second, a particular causal factor does not always lead to the same behavior even in a given individual. For example, being frustrated at a party might lead to a hostile act on one night but not on another. Being hungry might lead to the consumption of a hot fudge sundae on one occasion but to self-righteous abstinence on another occasion. Why the same condition leads to different behaviors on different occasions is part of the puzzle that captivates the motivation psychologist.

DEFINING MOTIVATION

Take a moment and try to define the word *motivation*. Psychologists also find this a difficult task. The word *motivation* is like so many other words, such as *learning*, or *development*, or *cognition*, that we all use, but don't really pin down with a concise definition. We feel we have the gist of the matter, or a good sense of what motivation refers to, but we all, psychologists included, fail when it comes to framing a universally acceptable definition.

The problem with the term *motivation* is that it encompasses so much. The diversity of the topics and concerns traditionally included under the rubric of motivation will be made clear from a glance through the subject index of this book.

Dictionary definitions of motives usually involve statements such as, "Something that causes a person to act" (Merriam-Webster, 1974). Although they are adequate for some purposes, these sorts of definitions leave a lot to be desired, as they are too vague and all-encompassing to be of much help.

Many modern psychologists have taken a different tack in trying to characterize motivation. Specifically, they have pointed out that when we speak of motivation we refer to factors which *initiate* and *direct* behavior, and to those that determine the *intensity* and the *persistence* of that behavior. We look at each of these aspects of the overall concept of motivation separately.

Initiation   Motivational factors initiate behavior. If we see a duck lying down in a meadow and suddenly the animal stands up and begins to walk, or quack, or both, we say, "Aha! Motivation at work." We may not know the exact nature of that motivation (who knows why ducks do all that quacking) but we are pretty sure it is operating. So when we see an animal shift from the absence of an activity to the performance of that activity, we say that motivation must be involved. Hunger initiates food seeking, loneliness initiates people seeking, pain initiates withdrawal or sometimes attack, fatigue leads to sleep, stress can lead to disease, and so on.

Direction   Motivation directs behavior and also initiates it. When we are hungry we move toward food, not toward pinball machines. When we are sleepy we seek rest, not sky diving. When we are motivated by a desire for thrills and excitement, we may well try sky diving. We certainly would not seek a darkened, quiet room. Thus, motivation gets us up and going, it energizes us, and it defines the direction or nature of the resulting behavior.

Intensity   Psychologists point out that motivational factors often determine the intensity of behavior as well as its initiation and direction. The longer we have gone without water the more intense our effort to locate water will be. If we find water, and drink it the motive and associated water-seeking behavior will be reduced. The speed with which we remove ourselves from the premises will be determined by the amount of fear we experience which, in turn, is determined by the size of that snarling dog rushing at us. As we see in upcoming chapters, the strength of a motive has important, and sometimes surprising and unexpected, effects on behavior.

Persistence   Closely tied to the preceding elements is the fact that the persistence of behavior is also determined by motivational factors. How long we keep at a particular activity is linked to our motives. If we want success we may work steadily for years in the pursuit of achievement. On the other hand, if we are not particularly achievement oriented, or if our desire for achievement wanes, we may give up quite soon.

It is a mistake to assume that as the intensity of behavior increases so does our persistence. The two can parallel one another, as in the case of an individual who works long, hard hours to attain a law degree. But sometimes the individual tries intensely for short periods of time and then gives up, as in the case of a seventy-three-pound nine-year-old trying to ring the carnival bell with a sledge hammer. Or another individual might never quite give up a goal but pursue it only in a desultory manner, as in the case of a person taking occasional, random college courses in the vague hope of someday attaining a degree.

In other words, even though initiation, direction, intensity, and persistence are all directly related to motivational factors, they are not related to one another in simple straightforward ways. Motivational factors, originating both from within and from without the organism, have a way of operating in tangled, interesting, and sometimes apparently contradictory ways.

Although we have presented the four characteristics of motivation in a straightforward manner, we must qualify this way of defining motivation. First, not all researchers agree that all four of these features are essential in characterizing motivation. Perhaps it is only the energizing quality of motives that is accepted by all thinkers in this area. Direction, intensity, and persistence are often seen as being more the result of learning and other factors than they are of motivational factors.

Some Reservations and Variations

Nevertheless, these four factors are often mentioned, alone or in some combination, and one should be aware that they constitute the major elements in most characterizations of motivation.

Another problem in the emphasis upon these four factors is that there may be *additional* characteristics of behavior which can be explained through the use of motivational variables. Some feel that these four factors are too few rather than too many.

For example, some point out that it is very difficult to speak of motivation without invoking the concept of *emotion* and without trying to account for the fact that motivational states lead regularly to emotional changes. Furthermore, some believe that the *variability* of behavior should be explainable in terms of motivational factors, as well as its energy, direction, initiation, and persistence. So, when thinking about a definition, remember that beyond the basic idea that motives energize behavior, there is considerable debate about exactly what motives do and do not account for.

Another point that ought to be kept in mind is that not all behavior is motivated. For example, when the doctor hits your knee with that little rubber hammer the knee-jerk response you display is not usually thought to be a motivated behavior; it is an automatic reflexive response which involves the spinal column and little else.

APPROACHES TO MOTIVATION RESEARCH

Levels of Analysis

When we try to understand anything at all, whether it be a person, a group, a country, a machine, or an animal, we can look at our subject matter from a number of different points of view. For example, if we are studying a nation, we can focus upon the people of that nation, its geography, its form of government, or its economy. Depending upon our interests and purpose we can look into one, more, or all of those components, as well as other facets of the overall picture. Knowledge gained on one level of analysis often facilitates understanding on other levels. For example, understanding of the economy of a particular country may well be enhanced by the fact that we know that particular country is landlocked, or alpine, or in the equatorial region. In other words, even though we often restrict our investigatory efforts to a single level, we should be aware that information obtained by other investigators, adopting a different focus or orientation, is also valuable.

The same is true in the study of motivation. Several different points of view have developed within this field. Certain investigators, because of their training and interests, emphasize one level of analysis over others, but none would argue that his is the only way to look at motivation.

The perspectives that have developed within the field of motivation include the *biological*, *learning*, *cognitive*, and the *social* approaches. Each of these points of view is valuable and interesting. Because the distinctions among them are so important in the field we look at each of them individually.

The Biological Approach

Psychologists who adopt the biological approach try to understand motivation by investigating its physiological underpinnings. They want to understand the complex *genetic*, *neural*, and *hormonal* factors that are involved in motivation. As an analogy, think of a computer.

Some people will be satisfied if they understand how to use the computer, but this will not be enough for others; they will want to look inside the computer and discover how its circuitry is laid out and how it operates. In a like manner, psychologists adopting the biological approach want to understand how that most complex of all machines, our body, works. They want to understand the electrical, mechanical, and chemical events that form the basis of observable behavior.

As an example, let us consider aggression as a form of motivated behavior that can be understood on a number of different levels. Certainly there is enough violence around us to compel us to try to understand, or at least minimize, it (because it is so important, we return to the study of aggression several times in this text). Obviously, the biological approach is not limited to a consideration of aggression; we merely present it as a convenient example.

Genetic Factors.   Some psychologists who have adopted the biological perspective have asked whether aggressive tendencies are partly or wholly inherited. The answer seems to be that genes do at least influence aggressive behavior. For example, you have probably already heard of fighting dogs and fighting cocks that have been selectively bred for aggressiveness. And in a controlled study, mice have been bred for both high and low levels of aggressiveness (Lagerspetz, 1964).

Neural Factors.   Psychologists who have adopted a biological approach are often interested in the neural underpinnings of the behavior they are studying. Thus, in connection with our sample behavior, it has been suggested that somewhat different neural systems and different parts of the brain are involved in different types of aggressive behavior (Moyer, 1976).

Hormonal Factors.   Hormones also appear to be heavily involved in aggressive behavior. Those of you who have watched a professional hockey game have noticed the aggressive and physical nature of the action. At least some of this highly paid aggressive behavior has been linked to the hormone testosterone. Scaramella and Brown (1978) found, that, among hockey players, testosterone levels correlated positively with degree of aggressive behavior.

Aggression As Instinct? Another issue that is discussed in greater detail later has to do with whether aggressive behavior is an innate, instinctive drive, or something that is learned and influenced by experience. This issue has generated a fascinating controversy with emphatic proponents on both sides.

The Learning *Approach* Although the biological approach, with its emphasis upon nerves, genes, and chemicals, is intriguing and valuable, it is not the only approach to understanding motivation. The second major tradition that has developed within the field may be termed the *learning approach.* Put very simply, this approach is concerned, first, with how motivation is learned or affected by experience, and, second, how motivation influences what we learn and how we express that learning.

Can Motivation Be Learned? One of the puzzles that interests psychologists adopting the learning approach is the extent to which motivated behavior is learned. For example, a controversy swirls around the idea that aggressive behavior is learned when it is rewarded. If a young child gets her way every time she bites or kicks she may adopt this form of behavior as one of her standard ways of dealing with her world. If, on the other hand, she is not rewarded for her aggressive behavior, or is even punished for it, then, according to the learning approach, she will not take on this form of dealing with the environment. Clearly, the issue of learned or acquired motivation is a complex one; it forms the basis of much of the discussion in Section III of this text.

How Does Motivation Affect Learning? We can turn the issue around and ask about the extent to which learning is affected by motivation. The impact is enormous. If two equally bright children enter the first grade, with one interested in learning to read whereas the other's primary goal is in creating hilarious disorganization in the classroom, these different kinds of motivation will be reflected in the reading levels of the two children at the end of the term. In other words, the proponents of this particular approach argue that to learn very much one must be motivated and rewarded for one's performance. (As you might suspect, other theoreticians argue that it is possible to learn in the absence of motivation.)

Another of the intricate relationships between learning and moti-

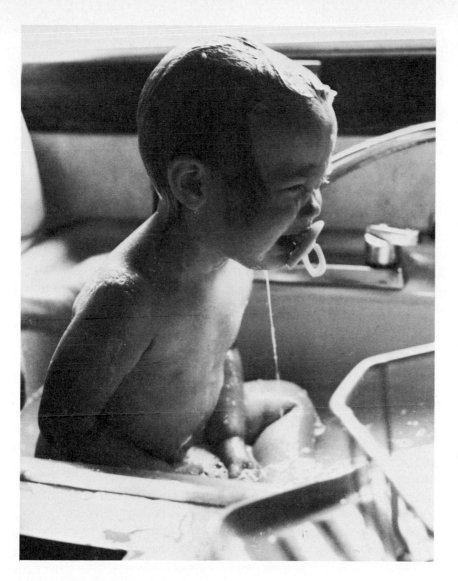

Can motivation be learned? If this child is rewarded for crying behavior while being bathed, she may be motivated to cry in the future. (Courtesy of J. D. Anker.)

vation is that expression of information that has been learned in the past, as well as new learning, will be affected by motivation. For example, suppose several equally bright children have learned a vocabulary list equally well; their past learning is the same. Now they are tested for their knowledge and it is found that their scores vary widely in spite of the fact that we know they had all learned the material equally well. Why? We must look for differences in motivation among these children to account for their different test scores. Perhaps we will find that one child was sick and thus disinterested in the test, whereas another may have been distracted by a recent family problem. Still another child might have panicked or froze during the test. The child that does the best on the vocabulary test will be the one whose motivational status is such that her full resources and concentration will be focused on retrieval of the stored words. In other words, motivation can block or facilitate the expression of previously learned information, just as it can block or facilitate new learning.

The Cognitive Approach   The third perspective within the field of motivation may be termed the *cognitive* approach. Although this approach has its roots in a great deal of earlier work, recent years have witnessed an upsurge of interest in cognitive process, not just in connection with motivation but as an area of research and thinking in and of itself.

Essentially, the study of cognition involves the study of complex mental events. The cognitive approach allows us, encourages us, to "look inside the head" and to investigate complex processes such as *knowing, perceiving, thinking, judging, reasoning, imagining, conceptualizing,* and *using language* (Houston, 1981).

In brief, the history of the cognitive approach is as follows. Early in the investigation of human psychology there was a willingness to try to explore and understand complex cognitive events. The "contents of consciousness" was a legitimate concern of the psychologist. But as the difficulties involved in trying to measure or quantify the contents of consciousness became apparent (how do you scientifically measure a mental image or a thought?) a reaction set in. Behaviorism, as the reaction is commonly labeled, maintained that we weren't getting anywhere by trying to study these elusive mental processes, and that the best way to practice psychology is to restrict our attention to overt, measurable, observable behavior. The idea was that because science requires strict measurement we must restrict our attention to what can be accurately measured (observable behavior) and must not confuse the picture by even attempting to study what "goes on in the mind."

But now the pendulum has swung the other way again; the cognitive approach is becoming increasingly popular. The feeling is that now that we have had time to develop new and better experimental techniques and methods of measurement, we can fruitfully study complex mental events.

The following examples show how complex cognitive events are an integral part of our overall motivational apparatus. Both examples emphasize the cognitive psychologists' contention that our thoughts motivate our behavior and both show that what we think about a situation will affect how aggressive we become.

It's All a Matter of Expectations. Imagine two students who have received a grade of C. One of the students is relieved and content; the other is furious and verbally assaults the instructor. How can it be that the same grade produces such different reactions? The difference lies in the students' expectations. The contented student expected a D or perhaps even an F whereas the disgruntled individual was sure he had earned an A in the class. Because of the ways they had been thinking about the situation, one student was overjoyed whereas the other was bitter and aggressive. This example demonstrates how cognitive factors, how we think about situations, can heavily affect our motivational status. In later chapters we see how the impact of expectations have been demonstrated in carefully controlled experimental situations (see Worchel, 1974).

He Didn't Mean It. Imagine two youngsters on a ballfield. Both are hit on the back of the head by stray softballs. One of the two becomes angry and aggressive whereas the other does not. Why?. Again the evocation of aggression has to do with the individual's evaluation of the situation, or her or his thoughts about what is going on. The youngster who reacted mildly concluded that the offending softball was not intentionally aimed at her head; it was an accident. The irate youngster concluded that the beaning was intentional and, as a result, he was steamed about it. The general principle here, which again demonstrates the role of cognition in motivation, is that the victim must perceive the event as intended to harm if it is to stimulate aggression (Kulik and Brown, 1979).

In summary, the cognitive approach, which is covered in greater detail in Section IV, emphasizes the enormous extent to which our own cognitive processes, our thinking, and our perception affect the initiation and persistence of a wide range of motivated states.

The Social
Approach

The social approach to the study of motivation emphasizes the extent to which people affect other people. This approach focuses upon the fact that people have a lot to do with evoking, modifying, maintaining, and terminating motivational states in other people.

You are correct if you are thinking that perhaps there may be a good deal of overlap between the cognitive approach and the social approach. The two approaches do have important points of contact. However, psychologists who adopt the social approach are particularly interested in the impact of people upon people. These psychologists focus on, or restrict their attention to, the motivational effects of other people.

Again, a few examples should help introduce you to this point of view which is considered in greater detail in Chapter 10.

Imitation: Bobo Dolls and Television Violence. Research has shown that people will imitate one another, or model their behavior after the behavior they observe going on around them. This kind of modeling occurs in connection with all sorts of behavior, ranging from language usage to violence and aggression. In other words, what we do often mimics the behavior of those around us.

In a now classic study, Bandura, Ross, and Ross (1961) had children watch adults interact with a five-foot inflated plastic doll called Bobo. In one condition the adults verbally and physically assaulted the doll, punching it, kicking it, and screaming at it. In a second condition the adults virtually ignored the doll. Then, some time later, the children were left alone for twenty minutes with a set of toys including a three-foot Bobo doll. The children who had watched adults abuse a Bobo doll were much more likely to behave aggressively toward their Bobo doll than were the children who had watched the adults ignore the doll. They punched, kicked, hammered, and shouted in a manner similar to that of the adults. In an unsettling manner, this study demonstrated that, through a process of imitation, children displayed increased aggressive behavior.

For some time now a controversy has swirled around the impact of media violence, and, in particular, television violence, upon violence and crime in our society. The fear has been that the substantial amounts of media violence witnessed by people will make them more aggressive. Through imitation and/or other processes, perceived violence may beget violence. Laboratory studies suggest that observed aggression does lead to increased aggression. However, at present, there is very little good, hard data to suggest that media violence leads to violence and crime in the world outside the laboratory (Freedman, Sears, and Carlsmith, 1981). We return to this fascinating and controversial topic in Chapter 11. For now, it is enough to understand that our motives and action do at least sometimes seem to be copied from those around us.

Crowding.   Studies on crowding may also serve as an example of the way that social conditions and interactions can affect our behavior. Freedman (1975) summarizes data which suggest that crowding can sometimes intensify whatever happens to be going on. Thus, if angry, hostile people are thrown together under crowded conditions, then we might expect an increase in aggressive behavior. On the other hand, if happy, excited people are pressed into a crowd then we might expect an increase in positive responses. In other words, the effects of people upon people, although substantial, are not simple, as we see in Chapter 11.

Thus far we have seen that several different approaches to the study of motivation have dominated the area, including the biological, learning, cognitive, and social points of view. Although any particular psychologist may work exclusively within one of these traditions and never stray far beyond the confines of that discipline, it would be unfair to say that these investigators are narrow-minded or possessed of inescapable tunnel vision. To the contrary, modern researchers are well aware of the full range of studies being done in the field, and are fully conscious of the value of that work. It is because of their training and their interests that these researchers focus on the field in a certain way. In addition, recent years have witnessed an increase in what we may call the eclectic approach. According to this approach, which tries to draw the best from the traditional approaches, we need to bring together, to somehow synthesize, the data gathered in diverse experimental settings and by diverse investigatory procedures. According to this approach, all points of view have something to offer, and a final, comprehensive understanding of motivation can only occur if we attend to the many available levels of analysis. Chapter 11 represents an example of the eclectic approach.

The Eclectic Approach

TOPICS VERSUS LEVELS OF ANALYSIS

Sometimes, in trying to organize their thinking about the field of motivation, or get a grip on the overall structure of the area, students welcome a distinction we can make between *topics* and *levels of analysis*. As we have already seen, levels of analysis refer to the particular focus we adopt when we look at motivation phenomena. Thus, we have discussed the various levels including the biological, learning, cognitive, and social. *Topics*, on the other hand, refer to the particular *kind* of motivation we are looking at, such as aggression, hunger, sex, love, thirst, or stress, and so on.

Now logically, and this is the important point, *any topic can be investigated on any level*. Thus, as we have seen, we can study the biological, learning, cognitive, and social aspects of aggression. The same can be said for any form of motivation. For example, hunger is something that can be approached on any level of analysis. We know a good deal about the biology of hunger, but we also have interesting data drawn from the learning level (e.g., learned habits affect obesity), the cognitive level (e.g., dieting is affected by how we think about ourselves), and the social level (e.g., other people have a lot to do with how much we eat).

It is important to keep in mind that data obtained on one level do not negate the importance of data gained on another level; quite the opposite is true. A full, comprehensive understanding of any motivation phenomenon must draw upon diverse sources of information.

By keeping in mind the distinction between levels of analysis and topics, the reader can sometimes avoid confusion and maintain a clear picture of exactly what is being discussed as we move through our chapters filled with varied and unique information.

THE PLAN OF THE BOOK

Because it provides a neat, helpful organization, this book is based upon levels of analysis rather than topics. Others (see Franken, 1982) have successfully used the alternative organization, which is based upon an attempt to look at many different topics on all levels. We begin, in Section II, by looking at those topics that are usually explored in connection with a biological approach. These include ethology, hunger, thirst, sex, arousal, stress, and sleep. In Section III we explore the learning approach including classical and instrumental conditioning, reinforcement, drive theory, and incentive motivation. In Section IV, the cognitive section, we discuss cognitive consistency, expectancy-value theory, achievement motivation, and attribution theory. In Chapter 10 we focus upon social motivation including topics such as conformity, obedience, morality, affiliation, liking, and loving. Finally, in Chapter 11, we analyze aggression on all four levels of analysis as an example of the eclectic approach.

SUMMARY

1. Motivated behavior is complex and diverse.

2. Behavior can be, and often is, multiply determined.

3. A single causal factor can lead to different kinds of behavior in different individuals and different behaviors in the same individual at different times.

4. Motivation is difficult to define.

5. Some people believe that motivational factors initiate and direct behavior and also account for its intensity and persistence.

6. Others believe that only the energizing quality of motivation is clear-cut. Still others believe that additional factors, such as variability and emotion, should be included in a characterization of motivation.

7. The biological approach to motivation focuses on genetic, neural, and hormonal factors.

8. The learning approach to motivation emphasizes the facts that motivation can be learned and that learning can be affected by motivation.

9. The cognitive approach to motivation looks at the influences of complex mental events such as knowing, thinking, perceiving, and reasoning upon motivation.

10. The social approach to motivation emphasizes the extent to which people affect other people.

11. An eclectic approach recognizes the complexity of motivation and draws upon all of these perspectives.

12. Any topic can be studied on several different levels.

Biological Mechanisms

SECTION II

CHAPTER 2

↓

Instincts and Ethology

WHAT IS AN INSTINCT?

After having dashed into traffic and pulled the child out of the path of an oncoming bus, the heroine is interviewed by the local newspaper reporter. She says, "I didn't even think about it. I just instinctively ran out and grabbed him."

We all use the word *instinct* occasionally. If asked for a definition of instinct, we would probably hesitate for a moment and then say something like, "It's when you react automatically to something." Even though we may not be very good at framing tight definitions of *instinct* we all have a pretty good idea of what we mean by the word. It refers to behavior that seems to be innate, predetermined, and unlearned. It is genetically determined behavior that does not have to be learned and it is relatively unaffected by experience. As Cofer and Appley (1964) put it, instinct is, "an inherited, specific, stereotyped pattern of behavior" (p. 60).

Most investigators emphasize two important aspects of instinctive behavior. First, instinctive behavior is assumed to be unlearned in the sense that its expression is not dependent on prior experience that the animal may have had. Second, it is assumed to be species-specific. Thus, if *all* members of a given species of bird build nests in exactly

INSTINCTS AND ETHOLOGY **21**

the same way (species-specificity), and they do so even if they have never seen other birds of the same species do so (unlearned) then that nest building is called instinctive.

Philosophical Roots of the Instinct Concept

The origin of the instinct concept can be traced to philosophical arguments rather than to scientific observations. Early philosophical systems set man apart from lower animals. Human behavior was seen as being stimulated by rational thought that, in turn, originated in the immortal soul. Animals, supposedly lacking souls and rationality, had to be understood in terms of some other mechanism. The concept of instinct was designed to explain the apparently intelligent acts of animals while, at the same time, denying them souls and maintaining the lofty status of the human (Beach, 1955).

The Rise and Fall of Instincts

Although the concept of instincts had been previously applied exclusively to so-called lower animals, attempts to explain human behavior in terms of instincts became very popular in the late 1800s and early 1900s (see Ayres, 1921). Part of this popularity probably stems from the theory of natural selection that was independently developed by Charles Darwin and by Alfred Wallace. These conceptions of evolution stressed the similarities rather than the differences among humans and the so-called lower animals. Since instinctive behaviors were evident among lower animals, it was only natural to extend the use of the concept to humans. If animals display instinctive behavior, and they are related to humans, then, the reasoning went, humans must be controlled by instincts, too.

The use of the instinct concept to explain human behavior expanded rapidly. For example, William James (1890) suggested that the instincts listed in Table 2.1 account for a great deal of human behavior. William McDougall (1908) compiled an even longer list containing 121 separate instincts. McDougall's position was more extreme than James's; McDougall believed that *all* human behavior had an instinctive origin. James, on the other hand, felt that learning and free will had a great deal to do with behavior. Unfortunately, these and other early conceptions of instinct failed clearly to differentiate learned from innate behaviors.

TABLE 2.1. Human Instincts Proposed by William James

Cleanliness
Constructiveness
Curiosity
Fearfulness
Hunting
Jealousy
Modesty
Parental love
Playfulness
Pugnacity
Rivalry
Secretiveness
Shyness
Sociability
Sympathy

Things began to get a little out of hand. Every time a behavior was observed an instinct was proposed to account for it. Atkinson (1964) states that by the second decade of the twentieth century almost fifteen thousand "instincts" had been proposed to account for almost all of human behavior.

But inventing instinct after instinct did not get us anywhere. Several devastating arguments were aimed at the instinct concept. First, it was pointed out that there was very little agreement about how many and exactly which instincts truly existed. Second as mentioned, no clear distinctions between learned and innate behavior were presented. Third, many so-called instinctive behaviors turned out to be heavily dependent upon prior experience. For example, Kuo (1930) showed that the "rat-killing instinct" in cats was strongly determined by life experiences. Fourth, and perhaps most importantly, the whole process of proposing new instincts to account for new behaviors was circular. Let us assume that an investigator saw an animal engage in a new piece of behavior. He would say, "Aha! That must be the result of the such-and-such instinct!" But when asked how he knew that the such-and-such instinct existed the investigator would smile and say, "This new piece of behavior I have found proves that the instinct exists!"

As a result of these and other objections the use of the instinct concept decreased drastically after about 1920. With some exceptions, few were willing to use and defend the word *instinct*.

Innate versus Learned Behavior? Few scientists would argue that behavior is totally free from innate or inherited influences. There are just too many clear-cut examples of species-specific innate animal behavior to argue that innate influences are nonexistent. However, it seems it is just as difficult to try to maintain that there are many behaviors which are *totally* innate and unaffected by learning and experience. Thus the question becomes one of trying to decide *how innate and learned behaviors interact and affect one another*. As we shall see in upcoming sections, this has proven to be a most difficult question.

ETHOLOGY

The instinct concept which has gotten itself something of a bad name, now appears in the literature much less often than it once did. However, this does not mean that investigators have given up on the idea that much of behavior is innately determined in an unlearned fashion.

Ethology is a special branch of biology concerned with the evolution, development, and occurrence of behavior in relation to the environment. Since many of the major battles concerning innate behavior occur within this field, we shall spend some time examining ideas and events within ethology.

Modern ethologists are deeply concerned with complex innate behavioral influences; in this sense, they carry on the instinct tradition. However, they differ from the earlier proponents of instinct in two important ways. First, they are much more willing to accept the fact that innate and learned factors interact; for them it is not an all-or-none (learned or innate) issue. Second, they have introduced a degree of rigor in experimental procedure, and a precision in language, that were unknown during earlier periods of investigation.

Instinctive behavior is not the only concern of the ethologists, but it does play an important part in their work. Much of the leadership in the field of ethology has come from Europe and has included the work of Konrad Lorenz, Nikolaas Tinbergen, and Karl von Frisch (the latter two shared a Nobel prize for their work).

Ethologists are interested in the behavior of animals in their environment; they want to know why an animal behaves the way it does. Tinbergen (1951) has observed that, once a male stickleback fish has established a territory, it will attack and attempt to drive off other males but it will not attack females. Let us use this small bit of behavior to introduce four concepts that have become central in the ethological tradition.

Four Principal Concepts

1. Reaction-Specific Energy. It is assumed that the behavior in question (attack) has a source or pool of energy that is available only for that specific behavior. Thus there is an energy pool associated with attack behavior. However, the male stickleback does not constantly attack; it only does so when it sees another male stickleback in its territory.

2. Innate-Releasing Mechanism. To account for the fact that the animal does not constantly attack, the concept of an innate-releasing mechanism is introduced. Think of this mechanism as a lock. It locks up the reaction-specific energy until something unlocks it.

3. Sign Stimulus. The key that opens the lock and releases the reaction-specific energy is called a sign stimulus (or sometimes a key stimulus). Sign stimuli tend to be fairly simple stimuli that have a dramatic effect upon the animal. For example, the crucial sign stimulus in the case of the male stickleback's attack behavior is the red belly of the intruding male. If the male sees a red belly (the key) the innate-releasing mechanism (the lock) is opened and out floods the reaction-specific energy (taking the form of attack). In a sense, the sign stimulus opens the floodgate. Another example is that of a bird feeding its young. The gaping mouth of the baby is the sign stimulus that opens the innate-releasing mechanism. This releases the appropriate behavior, which is, in this case, putting food in the youngster's mouth.

Tinbergen and his associates did some fascinating studies that demonstrated the specificity of sign stimuli. They made a group of models of male sticklebacks and showed them to a real male in its territory. They found that nothing else but that red belly mattered to the fish. The scientists could make models that were nearly perfect replicas of male sticklebacks, except that they did not have red bellies and the real male would ignore them. On the other hand, they made some very unrealistic models *with* red bellies and found that the male readily attacked them.

4. Fixed Action Pattern.   The behavior that is released is called a fixed action pattern because it tends to be rigid and stereotyped. There is not a lot of variation in the behavior. The male stickleback dashes toward the intruding male and drives it away every time it sees that red belly, without a lot of variety in its activity. The activity, once instigated, often, although not always, seems to run its course regardless of changes in the environment. Once the male sees the rival's red belly, it tends to execute the full attack response, independent of changes going on around it. Finally, the fixed action pattern seems to be somewhat immune to alteration through learning.

Additional Concepts   **Vacuum Reactions.**   If the animal has not been able to perform a given fixed action pattern because a sign stimulus has not appeared, the animal may tend to make the response anyway. For example, the male stickleback might attack a stimulus that is only pink, or, if enough time without responding has elapsed, it might attack something which does not resemble a rival at all.

   The idea here is that the reaction-specific energy builds up to a point where it is much more sensitive to triggering. Whether or not a vacuum reaction can occur in the total absence of some kind of sign stimulus remains unknown.

Displacement.   What happens when two sign stimuli appear at the same time if the responses these stimuli release are incompatible? For example, what does a stickleback do if we present a red-bellied rival and an equally powerful releaser of a flight response at the same time? It cannot attack and flee at the same time; the responses are incompatible. Displacement refers to the fact that the resulting behavior can sometimes be different from either of the expected behaviors. For example, the conflicted male fish may engage in a little nest building. Tinbergen argues that the energy accumulated in connection with the blocked motive somehow spills over into some other system (such as nest building).

Supernormal Stimuli.   If you give an oyster catcher an egg that is bigger than its own, it will incubate the larger egg. Plover's eggs have brown spots on a light brown background. If we give the plover a choice between its own egg and an egg that has black spots on a white background it will incubate the latter. These effects underline the rigidity of the behavior and the fact that learning seems not to play an important part in it. The behavior seems to be under the control of the sign stimuli.

ETHOLOGICAL MODELS

Both Tinbergen (1951) and Lorenz (1950) developed models of so-called instinctive behavior. We begin with Lorenz's hydraulic model, as depicted in Figure 2.1. According to this model the behavior in question, such as the attack behavior of the male stickleback, may best be thought of in terms of the action of water through a mechanical apparatus. Reaction-specific energy is assumed to accumulate like water in a reservoir. As the energy accumulates, the pressure to release it increases, like the pressure of water on a closed drain. The innate-releasing mechanism can be thought of as a rubber stopper held in place by a spring. Pulling against that spring, which has the effect of pulling the stopper out of the drain hole and releasing the reaction-specific energy (water), is the sign stimulus depicted by the weight in the pan in Figure 2.1. You can see that there are *two* forces working to unplug the drain. First, the filling of the reservoir increases the pressure on the innate-releasing mechanism (stopper). Second, the weight of sign stimuli perceived in the environment tends to pull the stopper out of the drain hole.

Lorenz's Hydraulic Model

Once water is released from the reservoir through the combined effects of the accumulating reaction-specific energy pushing the stopper out and sign stimuli pulling it out, the water or energy flows into a sloped pan with holes in the bottom. The more water released the deeper the water becomes in this sloped pan and the more different holes it flows through. This was Lorenz's way of accounting for the fact that behaviors are sometimes more complete than others. For example, on one occasion the male fish might just dash forward and then retreat, whereas on another occasion it might complete its attack and drive the intruder from the area. Each additional hole through which water flows represents one more component of the overall full-blown response.

Again you can see that two forces contribute to how partial or how

FIGURE 2.1
The hydraulic model of instinctive behavior. (Adapted from Lorenz, K. The comparative method of studying innate behavior patterns. In Symposia of the Society for Experimental Biology. Cambridge: Cambridge University Press, 1950, 4. 221–268. Fig. 1 on p. 256.)

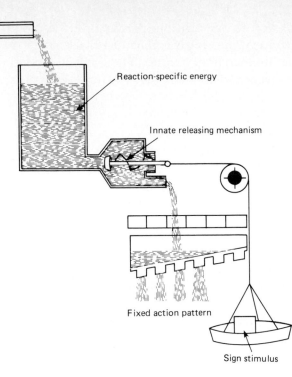

Reaction-specific energy

Innate releasing mechanism

Fixed action pattern

Sign stimulus

complete the fixed action pattern will be. The longer it has been since the animal attacked, the greater will be the pressure of the accumulated reaction-specific energy. And the more appropriate the sign stimulus the greater will be the pull on the stopper. Both of these lead to more released energy that, in turn, leads to water flowing through more holes (a more complete response).

The interesting thing about this simple model is that it can predict some of the effects mentioned earlier. For example, vacuum activity refers to the occurrence of a fixed action pattern in the absence of an appropriate sign stimulus. The model explains this activity in terms of the amount of accumulated reaction-specific energy being so great that the stopper is blown out of the drain hole by that pressure alone without any assistance from a sign stimulus. Similarly, supernormal stimuli may be thought of as stimuli with great weight that pull the stopper more effectively than do normal sign stimuli.

Tinbergen's hierarchical model is depicted in Figure 2.2. Tinbergen argued that energy for each general, major instinctive system (such as reproduction, feeding, or body care) accumulates in a specific brain center. In our following discussion of reproduction we will see how the system works.

First, energy associated with reproduction builds up, but its expression is blocked by an innate releasing mechanism that must be unlocked by an appropriate sign stimulus. The sign stimulus for this first level of the stickleback's reproductive instinct appears to be adequate space. If there is enough space available, the fish establishes a territory. If the area is too crowded, an effort to establish a territory will not occur; the reproductive energy will remain blocked. What happens when a territory has been established? According to Tinbergen, energy is available for a number of different activities associated with reproduction (e.g., fighting, nest building, mating, caring of offspring). But this energy is also blocked by innate releasing mechanisms. In other words, appropriate sign stimuli must be present for the behaviors in this second level of the hierarchy. For example, if

Tinbergen's Hierarchical Model

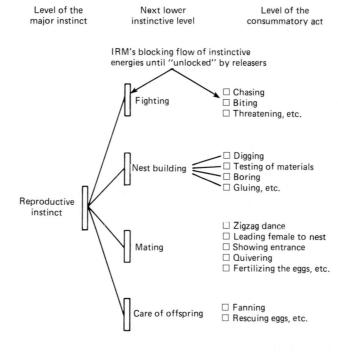

FIGURE 2.2
Tinbergen's hierarchical conception of the reproductive instinctive behavior of the male stickleback fish. (Adapted from Tinbergen, N. The study of instinct. Oxford: Oxford University Press, 1969. Fig. 89 on p. 104.)

sand and weeds are present, then the male will start nest building. But if sand and weeds (the releasing stimuli) are not available, then nest building remains blocked. Similarly, a rival male is needed for fighting to occur, a female is necessary for ritualistic courting behavior to occur, and the fish will not try to fan eggs unless eggs are present.

Tinbergen takes things to one final level in his hierarchical scheme. For example, exactly *which* fighting behaviors occur depends upon further sign stimuli. If the intruding male attacks (a sign stimulus), then the owner of the territory will also attack. But if the intruder flees (a sign stimulus) then the owner gives chase.

Tinbergen's model accounts for the great variety of behaviors that are observed to occur by assuming that energy is blocked at each successive hierarchical level until the appropriate sign stimuli are perceived. Depending upon what is perceived, the organism will display a wide range of released behaviors.

CRITICISMS OF ETHOLOGY

Although ethology is currently enjoying considerable popularity, this approach to the understanding of motivation has not escaped criticism (see Alcock, 1975; Bolles, 1975). One objection has been to the continued use of the word *instinct*. Many have believed that by calling a particular behavior instinctive we have perhaps obscured the true nature of that behavior. The use of the term *instinct* inhibits research because, if accepted, it eliminates the necessity of looking for as yet unidentified controlling variables.

Some have argued that the ethologist's references to physiological systems is unacceptable. For example, Tinbergen's hierarchical model includes references to energy being built up in particular brain sites. And yet there is no good evidence to support this claim; energy is not known to build up in the brain.

Further objections revolve around interpretations of experimental data. For example, consider the outline in Figure 2.3. When this model is moved to the right some birds will show flight behavior, but when the model is moved to the left, they do not flee. How do we interpret this? Tinbergen (1951) argued that the model resembles a bird of prey, such as a hawk, when it is moved to the right, because birds of prey have short necks. When moved to the left the model is assumed

FIGURE 2.3
Tinbergen observed that this pattern stimulated fear in some species of birds when moved to the right but not when moved to the left. (Adapted from Tinbergen, N. The study of instinct. Oxford: Oxford University Press, 1969. Fig. 26 on p. 32.)

to resemble a long-necked goose. Hence, according to Tinbergen, movement to the right serves as a sign stimulus that releases a fixed action pattern of flight, whereas movement to the left does not.

However, Ginsberg (1952) and others have argued that there is another way to think about these results which is contrary to the ethological interpretation. Specifically, they argue that when the model enters the visual field from the left side (short neck first) it is more startling, because of the abruptness of the change, than it is if it enters the visual field from the right side (long neck first). According to this way of looking at the data, there is no need to evoke fancy explanatory terms; it is just that the figure is more startling when it is brought in from one side than from the other.

By far the greatest problem researchers have had with the ethological approach has to do with the relationships between so-called instinctive behavior and learned behavior. The problem is a thorny one. Can basically innate patterns of behavior be affected by experience? How? When? Almost no one would argue today that purely instinctive behavior is very common, not even ethologists. Lorenz (1969) himself has described many situations in which experience seems to alter so-called instinctive behavior. He believed that instinctive behaviors can be modified by experience. For Lorenz, learning and instinct blend together to produce behavior. For example, he noted that the jackdaw does not know, innately, which materials are best for nest building. It knows that it has to select twigs and push them into a growing nest, but it doesn't choose the best ones until it has had a little experience. Through success and failure, some good twigs and some bad, the jackdaw learns which ones are best. In other words, the interplay of learning and innate impulses is bound to be complex.

The study of imprinting, to which we now turn, is important for two reasons. First, it is an enormously important area of current ethological research and, second, it makes clear the degree to which there is confusion about the interaction of learned and innate behaviors.

IMPRINTING

What Is It? The phenomenon of imprinting is interesting because it further illustrates the extent to which behavior is molded by, and limited by, innate factors as well as learning. In its simplest form imprinting refers to the fact that a newly hatched bird, such as a duck or goose, will often form a strong social attachment to the first moving object it encounters. Normally this moving object is the mother bird. Thus imprinting accounts for the pictures you have seen of ducklings following single file behind their parents.

However, the moving object to which the attachment is formed need not be the parent. Just about *any* moving object will become the target of this social bond whether it be a human, a football, a box, or a balloon. (Also, although most of our examples involve birds and visual stimulation, imprinting may occur in many other species, such as goats and shrews, and may involve sounds and smells as well as sights [Fantino and Logan, 1979; Hess, 1972]).

Lorenz (1937) was among the first to notice that if a newly hatched bird is first exposed to a walking human, then the bird will become imprinted upon that human and will, in the future, approach and follow that human in preference to its biological mother. Lorenz and other ethologists began by arguing that imprinting is genetically determined. They argued that when an appropriate stimulus (i.e., any moving object) is perceived the young bird will approach, follow, and form a lasting attachment to that object even if it has never perceived that object before. They argued that imprinting is not an instance of learning but rather that it is an innate predetermined sequence that is already "wired into" the animal.

Sample Procedures As you might expect, other investigators (see Rajecki, 1973; Hoffman and Ratner, 1973; Gaioni, Hoffman, De Paulo and Stratton, 1978) have been just as firm in arguing that imprinting is, after all, just another instance of ordinary learning. Before considering some of the argu-

ments and counterarguments concerning the true nature of imprinting, let us examine some of the procedures that have enabled
researchers to investigate imprinting in a precise, quantifiable way.
Hess (1959, 1972, 1973) has been one of the most influential investigators of imprinting. His apparatus is depicted in Figure 2.4. The
imprinting procedure is as follows: A duckling is hatched in an incu-
bator and then placed, by remote control, in the circular walkway. A
mechanical model of a female mallard duck begins to move around
the apparatus, emitting a "gock, gock, gock" sound through a built-
in speaker. The young duck follows the model, becoming imprinted
on it. When the experimenter wishes to terminate imprinting, a little
trap door is opened and the duckling tumbles harmlessly out of the
apparatus.

The strength of the imprinting can then be tested by giving the
duckling a choice between the model upon which it is imprinted and
its real mother. What is found is that the duckling often but not
always (see Hess, 1973) prefers the mechanical model, and will sometimes be willing to climb over barriers in order to stay with its
artificial "mother."

Hess has discovered some interesting facts using this apparatus.
For example, he wondered if the strength of imprinting was determined by how much *time* the duckling spent with the model or by
how much *distance* the duckling covered while following the model.
Hess set up conditions in which the speed of the model varied. In this

FIGURE 2.4
*Hess's circular walkway
used for imprinting.
(Adapted from Hess, E.
H. Imprinting. Science,
1959, 130, 133–141. Fig.
1, p. 134.)*

way he was able to vary the distance the duck traveled while keeping the time of exposure constant. In a constant time interval the ducklings traveled a greater distance when the model moved more rapidly. Hess (1959) found that the greater the distance traveled the greater the strength of imprinting. In another experiment Hess varied the time the duckling spent with the model while holding constant the distance traveled. He concluded, on the basis of the results, that time spent with the model is *not* particularly important in determining strength of imprinting.

The Critical Period
We now return to the question as to whether imprinted behavior is a learned behavior or an innate predetermined behavior pattern. Many researchers have lined up on both sides of this issue and have presented various kinds of evidence and arguments to support their positions. For our purposes, one example will suffice. Specifically, we consider the concept of a *critical period.*

It has long been known that whereas imprinting is very common in nature, it appears to be established only during a very short, critical period in the animal's life. This critical period seems to occur very early in the bird's life; somewhere between the ages of twelve and twenty hours seems to be when imprinting is most readily established. Early observations of the critical period were firmly substantiated by Hess (1959) in the laboratory. His procedure was to keep ducklings in comfortable darkened boxes for varying amounts of time before they were introduced into the apparatus depicted in Figure 2.4. As you can see in Figure 2.5 imprinting occurred very readily during the thirteen- to sixteen-hour age range. Before and after that time period successful imprinting dropped off dramatically.

Many investigators have argued that the existence of the critical period proves that imprinting is definitely not a case of ordinary learning because learning is not limited in terms of when it can occur. However, others have proposed counterarguments. For instance, it has been suggested that the critical period effect can be accounted for by two factors:

1. The fact that imprinting does not readily occur before the thirteen- to sixteen-hour period may be the result of the fact that the duckling is not yet very mobile. Just having come out of the egg it is still fairly wobbly; it cannot even walk very well yet. And if it cannot walk then it cannot follow, and if it cannot follow it cannot imprint.

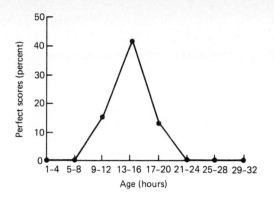

FIGURE 2.5
The relationship between age and imprinting. (Adapted from Hess. E. H. Imprinting. Science, 1959, 130, 133–141, Fig. 2, p. 135.)

2. The fact that imprinting after sixteen hours drops off dramatically has been attributed to the duck's maturing capacity to experience fear of strange or novel objects. When the duck is very young it does not react fearfully to novel stimuli. But, by the time it has spent sixteen hours in a cardboard box, the fear reaction is beginning to emerge. So when the sixteen-hour or older bird is dumped into the imprinting apparatus, the "gocking" model elicits fear rather than following behavior.

The argument here is that imprinting *could* occur both before and after the so-called critical period if (1) the animal could move at an earlier age and (2) if it did not react with fear at an older age. There is some evidence for at least one half of this interpretation. Investigators have been able to imprint much older birds if the fear reaction is first reduced (see Gaioni, Hoffman, De Paulo, and Stratton, 1978). The basic procedure has been to expose the birds to the novel stimulus for long periods of time without allowing them to flee or escape. Through this process of exposure the birds learn that the stimulus is not dangerous and they do begin to form social attachments to it. Thus, it appears that the critical period is not so critical after all.

The upshot of this line of research is that the critical period can no longer be accepted as clear proof of the idea that imprinting is something more than ordinary learning.

Further Arguments

The critical period is not the only arena in which the innate versus learned battle is fought. Hess and his associates have argued that there are other important differences between imprinting and learning. Some of these follow:

The Effects of Noxious Stimuli. Kovach and Hess (1963) ran an experiment in which ducklings were shocked during the imprinting process in the presence of the decoy. Shock increased the strength of the imprinting. Kovach and Hess argue that this is just the opposite of what one would expect if imprinting were ordinary learning. They point out that, in normal learning, if a shock is presented in the presence of a particular object or stimulus, the animal will flee from that object rather than approach it. Hess argues that his observed increase in the tendency to approach the model is just the opposite of what the principles of normal learning predict.

However, there are some problems with Hess's interpretation and experimentation. If we look carefully at the Kovach and Hess (1963) study, we find that the decoy was moved intermittently around the track, the bird was free to stand still or move, and no attempt was made to shock the bird only when it approached the decoy. Thus things were pretty complicated in this situation. The bird probably got shocked while it was standing still some of the time, and it may have been unshocked while following the decoy some of the time. To the extent that this happened the duck would be reinforced for running *toward* the decoy and *away* from the shock it received while standing still. In other words, Hess's situation cannot be compared to normal avoidance conditioning because it did not control when the shock was applied.

In a crucial study, Barrett, Hoffman, Stratton, and Newby (1971), after raising these issues, did control shock delivery. They made sure that the ducklings received a shock only when they approached and followed the model. In this case the birds quickly stopped following the model. In other words, when shock is delivered after the approach response is made, the ducklings stop approaching. This is what learning theory predicts. The bird does not increase its approach responses as Hess implies.

Hoffman and Ratner (1973) argue that the reason the shocked ducklings in the Kovach and Hess (1963) study actually showed an increase in their approach behavior was because the shock increased their overall level of arousal or excitement. Shock increased the ducklings' overall level of fear and motivation and therefore their performance. Whether this interpretation is correct is not overly important. The essential point of all of this is that imprinting cannot be clearly distinguished from ordinary learning on the basis of the effects of noxious stimulation.

Late Appearing Responses. Hess (1973) argues that imprinting differs from ordinary learning in that imprinting which occurs very early in life may not show up in behavior until the bird is mature. For example, it is possible to imprint one species of duckling on another species. Then, when the imprinted bird has matured, it will select and try to mate with members of the species to which it was imprinted.

Critics of this argument do not doubt the validity of this observed piece of behavior, but they do object to the implication that learned effects do not sometimes show a similar lag in appearance. Any number of theories of human development, for example, put great emphasis upon the idea that what we learn and experience as a very young child can have a profound effect on our adult behavior. For example, in Chapter 7 we see how the very essence of Sigmund Freud's theory of development revolves around the idea that early experience is crucial in determining adult behavior.

Long-Lasting Responses. Hess (1973) also tries to make a case for the difference between learning and imprinting by pointing out that imprinting is very durable and long lasting. He cites the fact that ducks imprinted on species A, and then forced to live with species B for up to seven years, will, when given the opportunity, still prefer and choose species A.

Again, Hess's implication comes under fire; in this case the implication is that ordinary learned behavior is *not* durable. But we know that this is simply not true. Life is filled with examples of the durability of learning. A prisoner released from jail after ten years will still know how to drive a car. Relatives who have not seen one another for long periods of time still recognize one another. And you can still dredge up many experiences and bits of learning acquired during your early years.

Irreversible Responses. Finally, Hess (1973) points out that imprinting is irreversible and cannot be eliminated whereas learned responses can be eliminated through extinction. Two objections arise here. First, there is some evidence that imprinting is not so irreversible as Hess claims. Gaioni, Hoffman, De Paulo, and Stratton (1978) report being able to imprint animals on a second object after they had been imprinted on a first object. Second, some kinds of learning seem to be pretty indelible. Can you imagine extinguishing your name? Do you think it is possible to lose the ability to drive a car?

In summary, the arguments used in support of a difference between learning and imprinting are interesting but far from conclusive.

Imprinting As Learning

Thus far we have been discussing how imprinting supposedly differs from ordinary learning. We now look at what supporters of the opposite point of view have to say, specifically, at some of the attempts to explain imprinting as an instance of learning.

Moltz (1960) gave the following explanation of imprinting. When it was first exposed to a novel stimulus, such as a decoy, at the age of a few hours, Moltz assumed that the duckling was in what he calls a "low-anxiety" state. The duck, because it was so young and immature, was not frightened or nervous. This state of low anxiety or tranquility became associated with the decoy. This association of low anxiety with the decoy is, as far as Moltz is concerned, the crucial bit of learning that underlies the imprinting effect.

The next step is to explain why the duckling follows the decoy at a later age. Moltz's explanation is this: When it is returned to the presence of the decoy at a later time, the duckling is no longer in a "low-anxiety" state. Quite to the contrary, it is now in a "high-anxiety" state. This is because the bird has matured to the point at which it is now capable of being frightened by novel external situations, whereas it was not yet capable of feeling fear when it was first exposed to the decoy. The bird is now frightened when it is taken from its home cage and put into the imprinting apparatus. The fearful little animal frantically looks about and sees the familiar decoy. The decoy elicits all of those low-anxiety feelings that were associated with it in the original early exposure session. So the duckling runs after the decoy.

The essential problem with Moltz's theory is the assumption that low anxiety existing during the original exposure accounts for imprinting. Several studies have shown that imprinting seems to be stronger when harsh rather than pleasant conditions exist during imprinting. For example, in a rather bizarre study, Salzen (1970) reports that chicks will imprint more strongly on a board if they are first given a light smack with that board. Others have found that a loud noise introduced during imprinting will enhance imprinting. These studies, in which better imprinting is obtained under high-anxiety conditions, cannot be explained by the Moltz theory.

Hoffman and Ratner (1973) have offered another theory that seems more likely because it holds that imprinting involves *both* innate and learned components. They argue that it is not an either-or situation but rather one that involves some complex mix of both learning and predetermined elements. The first assumption is that a certain general type of stimulus, such as any moving object, will innately elicit approach behavior. Thus, it makes no difference what the moving object is; as long as it is moving it will innately elicit following behavior.

If left at this point the theory would argue that an imprinted animal would follow any moving object. But we know that this is not the case. Birds become imprinted on *specific* moving objects and not *all* moving objects. To account for the specificity of imprinting, Hoffman and Ratner (1973) bring in a learned element. Assume that the object upon which the animal is imprinted is a blue ball. When it is first exposed to the moving blue ball the animal innately approaches it, not because it is blue or because it is a ball but because it is moving. At first the "blueness" and the "ballness" of the object are neutral and without power to elicit following behavior. But as the bird follows the moving ball it begins to associate the following response with these initially neutral aspects (blueness, ballness) of the moving object. In the future, then, through learning, the blueness and ballness of the stimulus become effective in eliciting the following response.

The tendency for modern researchers to think of imprinting as involving both learned and innate components seems to be growing. Some refuse to be drawn into the innate versus learned debate. For example, Gould (1982) prefers to speak of imprinting as a form of "programmed learning." Birds are equipped with the rule "memorize the appearance of the first moving object." But they are not entirely naive about what a parent should look like. According to Gould, "They are born with one or two general clues which they use if a decision between two moving objects becomes necessary. Hence, given a choice between say geese and people during its critical period, a duckling is programmed to pay attention to the more ducklike object" (Gould, 1982, p. 266). According to this position, birds seems innately prepared, or wired, to attend to certain kinds of stimuli (ducklings will innately attend to ducklike objects). At the same time, learning or memorization of the selected object is required. Hence, according to Gould and others, imprinting involves both innate mechanisms and learning.

How much, if any, of our own behavior, as compared to that of other animals, is innately determined? How much of our behavior might be called instinctive? These are complex questions, and have not yet been clearly answered. The best we can do at the moment is to suggest that there probably are innate factors operating in the determination of our behavior, but that these innate influences interact heavily with learned or experience-determined behavior. In this section we look at some of the data that support the tentative conclusion that humans do exhibit innate impulses but that these impulses are often shaped, molded, and altered by experience and learning.

Nonverbal Communication

One of the areas of research and thought that bears upon the issue of innate human behavior is that of nonverbal communication. This burgeoning field of investigation can stand on it own as a substantial area of concern. In fact, it has its own journal called the *Journal of Nonverbal Behavior*. But, for our purposes, nonverbal communication can best be mentioned in connection with the question of innate human behavior.

When we think of humans communicating we tend to think of language. Humans seem to thrive on verbal communication; we are constantly talking and listening to one another, we spend enormous amounts of time reading and writing. But there is another form of communication that, though perhaps more subtle than verbal communication, is just as important in our lives as is the use of language. Nonverbal communication refers to all of the different ways we communicate with one another without using language. Facial expressions, gestures, eye movement, and bodily posture can all be used to communicate various emotions. As we shall see, some of these seem to be innate but modifiable by experience. Consider, as an example, what happens when you are at a crowded party and you notice that someone is looking at you from across the room. You do not think much of it and you look away. But a few moments later you glance back and the person is *still* looking at you, and looking and looking. Something is communicated, isn't it? Most likely the nonverbal message is, "I'm interested in you." The longer the person looks the stronger is the message. In this social situation the communication is most likely to be a positive one. But suppose you received the same sort of look on a dark, deserted street late at night? Here there will also be a message, but it will probably make you uneasy. In other words, the strength of the message, whether it is positive or negative, increases as the length of eye contact increases. But whether the message is positive or negative seems to depend upon the circumstances, or the context, in which the eye contact occurs; it is a complicated situation. And it is but one of many different forms of nonverbal communication we use. As further examples, consider that you are using nonverbal communication when you wave, smile, beckon, nod, or gesture. Emotions, both positive and negative, seem to be easily communicated nonverbally.

Facial Expressions.   Facial expressions communicate an enormous amount of information nonverbally, both in humans and other species (see Miller, Caul, and Mirsky, 1967). Eibl-Eibesfeldt (1972) has concluded that many of these expressions are innate. He based this conclusion, which has proven to be somewhat controversial, upon his studies of various cultures, ranging from advanced to primitive societies, and upon his observations of deaf, blind, and retarded people.

Eibl-Eibesfeldt observed that humans born into vastly different cultures display the same expressions such as frowning, smiling, crying, and laughing. In other words, people laugh when something funny occurs, regardless of their cultural surroundings. The universality of the facial expressions convinced Eibl-Eibesfeldt that these expressions are innate. On the other hand, it is easy to see how these innate responses might also be influenced by experience. If a child is raised in a family in which "children are seen but not heard," then the laughter response, although it is innately patterned, may be modified in accordance with this social demand.

Figure 2.6 contains some examples of the eyebrow flick that Eibl-Eibesfeldt felt was an innate nonverbal form of greeting. Regardless of the culture involved, he found that people momentarily flick their eyebrow upward when they recognize someone. It may be a sign of recognition and friendliness. Whatever it is, it seems to be so pervasive as to make us think that is is innate.

Eibl-Eibesfeldt's conclusions concerning innate human behavior were bolstered by his observations of deaf and blind individuals. As Figure 2.7 shows, a deaf-blind girl displays the same facial expressions that the rest of us do, even though she has never had the opportunity to learn these expressions through the use of sight and hearing.

Thus facial expressions seem to be at least partially determined by

FIGURE 2.6a

The potentially innate eyebrown flick in, from top to bottom, the Waika Indian, Balinese, and Papuan cultures. In each case the right hand expression occurs after recognition, while the left hand expression occurs before recognition.

innate factors. However, we are a long way from understanding all of the intricacies involved in nonverbal communication through innate facial expressions. For example, Ekman and Friesen (1982) argue that at least three different kinds of smiles must be considered. *Felt* smiles are spontaneous reflections of positive emotions we are feeling, *false* smiles are those that we "put on" to achieve an end, and *miserable* smiles are those that appear when we feel bad but do not intend to do much about it.

The study of expressions is further complicated by the suggestion (Riskind an Gotay, 1982) that such expressions (as well as postures) have feedback properties. Not only do emotions determine expressions but expressions may determine emotions. For example, if we ask a subject to put her face into a frown without ever mentioning a frown, then she will actually feel negative. This can be done by asking the subject to bring her eyebrows together and drop the corners of

FIGURE 2.6b
These expressions of rage may also be innate, according to Eibl-Eibesfeldt. (Adapted from Eibl-Eibesfeldt, I. Love and hate: The natural history of behavior patterns. *New York: Holt, Rinehart & Winston, 1972. Figs. 2, 3, 6 on pp. 15, 16, 19.)*

the mouth without "tipping the subject off" as to what expression is desired. In other words, there may well be some complicated two-way causal relationship between expression and feeling.

Other Forms of Nonverbal Communication. Innate nonverbal communication is not limited to facial expressions. Eibl-Eibesfeldt listed, among other behaviors, flirting, kissing, threat gestures, and staring as forms of nonverbal communication that may have an innate basis.

Postures certainly communicate quite a good deal about what we

FIGURE 2.7
Possibly innate facial expressions in a deaf-blind female including relaxation, smiling, and crying. (Adapted from Eibl-Eibesfeldt, I. Love and hate: The natural history of behavior patterns. New York: Holt, Rinehart & Winston, 1972. Fig. 1 on p. 12.)

are feeling. For example, Weisfeld and Beresford (1982) found that both "tough," aggressive young people and successful young people have erect postures as depicted in Figure 2.8. People who felt less successful, and those who were more submissive, tended to adopt a more stooped posture. Whether this effect is innately determined remains to be seen.

Eye contact and a light touch on the arm have been shown to be more effective in getting someone to give up a dime that he has found in a phone booth than a downcast look and the absence of a touch on the arm (Brackner, Pressman, Cabitt, and Moran, 1982). This suggests that acts of intimacy may be perhaps innately effective in eliciting compliance.

Other Possibly Innate Human Behaviors

Eye Fixation. Although several forms of nonverbal behavior have been described as being innate, they are not the only kinds of human behavior that have been suspected of being innate. An example is the unquestionable tendency for us to fix our gaze upon the eyes of another individual. Is this an innate response? Although not conclusive, work by Haith, Bergman, and Moore (1977) suggests that fixating the face, and the eyes in particular, may be controlled by innate mechanisms. These investigators measured the tendency for very young infants to fix their gaze on adult faces brought before them. They found that seven-week-old infants would fixate the adult face almost 90

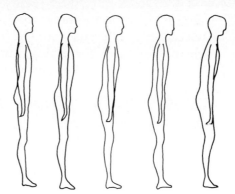

FIGURE 2.8
Scale used for rating erectness of posture. (Adapted from Weisfeld, G. E., & Beresford, J. M. Erectness of posture as an indicator of dominance or success in humans. Motivation and Emotion, 1982, 6, 113–131, Fig. 1 on p. 119).

percent of the time. In addition, the infants fixed their gaze upon the eyes even when the adult was speaking. In this case, one might have expected the infants to fix their gaze upon the mouth because of its movement. But they did not; their tendency to stare at the eyes may well prove to be an at least partially innate response designed to pick up important social cues.

Imprinting. We have already seen that many of the so-called lower organisms display imprinting. But what about humans? Do we imprint? At least one investigator (Bowlby, 1969) has argued that the bond formed between human infants and their parents or caretakers is quite similar to the imprinting observed in other mammals and in birds. It is true that children do not line up in single file behind their parent as do ducks and geese. On the other hand they *do* follow, even if in a less organized manner than the young birds. Children do sometimes react with fear when a strange adult approaches, and they will choose a familiar caretaker over a natural parent if that natural parent is unfamiliar.

Unfortunately, most of what we can say about human imprinting is speculative. We just do not have adequate experimental techniques for assessing the extent to which humans truly imprint. What roughly resembles imprinting may be nothing more than conditioning, or learning.

Language. Early theories of language acquisition emphasized the role of learning. Thus a child was taught to say "mama" because each time he did so the parents would reward the child with affection and praise. As the child matured, more precise language usage would be required before rewards would be delivered. Thus, a very young child might be rewarded for saying, "tricity" for electricity, whereas an older child would only be rewarded if some closer approximation to electricity was produced. In this way it was believed that language usage was shaped by the power of reward delivered by significant people in the environment.

But more recent thinking, especially that of the psycholinguists, has suggested that the learning interpretation cannot account for the human's generative, creative use of language. Children use language in new, unique ways that are not easily understood in terms of simple learning processes. For example, a child may use language in a way that has never been rewarded or used before. The psycholinguists argue that language learning involves the development and testing of hypotheses about how to use language more than it does the simple strengthening and shaping of responses through reward.

In addition, and this is the crucial point here, these psycholinguists argue that we are genetically prepared to use language. Biologically, we are more than ready to learn language. It is as though the sensitivity to, and the readiness to use language is inherited; it is "wired" into our nervous system.

Territoriality. In lower animals the defense of geographic territory seems to be fairly widespread. Many animals stake out their claims and fight to defend that claim. Territoriality has often been thought of as an instinctive and innate means of benefiting the species. For example, it spreads the species over a wide area and thus perhaps maximizes available food usage.

But do humans display territoriality? Ardrey (1966), and others, argue that territoriality does exist in humans. He mentions, for example, that humans rearrange themselves on elevators when someone gets off in such a way that maximum space exists among the remaining people. The fact that people want and pursue large homes on large plots of land also suggests territoriality. There is also the concept of *personal space.* What do you do when a stranger walks up to you and stands with his face four inches in front of yours? You back up, or at least want to back up. We do not like strangers to come that close to us. It is as though we each carry with us a bubble of space, our personal space, that we do not want others to invade. There are a few people we would *love* to have invade our personal space, but, in general, this small bit of territory seems to be important to us, and we will "defend" it to the extent that we will try to keep unwanted people out.

Is a concern for personal space innate? We are not sure, but it does seem to be something that exists in diverse cultures; it is pervasive enough to suggest an innate basis. But, as we have been emphasizing, even if this concern does have an innate basis, it also appears to be modifiable by experience. This is shown by the fact that different cultures seem to display different *sized* personal spaces. Whereas one culture may have a large personal space, others will have smaller spaces. These differences can cause some trouble when members of different cultures meet. A member of a large-spaced culture may think a member of a small-spaced culture is "pushy" whereas the small-spaced individual may regard the other as "aloof."

Sociobiology and Altruism

A man loses his life while trying to save his son from drowning. A woman dies trying to pull a stranger from a burning building. A pilot crashes in a field rather than parachuting to safety while his plane crashes in a populated area. We read and hear about these *altruistic* behaviors quite often: People actually give up their own life in order to save the lives of others.

These unselfish behaviors may very well be learned. But a group of investigators, calling themselves *sociobiologists* (Barash, 1977; Wilson, 1975), argue that such prosocial behaviors, and, in fact, all social behaviors, have a genetic or inherited nature. We are all familiar with the theory of natural selection that argues that individuals who are most suited to the environment will live to reproduce whereas less-suited individuals will be more likely to perish before reproducing. At first glance, the altruistic behaviors noted would seem to be contrary to the theory of natural selection. Specifically, if an individual carries a gene, or genes, for altruistic behavior, and dies in an altruistic act, then that gene should die along with the individual. But there are many examples of apparent altruistic behavior in the animal kingdom. In other words, altruistic behavior has not disappeared in flaming acts of heroism. Why not? The sociobiologists argue that the *individual* acts of fatal heroism ensure the safety, and therefore the reproduction, of the *group* to which the individual belongs. It is argued that all members of the group have the gene for altruism.

Individual acts of altruism help protect that group and help ensure the reproduction of that group. Thus the "altruism gene" does not die out.

Whether or not all social behaviors have a genetic basis, as some sociobiologists suggest, remains to be seen. The argument is an interesting one, and quite difficult to rebut.

SUMMARY

1. Instinctive behavior is described as unlearned, automatic species-specific behavior uninfluenced by experience.

2. The concept of instinctive behavior was popular around the turn of the century. But when it was lavishly applied to human behavior it lost its appeal because it involved circular reasoning, led to disagreement about what instincts actually operated, and failed to distinguish learned from innate behavior.

3. Ethology is a branch of biology that is concerned with the evolution and development of behavior in relation to the environment.

4. Ethologists represent the modern proponents of instinctive behavior and its interaction with learned behavior.

5. Ethological concepts included reaction-specific energy, innate-releasing mechanisms, sign stimuli, fixed action patterns, vacuum reactions, displacement, and supernormal stimuli.

6. Lorenz developed a hydraulic model of instinctive behavior.

7. Tinbergen's model of instinctive behavior is hierarchical.

8. Ethology has been criticized because it continues to use the word instinct, refers to unverifiable physiological factors, sometimes misinterprets experimental data and does not clarify the relationship between innate and learned behavior.

9. Imprinting is exemplified by the fact that newly hatched ducks and geese will follow and form strong social attachments to the first moving object they observe.

10. Hess has been very influential in studying and developing methods of studying imprinting.

11. Distance traveled by the duckling increases the strength of imprinting.

12. The concept of a critical period refers to the fact that, at first glance, imprinting seems to occur only during a short period of the bird's life soon after hatching has occurred.

13. Others have argued that the critical period is an artifact of the fact that the bird is essentially immobile before the critical period and afraid of the imprinting model after the critical period.

14. Imprinting cannot be distinguished from ordinary learned behavior on the basis of the effects of noxious stimuli, the late appearance of imprinted responses, the long-lasting quality of imprinted responses, or the irreversibility of imprinted responses.

15. Several theoreticians argue that imprinting can be accounted for with the principles of ordinary conditioning.

16. Humans probably display some innate behavior.

17. Many facial expressions seem to be innate.

18. Other behaviors, such as flirting, kissing, threat gestures, and postures, may be innate.

19. Human infants form attachments to their caretakers that some people believe are like imprinted attachments.

20. Some aspects of language usage may be innate.

23. Territoriality may exist in humans.

24. Sociobiology argues that all social behaviors have an inherited basis.

CHAPTER 3

Regulatory Mechanisms

THE CONCEPT OF REGULATION

Basic Physiological Needs

When one thinks of the vast array of human motives one tends to first think about rather complex needs and drives such as the motive to succeed, the need to find love and affection, and the need to express oneself creatively. These somewhat exhaulted motive systems are important, and they and others are discussed throughout the text. But we must not neglect the more basic *physiological* needs such as hunger, thirst, and sex, if we are to understand human motivation in any comprehensive manner.

Indeed these basic physiological motives remain crucial in our lives. The continuing importance of basic physiological motives is underscored by the fact that, as Maslow (1970) has pointed out, they can and often do take precedence over the so-called higher motive systems.

For example, the need to express oneself creatively cannot even begin to be satisfied if one is near death from starvation. Maslow (1970) and others argue that the more basic physical needs must be satisfied before higher needs, such as the drive toward self-actualization and fulfillment, can direct our behavior. If thirst is consuming us, the great artistic creation we have in mind will just have to wait until our thirst is reduced.

Because of the power of these basic motives in our lives, we explore what is and what is not known about the basic hunger, thirst, and sex motive systems. Then, in later chapters, we address the many higher, less obviously physiological motives.

Regulation Basic physiological needs are often thought of in terms of the body's tendency to regulate itself. The purpose of some physiological mechanisms is to maintain a steady state with respect to the needs of the body. To function properly, the body needs some food but not too much. Hence these mechanisms detect a falling level of nutrients within the body and initiate feeding behavior to bring nutrient levels back up to normal. Similarly, some mechanisms detect excesses in nutrients and stop feeding behavior in order to maintain some optimal level of food substances within the body.

Similar sorts of regulatory mechanisms function to maintain body water with a certain range. If our fluid drops too low, internal mechanisms detect the drop and initiate drinking behavior to correct the deficit. Drinking will normally terminate when the proper balance is restored.

Bodily regulation is somewhat analogous to what occurs in connection with machinery, such as an automobile. When the oil or gas levels fall too low, internal mechanisms in the automobile detect these states and signal us through a system of gauges. We correct the deficits by adding the appropriate substances. We refill the gas tank and add oil, but do not add too much. In this way we keep the oil level between the "add" and "full" mark on the dipstick.

Voluntary and Involuntary Regulation Some regulatory mechanisms, or parts of them, involve conscious voluntary effort on our part. For example, if we are hungry, we voluntarily seek food and make conscious decisions about how it will be obtained (Will it be tacos or hamburgers this time?). But sometimes regulatory mechanisms seem to be almost wholly involuntary. For example, we breathe without having to do so voluntarily. And when we become overheated we do not have to say, "Pores! Open up and sweat." They perform these functions for us automatically. As we shall see, the roles of consciousness and free will in regulation are complex and not yet completely understood.

Some regulation involves both automatic and voluntary action. The automobile automatically warns us when gas and oil levels are low, but it takes voluntary action on our part to correct the deficit. Other regulatory mechanisms, however, are fully automatic in the automobile. Some brakes are "self-adjusting." And in some cars the fan comes on automatically when the engine gets too warm and goes off when the engine cools down.

HUNGER AND EATING

Interest in, and speculation about, the mechanisms of hunger and eating are not new. Rosenzweig (1962) points out that Plato and Aristotle thought about these issues, even though they lacked experimental techniques. Down through the years attention seemed to focus upon the stomach as the source of hunger motivation. Some researchers believed that glandular activity in the stomach accounted for hunger whereas others believed that the rubbing together of the stomach walls created the sensation of hunger. Cannon and Washburn (1912) proposed that stomach contractions constitute the source of hunger.

Early Ideas: The Stomach

But these kinds of explanations, with their emphasis upon what goes on within the stomach were shown to be, at best, of limited value by two sorts of experimental data. First, when the vagus nerve, which carries messages to and from the stomach to the brain, is severed, the experience of hunger is not eliminated. Morgan and Morgan (1940) showed this effect with rats, and Grossman and Stein (1948) did it with humans. When the stomach can no longer communicate with the brain, hunger and eating still occur. The second kind of finding that demonstrates the inadequacy of the idea that events in the stomach constitute the source of hunger is even more dramatic. People whose stomachs have been entirely removed surgically still experience hunger (Wangensteen and Carlson, 1931).

So, even though these theories focusing on stomach events were popular, and were appealing on an intuitive level, they are inadequate.

Given that stomach events could not account for hunger and eating behavior, it is not surprising to learn that investigators turned to the central nervous system in their search for the answer to the riddle of hunger.

Dual Hypothalamic Control

As early as 1867, Schiff was suggesting that the brain must detect changes in the composition of the blood as the body uses up its fuel. But it was many years before good experimental demonstrations of this general idea appeared. Gradually it became clear that the *hypothalamus* (see Figure 3.1) must somehow be intricately involved in hunger motivation. More specifically, Hetherington and Ranson (1940) showed that if the *ventromedial hypothalamus* (VMH) was destroyed, extreme overeating and obesity would occur in a large number of species (the ventromedial portion of the hypothalamus is the front center area). This condition of obesity is called *hyperphagia*. Rats will grow to several times their normal weight when the VMH is damaged. The idea here is that the VMH must be some kind of "satiety center." When functioning normally, this center will detect when the animal has "had enough" food and will stop eating. When the VMH is destroyed, eating continues.

The next major step in the story came when Anand and Brokbeck (1951) showed that damage to the *lateral hypothalamus* (LH), or the sides of the hypothalamus, produced an effect that was just the opposite of that caused by destruction of the VMH. Specifically, lesions in the LH caused the animals to stop eating completely. Left to their

FIGURE 3.1
The location of the hypothalamus in the human brain.

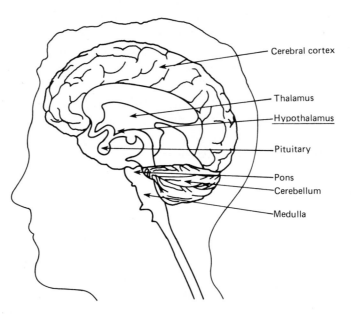

Cerebral cortex

Thalamus

Hypothalamus

Pituitary

Pons
Cerebellum

Medulla

own devices, these animals would not eat, which resulted in a condition known as *aphagia*, and would starve to death.

These discoveries led to the general idea that, through their intricate connections, the LH and VMH served together as a precise hunger control system. In a sense, the LH was seen as a kind of "on switch" whereas the VMH served as an "off switch."

Classical demonstrations of aphagia and hyperphagia have involved destruction of the appropriate areas of the hypothalamus, but similar effects can be obtained through direct electrical stimulation of the VMH and LH. As one would expect, if the LH is an "on switch," electrical stimulation of the LH by means of implanted electrodes results in ravenous feeding. As one would expect if the VMH is an "off switch," electrical stimulation of this area has led to abrupt cessation of feeding (Hess, 1957; Wyrwicka, 1976).

Glucostatic Theory: Short-Term Regulation

Lesions in and electrical stimulation of the LH produce inhibited and stimulated feeding, respectively, and lesions in and stimulation of the VMH produce the opposite effects. These are interesting effects, and they obviously implicate the hypothalamus in the control of hunger. But they really are nothing more than observations. They do not tell us *how* the hypothalamic mechanisms work. What is it, exactly, that normally goes on inside these two parts of the hypothalamus during the control of hunger and eating?

The answer to this question is far from clear, and, as we shall see in later sections, new and challenging ideas are emerging. But for now we want to examine two theories that have been very influential for a number of years. The first of these, the *glucostatic* theory, is discussed here, with the *lipostatic* theory to follow.

The idea behind glucostatic theory is a simple one; the notion is that the hypothalamus contains *glucoreceptors* (cells sensitive to glucose in the bloodstream) which somehow monitor glucose levels and initiate corrective action to maintain optimal levels of energy available in the body (Mayer, 1955). There is evidence for the existence of glucoreceptors in the VHM. For example, Oomura (1976) found that the firing rate of cells in that area can be increased by the application of glucose. And, as expected, application of glucose to the LH tends to decrease the firing of LH cells.

Unfortunately, although glucostatic theory has been very influential for many years, it has recently run into severe trouble. Too many recent findings run counter to the implications of a simple glucostatic interpretation of hunger control. The interested reader is referred to Cotman and McGaugh (1981) for a detailed analysis of the shortcomings of the glucostatic theory. For our purposes, we note a few of the problems facing the glucostatic theory. For example, it has been suggested (Stricker, Friedman, and Sigmond, 1975; Stricker and Sigmond, 1976) that damage to the LH results in the animal's having trouble reacting normally to stress. As a result, inhibited eating may be a secondary or derived result of this stress problem rather than a direct result of the LH lesion. Others (see Grossman and Grossman, 1973) have shown that damage to areas of the brain unrelated to the hypothalamus can have enormous effects on eating, which suggests that a simple glucose-monitoring system is inadequate as an explanation of all forms of eating. Additionally, Novin (1976) has reported evidence that suggests that the elusive glucoreceptors may not even be in the brain at all; they may be in the liver. Finally, the brain is not subject to wide swings in glucose level. The body "protects" the brain and tries to keep it in a steady state. Thus, even when we are extremely hungry the glucose level in our brain does not drop very much.

These and other troubling findings have not vanquished the old and venerable glucostatic theory, but they have raised serious questions about it. On the positive side, they have also stimulated new, fruitful lines of research.

Lipostatic Theory: Long-Term Control

The glucostatic theory, discussed in the previous section, has been developed in connection with what is known as the short-term control of hunger and eating, such as control of eating from hour to hour or day to day. But there is another kind of control, called long-term control, that has to do with the fact that we tend to maintain our weight, within a few pounds, over long periods of time. In this diet-conscious age it may seem like peoples' weights vary widely over time. But, with the exception of extreme conditions, such as disease and crash diets, we do tend to keep our weight fairly constant.

How do we do it? One influential idea is that our body monitors the amount of fat it contains and then regulates food intake such that this fat level is held fairly constant. This constant level may vary from individual to individual. Hence we think of some people as being "naturally" thin or "naturally" portly.

Keesey and his associates (Keesey, Boyle, Kemnitz, and Mitchell, 1976; Keesey and Powley, 1975), in their *set-point* theory, argue that the body does indeed maintain a "normal" weight by monitoring fat (fats are lipids). They argue that when the LH of an animal is damaged, and the animal shows a deficit in eating, the *ability* to eat has not been damaged. Rather, they argue, the LH damage merely resets the set-point at some lower level. The evidence for this idea is that animals with LH damage, once they have recovered, will eat in what seems to be a perfectly normal manner, except that they eat less and maintain a new lower so-called "normal" weight.

Keesey also suggests that the VMH may be involved in long-term control too. Specifically, he proposes that VMH damage may raise the set-point. After VMH damage the animal's so-called normal weight is now higher, which would account for the increased food intake following VMH damage. However, Keesey also points out that VMH-damaged animals do not maintain their new set point as firmly as do LH damaged animals.

Assuming that the LH and VMH are involved in long-term control of body weight, what is known about the exact stimuli which key off changes in eating behavior, or signal the hypothalamus? Not a great deal. The general idea is that some aspect of fat cells (such as their size) might be monitored by some mediating agent in the bloodstream, which then, in turn, "tells" the hypothalamus about the condition of the body's fat stores.

Wirtshafer and Davis (1977) have suggested that *glycerol*, a sweet, colorless substance in the blood, may be the agent involved in fat regulation. Glycerol content of the blood is related to fat cell size. Thus, if increased body weight leads to an increased glycerol level that in turn "tells" the hypothalamus to stop eating, then injections of glycerol should produce a reduction in eating. Wirtshafer and Davis did just this; they gave rats daily injections of glycerol and found a reduction in body weight. The body "thought" it was heavier than it actually was because of all that glycerol washing around in the bloodstream.

Another element that has been suspected of being involved in long-term control is *insulin* (see Keesey and Powley, 1975). Unfortunately, the exact mechanism, or mechanisms, controlling long-term weight levels are simply not well understood at the present time.

Let us return to the hypothalamic-glucostatic theory discussed earlier. This theory holds that the elusive glucoreceptors, or cells sensitive to glucose, are located in the hypothalamus. Thus the hypothalamus

The Liver

is thought to directly detect glucose level in the blood flowing through the hypothalamus.

Recent work suggests that the glucoreceptors may not be in the hypothalamus at all, but may be in the *liver* (see Novin, 1976; Vanderweele and Soaderson, 1976). The idea is that glucoreceptors in the liver detect changes in blood glucose levels and then signal the hypothalamus, via the vagus nerve, about these changes. Some results can be cited in support of these conceptions of the role of the liver. Injecting glucose into the hepatic portal vein, which goes through the liver, causes eating to drop. However, if glucose is injected into the jugular vein, which goes to the brain but does *not* go through the liver, there is no resulting reduction in eating. Finally, if glucose is injected into the hepatic portal vein *and* the vagus nerve is cut, no deficit is observed. It is as if the liver registers glucose levels but cannot convey the information to the brain.

Novin (1976) also did an experiment that suggests that the liver can initiate feeding as well as suppress it. Novin introduced 2-DG, a substance that blocks the use of glucose, into the hepatic portal vein and found that eating behavior picked up quite rapidly. The idea is that the liver reacted as though glucose level was low and initiated feeding via the vagus nerve.

Novin believes that glucoreceptors are located in the duodenum as well as in the liver. The intricate relationship between the functioning of the liver and the duodenum has not yet been worked out. Some, such as Russek (1963), feel glucoreceptors may be present in the stomach, liver, and hypothalamus.

Chemical or Neural Signals? CCK

The understanding of hunger is so incomplete that we do not know if glucoreceptors are in the brain or in the stomach or somewhere else. Similarly, we are not sure what kinds of signals are involved. Novin's work suggests that the liver sends *neural* messages to the brain via the vagus nerve, but recent work suggests that *chemical* messages may be involved too.

The most commonly suspected chemical agent is *cholecystokinin* (CCK), a hormone that is secreted by the upper intestinal tract (Smith and Gibbs, 1976; Straus and Yalow, 1979). The suspicion is that CCK is secreted when food enters the intestines. CCK then travels through the bloodstream to the brain where it serves as a signal to stop eating.

Several kinds of research support this picture of the role of CCK.

For example, Straus and Yalow (1979) compared the amounts of CCK found in normal and fat mice (these were mice that were naturally obese, and not made to be overweight by the investigators). They found that the levels of CCK in the brains of the obese animals were much lower than in the normal animals. Although not conclusive, this result is good circumstantial evidence for the idea that the overweight mice did all that overeating because they lacked sufficient levels of CCK to "turn off" the eating behavior.

Further evidence for the importance of CCK comes from Smith and Gibbs (1976), who injected CCK intraperitoneally and found that eating was reduced. They found this effect even when the vagus nerve was cut.

All of this work, involving the hypothalamus, liver, and intestines, as well as neural and chemical messages, underlines the complexity of the hunger mechanisms. It may eventually turn out that there are several receptor sites and several forms of messages. At this point it does not seem reasonable to anticipate a single simple biological hunger system.

Here is a particularly challenging result for the investigators of hunger. Geiselman (1983) varied the *rate* at which glucose was infused into the duodenum. Half of her rabbits received glucose at a slow rate and half received it at a fast rate. Slow-infused animals decreased their food intake as expected. But just the opposite effect was observed in the case of the fast-infused animals; they nearly doubled their food intake during the first half hour after the glucose infusion.

Rate of Infusion

Classical glucostatic theory cannot account for this result. We are faced with the fact that glucose appears to be able to stimulate hunger when it is taken quickly, and this is not something that the traditional glucostatic theory can explain.

In fact, no one can yet explain this intriguing result. In some as yet unknown way the body acts as though it is expecting more and more food when infusion is rapid. Then, when infusion ceases, and the expected food does not arrive, the body takes on more food through eating behavior.

Although traditional glucostatic theory has dominated the field of hunger research for thirty years, Geiselman's and similar results may be breaking new ground that will result in important gains in our knowledge about hunger.

Taste: Innate and Acquired

So far, in our consideration of hunger, we have focused upon possible biological factors that control the instigation and the cessation of eating without regard for such factors as flavor, smell, temperature, and texture. In a sense, we have been focusing upon the *quantity* of food eaten and have not yet considered the *quality* of that food. But taste factors are obviously very important in eating behavior. A hungry six-year-old may eat a complete pizza but turn up her nose at spinach. Rats will choose sweet-flavored food over bland food. Each and every day we make many choices concerning the flavor, temperature, smell, and texture of the food we eat.

In this section we discuss what is known or suspected about the role of these taste factors in eating behavior. As we shall see, one important distinction is between *innate* and *learned* preferences. Do we like salty or sweet foods innately, or have we learned to like them? A second important distinction is between *preferences* and *aversions*. We like some foods whereas others we detest. Are these aversions innate, learned, or both?

Learned Preferences.　When we stuff in those potato chips, or slice into that steak, are we doing so because we innately like those substances, because we have learned to like them, or both?

Clearly, some preferences are learned. For example, a sick rat who tastes a new food and then gets better will later show an acquired preference for that flavor (see Figure 3.2). We learn to like what is good for us. This is called the *medicine preference effect* (Richter, Holt, Barelace, and Hawkes, 1938; Rozin, 1967).

Innate Preference.　However, whereas some taste preferences appeared to be learned, others seem to be innate. For example, the preference for sweetness displayed by some species seems to be innate. The rat does not have to learn to like sugar through experience. The preference seems to be wired into the animal. Such innate preferences are often called *specific hungers*. Salt hunger appears to be another specific hunger. When they are salt deprived, many animals innately prefer salt. These animals do not have to learn to like salt by experiencing its beneficial effects (Cotman and McGaugh, 1980; Krieckhaus, 1970).

Taste Aversions.　Obviously some taste aversions are innate. If a baby bites into a new food for the very first time and discovers it to

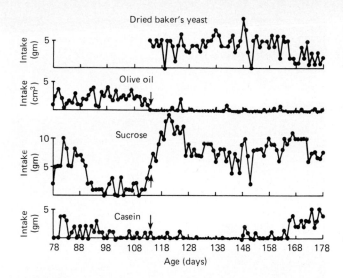

Dried baker's yeast

Intake (gm)

Olive oil

Intake (cm³)

Sucrose

Intake (gm)

Casein

Intake (gm)

Age (days)

FIGURE 3.2
An animal given a deficient diet will choose from the available food sources one which makes him feel better. This is called the medicine preference effect. If thiamine-deficient rats are given a choice only between fat (olive oil), carbohydrate (sucrose), or protein (casein), they will select fat since this is best for their health. When food containing thiamine (baker's yeast) is added to the choice, the rats consume the baker's yeast, resume a normal carbohydrate intake and decrease their consumption of fat. This shows a medicine preference effect not a specific hunger for thiamine. (From Richter, C. P., Holt, L. E., Barelace, B., & Hawkes, C. D. Changes in fat, carbohydrate and protein appetite in vitamin B deficiency. American Journal of Physiology, 1938, 124, 596–602. Fig. 2 on p. 598.)

be extremely salty and bitter, the expression on the child's face leaves no doubt in our mind about the innate quality of that particular aversion. The child did not have to learn to dislike that substance.

But many other taste aversions are acquired through complex learning processes. (We consider the intricate relationship between learning and motivation in much greater detail in Chapters 5 and 6.) Probably the best-known and most influential work on acquired taste aversions has been done by John Garcia and his associates (Garcia, Ervin, and Koelling, 1966; Garcia and Rusiniak, 1979; Garcia, Rusiniak, and Brett, 1977).

Essentially, animals will quickly learn to avoid flavors when the consumption of those flavors is followed by illness or other unpleasant consequences. A typical design used by Garcia and others is to have rats consume saccharin-flavored water while they are simultaneously exposed to X rays. X-irradiation is given in such doses that the animal becomes ill in an hour or so. Then, in subsequent tests, the rat will show a distinct aversion for saccharin. It is as if the animal has learned that the saccharin flavor is a danger signal.

The analogous situation in the life of a human is the one in which a new exotic food is consumed at a restaurant only to be followed by severe gastric distress later in the evening. It will probably be quite some time before the individual will try that particular dish again; just the thought of it will be enough to create a queasy sensation.

Some tastes are innate and some are learned. This child eating sweetened cereal may be exhibiting an innate preference. However, a preference for the octopus on sale in this fish market would most likely be learned. (Courtesy of J. D. Anker.)

This kind of learned taste aversion has been obtained with many different animals including mammals, birds, fish, and reptiles. Many different flavors, including sweet, sour, salty, and bitter ones, have been made aversive. The noxious condition has been established by X-irradiation, injected drugs, motion sickness, consumed toxic substances, and gamma irradiation, among others. In other words, the taste-aversion phenomenon is a very widespread phenomenon; it is not limited to rats and saccharin.

Garcia, Hankins, and Rusiniak (1974) summarize the experimental

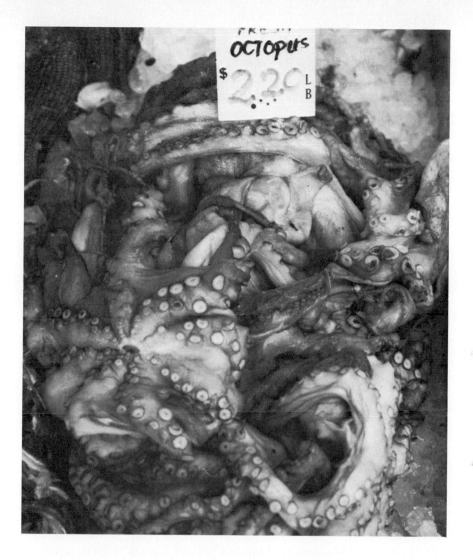

findings by noting that as the strength of the flavor increases the learned aversion will increase, the aversion will increase as the intensity of the illness increases, and the aversion will be less as the time between consumption and illness increases.

The novelty of the flavor also seems to be important. If a rat consumes two different flavors and is then X-irradiated, the subsequent illness is most likely to be associated with the more novel or unfamiliar of the two flavors. If you become ill after eating mashed potatoes and octopus, to which of these substances are you most likely to give credit for your discomfort? More than likely, it will be the novel taste of the octopus.

Even though the learning of taste aversions seems to be widespread and flexible, there does appear to be some kind of biological underpinning that limits the kinds of associations which are easily established. Garcia and Koelling (1966) X-irradiated rats while three different kinds of stimuli were presented. First, they drank saccharin-flavored water, second, lights flashed, and third, a noise was present. The question is this; to which of these three stimuli (taste, light, sound) will the illness be connected? Garcia and Koelling found that the illness was easily associated with the flavor but not at all with the other two stimuli. Neither light nor noise became aversive even though the two were paired as consistently with the illness as was the flavor. The argument here is that the animals were *prepared*, or neurally wired, to associate flavor with illness and unprepared to associate sights and sounds with illness. There seem to be biological, built-in limits to what will and will not be learned.

It makes sense from an evolutionary point of view, doesn't it? Animals that associate taste with illness are more likely to survive than animals that associate illness with sound or visual stimuli. (We deal with the whole topic of biological constraints or limits on behavior in greater detail in Chapter 6.)

The phenomenon of taste aversion has practical as well as theoretical implications. A few examples of the usefulness of taste aversion should suffice. First is the problem that coyotes create for themselves and others. Although their natural prey is rabbits and other small wild creatures, coyotes also love a tender young lamb now and then. This undeniable tendency for coyotes to prey upon domestic sheep creates an obvious conflict between stock raisers and environmentalists. It has been common to hunt and poison coyotes in large numbers (the use of poisoned bait is especially unfortunate because it kills many other innocent species, such as eagles).

Garcia and his colleagues (Garcia, Hankins, and Rusiniak, 1974; Gustavson, Garcia, Hankins, and Rusiniak, 1974) have proposed a solution that might satisfy ranchers and environmentalists alike. They fed coyotes bits of lamb flesh that have been dosed with lithium chloride, a chemical which makes the coyotes quite ill. After several meals of doctored lamb flesh, these coyotes were given a choice between rabbits and lambs. They very distinctly shied away from the lambs, but continued to attack their natural prey, the rabbits.

The ideal here is that coyote predation might be controlled by spreading, perhaps by airplane, bits of lamb flesh containing lithium chloride over the coyotes' range. After eating a few of these doctored pieces of bait, the coyotes would avoid the lambs and return to their natural diet.

Coyotes are not the only species that can be controlled through taste aversion; humans can too. In *aversion therapy*, which we consider in greater detail later, various human "bad habits" can be eliminated or at least reduced. The general procedure is to subject the person to some strong noxious stimulation while he is engaging in some undesirable behavior such as smoking, eating, or drinking. Electric shock and drugs are often used as the noxious stimuli. For example, if you are shocked as you inhale smoke, or are made to feel ill after drinking gin, then smoke and gin will become aversive through association with the noxious stimulation.

Obesity

It is no secret that our culture admires slenderness and ridicules heaviness. "Fat" jokes are commonplace, and the pages of *Vogue* magazine are filled with the near-emaciated. Many more people are trying to lose weight than to gain it. Being overweight can and does lead to a great deal of unhappiness.

Interestingly, even though it is abhorred by many, obesity is really quite difficult to define. Typically one is characterized as obese if one exceeds the average weight for one's age, sex, height, and bone structure by some percentage, such as 25 or 30 percent. But the average weight in a given culture is at least in part determined by that culture's attitude about obesity. As cultural norms change the weights that will be called obese change too. Thus, someone who is characterized as overweight today might have fallen within the normal range during an earlier era when plumpness was perceived as being more attractive than it is now. Standards of obesity are always relative to the culture's attitudes about what is pleasing and what is gross.

Differences in Eating Habits.   A number of very interesting potential differences between the eating behaviors of normal and obese persons have been discovered. Four differences listed in Table 3.1 bear mentioning.

TABLE 3.1. *Differences in the Eating Habits of Obese and Normal Individuals*

---

1. Obese people are stimulated into eating by external cues such as the presence of food or other food-related cues, whereas people of normal weight are controlled more often by internal cues such as internal hunger sensations.
2. Obese individuals seem to be less motivated to work for their food than are normal-weighted people.
3. Obese people are more particular about what they eat than are non-obese individuals.
4. Obese individuals often seem to have more trouble inhibiting their eating once it starts than do normal-weighted people.

Let us briefly look at some of the experimental data that support the differences contained in Table 3.1. Stanley Schachter (1971a, 1971b) has done a good deal of work related to the obesity issue. In one experiment he had subjects work at a task for several hours. Schachter misled the subjects with respect to what time it was by speeding up and slowing down the only available clock. Some subjects were led to believe that their normal dinner hour had arrived and some were led to believe that the dinner hour had not yet arrived. At this point crackers were offered to all subjects and Schachter observed how many crackers were eaten by the obese and nonobese subjects in the two time conditions. Overweight subjects ate many more crackers when they thought it was dinnertime than they did when they thought the dinner hour had not yet arrived. Normal-weighted subjects ate the same number of crackers in both time conditions. These results support point 1 in Table 3.1. Obese people judged their hunger on the basis of the external clock whereas nonobese people were not influenced by the clock; they seemed to rely on internal cues that were the same in both time conditions.

Point 2 in Table 3.1 states that obese people are less willing to work for their food than are normal individuals. In a study he did to support this proposition, Schachter (1971a) had obese and nonobese subjects fill out a number of personality tests. The subjects were offered almonds to munch on while they worked. Half of the subjects were offered shelled almonds and half were offered unshelled almonds. One would not think that shelling an almond would be a very significant bit of work, but it was. Half of the nonobese subjects were willing to shell almonds, whereas only one out of twenty overweight subjects was willing to do the same thing (see Table 3.2).

Point 3 in Table 3.1 indicates that obese people are more finicky and picky about what they eat than are nonobese people. Schachter (1971a) notes that obese Columbia University freshmen were more likely to terminate their meal contracts in the school cafeteria and less likely to renew them than were nonobese freshman. The idea here is that the less-than-delicious university chow was not quite tasty enough for the obese freshman who probably went elsewhere for better food. This same pickiness on the part of obese people has also been demonstrated experimentally. For example, Nisbett (1968) asked obese and nonobese subjects to evaluate ice cream. Normal ice cream and ice cream doctored with an unpleasant flavor were offered. Nisbett found that obese people were much more heavily affected by the flavor than were the nonobese in terms of how much they ate.

The fourth point in Table 3.1 points out that obese people have trouble stopping their eating behavior once it begins, which accounts for Schachter's observation that obese people are more likely to clean their plate than are nonobese individuals.

TABLE 3.2. *Effect of Work on the Eating Behavior of Obese and Normal Subjects*

Subjects	Nuts have:	Number who:	
		Eat	Don't eat
Normal	Shells	10	10
	No shells	11	9
Obese	Shells	1	19
	No shells	19	1

From: Schachter, S. Some extraordinary facts about obese humans and rats. *American Psychologist*, 1971, *26*, 129–144, Table 5 on p. 135. Copyright 1971 by the American Psychological Association. Reprinted by permission.

Biological Bases of Human Obesity

These behavioral differences between obese and nonobese individuals must be reflected, somehow, in biological differences. Whereas the exploration of these biological-behavioral relationships is just beginning (see Rodin, 1978), some interesting proposals have been made concerning the biological basis of obesity.

Human obesity has been suggested to be related to malfunctioning of the hypothalamus (Nisbett, 1972). As we learned earlier, lesions in the ventromedial hypothalamus lead to gross overeating in experimental animals. The behavior of these lesioned animals sometimes parallels the behavior of obese humans as outlined in Table 3.1. Thus lesioned animals will not quit eating once they start, and they tend to be quite finicky about what they eat (Teitelbaum, 1961).

The high degree of correspondence between these animal behaviors and the behaviors of obese humans leads us to suspect that hypothalamic malfunctioning may at least some of the time be a causal agent in human obesity. Although this kind of evidence is not conclusive, it is very suggestive.

Anorexia Nervosa

Anorexia nervosa is a poorly understood condition of severe undereating. It tends to strike young women often from midde- and upper-class families (Bemis, 1978). It is, in a sense, a form of self-imposed starvation. The sufferers are tremendously concerned about being overweight, and will be convinced that they are overweight when in fact they are severely underweight. In some cases force feeding is necessary to keep the patient alive, and death has been known to occur in some cases.

Table 3.3 contains the criteria used to diagnose this unfortunate condition.

The causes of anorexia nervosa are unknown. In a sense, anorexia is the opposite of obesity. Thus, a number of investigators have suggested that anorexia may involve malfunctioning of the hypothalamus, and the LH in particular (Lundberg and Walinder, 1967; Templer, 1971). These investigators point out that animals who have undergone hypothalamic lesioning display behavior which corresponds to that of the anorexic human.

Other investigators argue that the anorexic condition may have social and psychological in addition to physiological roots (Bruch, 1973). They argue that it is our culture's emphasis on, and apparent adoration of, slimness which helps drive young women to these excesses. Fear of being unattractive and a desire to be slender causes

TABLE 3.3.   *Criteria for Diagnosis of Anorexia Nervosa*

___

A.   Age of onset before 25.

B.   Anorexia with accompanying weight loss of at least 25% of original body weight.

C.   A distorted, implacable attitude toward eating, food, or weight that overrides hunger, admonitions, reassurance, and threats—for example:

    1.   Denial of illness with a failure to recognize nutritional needs.

    2.   Apparent enjoyment in losing weight with overt manifestations that food refusal is a pleasurable indulgence.

    3.   A desired body image of extreme thinness with overt evidence that it is rewarding to the patient to achieve and maintain this state.

    4.   Unusual hoarding or handling of food.

D.   No known medical illness that could account for the anorexia and weight loss.

E.   No other known psychiatric disorder, with particular reference to primary affective disorders, schizophrenia, and obsessive-compulsive and phobic neurosis. (The assumption is made that, even though it may appear phobic or obsessional, food refusal alone is not sufficient to qualify for obsessive-compulsive or phobic disease.)

F.   At least two of the following manifestations:

    1.   amenorrhea (absence of menstruation)

    2.   lanugo (a thick, soft, downy growth of hair)

    3.   bradycardia (persistent resting pulse of 60 or less)

    4.   periods of overactivity

    5.   episodes of bulimia (uncontrolled or excessive eating)

    6.   vomiting (may be self-induced)

___

From: Bemis, K. M. Current approaches to the etiology and treatment of anorexia nervosa. *Psychological Bulletin*, 1978, 85, 593–617, Table 1 on p. 594. Copyright 1978 by the American Psychological Association. Reprinted by permission.

some young women to eat less and less until their health is threatened. Interestingly, anorexics often have a wildly distorted perception of their own bodies. They are convinced they are fat when in fact they are starving, and they seem unable to accept the word of others concerning their actual physical condition.

Some, such as Bruch (1973), argue that this unfortunate condition must have its roots in something more than a simple desire to "look good." These investigators argue that poorly understood but disturbed family relationships must lead to confusion and conflict on the part of the patient. They argue that anorexia is an interpersonal problem.

Although the overall prognosis for anorexics is not good, the condition can sometimes be altered through training procedures. Garfinkel, Kline, and Stancer (1973) treated five women who had been hospitalized for anorexia. They rewarded the patients for weight gain with weekend passes and the opportunity to socialize with friends. As can be seen in Figure 3.3, the effects of such rewards can be dramatic. All five women regained almost all of their lost weight. So even though the disorder of anorexia is mysterious and difficult to treat, these kinds of training successes do hold out some hope for the future.

THIRST

A Steady State   Although not the most glamorous need, we are all aware of the powerful motivating effects of thirst. Few things are as demanding as a parching thirst and few events are as wonderful as the quenching of that thirst. Thirst may be thought of as a drive; it is such a strong drive that it ranks in importance with our need for air (Cotman and McGaugh, 1980). Without water life cannot be sustained. All meta-

FIGURE 3.3
The effects of rewarding weight gains in five patients suffering from anorexia. (Adapted from Garfinkel, P. E., Kline, S. A., & Stancer, H. C. Treatment of anorexia nervosa using operant conditioning techniques. Journal of Nervous and Mental Disease, *1973, 157, 428–433. Copyright 1973 by The Williams & Wilkins Co., Baltimore. Reprinted with permission.)*

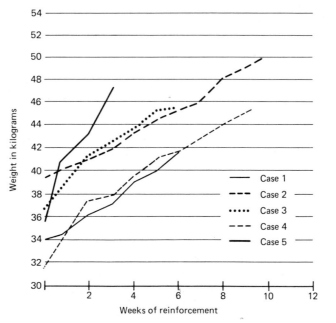

bolic processes require water, but elimination of waste, breathing, and sweating all result in the loss of water. Thus water must be replaced. Because the body requires a steady state with respect to fluid, mechanisms to replace this water, without overhydrating the system, must exist.

When our fluid level drops below an optimal level, the kidneys decrease the amount of water they excrete. This is one way that the body conserves water. However, even though this mechanism is helpful, it does not replace lost water; it merely helps to conserve a dwindling supply. Additional mechanisms, involving actual replacement through drinking, must exist.

Fluid is not distributed evenly throughout our bodies. Researchers have noted an important difference between what they call *intracellular* and *extracellular* fluid. Intracellular water is that contained *within* the cells. Intracellular fluid accounts for about two-thirds of the body's fluid. Extracellular fluid is all fluid outside the cells. This extracellular fluid is further broken down into fluid existing in the spaces between the cells and fluid in the blood. About four fifths of the extracellular fluid is located between cells and about one fifth in the blood.

Bodily Distribution of Water: Intracellular and Extracellular

It would be nice if there were one simple mechanism controlling thirst and drinking, but this does not seem to be the case. Apparently one mechanism controls drinking associated with extracellular fluid loss and a second separate mechanism controls thirst associated with intracellular fluid loss. For example, if a person is wounded and suffers a large loss of blood, the extracellular fluid volume drops. But no change occurs in intracellular water. The wounded individual becomes thirsty and drinks even though the intracellular water level is adequate. This suggests that two kinds of thirst exist, one related to losses from *within* the cells and one from fluid losses in the blood and spaces *between* the cells. We now turn to what is known about these two types of thirst.

Osmotic thirst refers to thirst caused by losses from *within* the cells. What mechanisms lie behind this form of thirst? Although controversial, the most popular current interpretation is as follows. You eat a salty substance. This raises the salt concentration in the extracellular spaces, leaving an imbalance across the cell membrane. In order for equilibrium to be established salt would have to penetrate into the

Osmotic Thirst

cell. Since this does not happen, water leaves the cells by osmosis in an effort to establish a balance. What this does, in effect, is dehydrate the cell.

Once the cells are dehydrated through this process of water moving out into the saltier extracellular spaces, what happens next? The best guess is that certain cells located in lateral preoptic regions of the brain close to the hypothalamus detect the condition in themselves and then initiate drinking behavior. These specialized receptors in the brain have been called *osmoreceptors* (see Blass and Epstein, 1971; Peck and Novin, 1971).

All of the cells throughout the body suffer from the same loss of fluid, but it is only the few osmoreceptors in the brain that use the detection of that condition to initiate drinking. Anderson (1971) showed this by injecting salt solution right into the osmoreceptor areas of the brains of rats that were not thirsty. They began to drink. The idea is that the osmoreceptors were tricked into acting as though the entire body needed intracellular water. In fact, the osmoreceptors themselves did need water, because of the locally injected salt solution, but the rest of the body cells did not need water. Thus, the message about a water deficit is not "carried to" the brain in any way. The osmoreceptors in the brain react on the basis of their own local conditions.

Volumetric Thirst We now turn to the second thirst mechanism. Loss of extracellular fluid, called *hypovolemia*, also results in thirst and drinking behavior. Extracellular loss can be caused by the following kinds of events:

> bleeding
> vomiting
> lack of drinking water
> diarrhea
> sweating

Although the existence of volumetric thirst is now widely accepted, the mechanisms behind this form of thirst are not well understood. As Cotman and McGaugh (1980) put it, "This thirst mechanism is a by far more complex and less well understood control than the cellular thirst mechanism. Its major receptors have not yet been identified" (p. 572).

Some progress has been made, however. The most widely noted

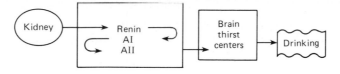

FIGURE 3.4
The role of renin in the initiation of drinking. When a fall in blood pressure or blood volume is detected, renin is released into the bloodstream from the kidney. In the bloodstream, renin splits a plasma protein into angiotensin I. (AI). When this decapeptide passes through the lungs, a converting enzyme located there splits it further into the octapeptide angiotensin II. (AII). The angiotensin II is then carried to the brain where it enters the cerebrospinal fluid and stimulates structures located near the ventricles to induce drinking. (From Coteman, C. W., & Mc-Gaugh, J. L. Behavioral Neuroscience New York: Academic, 1980, Fig. 13.4 on p. 574.)

mechanism involves *angiotensin*. The sequence is thought to go like this: A drop in extracellular volume causes the kidneys to secrete an enzyme called *renin*. Through a complicated chemical process renin instigates the production of angiotensin that circulates in the bloodstream. The best guess is that, once it reaches the brain, angiotensin stimulates specific receptors which then initiate drinking (see Figure 3.4). Although not well understood, it seems that the hypothalamus is the area in which these as yet unidentified receptors are located.

Evidence for the importance of angiotensin in producing drinking in response to hypovolemia comes from studies such as that of Epstein, Fitzsimmons, and Rolls (1970). They injected angiotensin into certain areas of the rat's brain. Satiated rats then began to drink. In addition, the more angiotensin they injected the more the rats drank.

Although the renin-angiotensin mechanism has been quite popular, it too is very controversial. For example, work by Stricker, Brodshaw, and McDonald (1976) suggests that even though renin-angiotensin will produce drinking, especially when present in abnormally large amounts, this mechanism may not be powerful enough to account for all volumetric drinking. The hint is that there are still additional volumetric mechanisms to be discovered.

In summary, there seem to be two thirst systems, one involving fluid loss within the cells and one involving losses outside the cells. The first is regulated by specialized osmoreceptors located in the lateral preoptic region. Losses of intracellular fluid cause cells there to initiate drinking behavior. The second form of thirst is less well understood but may involve the stimulation of as yet unknown receptors located in the brain by a kidney-renin-angiotensin system.

One of the most intuitively appealing ideas about thirst is that it can be stimulated by dryness of the mouth. You know, if you try to eat wall plaster you will become thirsty. Although popular at one time, this explanation of thirst has fallen on hard times. In general, it has been accepted that dry mouth can account for neither osmotic nor volumetric thirst.

Dry Mouth: Primary and Secondary Drinking

However, there really do seem to be times when dry mouth does lead to drinking. That mouth full of wall plaster does in fact lead to drinking.

Investigators make a distinction between *primary* and *secondary* drinking that is of value here. Primary drinking refers to drinking that is related to an actual loss of bodily fluid. Thus both osmotic thirst and volumetirc thirst lead to primary drinking.

But drinking does sometimes occur when our body has enough fluid, and even sometimes when we have an excess of fluid. For example, we may drink because we just cannot pass up the flavor of a chocolate soda. Or we may drink from habit as is the case of the individual who has two beers every evening to unwind even when his body fluid is adequate. This form of drinking, called secondary drinking, is very poorly understood. We have to await further research before secondary drinking is explained.

SEXUAL MOTIVATION

Differences from Hunger and Thirst

The study of sexual motivation is varied and complex. It ranges all the way from a concern for developmental issues (as we shall see in Chapter 7) to topics such as liking, loving, and attraction (as we shall see in Chapter 10). For now, we want to begin the exploration of sexual motivation by making some comments about what is known of the biology of sex. What are the neural and hormonal mechanisms that control sexual motivation?

Before turning to these mechanisms it should be pointed out that although it is certainly a basic biological motive, sex does differ in important ways from hunger and thirst. This chapter deals with regulatory mechanisms, and hunger and thirst are clearly examples of regulatory systems. But, even though this and other textbooks include sex in the chapter on regulatory mechanisms, sex does not fit the regulatory mold quite as neatly as do hunger and thirst. Sex motivation has enough in common with hunger and thirst to include it in a chapter on regulatory mechanisms, but, at the same time, the important, unique aspects of sexual motivation included in Table 3.4 should be kept in mind.

TABLE 3.4. *How Sex Differs*

1. Unlike food and water, sex is not essential for the survival of the individual. No one will die without sex. (You may think you are going to die, but you won't.) It is necessary for survival of species, of course, but not for the individual.
2. People seek arousal as well as reduction of the motive. Most people enjoy the feeling of being sexually aroused, but almost no one likes to feel too thirsty or too hungry.
3. Humans can be sexually aroused by an extremely wide range of stimuli—a much wider range, in fact, that will arouse hunger or thirst.
4. The arousal of the human sex motive appears to be less affected by deprivation than are the other drives. Except for a short period immediately following sexual orgasm, the sex motive seems to be arousable at almost any time, and does not show the regular increase over time that is displayed by the hunger and thirst drives.
5. Sexual behavior uses energy rather than replacing it.

From Houston, J. P., Bee, H., Hatfield, E., and Rimm, D. C., *Invitation to Psychology.* New York: Academic Press, 1979, p. 303. Reprinted by permission.

Hormones circulating in the bloodstream appear to have an enormous impact upon the sexual behaviors of lower animals (as we shall see, human sexual behavior is also determined by circulating sex hormones, but not quite so rigidly). In the female, estrogen and progesterone are produced by the ovaries. In the male, androgen (testosterone) is released by the male's testes. These hormones, collectively, are called *gonadal* hormones because they are released by the gonads.

What controls the amounts of gonadal hormones released by the ovaries and testes? It appears to be a complex situation, but the hypothalamus again seems to be involved. It seems that the hypothalamus influences the pituitary gland (often called the "master gland") which, in turn, releases a number of different hormones that control complex sexual motivation. Some of these hormones released by the pituitary move through the bloodstream to the gonads where they stimulate the release of the gonadal hormones.

So the hypothalamus appears to be involved in the production of testosterone, and estrogen, but only in an indirect manner; the hypothalamus acts on the pituitary, which, in turn, releases hormones that influence the production and release of the male and female sex hormones from the testes and ovaries, respectively.

Interacting Neural and Hormonal Factors

Animals versus Humans

Most sex research has involved lower animals for two reasons. First, rather drastic electrical, chemical, and surgical procedures can be used with animals but not humans. Second, restrictive cultural attitudes about studying human sex, or even talking about it very freely, have, until recently, tended to keep to a minimum what we know about human sexuality.

Researchers using animals as subjects hoped that by understanding animal sexuality they would also come to understand human sexuality. Animals research has, in fact, been extremely helpful. But, at the same time, there are important differences between animal and human sexuality that must be kept in mind:

Humans Are More Flexible. It is well known that lower mammals are in the strong grip of hormonally controlled sexual cycles. Females are sexually inactive most of the time, showing interest only during cyclical periods of *estrus* or "heat" during which the levels of sex hormones rise. At these times, and only these times, will the female seek out and engage in sexual activity. During the remainder of the time she will rebuff advances by males. Although seeking sex more constantly, males become especially aroused by cues, such as odor and calls, provided by the females during their receptive cycles. Clearly, human sexuality is much more flexible than this. Although human female arousal may be slightly cyclical (see Adams, Gold, and Burt, 1978), humans can and do engage in sex at any time; they are not restricted, as are the so-called lower mammals, by a hormonally determined cycle.

As we move up the phylogenetic scale, the dependence of sexual activity upon circulating hormones decreases. For example, a castrated male rat will quickly give up sexual activity of any kind. Castrated dogs show a decline in interest, even though not as abruptly as in the rat. But a castrated human male often will go on engaging in sexual activity as though nothing had happened.

The same kind of picture emerges when we compare the removal of ovaries in lower mammals and human females. Human females often continue to be interested in sex after removal of the ovaries, whereas females of most other mammalian species show a significant loss of interest in sex following the removal of their ovaries.

Sex and Learning. If hormones do not completely control our sex

life, what does? Learning and experience affect us much more than they do the lower species. We humans seem to be in the grip of some complex interaction between hormonal and learning factors.

Although some lower species, such as rats, mice, and birds, will engage in normal sexual activity even when they have been raised in total isolation, higher-order animals, such as primates, appear to be heavily affected by experience. Harlow (1971), in a classic series of studies, raised some monkeys in isolation and found that the development of normal sexual behavior was severely distorted. Somehow, in some complex manner, these monkeys must interact with one another if they are to develop normal, successful sexual behaviors. Presumably humans are even more susceptible to the impact of experience.

The Female Sexual Response   Prior to the work of Masters and Johnson (1966), very little objective information was available concerning the physiology of the sexual response. Kinsey and his colleagues (1948) had done some pioneering interview work. The upshot of their efforts was the idea that both men and women enjoy orgasm and that "normal" people engage in a wide variety of sexual practices and positions. Kinsey's work was heavily criticized because of sampling problems. Specifically, critics argued that Kinsey's sample of people did not represent the population in general. The very fact that Kinsey's subjects would even talk to a stranger about their sexual activity was thought to indicate that the subject was somehow abnormal or at least not representative of the general population. However, as time has passed, and the storm has died down, Kinsey's main point, that "normal" sex is very varied and enjoyed by women as well as men, has been substantiated.

Masters and Johnson (1966) took the investigation of human sexuality a step further by studying and taking physiological measures of people while they were engaged in sexual activities. Although some of the work done by Masters and Johnson is controversial, especially their therapeutic efforts (see Masters and Johnson, 1966; Cuniberti, 1983), much helpful information has been obtained.

Masters and Johnson propose that the human sexual response can be broken down into four stages: 1) excitement, 2) plateau, 3) orgasm, 4) resolution. Although not all people go through all of these stages in exactly the same manner, and the sexual response is understood to be continuous and not composed of discrete segments, Masters and Johnson argue that a good overall understanding of the human sexual response can be gained by thinking of it in terms of these stages. We look at the four female stages and then the four male stages.

1. Excitement.   When a human female is sexually stimulated, a number of physiological changes occur. The clitoris often increases in size through vasocongestion, vaginal lubrication occurs, the vagina lengthens and expands, the cervix and the uterus retract, nipples become erect, and a sex flush begins.

2. Plateau.   During this phase, vasocongestion of the vaginal opening reaches a peak. The clitoris draws back into the body. Nipple erection, breast enlargement, and sex flush continue. Heart rate and blood pressure increase.

3. Orgasm. During orgasm intense rhythmic contractions occur near the vaginal opening. Orgasms may vary in strength, some involving only a few contractions whereas others may involve as many as a dozen contractions. The clitoris remains retracted. Nipple erection and breast enlargement continue, while the sex flush ends abruptly. Heart rate and blood pressure peak during this stage.

4. Resolution. During this phase the vagina relaxes, vasocongestion decreases, and the clitoris returns to its normal position. Nipples and breasts return to normal as do heart rate and blood pressure.

The human male also goes through four stages in the overall sexual response.

The Male Sexual Response

1. Excitement. Through vasocongestion the penis becomes engorged and erect. The scrotal skin thickens and wrinkles, and the testes become elevated. In some males, but not all, nipple erection occurs. Some sex flush may occur.

2. Plateau. During this stage sexual arouses intensifies. The penis becomes fully distended and erect, and heart rate and blood pressure increases. There is a general increase in the changes first observed in the excitement phase.

3. Orgasm. During this stage the penis and the urethra contract rhythmically. The seminal fluid is forced out. Breathing, blood pressure, and heart rate all increase. Nipple erection and sex flush may continue.

4. Resolution. During this phase all of the arousal symptoms return to normal. The rate of return to normal varies from individual to individual and from symptom to symptom.

In this chapter we have emphasized the biology and physiology of sex. Obviously, there is a lot more to this topic, and we return to the issue of sexual behavior in the sections on the role of learning in motivation and the role of cognitive activity in motivation.

SUMMARY

1. Basic physiological needs, though perhaps less glamorous, are just as important as more complex and acquired motives.

2. Regulatory mechanisms maintain steady states with respect to the needs of the body.

3. Regulatory mechanisms may be under voluntary or involuntary control, or both.

4. Early suggestions that events occurring in the stomach control hunger have proved to be inadequate.

5. Dual hypothalamic control refers to the fact that the VMH serves as a kind of "off switch" whereas the LH serves as an "on switch."

6. The glucostatic theory refers to the hypothesis that the hypothalamus contains gluco-receptors which monitor blood sugar levels. This theory is usually applied to short-term control of eating.

7. The glucostatic theory has been heavily criticized.

8. The lipostatic theory suggests that the long-term stability of our weight is maintained through the monitoring of body fat.

9. Set-point theory is an example of lipostatic theory.

10. Glycerol may be involved in fat regulation. Insulin may be involved too.

11. Glucoreceptors may be in the liver and duodenum rather than the hypothalamus.

12. CCK may be a chemical signal involved in hunger.

13. Rate-of-infusion studies suggest that glucostatic theory is far from adequate.

14. Taste is important in eating behavior. Some preferences are innate and some are learned.

15. Learned taste aversions, such as bait shyness, are easily demonstrated. They may have important practical implications in areas such as the control of predation and bad habits.

16. Obesity seems to be related to important differences in the eating habits of fat and normal people.

17. Obesity may sometimes be related to malfunctioning of the hypothalamus.

18. Anorexia nervosa is self-imposed starvation.

19. Anorexia may have neural, social, and/or psychological bases.

20. Body water is constantly monitored and regulated.

21. Extracellular water, as distinct from intracellular water, is broken down into the water between the cells and the water in the blood.

22. Osmotic thirst refers to thirst caused by losses of water from within the cells.

23. Loss of extracellular water leads to volumetric thirst.

24. Angiotensin and renin may be in involved in thirst regulation.

25. Primary drinking occurs when an actual body loss of fluid occurs. Secondary drinking, poorly understood, occurs in the absence of a real need.

26. Sexual motivation is not as clearly a regulatory mechanism as are hunger and thirst.

27. Neural and hormonal factors interact in the control of sexual motivation.

28. Humans are less rigidly controlled by hormonal activity than are lower animals.

29. Human sexuality is strongly influenced by learning and experience.

30. According to Masters and Johnson, male and female sexual responses may be thought of as involving four stages: excitement, plateau, orgasmic, and resolution.

CHAPTER 4

$$\Downarrow$$

Arousal, Stress, Sleep, and Addiction

Everyone is aware of the fact that we are sometimes more aroused than others. We have all had the experience of feeling slow and sluggish, both mentally and physically, as we sometimes do when we wake up in the morning. And we have all had times when we have been feeling wide awake, alert, and "ready to go." At other times we feel "in between." In other words, our levels of physical and mental conditions can and do range all the way from very low to very high *states of arousal*.

The Arousal Continuum

Psychologists are interested in the causes and consequences of these arousal states. They want to know if they correlate with observable neurological changes, both in the brain and the rest of the nervous system, and they want to know how they relate to our feelings and our behavior. In the following sections we look at what psychologists have learned about the relationships between arousal and performance, emotion, and neural activity.

Performance and Arousal. We have all heard statements such as, "I was so keyed up I blew the exam." At other times people say, "I just couldn't get up for the exam and I blew it." These and similar

Arousal Theory: The Inverted U

statements suggest that our performance is dramatically affected by our state of arousal. The classic Yerkes-Dodson law (Yerkes and Dodson, 1908), depicted in Figure 4.1a, offers a summary statement of the relationship between performance and arousal.

As can be seen in Figure 4.1a, the argument is that *both* very high and very low levels of arousal interfere with performance. Thus if you are trying to play chess, but are half asleep, you will not be a very formidable player. On the other hand, if your opponent is overwrought and overly aroused she too may not perform up to her full capacity. According to the Yerkes-Dodson formulation, *intermediate* levels of arousal lead to maximum efficiency.

Figures 4-b and 4-c describe the proposed relationship between performance and task difficulty. The theory suggests that if the task is a simple one then a relatively high level of arousal will lead to the best performance (Figure 4-b). For example, if you are given endless

FIGURE 4.1
The inverted U relationship between arousal and performance (A), according to the Yerkes-Dodson law. The optimal arousal level is higher when the task is simple (B) and lower when the task is complex or difficult (C).

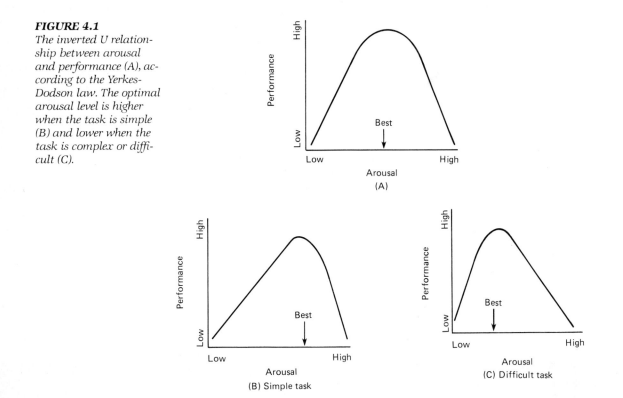

sheets of paper containing rows of random digits, and asked to cross out, endlessly, all the 2s and 6s, you will probably do better if you are highly aroused. Anything resembling low arousal will lead to poor performance. On the other hand, if the task is a difficult or complex one, such as playing chess, then you might not want to be too aroused (see Figure 4-c). Here it is better, according to the theory, to be only somewhat aroused.

Support for the theory has been good, but not perfect. For example, whereas some studies have shown that low levels of arousal hurt performance (Bexton, Heron, and Scott, 1954), others have suggested that the effect appears under some conditions but not others (Orne and Scheibe, 1964). Similarly, the idea that extremely high levels of arousal hurt performance is sometimes supported (Broadhurst, 1957) and sometimes not (Duffy, 1962).

Thus, although it is extremely appealing on a intuitive level, the Yerkes-Dodson formulation probably represents an oversimplification of the relationship between performance and arousal. It is probably fair to say that the theory is accurate under some conditions but not others, and that the precise natures of these conditions have yet to be worked out.

Emotion and Arousal. So far we have been speaking of the relationship between arousal level and *performance*. But what about the relationship between arousal level and *how we feel?* A substantial body of literature suggests that there is an inverted U relationship between emotion and arousal as well as between performance and arousal. Specifically, it has been argued that extreme levels of arousal, either high or low, are unpleasant and aversive. Intermediate levels of arousal are, on the other hand, preferred and associated with positive affect or emotion.

On an intuitive level this makes sense. Children like to go to the circus (moderately arousing) but do not want to be put right into the center ring (too arousing). Neither do they want to sit alone in their room all day (not arousing enough). We like to be stirred up but not *too* stirred up. We have an intermediate level of arousal that we prefer.

Let us now look at some of the experimental results that support the idea that there is a preferred level of arousal. First, consider the idea that we prefer moderate arousal to very low levels of arousal. Heron, Doane, and Scott (1956) paid human volunteers to take part in *sensory deprivation experiments* (See Fig. 4.2). Subjects spent, or tried to spend, long periods of time lying in a dimly lit, soundproof room. They wore goggles and gloves and had nothing to do. After a few days under these low-arousal conditions, most subjects could not stand it any longer and refused to stay in the room. They reported strong feelings of frustration and boredom. Some subjects reported having hallucinations after three days in this situation. The implication here is that they were underaroused, or below their preferred level of arousal. This interpretation is bolstered by the fact that subjects in this situation who were given the opportunity to press a button, which played a tape of a six-year-old lecturing on the evils of alcohol, would press that button repeatedly (Bexton, Heron, and Scott, 1954).

Berlyne (1958, 1966, 1971) has also been extremely influential in connection with this arousal issue by publishing a great deal of material demonstrating that we are *curious* animals driven to explore and perceive the world around us. He and others have shown that we are attracted to *novel* and perhaps *complex* stimuli, the perception of which presumably increases our state of arousal. For example, he found that humans would rather look at, and pay attention to, the unusual rather than the less novel stimuli shown in Figure 4.3.

FIGURE 4.2
A sensory deprivation situation. All sensory input is muffled, while electrical activity of the brain is recorded. (Adapted from Heron, W. The pathology of boredom. Scientific American, 1957, 196(1), 52–56. Fig. on pp. 52–53.

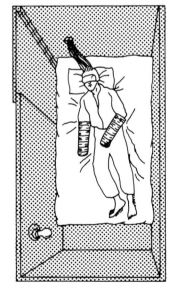

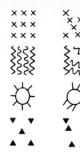
Irregularity of arrangement

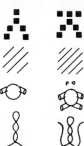
Amount of material

Heterogeneity of elements

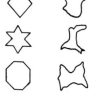
Irregularity of shape

Incongruity

Incongruous juxtaposition

FIGURE 4.3
Complex and simple materials developed by Berlyne. (Adapted from Berlyne, D. E. The influence of complexity and novelty in visual figures on orienting responses. Journal of Experimental Psychology, *1958, 55, 289–296. Copyright 1958 by the American Psychological Association. Reprinted by permission.)*

Demonstrations of what could be a desire for intermediate arousal are easy to find in the animal kingdom. For example, Harlow, Harlow, and Meyer (1950) found that monkeys will learn to open latches, and get better and better at doing so, without any extrinsic reward. Apparently they like to be involved in this activity for its own sake. Butler (1953) has shown that monkeys, confined in boring neutral boxes, will learn to solve problems when the reward they are given is the chance to look out of the box into the surrounding laboratory for a brief moment. The longer they have been deprived of sensory stimulation the higher their rate of instrumental behavior. The interest value of the sensory stimulation is important too; monkeys will show an increase in responding if a toy is placed outside the window rather than a blank wall. And Kish (1955) has shown that mice like a little variety too. He found that they would learn to press a bar when that bar press switched a light on for a moment. They will also learn the same bar-pressing response when it turns the light off.

These and many other studies show that animals and humans

prefer moderate arousal to very low arousal. But what about the other side of the argument? What studies show that very high arousal is unpleasant? Franken and Strain (1974) injected rats with methamphetamine, a drug that produces high arousal, and then gave the rats the chance to enter complex mazes which, by their complexity, would further increase the animal's arousal. In contrast to control animals that did not receive methamphetamine, the highly aroused animals were less likely to enter the complex mazes. It was as though they were experiencing enough, or too much, arousal from the drug and did not want to be stimulted further by the complex mazes. The control animals, on the other hand, showed a marked interest in the complex mazes.

Independence of Arousal and Emotion?

In the preceding sections we outlined many investigators' opinions of the relationship between feeling and arousal. The general consensus has been that intermediate arousal is pleasant whereas extremely high or low arousal is unpleasant. However, other investigators think that this is an oversimplification of the relationship between emotion and arousal.

Consider the following example. You are about to attend a concert that you have been looking forward to for some time. You are definitely aroused. You enter the crowded hall and the music begins. But the crowd does not respond favorably. They seem dissatisfied, restless, and irritable. The music draws a few "boos" and catcalls. You too begin to feel unhappy. You interpret your internal arousal as unpleasant. You use what is going on around you to interpret your feelings. If so many other people are disappointed then you must be too. In other words, emotion is the result of an interaction between internal arousal and your *cognitive appraisal* of what is going on around you.

Contrast this experience with one in which you enter the same hall, in the same state of arousal, and the crowd goes wild with appreciation. Here you would be caught up in the "mood of the crowd" and interpret your internal state of arousal in a positive manner. If so many other people are having such a good time, then you must be too. You use your perception of what is occurring around you to interpret your internal state of arousal.

According to this position, there is no simple inverted U relationship between emotion and arousal. What you feel depends upon what you are thinking. The same identical state of arousal can, depending upon what you are thinking, be experienced as either positive or negative emotion.

Schachter and Singer (1962) conducted the classic and, as it turns out, controversial experiment in this area. All subjects were first told that the experiment was concerned with the effects of "a new chemical compound" on vision. They were given an injection and asked to wait in a room and fill out a questionnaire. Experimental subjects were given an injection of epinephrine (adrenalin) which produces high arousal. One third of the experimental subjects were told nothing about the effects of the drug. One third was told, correctly, that the drug would increase their heart rate, their breathing rate, and a sense of edginess. The last third of the experimental group was misinformed. They were told that the drug would produce itching, a headache, and numbness. The other half of the subjects, or the control subjects, were injected with a saline solution that has no significant physiological effects. Then half of each group of subjects waited in the room with a confederate of the experimenter who acted angry. This confederate finally tore up the questionnaire and stormed out of the room. The other half of each group waited with a confederate who acted happy. This confederate smiled, giggled, and playfully threw paper airplanes.

The following results were obtained in the experiment. Subjects in the uninformed experimental and the misinformed experimental groups were both experiencing internal arousal that was unexplained, so they interpreted it in terms of what was going on around them. That is, when they were faced with an irritable confederate they too became irritable. When faced with a happy confederate they too acted happy. On the other hand, subjects in the correctly informed group, knowing that what they were feeling was a result of the drug, had no unexplained arousal to account for, and were thus unaffected by the confederates. And the control subjects, having no arousal to account for at all, were also unaffected by the confederates.

It is an interesting experiment and makes the point well: Our interpretation of what we are feeling can be affected by our state of arousal and our cognitive interpretation of what is going on around us. A study by Cantor, Zillmann, and Bryant (1975) offers further support for the idea. They had subjects watch an erotic film during three phases of recovery from exercise. In the middle phase when the subjects still showed autonomic arousal but no longer reported subjective feelings of arousal, the film led to higher sexual arousal. The subjects attributed their autonomic arousal to sexual factors.

However, even though other efforts to reproduce these effects have appeared (Erdmann and Janke, 1978) others have reported failures to replicate (Marshall and Zimbardo, 1979; Maslach, 1979). In other words, while understanding the idea behind the Schachter and Singer study we must await further experimentation before we draw firm conclusions concerning its validity (see also Plutchik, 1980).

We further discuss the impact of cognition on motivation in Section IV of this text.

Two Arousal Curves?

As we have seen, traditional thinking relates arousal to felt emotion with a single inverted U curve. According to this approach we prefer, or feel best, under conditions of moderate arousal. To a point that does seem to be true; we often find ourselves seeking moderate stimulation and avoiding very high and very low arousal conditions. However, there are times when we really do want and enjoy extremely high states of arousal, such as during sexual activity and during a rollercoaster ride. And there really are times when we want and enjoy very low states of arousal, such as taking a nap in the afternoon or simply sitting and watching the world go by. The inverted U conception does not easily account for these and other commonplace pleasures associated with very high and very low states of arousal. Accordingly, Walters, Apter, and Svebak (1982) have proposed that there are *two* arousal curves as depicted in Figure 4.4. According to these authors, there are two preferred levels of arousal, one high and one low; sometimes we like to be very relaxed and sometimes we like to be very excited. We can only prefer one of these states at a time. At any given moment we want to be high or low, but not both. We switch back and forth between these two preferred levels. The conditions that govern this switching back and forth between the two preferred states have not been well worked out. Presumably both simple and complex mechanisms govern this switching process. For example, we might switch from preferring high arousal to preferring low arousal simply because we have become fatigued. Or, at another time, we might switch from low to high arousal because of an attack of guilt over "wasting time."

In any case, this conception has the advantage over the simple inverted U conception in that it accounts for our occasional desire for

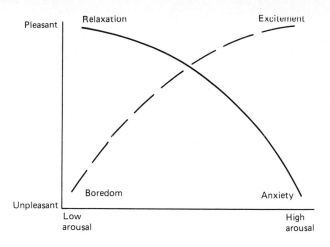

FIGURE 4.4
*Two arousal curves of
the type hypothesized by
Walters, Apter and Sve-
bak (1982) and ex-
plained in text.*

extremes. As you can see in Figure 4.4, intermediate levels of arousal
are seen as moderately pleasing, but the extremes are where intense
pleasure comes in.

So far we have been talking about arousal on a behavioral level. Now
it is time to turn to what is known about arousal on a more physiological level. What goes on within the body, and in particular the
nervous system, when conditions of arousal exist?

The RAS and Cortical Arousal

The *reticular activating system*, or RAS, has been implicated in both
cortical and behavioral arousal (see Moruzzi and Magoun, 1949,
Lindsley, 1951). Although it is somewhat difficult to visualize, the
RAS is a tangled mass of neuronal fibers that look criss-crossed, or
reticulated (the Latin word *reticulum* means "net"). This structure,
or system, can be thought of as the "core" of the brain stem (see
Figure 4.5) and it extends all the way from the hindbrain up into the
forebrain.

RAS involvement in arousal is thought to operate something like
this. Sensory signals coming into the brain from all of our sensory
systems (visual, auditory, and others) travel along afferent pathways
that project into sensory areas of the cortex. But, in addition, branches
of these afferent pathways also extend into the RAS (see Figure 4.5).
Thus sensory information goes to two places, the cortex and the RAS.
The signals reaching the RAS alert, arouse, or activate the cortex such
that sensory signals reaching the cortex can be acted upon. If the RAS
is *not* activated, then signals reaching the cortex do not seem to be
registered or acted upon. It is as though the cortex must be activated

FIGURE 4.5

Input from sensory sys-
tems goes into both the
cortex and the RAS. Out-
put from the RAS arouses
and readies the cortex
for input from the sen-
sory systems. (Adapted
from Magoun, H. Brain
mechanisms and con-
sciousness. Oxford:
Blackwell Scientific Pub-
lications Limited, 1954.)

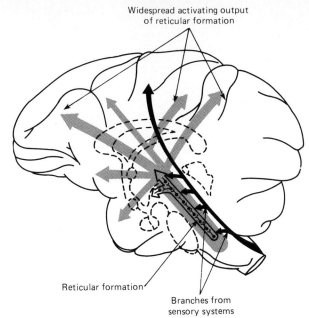

or readied by the action of the RAS before sensory signals will be processed by the cortex. Unless our RAS is activated and able to prime or ready the cortex, we will be unaware of events in our environment.

Cortical arousal is measured through the use of the electroenceph-alograph (EEG). The brain is an electrical organ, constantly emitting tiny electrical impulses. These impulses can be detected with the electroencephalograph, and displayed as ink lines on a strip of paper or tracings on an oscilloscopic display. The record of electrical activity is called an electroencephalogram. (Electroencephalograph is to electroencephalogram as telegraph is to telegram).

Our cortex emits different EEG patterns depending upon our state of arousal (see Figure 4.6). If we are excited and alert, our brain emits what are known as Beta waves. These are low-amplitude, high-frequency waves. When we close our eyes and relax, we emit what are called Alpha waves, or waves that have higher amplitudes and lower frequencies than Beta waves. When we are in deep sleep we display Delta waves as can be seen in Figure 4.6.

EEG records have often been used in studying the role of the RAS in arousal. For example, Moruzzi, and Magoun (1949) directly stimulated the RAS and found that this caused EEG arousal as well as

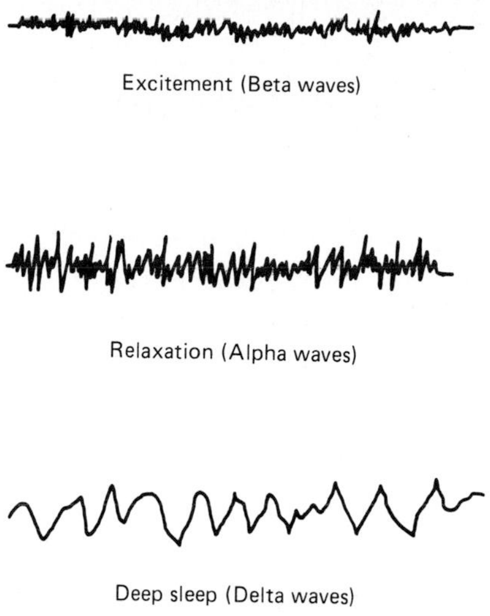

Excitement (Beta waves)

Relaxation (Alpha waves)

Deep sleep (Delta waves)

FIGURE 4.6
EEG records obtained under different states of arousal.

behavioral alertness. Stimulation of the RAS by the presentation of external stimuli, rather than direct electrical stimulation, also produces alertness. In other words, cortical arousal, RAS activation, and behavioral arousal all seem to go together, at least according to some studies. The assumption is that the RAS is responsible for cortical and behavioral arousal.

However, Routtenberg (1968) has noted that there is not *always* good correlation between EEG records, behavioral arousal, and RAS activity (see also Lacy, 1967). On the basis of some lesion work, Routtenberg concluded that there are at least two arousal systems in the brain. The first is the one involving the RAS. The second involves the limbic system, which is a system of several connected subcortical structures. Perhaps these two arousal systems (RAS and limbic) serve different functions rather than duplicating one another's activity. Even though Routtenberg's work has not been very influential, we cannot, at present, be too firm or precise in our statements about brain structures and arousal for there is still much to be learned.

Although the brain, and in particular the RAS and limbic system, is involved in arousal, other aspects of the overall nervous system also seem to be tied to arousal. Specifically, the autonomic nervous system seems to be responsible for many physiological changes that occur during arousal. For example, if we are exposed to strong external

The Autonomic System and Arousal

stimulation, such as injury, fearful circumstances, overwork, or certain drugs, our autonomic system goes into action. Our blood vessels construct and our heart rate increases. Digestion halts and the liver releases glucose for quick energy. Pupils dilate and perspiration increases. In other words, our body prepares for emergency. When the emergency has passed, the autonomic system returns the body to the normal nonaroused pattern.

Without going into great detail it should be clear that arousal seems to be related to changes both within the brain and in the autonomic subdivison of the peripheral nervous system.

Catecholamines and Arousal

Research into the nature of arousal has not been limited to investigation of specific brain structures, such as the RAS. Certain chemical substances, known as catecholamines, have also been implicated. Catecholamines are neurotransmitters, substances that allow a neural impulse to travel from one neuron to the next, across the synaptic gap. If there is a high concentration of a particular neurotransmitter in the area of the synapse, then the impulse is more likely to move from the first neuron to the next. Low concentrations of a neurotransmitter reduce the probability of the impulse moving from one neuron to the next.

The three catecholamines that have received the most attention in connection with arousal are dopamine, epinephrine, and norepinephrine. To one degree or another, all of these catecholamines seem to be involved in arousal. Although our knowledge about why and how these chemicals are released is still sketchy, we do know that their release seems to be associated with improved performance, increased arousal, and elevated mood (Mandel, Mack, and Goridis, 1975).

SLEEP

Sleep As an Active Process

Many consider sleep to be a state of either very low arousal, or no arousal at all. Thus it makes sense to talk about sleep research in conjunction with our section on arousal. Sleep may be thought of as the lower end of the arousal dimension.

However, it is a mistake to think of sleep as a state of "total blankness," or, "like being dead or unconscious." Even though sleep may represent low arousal it is quite a complicated process. Consider, for example, the common notions that when we are asleep we are (1) physically inactive, (2) unconscious, (3) insensitive to external stimuli, and (4) incapable of carrying out a plan. None of these is entirely true. Sleep can involve physical activity, as when you jerk your arm in the middle of the night. And consider the sleepwalker. Although not well understood, sleepwalking, a fairly common phenomenon, surely represents physical activity during sleep. When we are asleep we are not always unconscious either. In fact, a good portion of each night is spent dreaming, which is clearly a form of consciousness. And, when asleep, we do make fine discriminations among external stimuli. For example, parents with a newborn child may sleep right through the sounds of trashcans being tossed about outside their window. But let one little peep come from the new baby's room and the parent will be awake in a flash. We are, after all, sensitive to various kinds of external stimuli while we are asleep. Some of us can even execute simple plans while we sleep. For example, many of us can instruct ourselves to, say, "wake up at 7 A.M.," and then do it. No alarm clock is needed. Some of us that do need an alarm clock find ourselves waking up just before the alarm goes off. The point here is that sleep, although probably a state of low arousal, is still an active, dynamic, complex state.

EEG Patterns.   The electrical activity of our brain, as detected by the EEG, varies enormously as we sleep through the night. Repeated research has indicated that sleep can best be described as passing through five stages. These stages can be seen in Figure 4.7. When we fall asleep we tend to pass through these stages in the order in which they are depicted in Figure 4.7. As you can see, as we fall deeper into sleep, our brain waves become slower and of a larger amplitude. In stage 4 we find the lowest of all waves; these occur at a frequency of one or two a second whereas awake waves tend to occur at a rate of about 10 per second.

It usually takes thirty to forty-five minutes to drift down to stage 4, but then something unusual and significant happens. After spending some time in stage 4, we ascend back up through stage 3, stage 2, and then into what looks like stage 1 again. Instead of staying slow and infrequent our brain waves begin to look like those of stage 1 again; in fact, we have moved into the fifth stage, commonly called REM sleep or rapid eye movement sleep, which is now described.

REM and NREM Sleep.   What is this curious fifth stage of sleep?

Measurement of Sleeping and Dreaming: EEG and REM

FIGURE 4.7
EEG patterns correlated with various stages of wakefulness and sleep. (After A manual of standardized terminology, techniques, and scoring system for sleep stages of human subjects, Rechtschaffen, A., and Kales, A. [Eds.] National Institutes of Health, No. 204, 1968.)

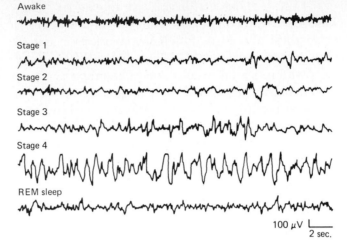

For the answer we must go back to Aserinsky and Kleitman (1953), who found that when the EEG patterns of sleeping people resemble stage 1, their eyeballs under their closed lids sometimes begin to show rapid movement. This rapid eye movement, occurring simultaneously with EEG activity similar to stage 1, has come to be known as REM sleep. Aserinsky and Kleitman found that if they woke people up when they were showing both rapid eye movements and stage 1 EEG patterns they would be very likely to report that they were dreaming. In other words, a *combination* of rapid eye movement and stage 1 EEG is a good predictor of dreaming. It seems we drift down through the first four stages of sleep without dreaming and then show a burst of rapid eye movement and stage 1 EEG indicating that we are dreaming, or at least that we are ready to recall a dream.

It has become customary to call sleep showing both rapid eye movements and stage 1 EEG activity *REM sleep*. All other stages of sleep are usually called NREM sleep or nonrapid eye movement sleep. In addition, rapid eye movements during REM are rapid relative to other sleep stages only. They are not particularly rapid relative to eye movements occurring during wakefulness.

Although stage 1 EEG activity occurring in conjunction with rapid eye movement is a good predictor of dreaming it is not perfect. Even though their reports are short, vague, and fragmentary, people do sometimes report dreaming in other stages and in the absence of

REM (see Vogel, 1978). However, these two factors together are good predictors and account for most of the dreaming we experience. It is reasonable to guess that from 75 to 80 percent of our dreams occur during REM sleep.

Muscular activity is so low during REM sleep that Dement (1972) states that we might even describe these intervals as periods of paralysis. It is as though, when dreaming, our minds and our eyes are most active while our bodies are least active. In fact, muscle activity is so low during REM sleep that it is often used in connection with rapid eye movements and EEG patterns to identify the occurrence of REM sleep.

We don't simply tumble down through the stages of sleep and stay at the bottom all night. To the contrary, there are some very interesting and consistent sleep patterns that we display each night. Consider Figure 4.8. This represents the sleeping pattern of a normal young adult. Enormous individual differences do exist, but Figure 4.8 can be taken as an "average" picture of what goes on during the night. First, observe that we go through several complete cycles during the night. We drift down to stage 4 in about thirty to forty-five minutes after sleep onset, and then we ascend back up and show a burst of REM sleep. The first burst of REM sleep tends to occur about sixty minutes after we have gone to sleep, and it lasts about five or ten minutes. Then we drop back down into stage 4 sleep only to return to REM sleep after another ninety minutes. We go through four or five of these cycles each night.

Notice further that the periods of REM sleep increase in length as the night goes on. Whereas the first burst of REM sleep might be five

Nightly Patterns of Sleeping and Dreaming: Jouvet's Theory

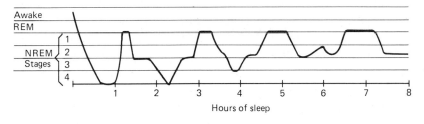

FIGURE 4.8
Periods of NREM and REM sleep during an 8-hour night. (Adapted from Van De Castle, R. L. The psychology of dreaming. Copyright 1971 General Learning Corporation [General Learning Press]. Reprinted by permission of Silver Burdett Co.)

minutes the last one may be as long as an hour. In other words, we do most of our dreaming later on in the night.

Finally, notice in Figure 4.8 that the depth of sleep tends to decrease as the night goes on. Although we usually drop right into stage 4 when we first fall asleep, the probability of going into stage 4 decreases as the night progresses. Thus we alternate periods of REM and NREM sleep during the night with REM periods becoming longer and NREM becoming more shallow as the night goes on.

Everyone agrees that we do go through these cycles each night. Just why we do so is another matter. The most widely held view seems to be that the RAS controls both REM and NREM sleep. Jouvet (1967) has shown that two different areas of the RAS control REM and NREM sleep. Specifically, the *raphe nuclei* control NREM sleep whereas the *locus coerulus nuclei* control REM sleep. Stimulating the raphe nuclei tends to increase NREM sleep whereas stimulation of the locus coerulus nuclei tends to induce dreaming.

These two sites tend to alternate in terms of their activity; either one or the other is active at any given time. This alternation seems to fit in with what we observe in terms of alternating cycles of REM and NREM sleep.

Although Jouvet's work is intriguing, much remains to be learned. For example, exactly why these two areas of the RAS alternate in terms of activity remains to be seen. We can relate EEG cycles to RAS activity, but we do not yet know what controls that RAS action.

The situation is further complicated by the fact that other areas of the brain also seem to be involved in the control of sleep. For example, areas in the hypothalamus, the thalamus, the frontal lobe, and the limbic system have been shown to be involved in the regulation of sleep (Williams, Holloway, and Griffiths, 1973).

Age and Sleep Patterns of both REM and NREM sleep vary as a function of our age too. For example, a newborn infant will take six or seven evenly spaced naps throughout a twenty-four-hour period whereas a young adult will sleep but once during the same period. Figure 4.9 shows the approximate sleeping patterns in which we engage as we are growing to adulthood.

Figure 4.10 shows total approximate amounts of both REM and NREM that occur as a function of age. Notice that the total amount of sleep required drops from about sixteen hours a day for a newborn to about six hours a day in advanced adulthood. Notice also that

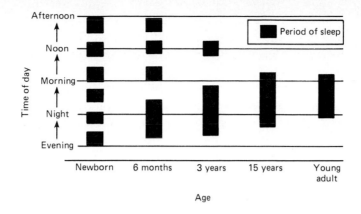

FIGURE 4.9
Approximate periods of sleep during a 24-hour day as a function of age. Note that the total amount of time spent asleep decreases with age, and the time spent sleeping is consolidated into fewer and fewer periods. (Adapted from Houston, J. P., Bee, H., and Rimm, D. C. Invitation to psychology. New York: Academic, 1983. Fig. 4 on p. 152.)

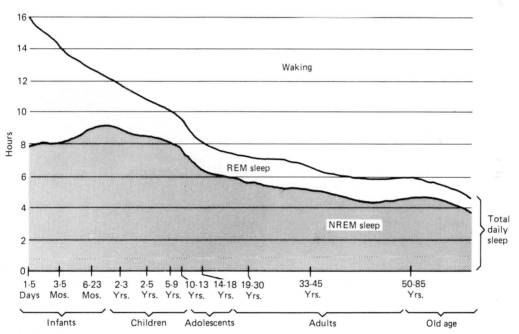

FIGURE 4.10
Total sleep, REM sleep and NREM sleep as a function of age. (Adapted from Roffwarg, H. P. Muzio, J. N., & Dement, W. C. Ontogenetic development of the human sleep-dream cycle. Science, 1966, 152, 604–619. Fig. 1 on p. 608.)

whereas total REM sleep drops from eight hours to about ninety to one-hundred minutes most of this drop occurs during the first five years of life. After five years the decrease in REM sleep becomes very gradual.

Individuals vary enormously in terms of the amounts of sleep they prefer. Some seem to be able to get along on three or four hours a night whereas others seem to need as much as nine, ten, or even more sleep each night.

The reduction in total sleep that occurs as we grow older tends to be the result of a loss in deep, or stage 4, sleep.

The Purpose of Sleep and Dreams

The Need to Sleep and Dream. We all know that if we are deprived of sleep we tend to feel tired, grouchy, and uncomfortable. If we are deprived of sleep for long periods of time we will feel anxious and our ability to perform will be impaired. It is obvious that we need to sleep. And so, too, we need to dream. In a classic study, Dement (1960) awakened a group of subjects each time they displayed REM sleep. Control subjects were awakened an equal number of times but not during REM sleep. Then, when allowed to sleep freely, REM deprived subjects showed an increase in REM sleep rela-

Sleep patterns vary with age. Children tend to sleep more, and more often, than adults. (Courtesy of J. D. Anker.)

tive to the controls. It was as though the need to dream built up during deprivation just as hunger builds up during food deprivation. This effect, where dream-deprived subjects dream much more than normal, is called *REM rebound*. Extra amounts of dreaming following REM deprivation can persist for several days.

So it seems clear that we need to both sleep and to dream. But *why* we need to do these two things remains something of a mystery. A lot of researchers are thinking about the problem; what follows are some of the "educated guesses" that have been forwarded.

Restoration. NREM sleep may well have a restorative function. Hartmann (1973) argues that NREM sleep allows us to replenish physiological elements and chemical compounds that are essential for smooth operation. He found that if we exercise strenuously we will increase our amount of NREM (particularly stage 4), but show no change in REM sleep.

REM sleep may also have a restorative effect in that it may help us deal with stress. Hartmann (1973) found that stressful situations, such as a death in the family or a marital conflict, can lead to increases in REM. More REM sleep tends to occur after days that are filled with worry and stress.

Programming. Bertini (1973) and others suggest that REM sleep serves an organizational or programming function. The idea is that new information we have received during the day is evaluated and related to existing information during REM. Reorganization, based upon the impact of the new information upon old information, occurs.

Consolidation. Broughton and Gastaut (1973) and others have proposed a related function of REM sleep. They argue that memories may become consolidated during REM sleep. The idea is that if REM sleep does not occur, then new memories will not have a chance to become permanent.

Energy Conservation. Finally, Webb (1971) argues that sleep may allow us to conserve energy when activity would be wasteful. We sleep at night because we are not a particularly effective species at night. We can not see that well at night; night activity would use up considerable energy at a time when we would be unable to replenish it. Bears hibernate during the winter because there is very little food available at that time to support them. The argument here is that sleep is related to the energy needs of the species and to the environment. Species are awake when they can gain energy. They sleep and conserve energy when to be active would be to experience a net loss in energy.

Freudian Dream Theory. So far we have noted that restoration, programming, consolidation, and conservation have all been mentined in connection with the purpose of sleep and dreaming. One final interpretation of dreaming should be considered, and that is Freudian dream theory.

Put very simply, Freud believed that we dream in order to satisfy unacceptable needs and impulses that we all have but are unaware of possessing. For Freud, the purpose of dreaming is wish fulfillment. According to Freud we all have strong impulses, such as sexual and aggressive urges, that are unacceptable to us and to society. To indulge these impulses would be to bring not only society's disapproval but also self-criticism. So we repress the urges. That is, without being aware that we are doing so, we keep the threatening impulse out of our consciousness.

For example, suppose you harbor deep, strong, even murderous, impulses. To indulge these desires would be to make yourself feel anxious and guilty, and might even land you in jail. So, through the use of the defense mechanism called repression, you keep these impulses hidden away, without being aware that you are doing so.

But, just because you repress them, these impulses do not disappear. They are still "in there" wanting to be satisfied. Freud believed that many of our problems of adjustment in life stem from blocked, unsatisfied, repressed impulses.

If you have strong impulses, of a sexual or aggressive nature, but cannot overtly satisfy them because both you and society will condemn their expression, what can you do? How can you gain some small measure of relief? According to Freud, you can dream about them. You can gain some satisfaction by expressing your impulses in a dream in which they will not actually hurt anyone. Through dream fantasy you can indulge some unacceptable impulses.

Suppose you do satisfy aggressive impulses by dreaming about hurting your mother? It is true your mother will not be harmed. But what about you? How are you going to feel in the morning when you wake up and remember gleefully abusing your sweet mother in the dream? Guilty? Anxious?

So, according to Freud, there has to be another step in the business of wish fulfillment through dreaming. Specifically, you have got to camouflage, distort, or hide the true meaning of the dream. One way this can be done is through the use of *symbols*. A symbol is anything that stands for something else. If we dream of symbols that stand for, but hide, the true meaning of a dream, then we can have the best of both worlds; we can fulfill our desires and not feel guilty about it. For example, we might dream of a calf being hurt in a farm accident. According to Freudian thinking, the calf might be a symbol for the person we really want to hurt and the farm accident might be a symbol for our own aggression.

As mentioned, Freud, rightly or wrongly, emphasized sexual and aggressive impulses. As a result, in the Freudian tradition a great deal of attention has been directed toward sexual and aggressive dream symbolism. Table 4.1 contains some lists of symbols standing for sexual organs and activities that are of a Freudian nature.

So, for Freud, dreams served an important function: They allow us

TABLE 4.1. *Examples of Sexual Dream Symbols.*

Male organs	Female organs	Sexual intercourse
Branches	Purses	Riding in a car
Snakes	Pockets	Climbing stairs
Pencils	Caves	Sliding on a bannister
Trees	Cabinets	Riding a train
Lamp posts	Closets	Moving on an escalator
Swords	Gloves	Airplane ride
Rifles	Parcels	Moving in an elevator
Hoses	Windows	Horseback riding
Flag poles	Tunnels	Amusement park rides
Weapons	Stoves	
Crowbars	Fireplaces	
Trains	Drains	
Hammers	Boxcars	
Any elongated object	Any opening	

These are of the type that might be included in Freudian dream interpretation.

to express desires that might otherwise remain bottled up or, even worse, burst out in some other unacceptable manifestation. But Freudian theory is far from universally accepted. In fact, it is downright controversial. Many people believe it is simply without foundation. The problem with Freudian theory is that there is very little experimental data available which either proves or disproves it. We have not yet become clever enough to design conclusive experiments. Most of the information we do have comes from clinical rather than from experimental settings, and that bothers a lot of people who want to keep psychology as scientific as possible.

So if tonight you dream about a huge bull smashing into a subway tunnel, tossing people this way and that, do not conclude in the morning that you are a fiend. No one really knows what dreams are all about.

Dreams May Be Meaningless. We should mention the logical possibility that dreams may mean nothing at all. They may represent random combinations of past events thrown together by low-grade cognition activity during sleep.

Primary Sleep Disorders Sleep disorders are many and varied. In fact, there is not much agreement about what a reasonable taxonomy of sleep disorders would look like. Because of its coherence and logic, we have chosen to describe a classification of sleep disorders developed by Hauri (1977). Hauri, who makes a distinction between *primary* and *secondary* sleep disorders, states, "Primary sleep disorders are those conditions in which various abnormalities related to sleep are the cardinal (and often the only) sign or symptom of the problem from which the patient suffers" (p. 35). Secondary sleep disorders are those that are the direct result of some other problem such as thyroid dysfunction or drug abuse.

1. Narcolepsy. The first of the primary disorders, narcolepsy, is a very specific disease in which people have trouble staying awake. They may fall into REM sleep no matter what they are doing. They may nod off while working, playing, talking, and even when they are driving.

The condition takes different forms. Sometimes the individual will go about her business normally but then be unable to remember what happened. In other cases the person may lose muscle control and slump to the floor. As you can imagine, this can be a difficult condition with which to live. Amphetamines are sometimes prescribed, but they have the drawback of leading to tolerance and demand for more and more of the drug.

2. Sleep Apnea.   This form of sleep disorder is more unfortunate than the garden varieties of insomnia. The person who suffers from apnea repeatedly wakes up gasping for breath. It is as though he loses the ability to breathe while asleep and can only begin to breathe normally when he wakes up. It appears that the effect is real and not imagined; the diaphragm, which controls our breathing, fails to contract properly when the individual is asleep. Sometimes the person will wake up gasping dozens of times in one night. There is no good cure for this condition. Sleeping pills which are normally used to reduce sleeping problems can actually aggravate this condition, as they tend to suppress respiration.

3. Insomnia.   Insomnia, or the failure to sleep, is the most common sleep disorder. Insomnia is not a simple condition. Webb and Agnew (1977) point out that there are several different forms of insomnia. Sometimes we experience sleeplessness when some significant or disturbing event has occurred in our life. We may have been fired from our job, or found a new love, or anticipate an upcoming intercontinental trip. These insomnias are temporary, and usually subside when the excitement dies down. Then there are times when we *think* we aren't sleeping well but actually are. A person may think there is something wrong because he needs half an hour to fall asleep and then only sleeps for six hours. But these figures are well within the normal range. The problem lies, not in the actual sleep, but in the individual's unfounded belief that something is wrong. People with this problem may sometimes be helped through education; they may benefit if they are simply told that nothing is wrong. Finally, insomnia sometimes seems to be caused by disruption of normal sleeping patterns. Let us say you suddenly get a job that requires you to be up at all sorts of odd times. Without your customary sleep pattern, you may find it hard to go to sleep and to stay asleep. Establishing as consistent a pattern as possible can help this condition.

Barbiturates are often prescribed in the treatment of insomnia. Initially, they seem to work, but, unfortunately, it seems that larger and larger doses are needed as time goes on. After considerable treatment with barbiturates, sleeping patterns become very unusual. Dement and Villablanca (1974) suggest that the disruption occurs because barbiturates seem to block or deprive the person of REM and stage 4. The individual gets into a state of constantly trying to "catch up" on REM and stage 4 sleep.

4. Myoclonus.   Myoclonus refers to a sleep disorder in which the sufferer's legs twitch in a highly stereotyped manner. According to Hauri (1977) these twitches occur every twenty to forty seconds. Periods of twitching last anywhere from five minutes to two hours. They alternate with periods of normal sleep. Although some drugs, such as Diazepam, have been used with some success, there is no completely adequate treatment for myoclonus at the present time.

5. Nonrestorative Sleep.   Sometimes people get adequate amounts of sleep, but the sleep does not seem to do them any good. When they are awake they complain of fatigue and malaise. This condition sometimes, but not always, seems to be related to chronic alpha intrusion into sleep. Unfortunately, there is no adequate treatment for this condition.

Sleep Disorders Secondary to Medical Problems   As mentioned, many sleep disorders are related to, or secondary to, other kinds of problems. Medical problems can lead to sleep disorders. For example, malfunctions of the thyroid system can cause trouble. Hyperthyroidism leads to broken, short periods of sleep, whereas hypothyroidism causes extreme sleepiness. Epilepsy can be tied up with sleep problems, too. Specifically, epilepsy seems to be aggravated by sleep; the sleeping patient suffers a special risk of having a seizure.

Sleep Disorders Secondary to Psychiatric Problems   Sleep problems often seem to be symptomatic of more general emotional and psychiatric problems. For example, broken, restless sleep is often associated with some kinds of depression. However, some deeply depressed patients sleep normally and others actually sleep more than normal. Thus, poor sleep often, but not always, occurs in cases of severe depression.

Psychotic patients, such as schizophrenics during an acute attack, may show disturbed sleep. Chronic schizophrenics, on the other hand, often sleep very well. Neurotics as well as psychotics may display disrupted sleep.

In summary, sleep disorders come in many forms. Some seem primary whereas others seem to be caused or at least influenced by other factors such as medical or psychiatric problems.

Stress and Arousal

So far in this chapter we have examined the arousal continuum and looked at sleep as a condition of extremely low arousal. In this section we attend to the other end of the arousal dimension and discuss stress, which, on a simple level, may be thought of as a state of extremely high arousal. Although stress can be thought of as extremely high arousal it can also be thought of in other ways. For example, stress may be thought of as what we experience when our body is required to adjust to substantial changes in our environment. Stressful reactions need not always be negative. For example, taking an unpleasant examination involves negative stress. On the other hand, getting married, or skydiving, may also be stressful, but not necessarily negative. Although difficult to define, stress may be thought of as a nonspecific set of responses the body makes to demands that are made upon it. Often these demands correspond to those that produce high arousal.

The Endocrine System and Stress

When we are faced with stressful conditions our bodies tend to react in a certain way. This stress reaction, or reaction to threat, involves the endocrine system. The endocrine glands are a set of glands located throughout the body that secrete their hormones directly into the bloodstream. The two endocrine glands that are of greatest importance in connection with stress are the pituitary gland and the adrenal glands (one located on top of each kidney). The pituitary gland, sometimes called the "master gland" because of its influence on other glands, is located at the base of the brain. Through a complicated mechanism, these two glands account for much of what we can describe as the "emergency reaction" of the body. They help ready the body to meet the attack or the stressor, by increasing muscle efficiency, speeding up breathing, increasing our heart rate, and so on. The body is readied for action. Once the threat is reduced, the action of these glands subsides and the body returns to normal.

The General Adaptation Syndrome (GAS)

Hans Selye (1956) has argued that our reaction to stress involves three stages, as depicted in Figure 4.11. When first confronted with a stressor we go into what Selye called the *alarm reaction*. It is during this initial phase that our body becomes fully and completely mobilized to face the stressor. Adrenalin is released into the bloodstream, heart and breathing rates accelerate, vasoconstriction of the viscera largely stops gastrointestinal activity, and the liver releases glucose into the blood system, thus facilitating vigorous activity. Pupillary dilation, increases in electrodermal activity, and a reduction in saliva flow may also occur. The alarm reaction lasts for a few moments to a few hours. If the stressor disappears, then our systems return to normal. However, if the stressor continues we do not maintain the high level of total mobilization observed in the alarm reaction. Instead we move into the second phase, which Selye called the *stage of resistance*. Alarm rections return almost to normal. Our body focuses on the specific threat at hand. Irrelevant systems are slowed while systems directly involved with the specific stressor are activated. In a sense, our body focuses on the specific problem at hand during the stage of resistance. It no longer engages in total mobilization as it did during the alarm reaction, probably because to do so would expend unneeded energy.

Finally, if the focused defenses of the stage of resistance fail to eliminate the stressor, we move into Selye's third stage, called the *stage of exhaustion*. Here the body again mobilizes totally in what

FIGURE 4.11
Selye's General Adaptation Syndrome (GAS).

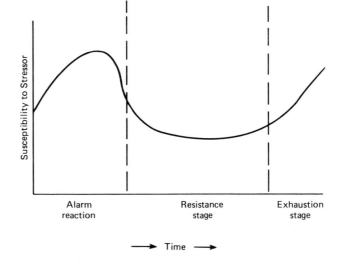

might be called a "last-ditch effort." If the resources added by this general reaction also fail to eliminate the stressor, the body, with its resources depleted, sinks into exhaustion, and finally dies (Selye, 1973).

The overall sequence of these stages is called the *general adaptation syndrome*, or GAS, by Selye. It is supposed to characterize our rection to all stressors, no matter what the specific nature of those stressors. It is a system designed to help us survive the onslaught of stressful elements in our life.

What Causes Stress?

Stress can be caused by physical elements such as bacteria, heat, cold, bone fractures, noise, crowding, and drugs. However, stress can also, and is often, caused by psychological factors, such as worry, anxiety, and guilt. In other words, stress is multiply determined.

Stress and Disease: Life Changes

Too much stress can lead to disease (Spielberger and Ying, 1982). The stress reaction is our way of meeting and dealing with stressors. But if we experience unremitting stressors, then the response of our body becomes, in a sense, self-defeating. This unfortunate consequence is exemplified by currently popular research being done on life changes.

This research is based upon the idea that many of the normal ordinary life changes we experience, such as job changes, marriage, and losses of friends, all constitute stressors. Some of these life changes are generally positive, whereas others are essentially negative. However, they are all seen as stressful, regardless of their valence. The second assumption made in this research is the idea that these changes can be reliably scaled in terms of their severity. Obviously, a jail term is more stressful than a parking ticket. And finally, it is assumed that the stressful effects of these life changes are cumulative. They pile up on top of one another such that stress increases as the number and severity of these life changes occurring at one time increase. If your mother dies, you are fired, and you face a jail term all at the same time, you really feel the impact of stress.

Researchers in this area have shown that as the number and severity of current life changes pile up, *the probability of the person becoming ill also increases*. Let us look at the details of this research by looking at the work of Thomas Holmes and his associates (Holmes and Rahe, 1967; Holmes and Masuda, 1974; Ruch and Holmes, 1971). They gathered together the forty-three life events contained in Table 4.2. They had large groups of people from different cultures and

TABLE 4.2. Significant Life Events and Their Stress Ratings*

Events	Scale of Impact
Death of spouse	100
Divorce	73
Marital separation	65
Jail term	63
Death of close family member	63
Personal injury or illness	53
Marriage	50
Fired at work	47
Marital reconciliation	45
Retirement	45
Change in health of family member	44
Pregnancy	40
Sex difficulties	39
Gain of new family member	39
Business readjustment	39
Change in financial state	38
Death of close friend	37
Change to different line of work	36
Change in number of arguments with spouse	35
Mortgage over $10,000	31
Foreclosure of mortgage or loan	30
Change in responsibilities at work	29
Son or daughter leaving home	29
Trouble with in-laws	29
Outstanding personal achievement	28
Wife begins or stops work	26
Begin or end school	26
Change in living conditions	25
Revision of personal habits	24
Trouble with boss	23
Change in work hours or condition	20
Change in residence	20
Change in schools	20
Change in recreation	19
Change in church activities	19
Change in social activities	18
Mortgage or loan less than $10,000	17
Change in sleeping habits	16
Change in number of family get-togethers	15

TABLE 4.2 *(continued)*

Events	Scale of Impact
Change in eating habits	15
Vacation	13
Christmas	12
Minor violations of the law	11

*Adapted from Holmes, T. S., & Holmes, T. H. Short-term intrusions into life-style routine. *Journal of Psychosomatic Research.* 1970, *14*, 121–132. Reprinted with permission of Pergamon Press, Ltd. Copyright © 1970 by Pergamon Press, Ltd.

different age groups rate these events in terms of how much adjustment would be required to cope with each of them. Coping with the death of a spouse was generally seen as the most difficult task while dealing with a minor violation of the law was seen as an easy task. (Of course, the stressfulness of any event can vary from culture to culture, and from time to time. For example, a $10,000 mortgage would be relatively easy to handle today.)

Once the *Social Readjustment Rating Scale,* as it is called, was established, two kinds of studies were done. In *restrospective studies* people were asked about when illnesses and life changes occurred in the past. Holmes then looked for a correlation between life changes and disease. The results suggested that people are likely to develop one or more serious diseases following a major life change, and that the more serious and numerous the life changes the greater was the probability of disease. However, this sort of *retrospective study* is marred by people's inability to recall accurately events from their past. Hence Holmes developed what are known as *prospective studies.* In this type of study, the subject is asked about current life changes and is then contacted six months or a year later and asked about any major health changes. Again it has been found that people tend to become ill following major and multiple life changes.

Although interesting, this kind of research has been criticized. For example, although the relationship between disease and life change holds true for large groups of people, it is very difficult to say anything about a particular individual. It is next to impossible to predict illness in one specific person. Still, the research does support the general idea that stress reactions can lead to disease.

Stress and Crowding

One obvious idea to come out of the work on stress is the question about whether crowding causes stress. A great deal of research has been done, both with animals and humans, and the answer to the question seems to be "sometimes." Freedman (1975) hypothesizes that it is not crowding per se that causes stress but rather a sense of loss of control that is sometimes, but not always, associated with crowded conditions. Many people actually enjoy and seek out crowded conditions, as when they attend sporting events or dance in packed nightspots. So we can't conclude that all crowding produces stress. It seems to Freedman that we begin to be stressed when the crowding begins to limit our options and interfere with our objections. For example, if the crowds at a sporting event are such that we can't see the game, find our seats, or get a hot dog, then we are stressed. If the dance hall is so crowded that we can't even edge onto the dance floor, then we are stressed.

Lundberg (1976) did an interesting experiment that supports this view. He compared commuters who got on a train at the beginning of the line with those who got on in the middle. The intuitive guess would be that those who got on first would more stressed by the end of the ride because they were on the train twice as long as the other

Crowding sometimes causes stress. A person unfamiliar with city life would probably feel stressed by this New York avenue, because of a loss of control and an increased interaction among individuals. (Courtesy of J. D. Anker.)

group. But measures taken at the end of the run indicated the opposite; the people who got on in the middle were more stressed. It seems the people who got on first felt they had more control. They got to pick the set they wanted and were able to stow parcels and generally settle in before the train became too crowded. People getting on in the middle were flustered as they bumped about searching for a seat and space to store their parcels.

Another interesting fact to come out of the crowding research is that it is not so much the actual density of the situation as it is the amount of required interaction that produces stress. For example, if we cage two rats together and twenty rats together, then the twenty rats will show more stress than the two rats even if we allow *more space per rat* in the twenty rat condition than in the two rat condition.

In summary, crowding is not necessarily stressful; in fact it is sometimes desired. On the other hand, crowding does seem to be associated with stress when it (1) produces a sense of loss of control, and (2) increases the amount of forced interaction among individuals.

Genetics, Experience, and Stress

People vary in terms of their reactions to stressful situations. Some people seem able to breeze through the most stressful conditions while others fall apart. A number of different factors may lead to these individual differences.

First, there may well be a genetic factor operating here; some people may inherit an ability to cope with stressors. The data are sketchy, but some animal research supports this conclusion. For example, it has been possible to breed strains of rats that differ in terms of their emotionality and reactions to stressors. Few data exist concerning inherited stress resistance in humans (because we can't go about selectively breeding people), but the animal data suggest that the trait may be influenced by genetic factors.

On the other hand, it has been clearly established that experience and learning can affect our ability to cope with the stresses and strains of life. In the upcoming section on coping with stress we examine some of the ways we can learn to control stress. For the moment let us look at some animal research that clearly indicates that early experience can affect an individual's later ability to handle stress. Levine (1960, 1971) subjected rodents to a number of stressful conditions when the animals were very young. They were picked up, handled, dropped a very short distance, and mildly shocked. These stressful conditions were continued for only a short time when the animals were very young. Then they were allowed to develop normally without further interference. When they reached adulthood they were tested for their ability to resist a range of stressful conditions. Animals subjected to early stress were much better able to handle adulthood stress than were animals that were unstressed in infancy. Interestingly, these effects only appeared when the handling occurred during the preweaning period of the animals' life, almost as though there is a critical period involved (see Chapter 2).

Positive Effects of Stress

The preceding section suggests that stress may not be all bad. Taken in a more general view, *some* stress may actually be a healthy thing to experience. People seem to operate well when they face a moderate challenge. We don't like to be completely unstimulated after all. We do like to give life a little fight. Dealing with moderate stressors can be rewarding. The trick is to set your life up such that you meet, face, and deal with moderate stress. We should establish goals for ourselves that require us to exert effort, but we should avoid setting goals which are clearly impossible to attain.

Type A, Type B, and Heart Attacks

Two types of people, who differ in terms of their probability of having a heart attacks, have been identified (Friedman and Rosenman, 1974; Glass, 1977). Type A people, who are two to three times as likely to have heart attacks as Type B people, are seen as extremely competitive, achievement-oriented, hostile, and aggressive. They display rapid, loud, explosive speech and arousal of the sympathetic nervous system. They are often dissatisfied and uncomfortable with job pressures, impatient with slowness, and try to concentrate on more than one activity at time. They have a sense of time urgency, are preoccupied with themselves, and often dissatisfied with life in general. They have a tendency to challenge others, and display free-floating hostility and aggression. They are impatient and annoyed when interrupted (Matthews, 1982).

Type B people, on the other hand, are much more easygoing. In many ways, they are the opposite of the Type A individual. They are more soft-spoken, satisfied, comfortable, and are less aggressive and achievement-oriented. They also have many fewer heart attacks.

Type A and Type B people react differently to stressors on a physiological level. For example, Type A people when faced with stressors will show a greater output of norepinephrine and greater increases in heart rate and blood pressure than Type B people. These physiological differences seem to appear primarily under conditions of stress. When faced with nonstressful conditions, Type A and Type B people do not differ on these physiological dimensions.

The causes for the differences between Type A and Type B people are not well understood. They may be at least partially determined by genetic factors, but it also seems likely that experience can influence these patterns as well. Attempts to alter these patterns have been somewhat successful, but not entirely satisfactory.

A concept related to the Type A–Type B distinction is that of the need for power (McClelland, 1982). People with a high need for power are seen as competitive, angry, and in need of the capacity to control. When frustrated, people with a high need for power will display heightened blood pressure and may develop disease. The exact relationship between the Type A–Type B distinction and the need for power concept has yet to be worked out.

Alcohol.   A large number of variables have been related to stress in the literature. We have picked two, alcohol and expectations, to provide some idea of the diversity of the research currently being done in connection with stress.

Stress, Alcohol, and Expectations

First, let us consider alcohol. Will drinking alcohol reduce stress? Will we feel better when we are faced with a stressful situation if we "knock back a few?" A lot of people seem to think so. The expression "driven to drink" seems quite common. But what does the research say about this question? Burish, Maisto, and Shirley (1982) did an interesting study that provides useful information. They had subjects either drink alcohol or not drink alcohol. Then the subjects worked a series of math problems under either stressful or nonstressful conditions. In the stressful conditions a time limit was imposed upon the subjects and they were verbally prodded by the experimenter as they tried to work the math problems. In the nonstress condition no time limit was imposed and prodding was omitted. Stress level was evaluated by measuring pulse rate and by asking the subjects how they felt.

The results indicated that alcohol did not help in the stressful situation. When prodded and pressed for time, people drinking alcohol felt just as stresed as people who did not drink alcohol. Perhaps the stress-reducing effects of alcohol were hidden by the fact that having one's ability impaired by alcohol might have been more stressful in itself. On the other hand, in the nonstressful condition, alcohol did reduce pulse rate and negative feelings. In other words, the effects of alcohol on the stress reaction are not simple, but alcohol does sometimes have calming effects.

Expectancies. Our experience of stress is affected by what we *think* as well as by the kinds of physical factors we have been discussing. The role of cognition in motivation is the central theme of Section IV of this text. For now, one example of the way that cognitive activity affects motivational states will suffice.

Klein (1982), in a role-playing situation, led subjects to believe that they would experience either mild or severe pain during a tooth extraction. A third group was told nothing about what to expect. Then, when the actual tooth extraction turned out to be extremely painful, Klein measured the subjects shock and dismay. The group that had been expecting mild pain registered greater shock on learning of the true nature of the painful extraction than either the subjects with no expectations or those expecting strong pain. In other words, quite simply, the severity of the stress we feel in any given situation can be heavily influenced by what we expected to occur in that situation.

Coping with Stress   Given that life is filled with stress, and that extreme stress is not only unpleasant but dangerous to our health, is there anything we can do about it? Yes, there are some techniques for dealing with stress that appear to have been at least partially successful.

In Chapter 6 we discuss a whole range of techniques used in dealing with our problems, including *systematic desensitization, assertion training,* and *biofeedback,* among others. As you read through the techniques for dealing with stress described in this section, keep in mind that you will be introduced to even more in Chapter 6.

Meditation. Meditation has been practiced in other cultures for centuries. In the United States it has only become popular in recent years. Meditation does seem capable of reducing not only the psychological but the physiological symptoms of stress as well.

Meditation techniques vary enormously. Some involve sitting quietly whereas others involve strenuous activity such as the dances of the Sufi dervishes. Still others involve chanting. But they all seem to involve an attempt to alter consciousness by exercising concentrated attention. In essence, meditation is designed to relieve us of the petty, noisy, stressful activity of our own minds and to deliver us into a state of peace, harmony, and tranquillity.

Meditation can involve sitting quietly and counting one's breaths or focusing on a point midway between the eyes, or "stepping back" and observing the uncontrolled flow of one's own thoughts. In all of these methods the aim is to achieve a state of tranquillity that is not normally experienced when we try desperately to deal, not only with the clatter of the world around us, but with the disturbing, endless chatter of our own nervous, edgy minds.

Meditation does seem to reduce stress. For example, it can reduce blood pressure (Benson and Wallace, 1972) as well as oxygen consumption (Wallace and Benson, 1972). Exactly why and how meditation works is unknown, but it does seem to do some good.

Relaxation.   Closely related to meditation is the concept of relaxation training. (In fact, some feel there isn't much difference between the two.) There are several different forms of relaxation training available. Each of them can help reduce stress. One of them goes like this: Sit in a quiet comfortable place. Close your eyes. Breathe evenly and regularly. Think about your scalp. If it feels tense relax it. If it doesn't feel tense, then tense it up intentionally and then relax it. (Sometimes the only way to become aware of tense muscles is to tense and relax them intentionally.) Now think about your face, concentrating on the muscles around the eyes and mouth. If they feel tense, relax them. Let the muscles melt and be pulled down by gravity. If they don't feel tense, tense them intentionally and then relax them so you will learn to become aware of the differences between tense and relaxed facial muscles.

Then concentrate on your neck and shoulders. Our muscles in these areas are often tense without our even being aware of it. Use the tense-and-relax technique to learn about these muscles, too. Relax these areas.

Then move on down your body in a similar manner. Concentrate on each successive area until you are sure you have relaxed it. Go back to earlier areas to make sure they have not tensed up again. While you are working on, say, your legs, your mouth may tense up again without your being aware of it.

By progressing from top to bottom, taking a section at a time, you can learn to relax completely. With a little practice you can learn to refresh yourself in just a few minutes.

Be Tricky. It's all well and good to relax or meditate once you already feel stressed. But there are things you can do to completely avoid stress, too. First, think about what it is in life that just drives you nuts, such as standing in line at the lunch counter or driving in traffic. Then arrange your life such that you avoid these problems. The difference between eating lunch at 11:30 or 12:00 can be astounding. Getting up and leaving for work a little early can be gratifying.

Another thing you can do is figure out when you tend to be best able to "handle" things. Some people can't "get going" in the morning and operate very well later in the day. Others are energetic at the crack of dawn and totally exhausted by 4 P.M. Arrange your life so that you protect yourself from stressors during your vulnerable periods. Unplug the phone when you are a basket case. Just let everyone know, for example, that you unplug in the evening because you need time alone. They can adapt; the world will go on.

DRUG ADDICTION

Addiction refers to an extreme dependence, either physical or psychological, upon drugs. Table 4.3 contains some of the major categories of drugs that are involved in drug addiction. Since many of these drugs can produce changes in arousal and emotional status, it seems appropriate to consider addiction in this chapter.

Throughout history people have used a wide array of substances in their efforts to relax, reduce pain, gain insight, stimulate themselves, and reduce anxiety. Just as persistently, human societies have tried to limit the use of these substances. Exactly which drugs are sanctioned seems almost random at times. For example, in the United States, alcohol has been acceptable at times but not at others. Similarly, the use of cocaine was once legal in this country but is now illegal.

Even though there has been some inconsistency in the application of sanctions against these drugs, the reasons for the sanctions are clear. As Table 4.3 indicates, most of these drugs have some very unpleasant consequences. As mentioned, many of them lead to *dependence.* In addition, *tolerance* may develop. What this means is that, as drug use continues, greater and greater amounts of the same drugs are required to produce the same effect. That can become extremely dangerous as well as expensive. If addiction progresses too far the user can get to the point where large amounts of some drugs are needed just to feel *normal. Withdrawal* can also develop in connection with the use of many of the drugs. What this means is that if the dependent person stops taking the drug a physically painful process of withdrawal will follow.

There are many theories about why people become addicted. Some of these theories emphasize physical factors whereas others emphasize psychological determinants. Some conceive of addiction as a disease whereas others see it primarily as learned behavior.

Solomon and Corbit's Opponent-Process Theory

One of the more intriguing and encouraging models has recently been proposed by Solomon and Corbit (1974). Their model is a general one, applicable to more than just drug addiction, but it is often discussed in connection with addiction because it does such a good job of explaining addiction. According to Solomon and Corbit, *all* experience produces an affective state; the experience feels either good or bad (see Figure 4.12). The strength of this affective reaction depends upon the intensity of the experience.

As the crucial notion in their theory, Solomon and Corbit argue that each time we feel a positive emotion we will, after a while, feel a negative emotion. This second opposite feeling is called the *opponent process.* Each time we feel a negative emotion then we are bound to feel an opponent positive emotion.

For example, if your shoes hurt and you take them off, the opponent feeling of relief and pleasure is more than just a return to a neutral state. And if you are having a wonderful time at a party, and then the party ends, the opponent "letdown" will be more than just a return to a neutral state. No matter what the experience, positive or negative, our bodies are wired to produce the opposite feeling when the first feeling is terminated. Soldiers feel cheerful after combat. Students feel great once their exam is over. "It feels good when it stops." Politicians feel depressed after a winning election night. Victory is often followed by the blues. A letdown follows a positive experience.

The next crucial aspect of the model is that as exposure to the first experience increases two things happen. First, the strength of the first emotion decreases and, second, the strength of the second opponent feeling increases. This is expressed by the change from Figure 4.12a to Figure 4.12b. For example, the first time we eat a new food our initial positive reaction will be strong and the letdown when we stop eating will be weak. But if we eat this food many times our

TABLE 4–3. Drugs Commonly Abused

Category	Name	Source	How taken	Medical use	Effect lasts (hours)	Typical dose
Narcotics	Morphine	Opium from opium poppy	Injected	Relieves pain	5–7	10–20 mg
	Heroin	Extracted from morphine	Injected; sniffed	None in U.S.	3–6	Variable
	Codiene	Extracted from opium and morphine	Swallowed; injected	Relieves pain	3–5	10–30 mg
	Methadone	Synthetic	Injected; swallowed	Relieves pain	4–6	10 mg
Hallucinogens	LSD (D-lysergic acid)	Ergot alkaloids	Swallowed	Experimental	5–15	100–500 μg
	Mescaline	Peyote cactus	Swallowed	None	5–15	200-400 μg
	Psilocybin	Psilocybe mushroom	Swallowed	None	4–10	25 mg
	Marijuana	Cannabis sativa plant	Smoked; swallowed	Experimental	2–5	1–2 cigarettes
Stimulants	Cocaine	From coca plant	Sniffed; injected; swallowed	Deadens pain	10–60 minutes	Varies
	Amphetamines Benzedrine Dexedrine Methedrine	Synthetic	Swallowed; injected	Relief of depression	3–5	2–10 mg
Depressants	Barbiturates Phenobarbital Nembetal Seconal Amytal	Synthetic	Swallowed; injected	Sedation	3–5	20–100 mg
	Alcohol	Fermented or distilled grains, potatoes, etc.	Swallowed	Antiseptic	1–5	Varies

TABLE 4–3 (continued)

Category	Name	Desired effects	Long-term effects	Physical dependence	Mental dependence	Physical damage
Narcotics	Morphine	Sense of well-being; prevention of withdrawal symptoms	Addiction; constipation; loss of appetite	Yes	Yes	No
	Heroin	Same as above	Same as above	Yes	Yes	No
	Codeine	Same as above	Same as above	Yes	Yes	No
	Methadone	Prevention of withdrawal symptoms	Same as above	Yes	Yes	No
Hallucinogens	LSD (D-lysergic acid)	Distortion of senses; insight; euphoria	Can precipitate psychosis	No	Perhaps	Unknown
	Mescaline	Same as above	None known	No	Perhaps	Unknown
	Psilocybin	Same as above	None known	No	Perhaps	Unknown
	Marijuana	Increases perceptions and sense of well-being	None known	No	Perhaps	Unknown
Stimulants	Cocaine	Exhilaration; excitement; sociability	Psychosis; convulsions; depression	No	Yes	Yes (?)
	Amphetamines Benzedrine Dexedrine Methedrine	Alterness; activeness; confidence	Loss of appetite; depression; psychosis	No (?)	Yes	Yes (?)
Depressants	Barbiturates Phenobarbital Nembetal Seconal Amytal	Tension reduction; sense of well-being	Addiction; convulsions; psychosis	Yes	Yes	Yes
	Alcohol	Tension reduction; sociability; sense of well-being	Neurological damage; cirrhosis of liver; psychosis	Yes	Yes	Yes

(Adapted from Houston, J., Bee, H., Hatfield, E., and Rimm, D. C. *Invitation to Psychology.* New York: Academic Press, 1979. Table 4–4 on p.p. 154–155).

FIGURE 4.12

The opponent-process theory. (Adapted from Solomon, R. L., & Corbit, J. D. An opponent-process theory of motivation. Psychological Review, 1974, 81, 119–145. Fig. 4 on p. 128.)

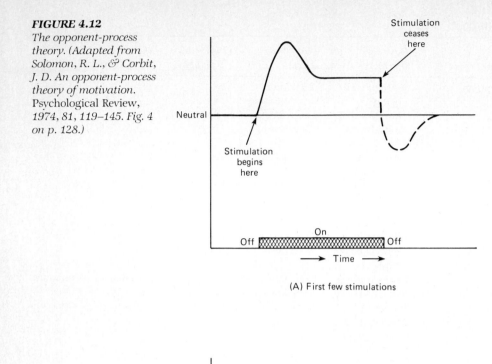

(A) First few stimulations

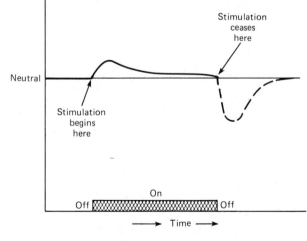

(B) After many stimulations

initial pleasure will decrease and the opponent negative reaction will increase.

What has all this to do with drug addiction? Suppose a person has just started to use heroin. At first the positive reaction will be big and the negative reaction small. But as his use of the drug continues the positive reaction will decrease and the opponent negative reaction will increase. This corresponds to the phenomenon of drug tolerance. The person will take more of the drug to regain the lost positive experience. But, unfortunately, when this is done the opponent negative reaction increases; the individual will feel even worse following drug use. So the person takes more. Now the individual is really caught. At first he took more and more of the drug to get back the positive state. But now he is taking more to eliminate the opponent negative reaction without realizing that to take more only makes that negative reaction worse.

In this system, withdrawal refers to living through the second opponent process without any of the drug to alleviate the symptoms. The more of the drug the person has taken the greater will be the negative opponent process and the more difficult the withdrawal process.

SUMMARY

1. Arousal ranges from very high to very low.

2. The Yerkes-Dodson law states that intermediate levels of arousal lead to maximum performance.

3. The performance of simple tasks can be facilitated by relatively high levels of arousal whereas the best level of arousal for complex tasks is somewhat lower.

4. Emotion has also been thought to relate to arousal in terms of an inverted U. We may often prefer an intermediate level of arousal.

5. However, what we feel, or how we interpret an internal state of arousal may be affected by our cognitive appraisal of what is going on around us.

6. There may also be two preferred levels of arousal, one high and one low, which we alternate between.

7. The RAS is involved in arousal.

8. The limbic system may also be involved in arousal.

9. The autonomic nervous system is involved in arousal.

10. The catecholamines are related to arousal.

11. Sleep is an active process sometimes involving physical acitivty, consciousness, sensitivity, and the execution of plans.

12. Sleep stages and dreams are detected with the EEG and by observing REM.

13. Sleep appears to involve five stages.

14. REM sleep is generally considered to be sleeping with dreams while NREM sleep includes all other stages.

15. Nightly sleeping includes several complete cycles through the five stages.

16. Jouvet argues that these cycles are related to RAS activity.

17. Sleep patterns change with age.

18. There is a need to sleep and a need to dream.

19. Sleeping and dreaming may involve restoration, programming, consolidation, and energy conservation.

20. Freud believed that dreaming involved symbolic wish fulfillment.

21. Sleep disorders include several types of insomnia as well as narcolepsy.

22. Stress has been characterized in several different ways but may be thought of as very high arousal.

23. The endocrine system is involved in stress.

24. The GAS interpretation of stress was developed by Selye.

25. Stress is caused by both physical and psychological factors.

26. Excessive stress may lead to disease and even death, as evidenced by life change research.

27. Crowding may cause stress when it leads to a sense of loss of control and forces excessive interaction.

28. Ability to resist stress may be determined by both genetics and experience.

29. Moderate stress may be good for us.

30. Type A people are two or three times as likely to have a heart attack as are Type B people.

31. Alcohol may not help reduce high stress.

32. Our expectations can affect how much stress we experience.

33. Meditation and relaxation can help reduce stress.

34. Stress can be avoided and dealt with through careful planning.

35. Drug addiction involves dependence, tolerance, and withdrawal.

36. Solomon and Corbit's opponent-process theory may prove to be helpful in understanding addiction.

Learning, Drives, and Incentives

SECTION III

CHAPTER 5

↓

Classical Conditioning, Instrumental Conditioning, and Reinforcement

THE LEARNING PERSPECTIVE

It should be clear by now that motivation cannot be clearly understood without at least some understanding of the role of learning in human life. Motivation and learning are so closely bound together, so dependent upon and affected by one another, that it is difficult to speak of one without some reference to the other. In this section we attend to the intricacies of this relationship. In Chapters 5 and 6 we look at some of the ways that the principles of classical and instrumental conditioning have been found to be involved in motivational issues. In Chapter 7 we turn to drive theory and its central notion that we are often energized or "pushed" into behavior by internal states of tension. Finally, in Chapter 7 we also discuss incentive motivation and its core idea that we are sometimes "pulled" or lured into behavior by aspects of the environment.

Just as motivation is difficult to define, so too is the word *learning*. Try to frame a definition for yourself. There have been many definitions proposed through the years (Donahoe and Wessells, 1980; Howe, 1980). One of the most appealing, because it is so comprehensive, was forwarded by Gregory Kimble (1967), who defined learning as a

The Definition of Learning

relatively permanent change in behavior potentiality that occurs as a result of reinforced practice. Kimble includes the term *permanent* in this definition because he thinks of new learning as involving long-lasting changes in behavior. To turn it around the other way, he wants to exclude from the realm of learned changes all *temporary* shifts in behavior that are the result of temporary changes in motivational states. For example, if you are tired of reading this book, your eyes ache, and you want to listen to some music, your behavior may change. You may drop the book and head for the stereo. This is a change in behavior, but it is not one that involves new learning because it does not involve a permanent change in behavior. Instead, it is a temporary change in behavior because of a shift in motivation. Temporary boredom and fatigue lead you to other behaviors. We are making the (perhaps overly self-confident) assumption that you will return to this text when boredom and fatigue subside. Many motivational shifts can lend to temporary changes in behavior that do not involve new learning. For instance, if we are hungry, we eat with knife and fork, if we are exhausted we sleep, and if we are thirsty, we drink. All of these involve temporary changes in behavior, but not new learning.

Let us look at another of Kimble's key terms. By including the term *practice*, Kimble wants to exclude from the category of learned changes many changes that are caused by factors other than practice. For example, changes that occur as a result of aging and maturation may lead to new learning, but, in and of themselves, do not involve new learning. As we age, our short-term memory may deteriorate, and our handwriting may become shaky. These are certainly permanent changes, but they do not involve new learning. When was the last time you heard someone say, "Hey, I'm really learning how to be forgetful. And I'm working on my loss of coordination, too"? Other factors, such as disease and accident, can lead to permanent changes in behavior that are not considered to be learned changes because they did not come about through practice.

Kimble also includes the term *potentiality*. He does this to emphasize that learning somehow resides within, ready to be expressed, but that it is not always expressed. For example, we all know, or have learned, the alphabet. But few of us are, at this moment, reciting it. It is stored somewhere within us, but is not constantly translated into behavior. And what is it that determines whether or not this potentiality will be expressed? Motivation. If we are motivated to recite the alphabet, we will do so. If we are not, then that learning will remain hidden.

Kimble also uses the term *reinforced* practice. For now, think of reinforcement as reward. Kimble is saying that we never learn anything unless we are rewarded for doing it. Thus a child learns to pick up her toys if her parents praise her. People learn jobs for pay, praise, and self-satisfaction. We learn to swim because it feels good and is self-satisfying. A child will learn not to touch a hot stove because escape from pain is rewarding.

Do not assume that everyone follows Kimble's lead with respect to this issue. To the contrary, many theoreticians are not convinced that reinforcement is absolutely essential for learning to occur. They believe that some, or perhaps all, learning can occur without the added factor of reward. In other words, the importance of reinforcement is controversial, and has been since the beginning of the study of learning and motivation. Most investigators believe that reinforcement facilitates learning, but only some of them are convinced it is absolutely essential.

The issue comes down to trying to identify an instance of learning that occurs in the absence of reinforcement. The problem is that rewards can be so subtle that it has been impossible to find learning occurring in their absence. For instance, what about the case where you drive along a highway and are then found to be able to remember billboard messages? Reinforcement theorists would argue that reading and remembering these banal messages was rewarded by a reduction in boredom or a satisfaction of curiosity. Some go so far as to say that simply processing information is rewarding, which is to come close to saying that learning is its own reward. If learning rewards itself then it would be logically impossible to find learning occurring in the absence of reward. So the issue stands unresolved. The entire concept of reinforcement is reviewed in greater detail later in this chapter.

In summary, Kimble's definition of learning is a good one because it is fairly representative of the kinds of definitions that are available. Yet it is not without its problems; some of its elements are controversial.

Finally, it appears to be impossible to frame a good definition of learning without referring to motivation. Specifically, Kimble includes the term *permanent* to distinguish between behavior changes that are learned and those that result from temporary fluctuations in motive state. He uses the term *potentiality* to emphasize the fact that motivation can lead to the expression of things which we have learned. And he introduces the term *reinforcement*, which is inextricably bound up with the notion of motivation.

Motivation Can Be Learned

In pursuing the complex relationship between motivation and learning, we should realize that some motivation is learned, or acquired. We may all be born with an innate capacity to be motivated by hunger and thirst but there are all sorts of motivational states that appear to be learned. Some of them are controversial, such as the need to affiliate, or be with other people. In this case we are not sure how much of the need is learned and how much is innate. The learning interpretation would argue that we learn to want to be with others because, in the past, being with others has led to good things. The innate position holds that the tendency to affiliate has been genetically selected; humans are more likely to survive in groups than alone. Perhaps both factors contribute to our need to be with others. Although affiliation is a controversial motive, other motive systems are clearly acquired or heavily influenced by experience. For example, avid antique collectors are driven by what must be a learned motive system. Certainly a motive to collect may be inherited, but the particular interest in antiques must have been learned.

Phobias, or strong irrational fears of such things as heights, snakes, germs, small spaces, open spaces, and so on, seem to be acquired, too. One is simply not born into this world with an abhorrence of horses or doorknobs. Those kinds of irrational fears are most likely learned.

If we accept the proposition that some motive systems are learned, then it becomes our task to understand how these systems are acquired and how, eventually, they may be controlled for the betterment of people's lives.

Motivation Determines New Learning

The relationship between learning and motivation is further fleshed out by the observation that new learning is dependent upon motivation. As stated in Chapter 1, it may well be that learning cannot occur unless the organism is motivated to learn. You will not rehearse and store the information in this text unless you are motivated to do so. A rat will not learn to climb over a barrier unless it has a reason for doing so, such as escape from shock or the need for food located on the far side of the barrier.

The dependence of learning upon motivation is almost universally accepted. However, the exact theoretical nature of that dependence is something else entirely. As we see in this and the following two chapters, the nature of the motivation-learning relationship has been perceived quite differently by various theoreticians.

The final facet of the complex relationship between learning and motivation revolves around the widely acknowledged distinction between learning and performance. In a nutshell, performance is the expression of learning that comes about through the involvement of motivation. Performance is observable behavior. Learning is stored information or associations that are only expressed as observable behavior when the animal is motivated to express them.

Motivation Translates Old Learning into Performance

As we have seen in our discussion of Kimble's definition of learning, the distinction between learning and performance can be a crucial one because undetected differences in motivation can lead us to false conclusions about how much learning exists. For example, teachers are always faced with the fact that school examinations are not perfect measures of how much a student has learned because the tests require the students to be motivated as well as knowledgeable if they are to do well.

CLASSICAL CONDITIONING

Having addressed several issues, definitions, and distinctions inherent in the learning approach to motivation, it is time to move on to some of the specifics. Exactly what do we know about different forms of learning and their relationships to motivation? In this chapter we address what is known as the conditioning approach, with a discussion of classical conditioning to be followed by an examination of instrumental conditioning.

Pavlov's Experiments. Ivan Pavlov, a Russian physiologist, was responsible for outlining the element of what is commonly called *classical* conditioning. More than likely you have already heard of his experiments with dogs, tones, and meat powder. Prior to the experimental procedure (Anrep, 1920), the dog was treated surgically such that saliva could be collected and measured accurately (see Figure 5.1). Then the dog was strapped in a restraining harness and a met-

Examples and Types

FIGURE 5.1
Pavlov's conditioning apparatus. (Adapted from Yerkes, R. M., & Morgulis, S. The method of Pavlov in animal psychology. Psychological Bulletin, 1909, 6, 257–273. Fig. 2, p. 264. Copyright 1909 by the American Psychological Association. Reprinted by permission.)

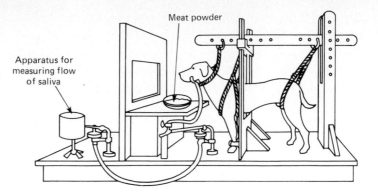

ronome, buzzer, or bell was sounded. A few seconds later the dog was presented with a dish of meat powder. At first, the meat powder caused the dog to salivate whereas the tone did not. But Pavlov persisted, repeatedly presenting the tone followed by the meat powder. After a number of such pairings Pavlov discovered that the tone by itself began to elicit saliva. The salivary response had been classically conditioned to the tone. (Classical conditioning is sometimes called *Pavlovian* conditioning and sometimes *respondent* conditioning.)

Classical conditioning is a widespread phenomenon; it is not limited to dogs, tones, and saliva. But for now, let us identify the four crucial elements of all classical conditioning situations.

1. The Unconditioned Stimulus. The unconditioned stimulus (UCS) in Pavlov's experiments was the meat powder. A UCS is anything that regularly and consistently, without any prior experience, elicits a response. Every time meat powder was presented it elicited salivation.

2. The Unconditioned Response. In classical conditioning, the unconditional response (UCR) is the response that is always elicited by the UCS. In Pavlov's situation the UCR was salivation in response to the meat powder.

3. The Conditioned Stimulus. The conditioned stimulus (CS) is any neutral stimulus that the animal can perceive which does not initially elicit a response. The bell or buzzer was the CS in Pavlov's situation.

4. The Conditioned Response.   When the animal salivates in response to the tone (CS), we call that salivary response the conditioned response (CR). It is the response that is learned. Be sure you understand the difference between the UCR and the CR. Although they are both salivary responses, the CR occurs in response to the CS whereas the UCR is evoked by the UCS. In addition, the CR is never as large as the UCR; it can be said to represent some fractional component of the UCR.

Further Examples.   Although Pavlov's experiments are the most famous of all, many more examples of classical conditioning are available. Many different animals, stimuli, and responses are involved. For example, eyelid conditioning is a widely used instance of classical conditioning because it allows precise measurement in the study of different aspects of conditioning. In this kind of experiment a puff of air (the UCS) is directed against the eyeball of the subject. If done properly, this regularly causes the subject to blink (the UCR). A tone, or bell, or any other perceivable neutral stimulus (the CS) is paired with the UCS on successive occasions. After a number of such trials, the CS alone (the tone or bell) will elicit a blink (the CR).

Conditioning is not limited to the so-called higher organisms either. For example, *planaria*, which are small, flat, freshwater worms, may undergo classical conditioning. In this procedure, a worm is placed in a dish of water through which controlled bursts of mild electrical current may be sent (see Figure 5.2). In addition, an ordinary household lightbulb is suspended over the dish. The burst of electric current is the UCS that elicits a constriction of the animal's body (the UCR). If turning on the light (the CS) is consistently paired with the UCS, then that light will begin to elicit bodily constriction by itself (Thompson and McConnell, 1955).

Other instances of reported classical conditioning involve pupillary dilation (Goldwater, 1972), human fetuses (Spelt, 1948), chick embryos (Hunt, 1949), human heart rates (Hall, 1976), and language (Maltzman, 1977), to mention but a few.

Classical Conditioning and Motivation

We have but scratched the surface of the interesting literature on classical conditioning (see Houston, 1981; Hulse, Egeth, and Deese, 1980). But that is reasonable given that our purpose is to illuminate the principles of motivation. What, then, from a motivational point of view, is the import of classical conditioning? Put very simply, *many*

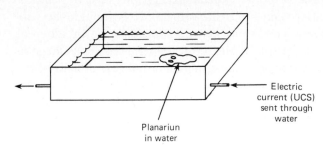

motivational states seem to be established through classical conditioning. Much of our motivated behavior appears to be the result of classical conditioning. This is a prime example of the way motivation is learned or acquired. We devote this section to some of the interesting ways in which acquired motivation comes about through this form of conditioning.

Experimental Neurosis. In a very early demonstration of the involvement of classical conditioning in the establishment of motive states, Pavlov reported what has come to be called experimental neurosis. First, on a screen in front, he projected to a dog either a perfect circle or an ellipse. When the circle (CS) was shown, meat powder was presented (UCS). As you might imagine, the dog learned to salivate (CR) when it saw the circle. When the ellipse was shown, Pavlov did nothing. Soon the dog did not respond to the ellipse. But then Pavlov began to make things a little more difficult. Over time he began to make the ellipse more and more like the circle by changing the ratio of the axes of the ellipse. At first, the slight changes in the ellipse did not bother the animal; it salivated when it saw the circle, but not when it saw the ellipse. But, as the ellipse more and more closely approximated the circle, the dog's behavior began to change. It could not form the difficult discrimination required of it. The conditioned salivary response finally disappeared completely. But even more alarming was the change in the dog's general behavior. It began to jerk around in the restraining harness, it tried to bite the apparatus, and it barked and resisted when it was being led to the testing room. Even when later returned to the simple circle-ellipse discrimination, the dog failed to respond appropriately. Pavlov pointed out that a good deal of the dog's behavior resembled neurotic human behavior. Although other interpretations are available (see Mineka and Kihlstrom, 1978), it appears that a powerful motivation to avoid the entire situation developed. It is as though the dog's capacity to discriminate had been exceeded, and that this was frustrating and disturbing. Imagine requiring a six-year-old child to discriminate between "idleness" and "laziness." Here, too, the child would be frustrated because the demand exceeded her capacity, and she might balk and become negative about the task. Whatever the final interpretation, Pavlov's demonstration of experimental neurosis stands as an early example of the involvement of classical conditioning in the alteration of motive states.

Everyday Emotions. It seems clear that many of our ordinary emotions, which have motivating properties, are established through classical conditioning. For example, imagine that you and one other person are being interviewed at the same time for the same job. The interviewer asks some simple questions that you stumble over. You feel stupid and embarrassed. Finally the interview is over and you flee. Later that week, you happen to see the other individual who was being interviewed with you. You feel awkward and dumb all over again. You avoid talking to the person. The initial embarrassment you felt in the interview was classically conditioned to the other individual.

In a similar manner, positive emotions, with their accompanying motivational properties, can be classically conditioned. For example, fond memories are often the result of classical conditioning. When one hears a fragment of a tune, or thinks of a particular person or place, the flood of affection and sentimentality may well be classically conditioned responses.

Fear and White Rats. Watson and Raynor (1920) conducted an experiment that suggests that the examples given are more than just guesses about how motivating emotions are conditioned. Albert, the eleven-month-old subject in the experiment, was first shown a white rat (CS). He was very placid about this exposure, and showed no fear. Then just as he touched the rat, a steel bar was struck with a hammer (UCS) causing Albert to almost jump out of his skin (UCR). After only seven pairings of the rat and the noise, Albert showed great fear (CR) when the rat alone was exposed. He would cry immediately and crawl away rapidly. In fact, Albert began to fear other objects that resembled the white rat. Furry objects such as a rabbit, a dog, and a fur coat also made him afraid. In other words, a powerful fear reaction with its associated motivational properties was classically conditioned.

Phobias.   Phobias are strong, apparently irrational fears. Thus, one individual might be deathly afraid of sheep whereas another might be terrified by fire. We are not speaking of ordinary fears we all have, such as a healthy respect for great heights, and a concern for fire. We are speaking of powerful, irrational fears that incapacitate the individual, such as a person who feels ill at just the thought of standing on a stepladder, or another individual who simply cannot leave the house for fear of open spaces. Table 5.1 contains some common phobias and their names.

There are many interpretations of phobic reactions. Some people believe that phobic reactions reflect deep inadequacies and severe personality problems. Others, looking at evidence such as that presented by Watson and Raynor (1920), are convinced that phobias may be the result of classical conditioning, wherein neutral stimuli are paired with traumatic events.

TABLE 5-1.   *Common Phobias**

Name of Phobia	Feared Stimulus	Name of Phobia	Feared Stimulus
Acrophobia	Height	Claustrophobia	Closed spaces
Agoraphobia	Open spaces	Cynophobia	Dogs
Ailurophobia	Cats	Equinophobia	Horses
Anthophobia	Flowers	Herpetophobia	Reptiles
Anthropophobia	People	Mysophobia	Contamination, dirt
Aquaphobia	Water	Nycotophobia	Darkness, night
Astraphobia	Lightning	Ophidiophobia	Snakes
Brontophobia	Thunder	Pyrophobia	Fire

*Adapted from Houston, J.P., Bee, H., and Rimm, D. C., *Invitation to Psychology*. New York; Academic Press, 1983. Table 1 on p. 595. Reprinted by permission.

For example, if an adult is found to be phobic with respect to red sunsets, then it would not surprise these psychologists to discover that, as a very young child, this person was held in a neighbor's arms as the child's house, and perhaps her family, burned at night. The UCS is the tragedy, the UCR is the fear, the CS is the red color of the fire in the evening sky, and the CR is the so-called irrational fear of red skies.

Some evidence for this conditioning interpretation of phobic reaction is to be found in the fact that a method for eliminating them, based on conditioning principles, has been used successfully. This method, called *systematic desensitization*, is outlined later in this chapter.

Masochism. Masochism refers to the tendency to derive pleasure from pain. You know how it goes. "Beat me, beat me, I love it." Again this particular form of behavior has been interpreted in many ways. Some feel it may reflect underlying self-hatred. The individual believes he deserves punishment. Others believe that masochistic behavior may be related to attention getting (punishment is at least *something*). Still others believe that masochism may come about through classical conditioning. (Probably the best way to look at masochism is that it may be related to all of these factors.) One can go all the way back to Pavlov for evidence that masochism is classically conditioned. He ran the following kind of experiment. A dog was conditioned to salivate. But in this case the CS was initially a very mild shock that did not disturb the animal. Then, very gradually, over a long series of trials, Pavlov increased the intensity of the shock serving as a CS. The dog did not react negatively to these increases. Finally, the shock was so intense that an untrained dog would have been terrified. But our conditioned dog continued to have a grand time in spite of the normally painful shock. It wagged its tail, cooperated, and seemed eager to jump up on the table for the next trial. It was as though the shock, even though intense, was still a cue for pleasure because it still signaled upcoming food.

Extending the analogy to the human condition, we might find a young adult who finds great pleasure in being hurt while making love. Tracing back the individual's history, it might be discovered that this person had a father who was much too rough when playing with the child. However, needing and wanting the father's love, the individual accepted the rough play and associated pain and pleasure in the sense that pain signaled pleasure. It's kind of like, "If it hurts I must be having fun."

Interoceptive Conditioning. As a final example of the way in which motivation and classical conditioning are tied together, we mention interoceptive conditioning. In standard classical conditioning, the CS and the UCS are events in the environment such as bells, buzzers, and puffs of air. But in interoceptive conditioning, which has been most widely reported in the Russian literature, either the CS, the UCS, or both are applied to internal visceral surfaces (Razran, 1961).

In *intero-exteroceptive* conditioning the CS is applied internally while the UCS is an external stimulus. For example, using a dog as a subject, the CS might be inflation of the duodenum with an inserted balloon whereas the UCS might be a shock to the paw. After a few pairings of these two stimuli it will be found that inflation of the duodenum will elicit paw withdrawal.

In *intero-interoceptive* conditioning both the CS and the UCS are applied internally. For example, the Soviets (Razran, 1961) used distention of intestinal loops as a CS and delivery of CO_2 to the lungs as a UCS. When we inhale CO_2 our breathing changes (the UCR). After a few pairings of CO_2 and intestinal distention the distention alone began to elicit the breathing changes.

In *extero-interoceptive* conditioning the CS is external and the UCS is internal. Thus a subject might have a balloon inserted in his bladder. Inflation of the balloon normally results in a strong urge to urinate. If some external stimulus is consistently paired with bladder inflation, then that external CS will begin to elicit reports of needing to urinate even when the bladder is not actually inflated.

Interoceptive conditioning suggests that our behavior may be strongly affected by internal events that we are not normally conscious of. In some cases we may not quite understand our behavior because it is tied to internal and external events through classical conditioning.

Classical Conditioning and Information

Recently, investigators have pointed out that classical conditioning is most effective when the CS *predicts* the occurrence of the upcoming UCS; the CS is said to be effective when it provides *information* about the future (see Dickinson and Mackintosh, 1978).

The idea is that a CR will only occur when the CS "tells" the subject that a UCS is about to occur. A subject, so goes the argument, will only blink in response to a bell if that bell means that a puff of air is about to be delivered. If the air puff is just as likely to occur *with* or *without* the bell, then no conditioning will occur (Rescorla and Wagner, 1972). In a sense, we are saying that the informational content of the CS motivates the subject to respond.

INSTRUMENTAL CONDITIONING

Another type of conditioning, called *instrumental conditioning*, is important in our discussion of motivation. The most widely mentioned example of laboratory-based instrumental conditioning involves a Skinner box (See Figure 5.3). The Skinner box is named after its developer, ex-Harvard professor B. F. Skinner, whose contributions to the study of learning have been enormous. Although Skinner boxes vary considerably, depending upon who built them and for what purpose, the essential elements are a stimulus to which the animal can respond, such as a lever, chain, rod, or panel to press, and a means of rewarding the animal, such as a food pellet delivery system, a liquid delivery system, or a means of terminating a shock.

Instrumental conditioning can be demonstrated by setting up the apparatus such that each time the rat (or other suitable subject) presses the lever a small pellet of food is delivered. When a hungry rat is first placed in the box it wanders about sniffing and exploring. But sooner or later it will press the lever and be reinforced or rewarded. Then it is only a matter of time before the animal learns to press the lever in a regular manner to obtain food. We say the lever-pressing bar has been instrumentally conditioned. The behavior of the animal (e.g., bar pressing) is instrumental in bringing about some change in the environment (i.e., reward).

Obviously, this form of learning is important beyond the confines of the laboratory. We all undergo instrumental conditioning. Students learn course material for grades, praise, and self-satisfaction. Telephone operators learn to use computers for wages and advancement. Children learn to throw temper tantrums, if they get their way by stomping and screaming.

Reward Training

Four types of instrumental conditioning need mentioning. The first, called *reward training*, is the one we have been discussing. The es-

FIGURE 5.3
A typical Skinner box.
(Photo courtesy of J. Hovancik.)

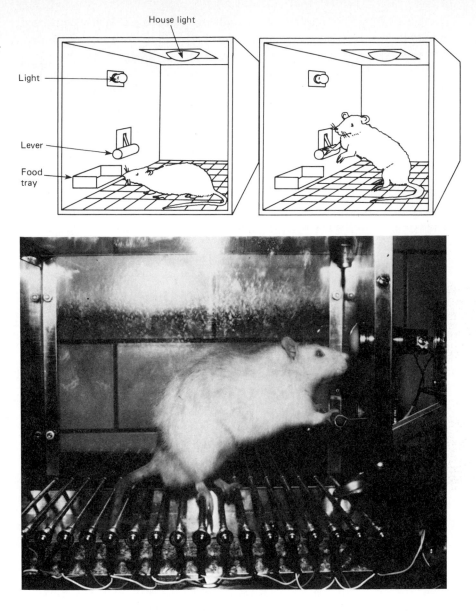

sence of reward training is that the animal *receives a pleasant reward if it makes a particular response*. Children learn to ask for candy because the request is often granted. Adolescents quickly learn to drive cars because driving is exciting and practical. Even garter snakes will learn to follow trails of earthworm scent through mazes if they are fed at the end of the trail (Kubie and Halpern, 1979). In other words, many of our behaviors, and the behavior of other animals, are molded by instrumental conditioning.

The second type of instrumental conditioning is called *avoidance training* and it may involve the apparatus depicted in Figure 5.4 (there are many other forms of avoidance apparatus. This is just a typical example). In avoidance training the animal is *punished if it fails to make a particular response*. The animal is placed in the box on the white side of the barrier. If the animal fails to scurry over the barrier to the black side of the box within a short period of time (say, 10 seconds) it receives an electric shock.

Avoidance Training

When first introduced to this situation the rat receives a substantial number of shocks. But quite rapidly it learns to leap over the barrier before it is shocked. In fact, after a while, it become so proficient that it never receives any more shocks at all.

What has all this to do with human motivation? It seems clear that many of what we called motivated behaviors are really instances of learned avoidance responses. For example, you may have known someone who is very shy about approaching members of the opposite sex. This may well be the result of some earlier bad experience. The person has learned to avoid punishment by escaping from the threatening situation. Each of us, whether we like to admit it or not, has learned to avoid certain circumstances because we have been "bitten" under similar conditions in the past.

A curious and unfortunate characteristic of avoidance conditioning is that we tend to go on avoiding long after any actual threat still exists. For instances, if we first train a rat to avoid shock by leaping a barrier, and then turn off the electricity completely, the rat will

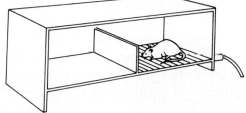

FIGURE 5.4
A typical avoidance conditioning apparatus.

continue to leap the barrier even though there is no danger. In a like manner, we humans may continue to shortchange ourselves because we fear punishing conditions that do not really exist. The person who is afraid to approach people in a social manner will, unless something is done, continue to avoid people even though all people are not punishing.

There are ways to break this vicious cycle (Mineka and Gino, 1979). Removing the punishment is not enough. The subject must be forced to remain in the threatening situation until he discovers that the danger is no longer present. The barrier in Figure 5.4 can be made so high that the rat cannot clear it. The animal will have a bad time of it for a while but will eventually relax. The socially inhibited human must be taken in hand and dragged to a warm, friendly social situation or else the avoidance response will continue.

Acquired Fear: The Two-Factor Theory. Some theoreticians have argued that avoidance training represents a situation when fear is acquired. If this is true then avoidance conditioning must truly represent the impact of learning on motivation, for, as we all know, fear is a powerful motivating factor.

The theory (Mowrer and Lamoreaux, 1946) contends that avoidance training involves two factors; first, the classical conditioning of fear and, second, instrumental escape from that fear. Let us look at each factor separately. When the animal is in the white side of the box, and is shocked (UCS), it feels pain (UCR). This fear associated with this pain becomes classically conditioned to the cues provided by the white area (CS), such that, on future trails, the animal experiences fear when it sees the white box even before the shock is delivered. The animal then learns to instrumentally escape from the fear by leaping over the barrier. Once on the "safe" black side fear is no longer experienced. Thus the two-factor theory holds that fear is first classically conditional and then instrumentally escaped. The powerful, acquired fear motivates the animal to escape.

There is a good deal of doubt about the validity of the two-factor theory and its emphasis on fear. For example, Wynne and Solomon, in an avoidance task, either lesioned the autonomic nervous system, which would disrupt fear, or injected a sedative, which would also reduce fear. Neither act affected performance on the avoidance task.

In escape training the subject *continues to suffer punishment unless a* | **Escape Training**
certain response is made. Imagine what would happen if the electric
current was left on at all times in the apparatus depicted in Figure
5.4. In this case, when the animal was placed on the white side, it
would receive at least a moment's shock no matter how fast it leaped
the barrier. No matter how hard it tries the animal cannot completely
avoid the shock; it can only escape from it. Learning is very rapid in
this situation.

In punishment training the animal *receives unpleasant stimulation if* | **Punishment**
it makes a particular response. Hence, we smack our dog with a | **Training**
newspaper if it jumps up on the couch. We scold our children if they
track in mud. Punishment training is used to eliminate a response
whereas the other three forms of instrumental conditioning are used
to establish or strengthen a response.

The effects of punishment are complicated. For example, not all
responses are equally affected by punishment. It's easier to eliminate
some response than it is others (see Shettleworth, 1978). In addition,
certain responses will be affected by one kind of punishment but not
another. In any case, it does seem clear that a good deal of human
behavior has been molded, shaped, and driven by punishment training. A recruit standing at attention in boot camp is not doing so for
sweet kind rewards. He or she is motivated by a drive to avoid punishment.

PRINCIPLES OF CLASSICAL AND INSTRUMENTAL CONDITIONING

Certain well-documented phenomena within the field of conditioning
are of particular relevance to the study of motivation. Specifically,
extinction, generalization, and *reinforcement* all deserve individual consideration.

Extinction refers to a *decrease in response strength with repeated non-* | **Extinction**
reinforcements. For example, suppose a rat has been trained to run
down an alley for food that it finds at the end of the alley. Then the
experimenter stops putting food into the alley. What will happen? At
first the animal will continue to run to the end of the alley. But

gradually, over a series of trials, it will stop doing so; the running response will extinguish.

Extinction occurs in classical as well as instrumental conditioning. For example, what will happen to the conditioned salivary response in a Pavlovian conditioning situation if the tuning fork is sounded repeatedly by itself, without any meat powder being presented? The salivary response will decrease over a series of CS presentations; it will extinguish.

Extinction is one of the most basic and fundamental of all learning phenomena. It is not limited to so-called lower species. Humans undergo extinction many times in their lives. A child who has learned to clown at home, because clowning brings parental attention, may drop the behavior when she enters school because horseplay is not rewarded there. An adult may play the stock market for a while but then cease when rewards are not forthcoming. Williams (1959) presents an interesting example of human extinction. A twenty-one-month-old child would routinely throw a tantrum each evening at bedtime. The parents had begun to stay in the bedroom each evening until the child dropped off to sleep in order to avoid the tantrum behavior. Then the child was put on an extinction schedule, that is, he was gently put to bed and left alone. As you can see from Figure 5.5, the child cried for almost an hour the first night, but after that the tantrum behavior extinguished quickly over a series of nights.

Extinction helps us understand some important motivational effects, especially those that appear to involve changes in motivation. For example, we may hear parents say things like, "I can't understand

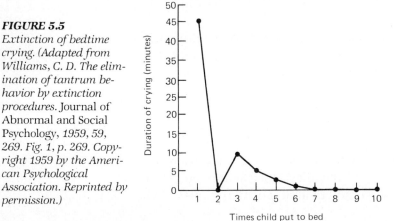

FIGURE 5.5

Extinction of bedtime crying. (Adapted from Williams, C. D. The elimination of tantrum behavior by extinction procedures. Journal of Abnormal and Social Psychology, 1959, 59, 269. Fig. 1, p. 269. Copyright 1959 by the American Psychological Association. Reprinted by permission.)

it. He's all of a sudden so polite. What's got into him? He used to be so rude." This shift in behavior may well be the result of some form of subtle, unrecognized extinction. The conditions that rewarded rude behavior may have evaporated as the child grew older, changed schools, or met new friends. In other words, what appear to be substantial changes in motivated behavior may sometimes be understood if we look for life conditions that might generate extinction. The trick is to discover what reinforcement has been removed from the individual's life.

Generalization

Generalization refers to the fact that *a response connected to one stimulus will tend to be elicited by similar stimuli.* The more similar the stimuli the more likely the response is to occur.

For example, if a dog has been conditioned to salivate in response to a particular tone, then similar tones will, when presented by themselves, also elicit salivation. But if the second tone is very different from the first one, then salivation will be weak. The more similar the second tone is to the first tone the more salivation will occur in response to that second tone.

When we drive into a new town and see a red light, we stop even though we have never seen that particular red light before. That is because the new red light is very similar to ones we have seen before. But if the light was orange and four feet off the ground we would hesitate. And if it were blue, octagonal, and one foot off the ground we would sail right on by.

This tendency for similar stimuli to elicit the same learned response is depicted in Figure 5.6.

Generalization provides another example of how motivated behavior is directed and controlled by learning. If we are driven by hunger we will eat things that are similar to things we have eaten before. But we will shy away from other foods, such as beetles and caterpillars, which are routinely eaten with pleasure in other cultures.

Reinforcement: Definitions and Parameters

Operational versus Theoretical Definitions. On a simple operational level there seems to be quite good agreement about the nature of reinforcement. Any stimulus is a reinforcer if its presentation or removal has the effect of increasing the strength or probability of a response occurring. But when we begin to wonder *why* reinforcers work, we begin to see some very divergent ideas appearing. As we see in the upcoming section on theories of reinforcement, there are a

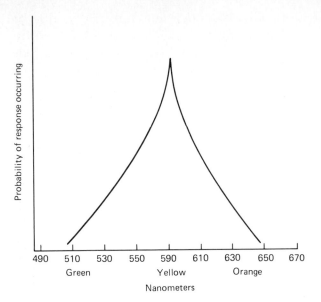

number of fascinating ways to think about reinforcement. But before we turn to the discussion of these theories of reinforcement a few additional topics need to be discussed.

Reinforcement in Classical Conditioning?

It is obvious that reinforcement is involved in instrumental conditioning. Rats learn to press levers for food, and humans learn their occupational skills for a wide array of reinforcers, or rewards. But what about classical conditioning? Does reinforcement operate here, too? In the past, it was assumed that instrumental conditioning involved reinforcement whereas classical conditioning did not. In fact, the absence of reinforcement in classical conditioning was, for a long time, taken as one of the fundamental differences between the two forms of conditioning.

But now our thinking has changed. Careful scrutiny of classical conditioning has led many to believe that reinforcement may be operating in classical conditioning after all. For example, consider eyelid conditioning. The previously undetected reinforcement operating in this situation may be avoidance of the air puff. In eyelid conditioning a CS (e.g., bell) is presented a brief moment before the UCS (air puff). If, upon hearing the bell, the subject can close or partially close her eye before the air puff is delivered then she has, in effect, been reinforced by avoiding the unpleasant puff. Think about the planaria that are conditioned with shock (UCS) and light (CS). It may well be that, upon sensing the light, the animal constricts in order to "brace" against the impending shock just as we brace against bumps, scrapes, or falls that we see coming. In other words, reinforcment may be operating in classical as well as instrumental conditioning.

1. *Amount of Reinforcement.* Several crucial variables have been investigated in connection with reinforcement. The first of these is the *amount* of reinforcement. What do you think the relationship is between the amount of reward you give an animal and how much that animal will learn? The situation is a complicated one, but you are correct if you concluded that perfromance increases as amount of reward increase, up to a point. After substantial increases in amount have been made, then further increases seem to be of little consequence.

2. *Delay of Reinforcement.* When we reinforce an animal we don't have to give it the reward immediately after it makes the response. We can delay the reinforcement as long as we wish. But when we do so we run the risk of greatly reducing performance. A rat's performance normally suffers if we delay reinforcement by as little as a few seconds.

Humans, on the other hand, seem to be able to perform quite well under long delays. For example you won't be tested and graded on this material for some time. Yet you keep going, slogging through page and chapter. Well, more than likely what is happening is that you are receiving rewards along the way. Reinforcement is not delayed that long. For example, you may congratulate yourself on having made it through another chapter. Or, miracle of miracles, some of this stuff may actually be interesting, and satisfy your curiosity. So, even in the case of the human, real delays in reinforcement probably lead to lessened performance.

3. *Schedules of Reinforcement.* Imagine a crazed little man in running shoes and a Hawaiian shirt standing in front of a Las Vegas slot machine. He is pumping coins into the machine as fast as he can. Is this motivated behavior? To be sure. But what is controlling this intense little segment of behavior? Why is he going about it so rapidly?

One of the controlling factors is that without necessarily labeling it at such, the casino has set the machine up so it operates according to a *variable ratio schedule of reinforcement.*

Schedules of reinforcement refer to the general idea that we need not reinforce every response an organism makes. We can pick and choose, and only reinforce certain responses. In a variable ratio schedule the subject must make differing numbers of responses before it is reinforced. Five responses might be required before the first reward is received, then fifteen more before the next reward, then seven, and thirty-two, and so on. It has been repeatedly demonstrated in the laboratory that the variable ratio schedule leads to very high rates of responding (see Hellenthal and Marcucella, 1978), in both animals and humans. It makes sense, doesn't it? You know that standing around won't get you anywhere, you do have to make lots of responses to get each reward, so you respond rapidly.

It is another example of the way motivated behavior is controlled by learning. All those Girl Scouts chasing about the neighborhood with boxes of strange minty cookies are in the grip of a variable ratio schedule. They have to push varying, unpredictable numbers of doorbells before they make each sale.

Many kinds of reinforcement schedules have been closely investigated. Three of the most common include *fixed interval, variable interval,* and *fixed ratio* (see Figure 5.7). In a fixed interval schedule the subject is rewarded for the first response it makes after a certain time interval has elapsed. When under the influence of this schedule, animals and humans tend to slack off on their responding after a reward has been received, presumably because they know some time must elapse before the next reward can be received. Then, as that interval nears its end, the rate of responding picks up in anticipation of the next reward. This schedule produces the characteristic *scalloping* pattern depicted in Figure 5.7. Students' studying behavior often displays this scalloping. After an exam, few study at all for a while. They all go to the beach. Then, as the next exam approaches, studying picks up again.

In the variable interval schedule the time intervals that must elapse before the next response is rewarded vary. This schedule produces steady responding without scalloping. The subject just "checks in" occasionally to discover when the varying intervals have elapsed.

Finally, in the fixed ratio schedule a certain unchanging number of responses must be made before a reward may be earned. Workers

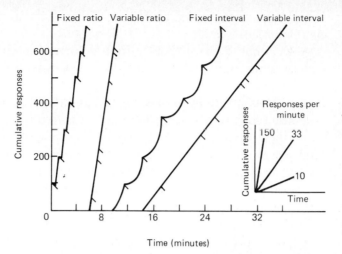

FIGURE 5.7
Cumulative response curves of the type obtained under the four most common schedules of reinforcement. (Adapted from Williams, J. L. Operant learning: Procedures for changing behavior. Copyright 1973 by Wadsworth Publishing Company, Inc. Reprinted by permission of the publisher, Brooks/Cole Publishing Company, Monterey, C A. Fig. 3.2, p. 46.)

doing "piecework" are subjected to this schedule. They must process a certain number of units before they earn money. For example, they might be paid by the number of baskets of peaches they pick or the number of toasters they assemble. As you might imagine, this schedule leads to high rates of responding.

Schedules of reinforcement are important in trying to understand motivation because they shape and influence behavior. Two equally hungry rats will behave very differently depending upon what schedule has been wired into the Skinner box.

So far, we have looked at amount, delay, and schedules of reinforcement, and at some of the effects these factors have on behavior. Now it is time to turn to some of the major theoretical interpretations of reinforcement. We turn from the realm of fact to that of hypothesis and theory.

Theories of Reinforcement

Drive Theory. Drive theory, and, in particular, the drive theory of Clark Hull (1943), is probably the best known of all theories of reinforcement. (Since Chapter 6 is, in large part, devoted to Hull's theory, this section will serve as an introduction to that discussion.)

According to drive theory, *reinforcement is equivalent to drive reduction.* If we are in a high drive state, make a response, and the drive state is reduced, then a reinforcing effect appears. That is, the response is strengthened because it was followed by a reduction in drive. Responses that lead to, or are followed by, drive reduction will be reinforced.

Now, what is drive? An animal is in a high drive state if it is experiencing some *homeostatic imbalance*, some kind of *strong negative stimulation*, or some *physiological need.* Thus if an animal is hungry it is normally in a state of heightened drive. If it makes a response (such as a lever press) that leads to a reduction in the drive state, then the lever-pressing response is strengthened and will more likely occur again under similar circumstances. As noted, drive is not related only to biological tissue needs such as hunger or thirst. External stimuli, such a shock, can lead to high drive, too. Responses that reduce the shock, and therefore the drive state, will be reinforced.

Drive energizes the organism, it gets the animal up and going. It is the "push" behind behavior. Drive reduction strengthens preceding responses and terminates behavior. The nature, strengths, and weaknesses of drive theory are more fully discussed in Chapter 6. The Lorenz and the Tinbergen models of instinctive behavior are discussed in Chapter 2. These two models are essentially drive models; in both, energy or tension is thought to build up only to be released or reduced by the occurrence of some response.

Optimal-Arousal-Level Theories.   Some investigators have pointed out that reinforcement does not always seem to involve a reduction in stimulation as implied by drive theory (Berlyne, 1969; Routtenberg, 1968). To the contrary, they point out that *increases* in stimulation and arousal quite often appear to be reinforcing. For example, some rock music is played at concerts above the pain and ear damage level. Yet, to judge from gross receipts, this intense increase in stimulation is reinforcing.

Facts such as this have led to theories that maintain that there is some *preferred level* of stimulation which the animal seeks to maintain. If arousal is too high, then responses that reduce arousal will be reinforced. But if arousal is too low, then responses that increase stimulation will be reinforced.

You know, if you have been to a party everyday for the last two weeks you may seek the solitude of your apartment. But if you have been trapped in that apartment for two weeks you will try to stir up some excitement. Responses that keep you in your preferred level, whether they increase or decrease arousal, will be reinforcing. This form of theory has been discussed in Chapter 4.

Although different in many ways, optimal-arousal-level theories are similar to drive and instinct models in that they involve tension which is somehow adjusted.

Stimulus Theories.   Drive theory and optimal-arousal-level theories both hold that reinforcement is correlated with the maintenance of some internal state. Other psychologists have pointed out that there seems to be still more to this business of reinforcement. They emphasize the impact of external stimuli rather than internal states on reinforcement. (Berlyne, 1960; Dember and Earl, 1957; Fiske and Maddi, 1961).

Some stimulus theories (McCall, 1966) argue that any *stimulus change*, up to a point, will be reinforcing. Still other stimulus theories emphasize *quality* rather than *quantity* of stimulation (Pfaffman, 1969; Young, 1966). These theories maintain that certain stimuli, such as sweet ones, are preferred, and that this preference is inherited. Any act that leads to the attainment of these preferred stimuli will be reinforced. The stimulus does not have to have anything to do with tissue need reduction, as is evidenced by the fact that saccharin solutions will do very well as reinforcing stimuli even though they are completely nonnutritive.

Response Theories: Premack's Principle.   So far we have mentioned drive, optimal-arousal, and stimulus interpretations of reinforcement. The final type of theory is called the response theory. These theories, although they vary considerably, argue that the making of a consummatory response is what reinforcement is all about (see Glickman and Schiff, 1967; Sheffield, 1966). If a particular response is followed by the occurrence of some consummatory response (e.g., eating, chewing, drinking, copulating, manipulating, swallowing) then that response will be reinforced. Consummatory theories do not focus on external stimuli, or on internal state of arousal. They focus on the idea that it is reinforcing to make consummatory responses.

Premack (1959, 1965) has presented an influential variation on the consummatory theme. According to Premack (1959, p. 220), "Any Response A will reinforce any other Response B, if and only if the independent rate of A is greater than that of B." One response can be used to reinforce a second response, but only if the first response is more likely to occur, in general, than the second. For example, if a rat is observed to lick a water tube more often than it presses a lever, then lever pressing can be reinforced by allowing the animal to lick the tube after it presses the bar. Premack gave children the choice of operating a pinball machine or a candy machine. He found that children who preferred to play pinball could be induced to increase their operation of the candy machine if it was reinforced by allowing the child to play pinball. Similarly children who preferred to work the candy machine would increase their pinball playing if pinball playing was followed by a chance to work the candy machine.

Conclusion.   There are many theories of reinforcement, which are referred to throughout the text. It seems that this business of reinforcement is not simple. There may be no single, simple way to look at reinforcement; the effect may be many faceted, and quite different internal and external events may be reinforcing under varying conditions.

Secondary Reinforcement

A secondary reinforcer is any neutral stimulus that, through repeated pairings with a primary reinforcer, acquires reinforcing properties. For example, first we train a rat to run down an alley to a distinct black (or white) goal box where it is fed. Then we construct a T maze such that one arm of the T is the distinct goal box and the other arm is a new neutral color (e.g., white if the goal box used in the straight alley training phase was black). We then give the animal the opportunity to run down and turn into one of the two arms when food is *never* present in either arm. It has been found repeatedly that the animal will learn to turn into the distinct goal box that has been previously paired with food. The distinct box has become a secondary reinforcer.

Money is a prime example of secondary reinforcement in human life. Those little green paper rectangles certainly do not have much inherent value. Aside from a passing curiosity an infant shows little interest in them. Adults, on the other hand, sometimes even kill one another for them. Because they have been paired with almost every imaginable primary reinforcer (food, sex, drink, freedom, travel, possessions, and so on), they have become extremely powerful secondary reinforcers. They direct, maintain, and control an enormous amount of our behavior.

1. Learning and motivation are closely bound together and influence one another heavily.

2. Learning may be defined as a relatively permanent change in behavior potentiality that occurs as a result of reinforced practice.

3. Motivation can be learned.

4. Motivation determines new learning.

5. Motivation translates old learning into performance.

6. Classical conditioning involves unconditioned stimuli, unconditioned responses, conditioned stimuli, and conditioned responses.

7. Many different organisms, stimuli, and responses can be involved in classical conditioning.

8. Many different motivational states appear to be established through classical conditioning. Examples include experimental neurosis, everyday emotions, fear, phobias, masochism, and interoceptive conditioning. Conditioning may be most likely when the CS signals the occurrence of the UCS.

9. Instrumental conditioning includes reward, avoidance, escape, and punishment training.

10. Extinction refers to a decrease in response strength with repeated nonreinforcements.

11. Generalization refers to the fact that a response connected to one stimulus will tend to be elicited by similar stimuli.

12. Reinforcement may operate in classical as well as in instrumental conditioning.

13. Parameters of reinforcement include amount, delay, and schedules.

14. Theories of reinforcement include drive theory, optimal-arousal-level theories, stimulus theories, and response theories.

15. The Premack principle states that if one response is more likely to occur than another, then the first response can be used to reinforce the second.

16. A secondary reinforcer is any neutral stimulus that, through repeated pairings with a primary reinforcer, acquires reinforcing properties of its own.

CHAPTER 6

Motivation and Learning: Extensions and Applications

In Chapter 5 we discussed the intricate relationship between motivation and learning, pointing out that they influence one another heavily. In this chapter we introduce some fascinating areas of research, including coping through behavior modification, depression, learned helplessness, biofeedback, and biological constraints on learning. In a sense, many of these topics supplement our coverage of coping with stress given in Chapter 4. Each of these topics can stand on its own as a legitimate area of research. And yet each is bound up closely with the motivation-learning marriage. So to discuss them together in one chapter is to further illuminate the relationship between motivation and learning while simultaneously covering some of the most interesting topics in the field of motivation.

COPING THROUGH BEHAVIOR MODIFICATION

Behavior modification, or behavior therapy, refers to the control of behaviors through the application of the principles of conditioning we discussed in Chapter 5. Essentially, the behavior modifier believes that all behaviors, including abnormal or disruptive behaviors we might want to change, are learned and that if they are learned then

Definition

they should be subject to change and alteration through the application of the principles of learning and motivation, such as reinforcement, extinction, and generalization. Behavior disorders, in all their complexity, are, according to behavior modifiers, subject to the same rules and principles that govern any learned behavior. In this section we see that this approach, now very popular, has led to some striking results.

Relationship to Clinical Approaches

Generally speaking, behavior modification differs from the more traditional clinical procedures in that it deemphasizes personal interaction with the patient. Whereas a traditional clinical approach might involve long discussions between patient and therapist, during which an effort is made to uncover and remedy underlying causes of behavior problems, the behavior modifier pointedly avoids such contact. Behavior modifiers are more concerned with altering symptomatic behavior than they are with delving into subconscious and unconscious conflicts. Although this position is softening, as we shall see when we discuss cognitive behavior modification, strict behavior modification deals more with observable behavior than it does with the "contents of the mind."

Token Economies

Many examples of behavior modification are available in the literature. *Token economies* are most often used in mental hospitals, schools, prisons, or other institutions. They involve efforts to alter behavior through the use of rewards that are delivered immediately after the occurrence of the desired behavior. For example, consider a ward for severely disturbed patients in a large state mental hospital. Most of the patients are on medication. Many of them are slowed down and apathetic. Simple things, such as combing one's hair, cleaning up one's sleeping area, being nice to one another, and attending hospital social and therapeutic activities tend not to get done. In a case such as this a token economy can be helpful. Tokens, poker chips, or marks on a sheet of paper are given to the patients by the ward attendants each time the patient is observed engaging in one of the desired behaviors. These tokens can be accumulated by the patients and later used as money in the hospital store or exchanged for other privileges such as extra television or sports time. These procedures can lead to dramatic changes in behavior (see Klein, 1979; Schaefer and Martin 1966).

Figure 6.1 contains some of the results reported by Dapcich-Miuri

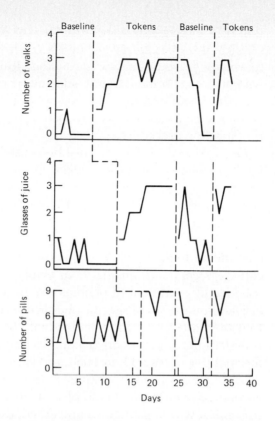

FIGURE 6.1
Adherence to a complex medical program as influenced by token reward. (Adapted from Dapcich-Miura, E., & Hovell, M. F. Contingency management of adherence to a complex medical regimen in an elderly heart patient. Behavior Therapy, 1979, 10, 193–201. Fig. 1, p. 198).

and Hovell (1979). These results indicate what was done with an eighty-two-year-old retired heart patient who, for one reason or another, did not do the things he was supposed to do to ensure his health. He did not like to take walks and he often neglected to drink liquids and take pills. Then he was put on a token schedule where each time he did do one of these things he was given a token. Accumulated tokens could then be exchanged for the opportunity to select a dinner menu or to choose and dine at a restaurant. As you can see, the desired behavior increased dramatically during periods when tokens were given. The desired behavior dropped out when the tokens were no longer given. In other words, reinforcement must be continued or the reinforced behavior will extinguish.

Tokens are not the only reward used by behavior modifiers. In fact, anything that people like, want, and value can be used to reinforce desired behavior directly without the mediating token. For instance, Powell, Felce, Jenkins, and Lunt (1979) report the dramatic finding

Other Reinforcers and Behaviors

that rest-home guests were stimulated to engage in healthy social and physical activities by rewarding these activities with the opportunity to engage in some indoor gardening. Knight and McKenzie (1974) were able to eliminate thumb sucking by rewarding nonthumb sucking with a bedtime story. Money, food, praise, recreation, and social activities can, and have been, used as effective rewards in behavior modification procedures.

Just as many reinforcers have been used, so too have many behaviors been altered, including weight losses (Wilson, 1979), energy consumption (Winett, Neale, and Grier, 1979), bed wetting (Azrin, Hontos, and Besalel-Azrin, 1979), and fetishism (Raymond, 1956), to name but a few.

Systematic Desensitization

One of the most widely acclaimed examples of behavior therapy is called *systematic desensitizatioin* (Wolpe, 1973). This is a technique used in the treatment of phobias. We have already seen that phobias are irrational fears of specific objects or events which are so powerful that they interfere with the individual's life and sense of well-being.

Systematic desensitization assumes that phobias are classically conditional responses and, as such, are subject to the principles of conditioning as outlined in Chapter 5. In particular, if a phobic reaction is conditioned, then it should be extinguishable. Systematic desensitization is a way to extinguish unwanted, disruptive fears.

The procedure involves two steps. In the first step, the phobic patient is taught to relax. In the second step, the subject is asked to make up a list of stimuli, objects, or situations that cause fear and to rank these fear-producing stimuli in terms of how powerful they are. These lists of ranked fear-producing stimuli are called *hierarchies.* Examples of hierarchies are contained in Table 6.1.

How is a conditioned response extinguished in any classical conditioning situation? The CS is presented repeatedly without the UCS. This causes the CR to diminish gradually. Applying the same principle to the phobic problem, we could present the most powerful fear-producing stimulus from the hierarchy first. But if we did that the patient might be unnecessarily frightened. So instead we present the *weakest* of the stimuli first. Typically the patient is asked to get into a comfortable position and to relax as she has been taught to do in the first step of the desensitization procedure. Then she is asked to think about the weakest fear-producing stimulus while relaxing. This procedure is assumed to have two effects. First, the fear that has been

TABLE 6.1. Examples of Anxiety Hierarchies*

A. *Claustrophobic Series*
   1. Being stuck in an elevator. (The longer the time, the more disturbing.)
   2. Being locked in a room. (The smaller the room and the longer the time, the more disturbing.)
   3. Passing through a tunnel in a railway trian. (The longer the tunnel, the more disturbing.)
   4. Traveling in an elevator alone. (The greater the distance, the more disturbing.)
   5. Traveling in an elevator with an operator. (The longer the distance, the more disturbing.)
   6. On a journey by train. (The longer the journey, the more disturbing.)
   7. Stuck in a dress with a stuck zipper.
   8. Having a tight ring on her finger.
   9. Visiting and unable to leave at will (for example, if engaged in a card game).
  10. Being told of somebody in jail.
  11. Having a polish on her fingernails and no access to remover.
  12 Reading of miners trapped underground.

B. *Death Series*
   1. Being at a burial.
   2. Being at a house of mourning.
   3. The word *death*.
   4. Seeing a funeral procession. (The nearer, the more disturbing.)
   5. The sight of a dead animal (For example, a cat).
   6. Driving past a cemetery. (The nearer, the more disturbing.)

C. *Illness Series*
   1. Hearing that an acquaintance has cancer.
   2. The word *cancer*.
   3. Witnessing a convulsive seizure.
   4. Discussions of operations. (The more prolonged the discussion, the more disturbing.)
   5. Seeing a person receive an injection.
   6. Seeing someone faint.
   7. The word *operation*.
   8. Considerable bleeding from another person.
   9. A friend points to a stranger, saying, "This man has tuberculosis."
  10. The sight of a blood-stained bandage.
  11. The smell of ether.

TABLE 6.1 Continued

12. The sight of a friend sick in bed. (The more sick looking, the more disturbing.)
13. The smell of methylated spirits.
14. Driving past a hospital.

*From Wolpe, J. The systematic desensitization treatment of neuroses. *Journal of Nervous and Mental Disease*, 1961, *132*, 189–203, p. 197. Copyright 1961 by The Williams & Wilkins Co., Baltimore. Reprinted by permission.

classically conditioned to the stimulus will extinguish because the CS (the weak stimulus) is being presented (thought about) by itself without a UCS. Second, the relaxation response is becoming conditioned to the weak fear stimulus. An old response (fear) is being extinguished while a new response (relaxation) is being conditioned to the weak fear stimulus.

The patient is instructed to continue to dwell upon and relax in the face of this weakest of all fear stimuli until no more fear is felt and the subject feels comfortable with that stimulus. Then the therapist asks the subject to think about the next most powerful fear-producing stimulus from the hierarchy. When the fear elicited by this stimulus is extinguished and replaced by relaxation, the subject moves on to the next stimulus in the hierarchy, and so on. This step-by-step, or systematic, procedure is followed until all phobic stimuli have been desensitized.

Notice that *thinking* about fear-producing stimuli appears to be adequate. There is no need to present the actually physical objects or events to ensure the success of this procedure.

Systematic desensitization represents one more way in which powerful motive systems can be altered and, in this case, eliminated, through the principles of conditioning (see also Rimm & Masters, 1979).

Aversion Training   Aversion training, or aversion therapy as it is sometimes called, is another technique for altering motivated behavior through the use of conditioning principles. Aversion therapy is often used to eliminate "bad habits." For example, consumption of alcoholic beverages can sometimes be reduced through aversion training (see Morosko and Baer, 1970; Wilson, Leaf, and Nathan, 1975). In a typical training situation the subject will be given, say, eight glasses of liquid. Six of the glasses contain nonalcoholic beverages (juice, water, and so on) whereas the remaining two contain alcoholic beverages (e.g., gin and wine). Initially, the subject is required to drink all eight liquids. When the nonalcoholic liquids are swallowed, nothing happens. But when the subject drinks the alcoholic substances, electric shock is delivered. Needless to say, this is not a pleasant experience. In fact, on subsequent trials when the subject can refrain from drinking alcoholic beverages, many subjects show a marked drop in their consumption of alcohol. Apparently the effect can persist beyond the confines of the laboratory. People undergoing this sort of aversion therapy can be helped in their efforts to curb their everyday drinking.

Aversion therapy has been used to reduce a wide range of behavior. For example, it is very uncomfortable to have your own voice played back to you a second or two after you speak. This kind of negative event has been used to reduce stuttering (Goldiamond, 1965). Subjects were asked to speak sentences. When they spoke without stuttering nothing happened, but when they stuttered they received delayed feedback of their speech. A reduction in stuttering was noted.

Smoking, overeating, hair pulling, and just about any bad habit you can think of seem to be susceptible to aversion training. Of course, the ends must justify the means. We cannot indiscriminately administer aversive stimuli without first weighing carefuly the costs and benefits of such action.

Aversion therapy is sometimes thought of as an example of punishment training in that if the subject makes a particular response (e.g., eating or stuttering) aversive stimulation is applied. Others think of it as an example of avoidance conditioning in which an inhibitory response is learned in order to avoid punishment. According to the two-factor theory of avoidance conditioning, fear is initially classically conditioned to a particular stimulus or act (e.g., fear produced by shock is classically conditioned to the act of drinking alcohol). Then the fear is instrumentally avoided by staying away from the fear-producing stimulus or act (e.g., by not drinking alcohol). Whatever the interpretation, aversion therapy appears to be a fairly powerful tool in eliminating, or at least reducing, bad habits.

In most of the examples given so far, efforts have been made to alter behavior without having to consider what the subject is thinking about. Cognitive factors have been ignored. Thus, if a patient straightens up her sleeping area she receives a token regardless of what she is thinking or feeling. An alcoholic is shocked if he drinks alcohol regardless of what he is thinking or feeling. These are examples of traditional behavior modification in which the emphasis is upon changing overt, observable behavior without dealing with cognitive events. But, beginning in the mid 1970s, a new approach to behavior modification has developed called *cognitive behavior modification* (CBM). Quite simply CBM argues that *if we can change the way people think, then we can change their behavior.* This is a radical departue from the strict traditional behavior modifier's position that took a very dim view of anything which smacked of cognitive activity.

Proponents of CBM argue that the traditional point of view is too limiting and that, in fact, it is illogical when it eliminates thought from consideration. Specifically, they argue that a thought is just as much a piece of behavior as is throwing a baseball. The thought may be more difficult to measure, it may be much more elusive than physical activity, but it is a behavior nonetheless. And, as behavior, thought should be subject to the principles of conditioning just as is any other piece of behavior.

The critics of CBM cry out that to take this position is to return to the dark days when unmeasurable mentalistic concepts were bandied about in a most unscientific manner. They look at CBM as a step in the wrong direction.

However CBM appears to be here to stay. A great number of researchers are adopting this point of view and expanding upon the number of available CBM techniques (see Meichenbaum, 1979; Mahoney and Kazdin, 1979).

Assertion Training

Assertion training is a technique that serves as a good example of this new emphasis upon cognitive activity. It really represents a blend of the old traditional point of view and the new cognitive approach.

How many times have you given in to unreasonable demands made by others? "I could take the bus but it would be so helpful if you could drive me to the airport at 1 A.M." "Would you watch my laundry in the dryer while I slip next door to grocery shop?" "Could you lend me fifty dollars until payday?" These sorts of requests appear often in life. Once in a while they are acceptable, but if too many of them appear, or the same one appears too often, we feel frustrated and used after we give in to the demand. We feel like a chump. We feel as though we should have been more assertive and in a polite but firm manner said, "No."

In a similar manner there are often times when we fail to ask for what we reasonable and fairly deserve. The typist who has been working faithfully for years in the same law firm might reasonably expect a raise. But, because of timidity, the request for the raise is never made. "Oh, I don't want to bother the boss." "Wouldn't it be embarrassing if I were turned down?"

Both of these conditions, the one where we agree to unreasonable demands and the one where we fail to ask for what we deserve, are far from ideal. In assertion training steps are taken to enable us, by analyzing and changing our thoughts as well as our behavior, to become more assertive.

The steps in assertion training are outlined in Table 6:2. As you read through them, focus on the fact that they represent CBM in that the emphasis is upon changing behavior by first changing thought.

The Problem of Generalization

It is all well and good to sit an individual down in front of a line of cups of liquid and shock them each time they drink alcoholic beverages. Of *course* the subjects will stop drinking the alcoholic beverages. They would have to be pretty foolish to keep on drinking and being shocked. But, and this is the crucial question, what happens after the subjects leave the experimental setting? Will they continue to refrain from drinking alcohol? Or will they all get together at the local pub to celebrate the end of the experimental session by "knocking back" a few? In other words, will the changed behavior generalize beyond the confines of the laboratory? We have already noted a few studies that seem to indicate that some treatments carry back into the subject's everyday life. However, it would be a serious error to conclude that all, or even most, behavior modification effects are stable and strong enough to influence everyday nonexperimental life. In fact, many experimental effects do *not* appear to generalize; they are strong within the experimental setting but are extremely weak or nonexistent beyond the confines of the laboratory.

TABLE 6.2 *Assertion Training Procedures**

1. Examine your interactions. Are there situations that you need to handle more assertively? Do you at times hold opinions and feelings within you for fear of what would happen if you expressed them? Do you occasionally blow your cool and lash out angrily at others? Studying your interactions is easier if you keep a diary for a week or longer, recording the situations in which you acted timidly, those in which you were aggressive, and those that you handled assertively.

2. Select those interactions where it would be to your benefit to be more assertive. They may include situations in which you were overly polite, overly apologetic, timid, and allowed others to take advantage of you, at the same time harboring feelings of resentment, anger, embarrassment, fear of others, or self-criticism for not having the courage to express yourself. Overly aggressive interactions in which you exploded in anger or walked over others also need to be dealt with. For each set of nonassertive or aggressive interactions, you can become more assertive, as shown in the next steps.

3. Concentrate on a specific incident in the past. Close your eyes for a few minutes and vividly imagine the details, including what you and the other person said, and how you felt at the time and afterward.

4. Write down and review your responses. Ask yourself the following questions to determine how you presented yourself:

   a. Eye contact—did you look directly at the other person, in a relaxed, steady gaze? Looking down or away suggests a lack of self-confidence. Glaring is an aggressive response.

   b. Gestures—were your gestures appropriate, free flowing, relaxed, and used effectively to emphasize your messages? Awkward stiffness suggests nervousness; other gestures (such as angry fist) signal an aggressive reaction.

   c. Body posture—did you show the importance of your message by directly facing the other person, by leaning toward that person, by holding your head erect, and by sitting or standing appropriately close?

   d. Facial expression—did your facial expression show a stern, firm pose consistent with an assertive response?

   e. Voice tone and volume—was your response stated in a firm, conversational tone? Shouting may suggest anger. Speaking softly suggests shyness, and a cracking voice suggests nervousness. Tape recording and listening to one's voice is a way to practice increasing or decreasing the volume.

   f. Speech fluency—did your speech flow smoothly, clearly, and

TABLE 6.2 Continued

slowly? Rapid speech or hesitation in speaking suggests nervousness. Tape assertive responses before you try them out in problem situations, so you can practice and improve your fluency.

g. Timing—were your verbal reactions to a problem situation stated at a time closest to the incident that would appropriately permit you and the other person time to review the incident? Generally, spontaneous expressions are the best, but certain situations should be handled at a later time—for example, challenging some of your boss's erroneous statements in private rather than in front of a group that he or she is making a presentation to.

h. Message content—for a problem situation, which of your responses were nonassertive or aggressive, and which were assertive? Study the content and consider why your responded in a nonassertive or aggressive style.

5. Observe one or more effective models. Watch the verbal and nonverbal approaches that are assertively used to handle the types of interactions with which you have been having problems. Compare the consequences between their approach and yours. If possible, discuss their approach and their feelings about using it.

6. Make a list of various alternative approaches for being more assertive.

7. Close your eyes and visualize yourself using each of the above alternative approaches. For each approach, think through what the full set of interactions would be, along with the consequences. Select an approach, or combination of approaches, that you believe will be most effective for you to use. Through imagery, practice this approach until you feel comfortable that it will work for you.

8. Role-play the approach with someone else, perhaps a friend or counselor. If certain segments of your approach appear clumsy, awkward, timid, or aggressive, practice modifications until you become comfortable with the approach. Obtain feedback from the other person as to the strengths and shortcomings of your approach. Compare your interactions to the guidelines for verbal and nonverbal assertive behavior to Step 4. It may be useful for the other person to role-play one or more assertive strategies, which you would then practice by reversing roles.

9. Repeat Steps 7 and 8 until you develop an assertive approach that you are comfortable with and believe will work best for you.

10. Use your approach in a real-life situation. The previous steps are designed to prepare you for the real event. Expect to be somewhat anxious when you first try to be assertive. If you are still too fearful of attempting to be assertive, repeat Steps 5 through 8. For those few individuals

TABLE 6.2 Continued

who fail to develop the needed confidence to try out being assertive, professional counseling is advised—expressing yourself and effective interactions with others are essential for personal happiness.

11. Reflect on the effectiveness of your effort. Did you "keep your cool?" Consider the nonverbal and verbal guidelines for assertive behavior discussed in Step 4; what components of your responses were assertive, aggressive, and nonassertive? What were the consequences of your effort? How did you feel after trying out this new set of interactions?

12. Expect some success with your early efforts, but not complete personal satisfaction. Personal growth and interacting more effectively with others is a continual learning process.

*Adapted from Zastrow, C. How to become more assertive. In C. Zastrow and D. H. Chang (Eds.), *The Personal Problem Solver.* Englewood Cliffs, New Jersey: Prentice-Hall, 1977, pp. 238–240. Reprinted by permission of Prentice-Hall, Inc., Englewood Cliffs, New Jersey.

The situation is complicated by the fact that at least two factors can lead to the loss of a behavior modification effect outside the laboratory.

1. The effect may simply extinguish because the reinforcers are no longer delivered. For example, if children are paid for picking up street trash in their neighborhood, they will only do so as long as that pay is forthcoming. Once the reinforcement is removed the behavior quickly drops out or is extinguished (Chapman and Risley, 1974).

2. The laboratory setting may be so different from the subjects' everyday life that the laboratory-based learned response simply does not generalize. There isn't enough similarity between the laboratory and everyday life for responses learned in the laboratory to carry over into the subject's normal life.

Many studies do not adequately test for generalization of the critical response, or for its persistence over time. One study might demonstrate that children will stop hair pulling if they are punished each time they do so in the laboratory. But the same study will fail to test for the effect (a) in different situations and (b) after substantial time since training has elapsed.

Thus, although behavior modification, both traditional and cognitive, is extremely encouraging it must still undergo additional evaluation before it can be accepted as a proven method of sustantially altering motivated behavior.

In the discussion of classical and instrumental conditioning in Chapter 5 we spoke as though these two types of conditioning are distinctly different forms of learning. Traditionally, classical conditioning has been thought to involve *involuntary* responses whereas instrumental conditioning has been thought of as involving *voluntary* responses. In a sense, the argument has been that we are neurally "wired" in two different ways; one to modify involuntary visceral behavior through classical conditioning and the other to modify voluntary responses through the procedures of instrumental conditioning.

Involuntary responses such as eyeblinks, heart rates, and salivation have been modified by classical procedures whereas more complicated voluntary responses such as bar pressing and picking up toys have been modified by instrumental procedures.

But recent research has cast doubt on this simple, pat distinction. Neal Miller and his associates (Miller, 1973, 1978) have stimulated the scientific community by reporting what appears to be *instrumental conditioning of so-called involuntary responses.* If it turns out that involuntary responses can, in fact, be instrumentally conditioned, then the time-honored distinction between classical and instrumental conditioning must be seriously questioned, if not actually laid to rest.

How does Miller do it? In one study Miller first paralyzed the skeletal muscles of a rat with curare. (Curare is a poison sometimes put on the tips of arrows by South American Indians.) By paralyzing the voluntarily controlled skeletal muscles, Miller was effectively eliminating them as a source of confusion and confounding in his experiment. They were "out of the way." Then Miller carefully monitored the rat's heart rate. Heart rate is not absolutely constant; it varies a little over time. Each time the rat showed an increase in heart rate Miller rewarded it by removing shock from the animal's tail or by electrically stimulating areas of the brain in a way that is known to be reinforcing.

Here we have a rat, all strapped in, paralyzed, and undergoing shock. Doesn't it seem overly optimistic to expect this creature to increase its heart rate in order to escape from the shock? But that is exactly what it does as Figure 6.2 shows. Miller found that rats will increase their heart rate by as much as 20 percent in order to escape from shock.

Now you might object to this result by suggesting that the increase

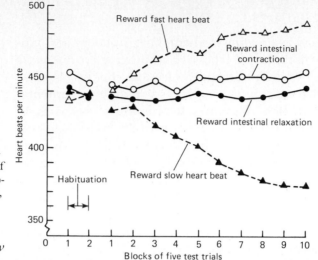

FIGURE 6.2

Heart rates in rats rewarded for increases or decreases in heart rate. Also heart rates in rats rewarded for changes in intestinal contraction. (After Miller, N. E., & Banuazizi, A. Instrumental learning by curarized rats of a specific visceral response, intestinal or cardiac. Journal of Comparative and Physiological Psychology, 1968, *65, 1–17. Fig. 4, p. 5. Copyright 1968 by the American Psychological Association. Reprinted by permission.)*

in heart rate might be caused by an overall increase in the rat's level of arousal, rather than learning. After all, the animal is undergoing quite an unusual experience. Miller did two things to eliminate this possiblity. First, he tried rewarding decreases in heart rate rather than increases. As Figure 6.2 shows, the rats significantly decreased their heart rates, indicating that the effect is something more than an increase in overall excitement or arousal level. Second, Miller rewarded intestinal contraction or relaxation and looked at heart rate while he did so. As Figure 6.2 shows, heart rate was unaffected in this case, again indicating that the effect could not be attributed to general arousal level.

Miller's work was not limited to heart rates. For example, he found he could increase or decrease the rate at which rats' kidneys produced urine by appropriately rewarding monitored increases and decreases. He has also reported being able to teach a rat to blush in one ear but not the other. In other words, at least with the rat, there appear to be some so-called involuntary responses that can be instrumentally conditioned. Although Miller (1978) has reported some skepticism about his own results, they have been widely interpreted as suggesting that the traditional voluntary-involuntry distinction between instrumental and classical conditioning must be at least modified.

Critics of the research purportedly demonstrating instrumental conditioning of involuntary responses do not deny the reported effects. Instead they argue that the effects may be *mediated* by undetected or uncontrolled voluntary responses. For instance, what would you do if someone said he would give you a substantial sum of money if you could increase your heart rate? You would do some quick exercises, thereby increasing your heart rate, and collect your reward. The heart rate would be indirectly rather than directly affected by the reward contingency. In other words, the involuntary response may not be directly alterable by instrumental conditioning after all.

But, as we have seen, Miller anticipated this objection and paralyzed his rats. Their involuntary response changes could not have been mediated by voluntary action because all voluntary physical action was blocked. In addition, Miller (1978) and Bracker (1977) report cases in which paralyzed humans were able to alter their blood pressure in response to instrumental reward contingencies. Thus there is some evidence, involving both animal and human data, that suggests that not all instances of instrumentally conditioned involuntary responses can be attributed to voluntary physical mediation.

However, there is an even more serious objection to this research of which Miller (1978) is also aware. He describes two paralyzed humans who could alter their blood pressure by *thinking* about exciting events such as horse races and sex (see also Hatch and Gatchel, 1979). In other words, it is possible that what appears to be direct control of involuntary responding is, in fact, control through voluntary *mental* mediation. Through voluntary cognitive activity, we are able to mediate what at first might appear to be direct control of involuntary responses. The perfect example of unmediated direct control of involuntary responding has yet to be forwarded.

Physical and Mental Mediation

However, as some have pointed out, the question of mediation, although crucial to the theoretical distinction between instrumental and classical conditioning, is irrelevant when one addresses the *usefulness* of the control of so-called involuntary responses. It is becoming clear that humans are much more able to control so-called involuntary responses than was previously believed in Western societies. Whether this control is mediated physically, mentally, or not at all is unimportant when one considers the applications of such control.

Control of so-called involuntary responses apparently has been

Applications

commonplace in some Eastern cultures. For example, Wallace and Benson (1972) report cases in which Zen meditators significantly decreased their consumption of oxygen and decreased their output of carbon dioxide while they were meditating. Wenger, Bagchi, and Anand (1969) found that several Yogis, although they did not actually stop their hearts, were able to cause their hearts to pump so little blood that the ordinary signs of heart activity temporarily ceased (see also Green, 1973).

In Western societies, playing catch up, investigators have used the term *biofeedback* to refer to cases in which so-called involuntary responses are brought under voluntary control. Typically, the subject is given information about some involuntary system, such as blood pressure or heart rate, that is normally beyond his awareness. Then, as desired changes occur in that system, the subject is rewarded. Rewards can be self-delivered or delivered by an experimenter, and they can include, among other things, money, praise, and self-congratulations. For example, a subject might be attached to equipment that makes a clicking sound each time the subject's heart beats. Then, when desired decreases in heart rate appear, the subject will be reinforced in some appropriate manner. The following represent some, but not all, of the so-called involuntary responses that have been reported as being altered by biofeedback techniques (Houston, 1981):

heart rate	fever
blood pressure	headaches
electrical brain activity	epilepsy
skin temperature	neuroses
salivation	anxiety
vomiting	insomnia
electrodermal activity	bruxism (grinding of teeth)
gastric distress	enuresis (bed wetting)

Obviously, the potential benefits to society are enormous. Just as obviously, most of this work is experimental and extremely controversial. We will have to wait for some time before the final value of biofeedback techniques becomes apparent.

Martin Seligman and his colleagues have discovered a powerful phenomenon, called *learned helplessness*, that further fleshes out the relationship between learning and motivation (see Maier and Seligman, 1976). In the original animal studies (Seligman and Maier, 1967) dogs in one group were first subjected to repeated, inescapable shocks. The shocks were painful but not physically damaging. A second group was shocked but was able to escape from the shock by pressing a panel with its heads. Dogs in these two groups received the same amount of shock; this was accomplished by having the shock in the first group terminate when the animals in the second group terminated their shock. Dogs in a third group received no shock.

Then, twenty-four hours later, all these groups (inescapable shock, escapable shock, no shock) were put into a shuttle box similar to the one described in connection with avoidance conditioning in Chapter 5. In this situation the apparatus was set up such that if the animal failed to leap over a barrier within ten seconds it was shocked. As we learned in Chapter 5, naive animals will learn to avoid shock entirely in this type of situation by jumping over the barrier before the shock comes on. As can be seen in Figure 6.3, dogs in the no shock and escapable shock conditions did, as expected, learn to escape from the shock. But dogs in the inescapable shock condition behaved very differently; almost two thirds of them failed to avoid or escape from the now escapable shock. They just "took" the shock as though they were helpless and hopeless.

The fact that the dogs in the escapable shock condition learned during the second phase of the experiment shows that the failure of the dogs in the inescapable shock condition to learn could not be attributable to shock alone. Specifically, dogs in both of these conditions received the same amount of initial shock, but only the dogs in the inescapable condition failed to learn during the second phase, thereby indicating that it was the inescapable quality of the shock which caused the observed failure to learn.

So now you know something about dogs and helplessness. Several studies indicate that humans can suffer from the same sort of learned disability. For example, Hiroto (1974) replicated the Seligman effect using humans as subjects and a loud unpleasant noise as the noxious

Animal Research: The Triadic Design

Humans and Helplessness

FIGURE 6.3

The learned helplessness effect. The figure shows the failure of dogs to escape after having received escapable shock, inescapable shock, or no shock at all. (From Seligman, M. E. P., & Maier, S. F. Failure to escape traumatic shock. Journal of Experimental Psychology, 1967, 74, 1–9. Copyright 1967 by the American Psychological Association. Reprinted by permission.)

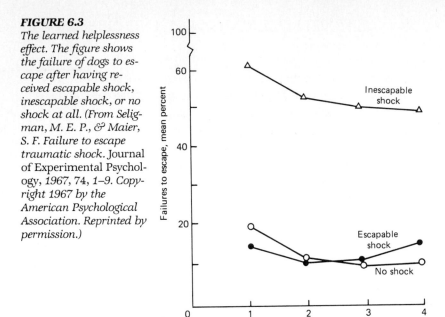

stimulus. Just as in the Seligman situation, one group could not escape the sound, one group could escape by pressing a button, and one group received no noise. Then all three groups were put into a situation in which they could all escape the noise by moving their hand from one side to the other. Most of the subjects that had experienced inescapable shock merely sat passively and accepted the unpleasant noise, whereas subjects in the other two conditions quickly learned to terminate the noise.

Seligman interprets these results in terms of learned feelings of hopelessness and helplessness. "What's the point? I've tried and tried and it's done no good. So why bother trying again?" It's something like what an undergraduate might experience if she arrived on campus, full of hope, and received Ds in her first fourteen courses. She might stop trying.

Strassman, Thaler, and Schein (1956) report that there are two types of prisoner of war, those who try to escape and cause trouble for their captors, and those who do not. When interviewed after release it turns out that the ones who tried to escape always felt there was hope; they felt as though they were not entirely helpless. Those who did not try to escape believed they were without power to better their condition. If anything, they believed that to try to escape would have made things worse.

1. Failure to Initiate Action.   According to Seligman, there are at least three components of the overall helplessness effect. The first of these is the fact that animals and humans who have undergone helplessness training appear unable to initiate new responses in new learning situations. They become passive. For example, the animals in the original Seligman studies crouched and remained relatively motionless when put into the escapable shock situation. They didn't try. There was no way they could learn to escape if they didn't try a few responses.

2. Failure to Learn.   Seligman believes that, in addition to not trying, helplessness trained animals also show a newly acquired inability to learn. He is arguing that even if the animals *did* initiate some responses (which they seldom do), successful responses would not be learned. In fact, helpless dogs in the original studies *did* occasionally leap the barrier and escape from shock. But they did not profit from this experience. They did not learn anything from these successful escapes.

So the problems of the helpless organism are complex. If we have learned to be helpless we are doubly damned; not only do we seldom try to overcome our difficulties, but when we occasionally do make an effort that proves to be successful we don't learn anything from the experience.

2. Emotional Problems.   Things are made even worse by the fact that certain emotional reactions appear to go hand in hand with the passivity and learning problems associated with helplessness. Seligman argues that organisms exposed to uncontrollable events experience traumatic emotional events. For instance, Roth and Kubal (1975) asked humans about their feelings following uncontrollable experiences. These subjects said they felt frustrated, depressed, incompetent, and helpless.

The most interesting aspect of the helplessness hypothesis lies in Seligman's (1975) contention that it can serve as a model for certain types of depression. According to this proposal we feel depressed

Three Aspects of Helplessness

Relationship to Depression

when we expect that we will be unable to control events. The type of depression that is supposed to be best thought of in terms of helplessness is called "reactive depression." Reactive depression, which is often thought to account for most depressions, is the kind we feel when something unpleasant, and beyond our control, occurs in the external environment. Events such as loss of a job, death of someone close, financial problems, rejection by a desired person, and physical disability are thought to be of this reactive variety. In all of these, depression is assumed to be the result of our belief that we can't do anything at all that will help things get better.

Table 6.3 contains the similarities that Seligman sees between learned helplessness and depression. It's quite an impressive list.

Objections and Reformulation

Seligman's work has stirred enormous interest, not only in the fields of motivation and learning but in the field of clinical psychology as well. Since depression is widespread, and incapacitating, anything that might help us understand and control this unfortunate condition is heartily welcomed.

Unfortunately, a number of serious objections to Seligman's original formulation have arisen. Generally speaking, these objections point out that Seligman's original ideas were too simplistic, and did not account for the heavy involvement of *cognitive* processes in depression. Partly in response to these criticisms Seligman (Abramson, Seligman, and Teasdale, 1978) has proposed a revised theory of depression. This reformulation takes into account our beliefs about who or what is reponsible for our lack of control. For instance, the depression we feel might differ depending upon whether we think it is our fault or caused by some uncontrollable external event. Because this reformulated theory relies heavily upon the concepts and principles of attribution, a detailed discussion of it is delayed until Chapter 9, which is devoted entirely to attribution theory and research.

For now, it is enough to realize that Seligman's influential interpretation of depression (1) began with the study of avoidance conditioning and (2) argues that depression is a learned or acquired motivational state.

Helplessness and Competing Responses

So far, we have seen that the major thrust of Seligman's work has been to argue that we feel hopeless and helpless when we experience a lack of control. This line of thinking has led to Seligman's formulations and reformulations with respect to the relationship between

TABLE 6.3. *Similarities Between Learned Helplessness and Depression**

	Learned helplessness	*Depression*
Symptoms	Passivity	Passivity
	Difficulty learning that responses produce relief	Negative cognitive set
	Dissipates in time	Time course
	Lack of aggression	Introjected hostility
	Weight loss, appetite loss, social and sexual deficits	Weight loss, appetite loss, social and sexual deficits
	Norepinephrine depletion and cholinergic activity	Norepinephrine depletion and cholinergic activity
	Ulcers and stress	Ulcers (?) and stress
		Feelings of helplessness
Cause	Learning that responding and reinforcement are independent	Belief that responding is useless
Cure	Directive therapy: forced exposure to responses that produce reinforcement	Recovery of belief that responding produces reinforcement
	Electroconvulsive shock	Electroconvulsive shock
	Time	Time
	Anticholinergics; norepinephrine stimulants (?)	Norepinephrine stimulants; anticholinergics (?)
Prevention	Immunization by mastery over reinforcement	(?)

*Adapted from Seligman, M.E.P. *Helplessness: On depression, development, and death.* San Francisco: W. H. Freeman, 1975. Table 5-1. p. 106.

depression and helplessness. However, additional ways of looking at the learned helplessness phenomenon require reference neither to depression nor to a sense of helplessness on the part of the subject (see Minor and LoLordo, in press.)

For example, a number of investigators go all the way back to the original helplessness studies and interpret them in a very different way. According to these thinkers, the delivery of so-called inescapable shock leads to the learning of responses that are incompatible with later escape responses. During shock the dog may find that crouching and holding still is the best (least punishing) way to take the shock.

So this crouching response is learned. Later, when given the opportunity to escape, the animal fails to do so, not because it feels hopeless, but because it continues to do what has been rewarded in the past; it crouches and braces because it has learned that to do so is to make the best of a bad situation (see Anderson, Crowell, Cunningham, and Lupo, 1979; Bracewell and Black, 1974).

BIOLOGICAL CONSTRAINTS

In Chapters 5 and 6, we focused upon the intricate relationship between motivation and learning, pointing out how motivation can affect learning and how motivation can be learned. In this section we want to further flesh out this relationship by outlining some of the ways that innate mechanisms limit the extent to which behavior is modifiable by learning; biology sets the limits on what can and cannot be learned.

Preparedness   It has been traditional within the field of learning to assume that, given comparable levels of complexity, all responses can be learned with equal ease. Thus it has been thought that jumping, bar pressing, head moving, licking, and so on can all be learned about equally easily. It has been assumed that reponses are "interchangeable" in the sense that, given comparable complexity, one response is no more difficult to learn than another (Houston, 1981).

Similarly, it has been assumed that, given equal salience, all stimuli can be utilized in learning with equal ease. The assumption has been that lights, colors, buzzers, tastes, and so on can be substituted for one another without creating any differences in the learning process.

But both of these assumptions, that of response interchangeability and that of stimulus interchangeability, have proven to be false. As it turns out some responses just seem to be harder for some species to learn than others. And some stimuli are much less easily utilized as effective cues than others, even when they are equally salient.

For example, on the response side, you can easily teach a dog to leap over a barrier for food. But if you try to teach a dog to *yawn* for food you are in for a long and frustrating time (Konorski, 1967). You can teach a cat to escape from a box by pressing a lever. But if you try to teach the same cat to escape by licking itself, you are going to be disappointed. In some very basic, probably innate manner animals are *prepared* to learn certain responses and unprepared to learn others. Seligman (1970) argues that it is best to think of a continuum of preparedness, ranging from high preparedness to very low preparedness. It is not an all-or-none situation; there are, according to Seligman, intermediate degrees of preparedness.

Different species are prepared to learn different sorts of responses. Thus modern linguistic theory suggests that humans are highly prepared to learn languages whereas other species have their own, probably survival-related, sets of easily learned responses.

On the stimulus side, there appear to be certain stimuli that are more easily utilized by a given species than others. For example, birds seem highly prepared to utilize visual cues but much less prepared to use olfactory cues.

The preparedness notion bears directly upon the relationship between motivation and learning. What is implies is that there is more to behavior than response systems modifiable by learning and motivational factors as we have discussed them so far. Innate biologically determined factors predispose the animal to behave in certain ways.

Instinctive Drift

Instinctive drift (Breland and Breland, 1961) is another example of the ways in which motivated behavior is affected by more than the principles of conditioning. Instinctive drift refers to the observation that learned behavior will, with time, drift back toward instinctive, or innate behavior. For example, a pig can be taught to pick up wooden coins and carry them to a bank for a reward. But after this response is established a curious thing happens. Instead of briskly and efficiently picking up and carrying the coins, the pig begins to root them, pick them up, drop them, and root them again. Rooting is a basic urge upon the part of the pig, and the animal seems determined to engage in that behavior regardless of what kind of conditioning the psychologist establishes. The Brelands have shown that the pig, by rooting about, actually gains fewer experimenter-delivered rewards that it would if it refrained from rooting. There seems to be a more basic motive, probably innate, that drives the animal to root. Biological motives or urges take precedence over learned behavior.

Another example of instinctive drift involved a raccoon. This animal was taught to pick up and bank coins in order to receive a reward. In this case the experimenters observed that, after a while, the animal began to rub the objects together as though it were washing them. This washing behavior led to fewer rewards, but it still crept into the animal's behavior. Once again behavior drifted toward the instinctive at the expense of conditioned behavior.

Species-Specific Defense Reactions (SSDR)
We have already noted that certain responses are more easily learned than others. Among these are escape and avoidance responses. Certain species are much more likely to learn certain avoidance responses than they are others. Thus a dog will easily learn to escape from shock by leaping over a wall but will have trouble learning to scratch in order to escape. Bolles (1970) has introduced the concept of *species-specific defense reactions* (SSDR) to account for these differences. An SSDR is an innate, predetermined defensive reaction that the species has to new, novel, or suddenly introduced stimuli. The most common SSDRs are flying, fleeing, fighting, and freezing. If an antelope is suddenly shown a large piece of cardboard it will flee because that response is that species' SSDR. Other species, such as the rabbit, will freeze in response to a sudden, potentially dangerous stimulus. Pigeons fly rather than freezing or running.

Bolles argues that the differences we observe in laboratory-based avoidance conditioning experiments can be accounted for in terms of SSDRs. He proposes that responses which are easily learned in avoidance conditioning situations are, in fact, SSDRs. He goes so far as to suggest that *only* SSDRs can be easily established in avoidance-conditioning situations.

Instincts and Imprinting
Although we do not here discuss these topics in detail, as we have already done so in Chapter 2, the reader should keep in mind that instinctive behavior, and such ethological topics as imprinting, bear upon the general issue of biological constraints on learning. There exists a controversy about how both of these relate to learned behavior. The general consensus seems to be that learned and innate behaviors are entangled in some as yet undefined ways.

SUMMARY

1. Motivation and learning are intricately related.

2. Behavior modification refers to the control of behavior through the application of the principles of conditioning.

3. Behavior modification deemphasizes the personal interaction between therapist and patient that is emphasized in traditional clinical work.

4. In a token economy the subject's desirable behavior is rewarded immediately with tokens that can later be spent like money for valued objects and privileges.

5. Many different reinforcers have been used to alter many different behaviors through behavior modification.

6. Systematic desensitization is a technique used to eliminate phobias.

7. The patient is first taught to relax and is asked to make up a hierarchy of fear-producing stimuli and events. The subject then relaxes while thinking about the least powerful stimulus. Through extinction and counterconditioning fear is eliminated, enabling the subject to move on up through the hierarchy of fear-producing stimuli.

8. In aversion training, which is used to eliminate bad habits, noxious stimuli are paired with the undesirable behavior.

9. Aversion training has been thought of as punishment training and as avoidance training.

10. Cognitive behavior modification is based on the idea that we may be able to change people's behavior if we change the way they think.

11. Assertion training is a blend of cognitive and traditional behavior modification. It is designed to help us ask for what we deserve and to say "no" to unreasonable requests.

12. Behavior modification effects do not always generalize beyond the experimental setting.

13. Neal Miller appears to have been able to instrumentally condition a number of so-called involuntary responses.

14. Apparent direct control of involuntary responses through instrumental training may, in fact, be the result of either physical or mental mediation effects.

15. Biofeedback techniques may eventually prove to be very useful in reducing a wide range of human problems.

16. Learned helplessness refers to the fact that animals, when given the opportunity to learn avoidance responses following inescapable noxious stimulation, will often fail to learn those responses.

17. Humans as well as animals seem to display learned helplessness.

18. Learned helplessness seems to involve failure to initiate action, failure to learn, and emotional problems.

19. Seligman argues that there is a strong correspondence between human depression and learned helplessness. A recent reformulation of his theory is discussed in Chapter 9.

20. Others have argued that learned helplessness can be explained in terms of competing responses without reference to emotional disturbances.

21. Learning is limited by biological constraints.

22. Preparedness refers to the fact that some stimuli and some responses are much more easily involved in learning than others in certain species.

23. Instinctive drift refers to the fact that learned behavior will, with time, drift back toward instinctive behavior.

24. Species-specific defense reactions are innate reactions to suddenly introduced novel stimuli. They include flying, fleeing, fighting, and freezing.

25. Bowles believes that only species-specific defense reactions (SSDRs) can be readily learned in avoidance-conditioning situations.

CHAPTER 7

↓

Drives, Incentives, and Sensation-Seeking Behavior

DRIVES AND INCENTIVES: PUSHING AND PULLING

Many of us tend to think of our behavior as being "driven" from within. For us, motivation is often thought of in terms of the energizing and directing effects of internal states of tension or arousal which we label as drive. We say, "He's a driven man," or, "I was driven to the snack bar by hunger." Although we tend not to define our concept of drive in any precise manner, we all have a pretty good idea of what we mean by it. Drive refers to some internal state of arousal that energizes us. It gets us going and keeps us going. It *pushes* us from within. The push or drive may be related to something as basic as a biological need such as hunger or thirst, or it may be a more complicated push, such as that associated with wanting to get into medical school.

It is not surprising, then, to learn that this general idea of motivation as an internal pushing process has been incorporated into psychological theories and interpretations of motivation. In this chapter we review some of the major theories of motivation that attempt to explain motivated behavior by using the drive concept.

***The General
Concept of Drive***

Drives versus Incentives: Push versus Pull

However useful the concept of drive, it is not enough to explain all of motivated behavior. For example, suppose it is lunchtime and you go to the snack bar for lunch. You are motivated to get that far by the internal state of hunger. But wait a minute, the line is enormous. You hesitate, trying to see the menu over the heads of the crowd. At first you see, "liver and bacon," and get depressed. You are about to forget lunch when you see that the special is fried chicken, your favorite. You happily enter the line and wait your turn.

In this case something else besides your internal hunger affected your motivation. Specifically, your motivation to stand in line was *increased* by the goal object (fried chicken) even though your internal hunger state remained constant. You were *pulled* by the goal as well as pushed by the hunger. When a goal object pulls us, or increases our motivation, over and above the push from within, psychologists say we are dealing with *incentive motivation*. Generally, an incentive is a goal that motivates us or affects our level of motivation. Our behavior is motivated in two ways; we are driven or pushed from within and we are pulled or attracted from without.

You can see how a consideration of incentives is crucial in trying to understand motivated behavior. A person experiencing a constant level of hunger will behave in very different ways depending upon what goals are available. You might walk a mile for a taco but wouldn't eat at all if *All Bran* were the only available food.

Because incentives are so important in determining our behavior, the latter portion of this chapter is devoted to what is and what is not known about the pulling power of goals.

FREUD'S PSYCHOANALYTIC THEORY

We begin our consideration of the drive approach to motivation with a discussion of Freudian theory. Although in many ways radically different from the other theories we consider, Freud's theoretical approach was a drive approach. He believed, as do all drive theorists, that our behavior is activated and directed through the operation of strong internal states of tension.

Freudian theory is not easily grasped. Depending upon which summary you read, you may come away with an impression that differs from that provided by other sources. One reason for this is that

Freud's thinking changed and developed through the years. His thinking was not stagnant. Another reason for much of the controversy (and sometimes confusion) surrounding the theory has to do with the fact that it is based upon Freud's clinical observations rather than upon experimental data which can be replicated. Finally, Freud's language, although perceptive and picturesque, often lacks some of the rigor that characterizes modern psychological theorizing. For the student truly interested in grasping Freud's way of thinking, a reading of at least some of his original writing is a must (see Freud, 1933).

In spite of its difficulty and occasional ambiguity, Freud's psychoanalytic theory has had an enormous impact, not only upon the way psychologists think but upon the way the general public thinks as well. For example, when you hear or use words and phrases such as "Freudian slips," "unconscious desires," "the Oedipal conflict," and "psychoanalysis," you are using terms that Freud developed.

So in spite of the fact that Freudian theory no longer represents the frontier of psychological investigation, we should keep in mind that it has been extremely influential throughout the years.

Freudian Instincts

Freud believed that all behavior is caused by the operation of certain basic internal drive states he called *instincts* (his term *treib* may also be translated as "impulse" or "provocation" to action). These instincts serve to satisfy bodily needs. They demand immediate gratification. The aims of instincts are the maintenance and reproduction of life. Gratification of an instinctual drive is pleasurable. Although he has been criticized for doing so, he emphasized sexual and aggressive instincts. Gratification of the sexual instinct does two things: (1) it reproduces life and (2) it produces pleasure.

Thus, for Freud, the basic driving forces behind all our actions are instincts tied to the needs of the body. These instincts demand immediate pleasurable gratification although they don't always get it. A state of unpleasant tension set up by the instinctual system drives the organism into activity that will reduce that tension; this reduction is experienced as pleasure.

Id, Ego, and Superego

As you sit there reading this text somewhere within you, according to Freud, are strong, raw, primitive, instinctual drives. You are a cauldron of seething sexual and aggressive impulses, each and every one of them demanding immediate gratification. But you are not now raping and killing; you are outwardly calm and collected. So there must be more to motivation and behavior than the primitive instinctual drives.

To account for the disparity between overt behavior and the hypothesized internal states of tension and demand, Freud elaborated his theorizing. Specifically, he argued that there are three aspects to our personality. First, the *id* is that part of our makeup that contains all of the blind, demanding, unreasoning instinctual drives to which we have been referring. The id operates according to the *pleasure principle*, which means that the id wants gratification at this very moment and damn the consequences. Freud felt that these id impulses are *unconscious*; thus you are currently unaware of all the tumultuous demands seething around inside you.

The id is constantly pushing for immediate gratification. This can be accomplished in two ways. First, direct expression can occur; some people do, in fact, attack other people sexually and/or aggressively. Second, the id can attain satisfaction through *wish fulfillment*. Wish fulfillment refers to the gratification one can gain by imagining the objects or events that would provide satisfaction. Just thinking about sexual or aggressive events can, for example, provide some degree of relief. Dreams, as we saw in Chapter 4, represent a fertile ground for wish fulfillment. As previously noted, dreams, according to Freud, represent hidden or disguised instances of wish fulfillment.

What would happen if the id was all there was to our personality? Obviously we wouldn't last too long. We can't go about indulging our most basic and brutal impulses without suffering for it. Accordingly, Freud believed that additional facets of our personality develop as we grow and mature. These additional components allow us to live more harmoniously with society, and they reduce the danger to ourselves and those around us.

But the id remains strong throughout our lives. It continues to be the source of energy for all psychological activity. We are not normally aware of the id's constant presence, as id impulses are unconscious, but they are still there, powerful and demanding as ever.

Freud did not believe that the id was a "thing," such as a location in the brain, or some kind of physical structure; he merely used the term *id* to refer those aspects of our overall personality which are best described as basic, primitive, instinctual drives.

The second component of the overall psychological structure, the *ego*, according to Freud, is that aspect of our personality that tries to satisfy the demands of the id without getting us into trouble. It mediates the conflict between the id's demands and the correspondingly powerful demands of reality. The ego operates according to a *reality principle*, which means that it tries to find reasonable, logical, *safe* ways to satisfy the demands of the id. In a sense, the id says, "Gimme, gimme, gimme," while the ego says, "Take it easy. Let's figure this out. I'll get it for you if I can" (Houston, Bee, and Rimm, 1983). The id is impractical and dangerous, whereas the ego is practical, logical, and problem-oriented.

Even though the ego is discreet and helps dampen the reckless demands of the id, there is more to us than id and ego. For example, suppose your id demands revenge and your ego figures out how to get that revenge without suffering for it. Will you take revenge? Not necessarily. Your conscience, or your sense of right and wrong, may inhibit you. Freud referred to this moral, or ethical aspect of our personality as the *superego*. The superego is the set of rules about what is right and wrong that we learn from our culture.

In summary, although this is something of an oversimplification, the id, ego, and superego may be thought of as blind desire, reason, and conscience, respectively.

As seen in Figure 7.1, Freud believed that most of the action of all three psychological elements is unconscious. About all that sees the light of consciousness is a little bit of the superego and some of the ego. Thus, for Freud, little of our behavior is consciously guided and determined; it appears that we are in the grip of largely unconscious psychological events. As you might expect, Freudian theory has been heavily criticized for this emphasis upon unconscious psychological events that leave us essentially without conscious control over our behavior. Most of us would prefer to think of ourselves as at least occasionally being in the driver's seat.

According to Freud, many of the psychological problems we experience in life are caused by the conflicts that arise among the id, ego, and superego. For example, if your superego maintains that it is wrong to steal, but your id wants some quick thievery, then you have a problem. The ego may be caught in the middle, trying to satisfy both id and superego at the same time. The result of this sort of conflict is *anxiety*, that unpleasant sense of uneasiness and foreboding that resembles fear but tends to be less specific. Anxiety, for Freud, lies at the basis of many neurotic conditions.

The War Among the Elements

FIGURE 7.1
The relationship of the Freudian personality structures to levels of awareness. According to Freud, the mind is much like an iceberg, with only the tip projecting into the level of conscious awareness. All of the id, most of the superego, and a good portion of the ego operate on an unconscious level. Preconscious thought is thought that is now unconscious, but can become conscious. (Adapted from Houston, J. P., Bee, H., & Rimm, D. C. Invitation to Psychology. *New York Academic, 1983. Figure 2 on p. 493.*

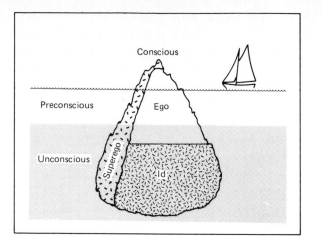

Defense Mechanisms

If anxiety becomes too acute, if the war between the three elements becomes too painful, we often turn to the use of *defense mechanisms*. Defense mechanisms are techniques we all use, to one degree or another, in our efforts to alleviate anxiety. Occasional use of defense mechanisms is well within the range of ordinary behavior. However, if an individual is so acutely anxious that defense mechanisms become the predominant mode of relating to the environment, then they can become incapacitating. So don't be surprised if you recognize some of these defense mechanisms; sooner or later most of us turn to them temporarily in order to help us over the difficult spots in life.

Suppose someone cheats on an exam. Now some people would feel no anxiety (weak superego). But most of us will feel some guilt and remorse. What can we do to reduce these negative feelings? We can say to ourselves, "I didn't cheat very much. It probably won't affect my grade anyway." In other words, we can *rationalize* our act; we can act as though we didn't do anything wrong. If you fail to get into medical school you can rationalize by saying, "I didn't *really* want to go," or, "It's a good think I found out so soon that I'm better off in another field." We all rationalize at some time in our life. Table 7-1 contains some additional defense mechanisms.

TABLE 7.1. *Some Freudian Defense Mechanisms**

Mechanism	One possible manifestation
Repression Keeping painful or dangerous thoughts in the unconscious; this is thought to be the most basic of defense mechanisms.	A soldier comes very close to death, but remembers no details of the event.
Rationalization Attempting to prove that one's behavior is "rational" and justifiable.	A grown man who loves his mother too dearly treats her with extreme consideration, kindness, and devotion but convinces himself that he is motivated by duty and not by love.
Compensation Covering up weakness by emphasizing another trait.	A person unsure of sexuality becomes a bookworm.
Fantasy Gratifying frustrated desired in imaginary achievements.	A baseball player dreams of hitting the winning home run.
Reaction formation Behavior is the opposite of what the individual would like it to be.	A woman loves an unobtainable man and behaves as though she dislikes him.
Projection Persons come to believe that their own undesirable feelings or inclinations are more descriptive of others than of themselves.	A claustrophobic person who unconsciously avoids closed spaces is amazed at the number of persons who suffer from claustrophobia.

*From Lefrancois, G. R. *Psychology.* Belmont, Calif.: Wadsworth, 1983. Table 13.4, p. 396. Reprinted by permission.

There are three essential characteristics of *all* defense mechanisms:

1. Defense mechanisms are unconscious efforts to reduce anxiety. We are not aware when we are using them. What good would it do to rationalize if we knew we were just kidding ourselves?

2. All defense mechanisms involve distortion of reality. In a sense, we deceive ourselves in order to feel better when we use defense mechanisms.

3. Defense mechanisms when used in moderation can help us through troubled times without necessarily being unhealthy. However, if they are our predominant means of dealing with anxiety, they can form the basis of severe mental disturbances.

Psychosexual Stages

Freud believed that, in growing to be fully matured adults, we pass through several very important *psychosexual stages.* These five stages are seen as important because, even though we normally move on through them, each can have a significant impact upon our adult behavior. It is the influence of these stages upon adult behavior that forms the basis of Freud's widely recognized belief that our earliest experiences have an important impact upon later life.

Each of these five stages is associated with the area of the body through which pleasure is obtained at a given time in early life. Essentially, Freud believed that the sexual instinctual drive seeks expression and gratification through different parts of the body at different times in the child's life. First, during the *oral* stage (0 to 1½ years) the child is most likely to experience pleasure through oral activities such as sucking, chewing, and biting. Second, during the *anal* stage (1½ to 3 years), eliminating and holding in feces seem to be the activities that yield the most pleasure. Third, during the *phallic* stage (3–7 years), all children are assumed to obtain pleasure primarily through genital activity such as masturbation, showing their genitals to others, and being shown others' genitals. Fourth, during the *latency* period (7–12 years) the sexual instinctual drive is relatively inactive. Fifth, with the onset of puberty, the child enters the *genital* period during which an interest in sexual activity is revived. But in this stage, sexual activity is of a more mature variety than that observed in the phallic stage. Here, interest is centered upon mature, appropriate sexual relationships with significant others. The genital phase lasts throughout adult life.

Fixation

The significance of these stages lies in the fact that Freud believed they could influence adult life. Specifically, he believed that, instead of passing normally through the stages, people can become *fixated* at one stage or another. Fixation means that the characteristics of an earlier stage are maintained through later stages. Fixation can occur in two ways. First, and most commonly, if gratification at a particular stage is *frustrated*, then the individual may continue to seek pleasure from that zone during later times. Second, and less frequently, *too much* gratification at a particular stage can also lead to fixation.

Let us look at some specific examples of what Freud meant by fixation. If a child is frustrated at the oral stage by parents who do not feed the child often enough and/or implement harsh weaning procedures, then that individual may become fixated at the oral stage. That person may, as an adult, smoke, eat, or drink too much in an effort to obtain the oral gratification that was not allowed during the appropriate period of early life. Similarly, if an individual is subjected to severe toilet training procedure she may, as an adult, become what Freud referred to as anal retentive, or tight, controlled, and frugal. On the other hand, if the child is overindulged during the anal stage, and is subjected to very loose, casual toilet training procedures, then he may become what is known as *anal expulsive*, or sloppy, disorganized, and messy. In general, Freud believed that many of the problems adults have in getting along in the world may be traced to fixation.

A discussion of Freud's work would be incomplete without mention of the famous *Electra* and *Oedipus* complexes. During the phallic phase females are sexually attracted to their fathers and resent their mother. Males, on the other hand, are sexually attracted to their mothers and resent their fathers. Since both children want to, but cannot, possess the opposite-sexed parent and replace or eliminate the same-sexed parent, they suffer distress. The resolution of the Electra complex in females and the Oedipus complex in males is seen as a crucial step in the development of all children. Resolution is accomplished by repressing the desire for the opposite-sexed parent and by identifying with the same-sexed parent. As the female learns to identify with the same-sexed parent ("I'm a woman like Mommy"), she begins to take on the rules and standards of behavior that her society requires. In other words, her superego begins to develop out of the resolution of the Electra complex. Similarly, the male child represses his desire for his mother and, by identifying with his father ("I'm a man like Daddy"), begins to internalize the prevailing societal standards that will define his superego.

Development of the Superego

Freudian theory has been heavily criticized through the years:

Criticisms of Freudian Theory

1. Many people have argued that Freud's theory can never be anything more than that . . . a theory. They point out that the theory is supported by very little experimental data. Most of Freud's ideas were based upon his clinical observations, and many modern researchers are simply not willing to accept that kind of data because it is too

loose, fuzzy, and subject to various interpretations. Demanding, rigorous, conclusive experiments are difficult, if not impossible, to devise in connection with Freud's thinking.

2. Others have argued that Freud was overly concerned with sexual and aggressive impulses. They argue that to conclude that most adult problems are based upon sexual and/or aggressive impulses is to oversimplify human life.

It may well be that sexual problems were more commonplace during the restrictive era when Freud worked. However, at the present time, when sexual codes are much less strict than they once were, we still have a lot of troubled adults, which suggests that there is more to mental disturbance than sexual conflict.

3. Freud based his ideas upon his observation of neurotic patients. Some have argued that this is an inadequate population if one is to develop a model of *all* human behavior. To be truly representative, a theory must be based upon observations of normal as well as neurotic individuals.

4. Finally, Freudian theory falls down because it can interpret any behavior as maladjusted. Suppose, for instance, you act aggressively toward others. Freudian theory argues that your unconscious impulses are breaking through. But suppose you don't act aggressively. Freudian theory can still argue that you are aggressive; you are merely repressing your impulses.

In spite of these and other objections, Freudian theory has been very influential. And it does represent an early drive interpretation of motivation. As we pursue additional drive theories we have the opportunity to see how Freud anticipated some of the drive concepts that were incorporated into later, more rigorous, conceptions of motivation.

HULL'S DRIVE THEORY

Clark Hull's (1884–1952) drive theory represents an enormous departure from the earlier Freudian approach. However, as we move through our discussion of Hull's theory, keep in mind that it is, after all, a drive theory, and in that sense, it is very similar to Freud's theory. Both Freudian and Hullian theories argue that, among other things, internal states of tension drive the organism into activities that reduce the state of tension and which are experienced as pleasurable.

Hull As a Behaviorist

Strict behaviorists are psychologists who believe that the proper way to study behavior is to do so by attending only to factors that can be directly observed and accurately measured. Hence, behaviorists focus upon overt, observable behaviors such as running, jumping, and making sounds. Behaviorists believe that it is wrong to attend to the "contents of the mind." They feel, as we have seen in our discussion of behavior modification, that it is silly to try to deal with such elusive factors as thoughts, cognitions, images, and ideas because it is impossible to observe and measure them directly.

Modern psychologists have moved away from the strict behaviorist position; most of them now admit to the importance of the contents of the mind. Cognitive psychology, in fact, is now one of the most active areas of investigation and its primary concern is thinking. But Hull was a true behaviorist. Hence, you will find no mention of the contents of the mind in his work. In this sense his work was very different from Freud's, who not only wanted to explore the mind but was convinced that the *unconscious* mind was important as well. But again this basic difference between Hull and Freud should not obscure the fact that they both believed drive factors to be responsible for motivated behavior.

Hull's Master Theory

Hull was one of the last psychologists to try to outline a complex theory that might eventually encompass *all* behavior, not only the behavior of white rats but all behavior of all humans as well. He presented his principles in three books spanning almost ten years. Although Hull himself realized that his work was preliminary, the titles of these books reveal something of Hull's interest in encompassing all behavior: *Principles of Behavior* (1943), *Essentials of Behavior* (1951), *A Behavior System* (1952).

Hull's work dominated the field for many years. Hundreds of studies relating to his work appeared in the literature. However, modern psychologists have moved on, leaving Hull's system as an enormously ambitious project that didn't quite make it; this system was not as all-encompassing as Hull hoped it would be. It did not, after all, account for all behavior. Still, like Freud, Hull had a tremendous impact upon the field. Even though his theory is not presently in vogue, and few still base their work on it, he influenced the ways in which later generations of younger psychologists were to think about and approach problems.

Perhaps the very rigor that Hull hoped to impose upon his system contributed to its demise. The system was mathematical and very precise; perhaps *too* precise. For example, consider the following quote from Hull (1952):

A. When a brief stimulus (S) impinges upon a suitable receptor there is initiated the recruitment phase of a self-propagating molar afferent trace impulse (s'), the molar stimulus equivalent ($\dot{S}'$) of which rises as a power function of time (t) since the beginning of the stimulus, i.e.,

$$\dot{S}' = 465{,}190 \times t^{7.6936} + 1.0,$$

$\dot{S}'$ reaching its maximum (and termination) when t equals about .450.

This is but one of many principles forwarded by Hull; it is representative of his language. It may also be representative of his misguided belief that incredible precision could be brought into the study of behavior. Perhaps sometime in the future we will be able to deal with time raised to the 7.6936th power, but not now; we simply do not know enough yet to be so precise.

Hull's Behavior Equation

Hull's system grew and changed throughout his working life. He was always tinkering with it. It may be summarized, in a *very* simplified form, by the following equation:

Response Probability $= (D \times H \times K \times V) - (I)$

According to this formula, the probability of any organism making a particular response is a function of five important variables. Let us look at each of these factors separately. Although the notation looks somewhat imposing, Hull's conception of the causes of behavior has an appealing common-sense basis.

Drive (D)

In his early formulations, Hull proposed that biological needs, such as the needs for food and water, lead to an internal state of arousal, which he called *drive* (D). It is this drive, or state of internal tension, that pushes the animal into action. If a response is then made that reduces the biological need (e.g., the animal finds and eats food) then the drive is reduced, which means that the animal is no longer pushed into further behavior. When drive is at zero, the animal is inactive. The system is a survival system. The more the body needs food the more driven the animal is. The more driven the animal the more it acts. The more it acts the more likely it is to make a response that will reduce the biological need and, consequently, the drive state.

1. Drive and Need. One might reasonably ask the following questions: Why bother with the drive concept at all? Why isn't the biological need sufficient to account for behavior? These are good questions, but there is an answer. If we increase biological need, we *initially* get an increase in aroused behavior. But the relationship does not hold for all levels of biological need. As the need becomes extreme (e.g., starvation) arousal seems to lessen. Hence, we need the drive construct to account for the curvilinear relationship between biological need and aroused behavior.

2. Drive and Time of Deprivation. Drive is a hypothetical construct. It is not something you can see or touch. But Hull, being a good behaviorist, was careful to tie his drive concept to something measurable. He argued that D could be measured in terms of time of deprivation. The longer an animal is deprived the greater is its drive state, up to a point as we have seen.

Time of deprivation, as a measure of drive, has been criticized. For example, some have pointed out that you can take a thin rat and a fat rat and deprive them of food for the same amount of time. According to the simple notion that drive can be measured in terms of time of deprivation, these two rats should be equally motivated. But they are not because the impact of the deprivation will be greater on the thin rat than it will be on the heavier animal. Hence, some have suggested that the proportion of weight loss to body weight would be a better estimate of drive level than time of deprivation.

3. Generalized Drive. Hull made the somewhat surprising claim that D is a general factor that energizes *all* behavior. If we are hungry it is not just our hunger-related behaviors that are energized. *All* behaviors will be energized. The hungry person will, according to this view, run faster, read faster, think faster, and jump higher than a nonhungry person. Drive, instigated by various kinds of deprivation, is supposed to energize all behavior and not just behaviors related to the specific forms of deprivation.

This proposal, because it is so counterintuitive, stimulated a great deal of experimentation. In summary, the results of these many studies were contradictory. Some supported the generalized drive notion and some did not.

4. Drive Stimuli (S_D). If one accepts at face value Hull's idea of a generalized drive state, then certain behaviors cannot be explained. Suppose, for example, you are playing tennis. As you play you become more and more thirsty. This water deprivation leads to an increase in D. If D is a general factor, energizing *all* behaviors, you should play harder. But you don't; you quit playing altogether and head for the water fountain. Hull was aware of this shortcoming of the generalized drive interpretation and had a solution for it. Specifically, he proposed that there are *two* consequences of any biological need state. The first is D as we have seen. But, in addition, Hull argued that biological need states lead to what he called *drive stimuli* (S_D), such as hunger pangs. Each specific form of deprivation leads to its own set of distinct drive stimuli.

According to Hull, D energizes all behavior whereas the S_D *direct* behavior, or guide it in a direction related to that specific need. When we are hungry, we eat rather than drink because of the drive stimuli associated with hunger. Similarly, the drive stimuli associated with thirst lead us to drink rather than eat.

How does the guiding action of the drive stimuli come about? According to Hull, it happens through the action of classical conditioning. Consider the fact that babies suck (rather than, say, blink their eyes) when they are hungry. Hull analyzed the situation as follows. Food (milk) is the UCS. Sucking is the UCR. The drive stimuli associated with hunger serve as the CS. Through repeated pairings of the CS (S_D) and UCS (milk) that occur when the baby is fed the CS (S_D) takes on the capacity to elicit a conditioned sucking response (CR) similar to the UCR. Then, in the future when the baby is hungry, D activates or energizes all behaviors, whereas the drive stimuli, serving as conditioned stimuli, elicit eating rather than some other form of behavior. Thus, it is through classical conditioning that behavior appropriate to a particular need develops.

5. Other Sources of Drive. Hull's theory emphasized the importance of biological needs in determining motivation. However, he was not unaware of other sorts of stimulus conditions that can establish motive states, and he made an effort to include them in his system.

Let us mention three sources of drive that do not seem to be related to deprivation-induced biological needs. First, Hull acknowledged that strong noxious environmental stimuli, such as shock, can lead to an increase in drive. Electric shock, although it does not threaten the animal's life and is unrelated to a state of biological deprivation, can still motivate defensive or escape behavior. Second, a whole series of studies (see Sheffield and Roby, 1950) demonstrate that animals will work for, and learn instrumental responses in order to obtain, saccharin, even though saccharin has no nutritional value. Thus it is clear that animals can be motivated in the absence of biological need states. Third, internal cyclical biological systems, such as reproductive cycles, seem to motivate behavior in the absence of deprivation. In fact, the sexual behavior of a female cat seems to be more determined by the *addition* of something (estrogen) than it is by the absence of something.

Habit (H)

Now let us move on to the second element in Hull's equation. We have just made clear the fact that Hull believed that behavior is at least, in part, a function of internal motive states. What else will affect whether or not an animal or a human will make a particular response in a particular situation? Suppose a hungry rat is in a Skinner box, or a thirsty child is in the hallway of her school. What else, besides thirst, will determine whether or not these two organisms will act? It seems clear that their *experience* with the situation will have some effect. If the rat has pressed the lever in the past, and been given water, it will be more likely to do so now. Similarly, if the child has used the school water fountains before she will be more likely to do so now.

This role of experience, or learning, is what Hull was referring to when he spoke of habit (*H*). As habit, or learning, goes up so does the probability of the response occurring. The more times the rat presses the bar, and receives water, the larger *H* becomes, or the better the pressing response is learned. We do what we have been reinforced for doing in the past.

Hull measured *H* (another construct) in terms of *number of reinforced responses*. The greater the number of reinforced responses the greater *H* becomes, up to a point.

What is reinforcement for Hull? Initially, he tied reinforcement to need reduction. A reduction in a biological need was seen as the reinforcing event. Thus, learning, or an increase in H, was seen as the result of a biological need being reduced. If a thirsty animal ate dry food, no need would be reduced and no learning would occur. However, if the thirsty animal drank, then the need would be reduced, which, in turn, would reinforce or strengthen the drinking response.

However, this elegantly simple conception of reinforcement proved to be too simple. When an animal eats, considerable time must pass before the food is actually broken down and absorbed into the bloodstream. It takes time for the biological need to be reduced. But reinforcement effects can be shown to appear right after the food is eaten. In other words, there must be more to reinforcement than need reduction. Later Hull tried to account for this shortcoming in his theory by arguing that reduction in *drive stimuli* is what is actually reinforcing. For example, Hull later argued that an immediate reduction in hunger pangs, rather than biological need reduction, is what is reinforcing.

Before we move on to the next element in Hull's equation, notice that D and H interact in a multiplicative fashion. Two points need to be made here. First, the relationship might have been additive (i.e., $D + H$ instead of $D \times H$). Why did Hull present the relationship as multiplicative? He did not pull it out of a hat. A series of studies (see Perin, 1942) varied drive level and habit and found that the two variables do interact in a multiplicative fashion. The second point that needs to be made is that if either H or D are zero, then no behavior occurs. In a sense, D activates H in the same sense that performance is the result of an interaction between motivation and learning.

Incentive (K)   So far we have seen that motivation (D) and learning (H) affect whether or not our thirsty rat and our thirsty youngster will drink. There must be other factors that contribute to the tendency to respond. It seems likely that the quantity and the quality of the goal or reward should have some impact on performance. For example, if we provide our rat and child with small amounts of stale, lukewarm water they will be less motivated than they will be if we use larger amounts of cool, sweet-flavored water as rewards. In other words, our level of motivation seems to be increased as the size of the reward is increased and as the attractiveness of that reward is increased. We might work for a pizza but not for a bowl of oatmeal, even if our level of hunger remained constant.

Hull introduced the concept of *incentive motivation* (*K*) to account for these kinds of phenomena. Incentives motivate us, just like drives do, but they do so by *pulling* us toward more attractive and sizable goals, whereas drives *push* us from within.

Although Hull was basically a drive theoretician, he was aware of the importance of incentive motivation. He tied his *K* concept to the quantity and the quality of the goal. In this section we discuss several of the interesting issues surrounding Hull's *K* construct.

Learning or Motivation? In his earlier thinking, Hull assumed that the value of the reward affected learning and not motivation. He assumed that the bigger and better the reward the greater was the reduction in drive and, therefore, the greater the learning. The quality and quantity of the reward were assumed *not* to affect level of motivation.

However, various studies showed this assumption to be wrong and led to Hull's eventual inclusion of the *K* construct in his model that encompassed the idea that the value of the reward does, after all, affect motivation level and not learning per se.

The most famous of these studies, showing that the value of the rewards affect motivation, was done by Crespi (1942) (See Figure 7.2). Three groups of rats were given either 1, 16, or 256 pellets of food when they ran down and reached the end of an alley. As one might expect, the larger-reward group ran most rapidly whereas the small-reward group ran the most slowly. Then, on the twentieth trial, Crespi began to give all three groups 16 pellets for running down the alley. Now, if amount of reward affected learning, what would we expect would happen to the performance of the group when the reward shifted from 1 to 16 pellets? We would expect a *gradual* increase in running speed as the animal slowly learned to run faster. However, as can be seen in Figure 7.2, that is not what happened. Within just three trials the 1 to 16 pellet group was running as fast as the 16 to 16 pellet group. This *rapid* jump in running speed is taken as evidence for the idea that amount of reward affects motivation and not learning; the 1 to 16 pellet rats did not slowly learn to run faster when the reward size was increased. They were *immediately* pumped up and motivated to run faster.

FIGURE 7.2
The Crespi effect showing that amount of reward affects motivation and not learning. (Adapted from Crespi, L. P. Quantitative variation of incentive and performance in the white rat. American Journal of Psychology, *1942, 55, 467–517.*

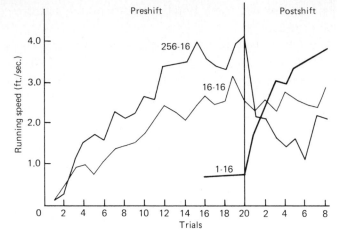

In a similar fashion, the 256 to 16 pellet rats showed an almost immediate decrease in running speed following the shift in reward size, again supporting the idea that amount of reward affects motivation and not learning.

The r_g–s_g Mechanism

Once it was established that amount of reward was a motivating factor, both Hull and one of his most famous students, Kenneth Spence (1956), worked out an analysis of exactly how incentive motivation operates. Here is their explanation. When the animal eats the food in the goal box, classical conditioning occurs. The food is the UCS. The act of eating is the UCR. The CS is composed of various aspects of the goal situation (e.g., the color, the texture, the brightness). The CR, which becomes conditioned to these various stimuli, is something like the UCR; it is a partial consummatory response. Thus when the rat sees the CS (the distinct goal box), CRs (such as partial licking and chewing responses) occur, as when your mouth waters when you enter a favorite restaurant. This *fractional anticipatory goal response* is called an r_g.

Now think about what happens to the rat as it is moving down the alley toward the food. To the extent that the alley resembles the goal box (e.g., same smell, brightness) the alley will serve as a CS and elicit the CRs, or the r_g response. You say, "So what? The animal's mouth waters a little in anticipation of the food." This is where Hull and Spence took the big step. They argued that the conditioned anticipatory r_g has *stimulus properties* (called s_g) that *motivate* the animal. Salivating or making small chewing movements (r_g's) in response to the alley cues have motivating stimulus properties (s_g) that energize the animal.

When you see the restaurant in the distance you salivate a little, and this act of salivating prods you onward and motivates you to move toward the restaurant more rapidly. The closer you are to the goal the more similar the environmental cues are to those in the actual goal box and, therefore, the more highly motivated you are likely to be through the operation of this r_g–s_g *mechanism*.

Although intriguing, the r_g–s_g mechanism has not been entirely substantiated. For example, attempts to actually locate and measure r_g's have not been particularly successful (see Bolles, 1975; Hulse, Egeth, and Deese, 1980).

Hull became aware of the fact that intense stimulation seems to increase the probability of our responding in any given situation. For example, if you are studying for an exam and an airplane flies overhead at a reasonable height, you may continue to study. But if the same plane flies over at a low altitude, creating more of a racket, you are likely to get up, disgruntled, and close the window.

To account for the impact of stimulus intensity on behavior, Hull introduced *stimulus intensity dynamism* (V). V is measured in terms of stimulus intensity and is related to D, H, and K in a multiplicative fashion. Hull's conception of V was not well worked out, and V has not taken a prominent position in the Hullian school of thinking.

Stimulus Intensity Dynamism (V)

Inhibition (I) in Hull's equation *subtracts* from the tendency to respond, whereas all the other factors we have discussed (D, H, K, V) contribute positively to the tendency to respond. Thus, if we are to understand I, we must look for something that decreases, rather than increases, the probability of a response occurring. What about the rat in the Skinner box? What will decrease its tendency to respond? *Fatigue* will do it; fatigue is what I is all about. The more times the animal makes the response, and the more work it takes to make that response, the greater will be the fatigue and the less likely the animal is to respond again. I is like a negative drive. It builds up as responding continues. If the animal responds for a very long time, I can build up to a point where it overshadows H, D, K, and V, and responding stops altogether (the animal is too tired to continue).

Inhibition (I)

Actually, Hull identified two types of inhibition. The first, called *reactive inhibition* (I_r), is what we have been discussing so far. This is a negative, or subtracting, drive. It builds up as responding continues and dissipates when the animal rests. The second form of inhibition is called *conditioned inhibition* ($_sI_r$) and is considered to be a permanent, learned form of inhibition. $_sI_r$ may be thought of in this way: Each time the animal refrains from responding I_r goes down. A reduction in I_r is like any other form of drive reduction in that it is reinforcing. Refraining from responding is rewarded by a little rest. Hence, the "response of not responding" is rewarded and learned. This tendency not to respond is learned because it is reinforced by a reduction in I_r. It is called conditioned inhibition.

The Status of Hull's Theory

Hull's theory was expressed in mathematical terms, but its foundations are found in commonsense observations about behavior. Specifically, Hull's theory states that behavior is a function of need, what has been learned, the attractiveness of the available goal, the intensity of the stimulation, and fatigue.

Although Hull's work has had an enormous impact upon the way we think about behavior, the theory itself has faded into the background. For example, few current studies are concerned with the intricacies of the theory. This is in contrast to the hundreds of investigations of the theory that appeared in the 1940s, 1950s, and 1960s.

The shortcomings of the theory need not be detailed here. It is sufficient to point out that it cannot account for all motivated behavior. For example, drive theory argues that we always seek to *reduce* arousal and tension. Our ideal state is one of nonarousal. And yet anyone who has had his curiosity aroused, or who has wanted to sit close to a rock band knows that we sometimes want to *increase* rather than decrease arousal (see Sheffield, 1966). As we see in a later section, curiosity and exploratory impulses are not easily explained by a drive reduction theory.

Other problems that have already been mentioned include the fact that support for the notion of a generalized drive was, at best, weak. And the relationships between need reduction and reinforcement were never cleared up. The reader interested in pursuing the intricacies of Hull's theory is referred to Bolles (1975).

Acquired Drives

Mention should be made of the idea of acquired drives. Although Hull focused upon innate, predetermined drives such as hunger and thirst, he also pointed out, in 1943, that external, previously neutral stimuli can probably acquire the ability to evoke internal drive states, once again, through classical conditioning. This basic idea that some drives are learned, or acquired, has been pursued by a considerable number of psychologists (see Miller, 1948; Mowrer and Lamoreaux, 1942; Brown and Farber, 1951). Both appetitive and aversive drives have been suspected of being acquirable.

One example of an acquired drive should suffice, particularly since we have already discussed the idea in Chapter 5. Avoidance conditioning is the situation in which an animal is punished if it fails to make a response within a certain time interval. A rat can be placed in a white box, separated from a black box by a low barrier. If the animal is still in the white box after, say, ten seconds, it is shocked. However, if it moves over the barrier into the black box before the ten seconds elapse it is not shocked.

Although criticism of this interpretation was outlined in Chapter 5 (see Hineline, 1970; Levis, Smith, and Epstein, 1978, Solomon and Wynne, 1954), the theory argues that conditioned fear (a learned drive) develops in avoidance conditioning. When the animal is first shocked in the white box, fear is classically conditioned to the white box. The shock is the UCS. Fear in response to the shock is the UCR. The white box is the CS and fear in response to the white box is the CR. Then, once the fear is learned it serves as a drive in that escape from the white box is reinforced through reduction of that acquired fear drive. First, fear is classically conditioned. Then the barrier-crossing response is rewarded by a reduction in that learned fear or acquired drive.

This interpretation may or may not prove to be adequate. But the phenomenon of avoidance conditioning seems to provide support for Hull's original idea that both learned and innate motive states determine our behavior.

Conflict refers to the simultaneous arousal of two or more incompatible motives. In a sense, the following analysis of conflict can be thought of as what happens when conflicting drives, either innate or acquired, clash head to head. We all experience conflict at one time or another. You are in conflict if you say, "I want to eat that pie, but it is fattening." You were in conflict when your mother said, "Eat your spinach or go to bed." And you are even in conflict when you can't decide which of many delicious entrées to choose from a menu. The

The Analysis of Conflict

essence of the conflict situation seems to be that if you satisfy one motive or drive then you automatically cannot satisfy the other. You can't have your cake and eat it.

Psychologists, notably Miller (1944) and Brown (1948), have identified three major varieties of conflict:

1. The Approach-Avoidance Conflict. This is the situation in which the same goal has both positive and negative attributes. You want to swim with friends but the water is too cold. You want to drink beer but it's bad for you. You are attracted to someone but he has the disquieting tendency to call you a geek in public.

2. The Avoidance-Avoidance Conflict. This is the situation in which you have to do one of two unpleasant things but don't want to do either. Study or flunk the exam. Pay your taxes or go to jail. Go to the party with someone you dislike or miss out on the party entirely.

3. The Approach-Approach Conflict. This is the best of all conflicts. You must choose between two attractive goals, but attaining one means you can't have the other. Go to movie A or movie B. Eat Mexican food or Italian food. Read a book or drop off to sleep.

How do we act in these situations? What are our most common responses when we are faced with these various conflicts? The work of Miller (1944) and Brown (1948) led to the following analysis of the approach-avoidance conflict situation (see Figure 7-3). Rats were trained to run down an alley to food. By attaching a harness to the rat, it was discovered that the rat pulled harder as it came closer to the goal. This *approach tendency*, which increases slightly as the animal moves closer to the goal, is depicted in Figure 7-3. Other rats were shocked at the end of the alley instead of being fed there. They ran away from the end of the alley. It was discovered, as one might expect, that the rats pulled harder in their harnesses when they were close to the place where they had been shocked. But notice in Figure 7-3 that the resulting *avoidance tendency* is *steeper* than the approach tendency. That is, near the goal box shocked rats pull harder trying to escape than do fed rats trying to approach. However, when far way from the end of the alley, the situation is reversed; the tendency to approach is greater than the tendency to avoid.

There is a point at which the two gradients cross one another. It is at this point that we would predict hesitancy and vacillation if one

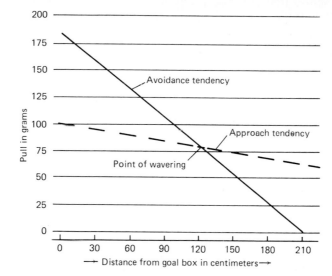

FIGURE 7.3
Judson Brown's analysis of approach—avoidance behavior. If the rat is closer to the goal box than 120 cm it will move away, because the avoidance tendency is stronger than the approach tendency. At all points further than 120 cm from the goal box the rat will approach. If left alone the rat will waver around the 120-cm point.

rat had been both shocked and fed in the end of the alley. Brown (1948) did just that; the same rat was first fed and then shocked in the end of the alley. Then it was allowed to do what it wished in the alley, unrestricted. In accordance with this analysis of the approach-avoidance conflict, the rat vacillated at some midpoint. Presumably if it tried to approach further the rat would be driven back by the avoidance impulse. But it could not leave entirely; if it moved too far from the end of the alley, the approach impulse took over and sent the animal back toward the goal.

This research suggests that approach-avoidance conflicts can be difficult to resolve, and that they will result in vacillation. You must know, or have heard of, a couple that is constantly breaking up only to make up again. When the two people are apart all they can remember are the positive aspects of the relationship. So they rush back into one another's arms, only to rediscover all that drove them apart in the first place.

Of course, an approach-avoidance conflict can be resolved by raising or lowering a gradient. Suppose we deliver a tremendous shock to the rat in the end of the alley. This may have the effect of raising the avoidance gradient so high that approach is never attempted. Similarly, we can deprive the rat of food for a long, *long* time, thereby raising the approach gradient to the point at which it never falls below the avoidance gradient.

So much for the resolution of the approach-avoidance conflict. What about the other conflicts? The avoidance-avoidance conflict is tough to break because each time you move toward one negative goal it becomes more repulsive. It is stable. If your parents didn't finally resolve the conflict for you, you might sit there all night staring glumly at your cold turnips but not going to bed either.

The approach-approach conflict isn't so bad. If life were filled with nothing but positive alternatives we would not be too discontent. The Miller-Brown analysis suggests that once we make a move toward one of two equally attractive goals we should continue to move in that direction because the approach tendency associated with that goal is increasing in strength while the other approach tendency is weakening. This conflict situation is often described as being unstable because resolution is so likely to occur. If you want to go to a movie and to a dance, and choose the movie, then your problem should be over because you should feel more and more positive about the movie as you approach it.

Summary of Drive Theory

In summary, the drive approach to the understanding of motivation is widespread and takes many forms. But in each case the emphasis is upon some internal state of arousal or tension that "pushes" us into behavior. Although the theories of Freud, Hull, and the ethologists differ remarkably in many ways, each is a drive theory.

We have also seen that incentive motivation, which emphasizes the "pulling" aspects of the environment, has been an important way of thinking about motivation. As we learned in an earlier section, work on incentive motivation tries to account for the fact that there is more to motivation than internal drive states. Specifically, our level of motivation can be affected by out perception of the nature of the goal. The more attractive the goal, the more motivated we become.

SENSATION-SEEKING BEHAVIOR

Some Examples

We now turn to another area of research and thinking that has played a dominant role in the field of motivation. We refer here to the fact that many studies have shown that both animals and humans will seek out, and expend energy in their efforts to obtain, stimulation apparently unrelated to any known biological drive. Animals are curious, they like to explore, and they seem to enjoy a certain amount of sensory stimulation that is novel, changing, and complex. You can contract "cabin fever" even though all your known biological drives are satisfied; you will want to get out of a confining situation and be stimulated.

Let us look at a few of the classic laboratory demonstrations of exploratory and curiosity behavior, and then discuss how these findings relate to drive theory and what kinds of explanatory systems have been developed to account for them. Butler (1954) discovered that monkeys would learn to press a bar that opened a window allowing them to look at an electric train for a very brief period of time. They were not rewarded with food, liquid, or anything else related to known biological needs; yet they learned that bar press response. In a related study, Butler and Harlow (1954) set up the situation so that a correct response gave the monkey the opportunity to look around the laboratory for thirty seconds. The monkeys seemed highly motivated; they would go on opening that window for *twenty hours* without showing a loss of interest. Now that's motivation. As mentioned in Chapter 4, Kish (1955) found that mice would learn to press a lever in order to turn a light off for a brief period of time. One might argue that the mouse was afraid of the light. So Kish reversed the situation so that a response turned the light on for a brief period of time. The mice would learn this response too. They didn't care if the light was turned on or off. As long as something happened, something changed, they would learn. Harlow, Harlow, and Meyer (1950) demonstrated that monkeys will work for hours trying to open a lock mechanism. If they succeeded, no reward was given; the monkeys merely locked the lock themselves and began all over again. The list of studies demonstrating curiosity, exploration, manipulation, and the rewarding properties of complex, novel, and changing stimuli is extensive. The reader interested in pursuing these many studies should refer to Cofer and Appley (1964).

What has all this to do with drive theory? Put quite simply, it depends upon to whom you talk. Some people believe that drive theory can easily account for these results whereas others are completely convinced that new theories will have to be developed to account for them.

Let us look at both sides of the argument; first, the pro-drive position. These investigators point out that, with the postulation of a few new drives, such as an exploratory drive, a curiosity drive, a manip-

Relationship to Drive Theory

ulatory drive, and perhaps an activity drive, most of these data can be accounted for. They argue that, just because we have not yet been able to identify the biological bases of these drives, we should not deny their existence. In a sense, the pro-drive psychologists are arguing that there may well be biological bases for these drives but that we have not yet found them.

In support of their argument these psychologists point out that many of the so-called sensation-seeking drives seem to parallel the traditional drives in many ways. For example, sensation-seeking drives seem to increase in strength as deprivation increases (the longer you stay trapped in your apartment, the more stir-crazy you become). Furthermore, these drives seem to be reduced with exposure to the appropriate form of stimulation (once out of your confining apartment you become less agitated and more satisfied). Finally, as with the basic drives, reductions of the so-called sensation-seeking drives seem to be reinforcing. You will learn whatever response brings you sensory stimulation.

1. Sensory Deprivation. In a sensory deprivation study (see Bexton, Heron, and Scott, 1954; Zubek, 1969) subjects are artificially cut off from many normal sources of external stimulation. The subjects lie in a sound-deadened room for twenty-four hours a day, wearing translucent goggles and gloves with stiff cuffs. They are paid twenty dollars per day to lie there. Most subjects can stand no more than a day or two of this kind of sensory deprivation. Although extreme individual differences showed up, many subjects reported boredom, irritability, and a tremendous desire for stimulation. Some even reported vivid hallucinations and disrupted thought processes. No one *liked* the experience, to say the least.

These studies can be used as evidence for the drive interpretation of sensation-seeking behavior in that they seem to suggest that an aroused drive state develops as time of deprivation increases. But, curiously, as we see in the next section, these same data have been used in arguments *against* drive theory.

2. Deprivation Dwarfism. The core idea behind the drive interpretation of sensation-seeking behavior is that there is an undetected biological *need* for sensory stimulation. Dramatic studies of *deprivation dwarfism* can be used as evidence for this kind of need. These studies suggest that sensory deprivation can lead to physical problems just as deprivation of food and water can damage the machine we call our body (see Gardner, 1972; Money, 1977).

Deprivation dwarfism studies have shown that the lack of stimulating home conditions can result in retarded physical growth. The heights of some of these deprived children were much less than normal, even though their diet was normal. The home conditions from which they came were often hostile, disruptive, unfriendly, neglectful, and uncaring. In addition to having stunted growth these children seemed withdrawn, sad, and lethargic.

Obviously, this situation is complicated. There is more missing in the lives of these children than the opportunity to explore and exercise curiosity; they are emotionally unsupported as well. Some investigators have argued that the pituitary gland, in an as yet undesignated way, is involved in the production of these symptoms. However, deprivation dwarfism can be thought of as something that is consistent with the drive theory suggestion that there is some kind of biological requirement for stimulation.

So far we have seen that drive theory has been applied to the sensation-seeking data. What about the other side of the argument? What kinds of arguments have been marshalled against the drive interpretation of sensation seeking?

1. Increased Arousal.

According to drive theory, the organism is bound and determined to reduce all its drives. Its primary goal is "zero drive level," or a state of total nonarousal. According to drive theory we should be most happy and content when we are sitting in a corner like a lump with all our biological drives satisfied.

But the sensation-seeking phenomena suggest a very different picture of life. They suggest there are time when we actively, sometimes even almost desperately, seek out *increases* in arousal, rather than decreases as drive theory proposes. We *want* to be in a state of tension and arousal, at least part of the time.

Many have argued that drive theory cannot explain this very basic interest in increasing rather than decreasing arousal. The argument is a good one. Although it may not necessarily invalidate all drive considerations, it does suggest that some modifications in drive theory would be necessary if that theory is to be comprehensive.

2. Unknown Drives?

Opponents of the drive position argue that it

is legitimate to discuss, "as yet undetected biological bases for the sensation-seeking behaviors," but they feel that such a position really isn't adequate. After all, it is based upon an assumption that may very prove to be false. Until we know for sure whether or not sensation-seeking behaviors have a basis in some biological need system the opponents of the drive position argue that it would be better to avoid such a risky assumption.

3. Too Many Drives?   The final objection the antidrive theoreticians have is that drive theoreticians are always making up new drives to explain things they can not explain with the drives they have already proposed. If a new, inexplicable piece of behavior turns up, they invent a new drive to account for it. Exploratory, manipulatory, activity, and curiosity drives have been proposed. Opponents ask, "When will it all stop?", and they point out that labeling behavior as being determined by a newly invented drive does not get us very far. It simply does not tell us very much.

You can see that there is plenty of disagreement about the nature and importance of sensation-seeking behaviors. It is probably fair to say that the drive interpretation has come out of the controversy on the losing side. Most motivation psychologists would argue that there is more to sensation seeking than heretofore undetected drives. In a later section, we look at some of the theories that have been offered as alternatives to the drive interpretation.

Relation to Incentive Motivation   At this point some readers may say, "Hey, wait a minute. What is the difference between incentive motivation and all of this sensation-seeking behavior?" The two sets of principles and data are related, but there are important differences too.

Both refer to the "pulling" or motivating aspects of the environment that we have been discussing. In this sense, both incentive motivation and sensation-seeking behaviors stand distinct from the drive interpretation with its emphasis upon internal "pushing" states.

However, when we discuss incentives and sensation seeking our focus or emphasis is different. Specifically, when we discuss incentives, we focus on the "pulling" aspects of *goals that are directly related to known biological needs*, such as the attractiveness or value of food and water. In contrast, when we study sensation-seeking behavior we focus upon the "pulling" power of external stimuli that are *not* related to known biological needs, such as stimulus complexity and novelty (of course, if one adopts a drive interpretation of sensation seeking then the two become equivalent).

We have seen how drive theoreticians have tried to include sensation seeking within their general theoretical framework. And we have seen how other theoreticians have tried to invalidate the drive interpretation. In this and the following sections, we discuss some of the alternatives to the drive interpretation.

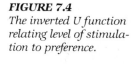
Optimal Level Theory

During the 1950s and 1960s a number of psychologists came up with similar explanations of sensation-seeking behavior (see Berlyne, 1971; Dember and Earl, 1957; Walker, 1980; Walters, Apter, and Svebak, 1982). Although the specifics of their theories differ, they do agree on two important points. First, they all argued that *there is some optimal, or preferred, level of arousal or stimulation.* Second, they all agree that this is a better theory of sensation-seeking behavior than the drive interpretation.

Optimal level theory is quite simple as we already know from Chapter 4. Only three principles are involved.

1. The Inverted-U. The first of the three principles states that for each organism there is some preferred level of stimulation that organism tries to maintain. Figure 7.4 contains a schematic representation

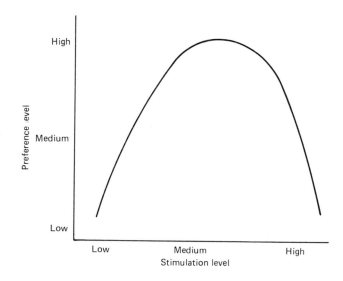

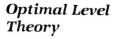
FIGURE 7.4
The inverted U function relating level of stimulation to preference.

of this principle. Stimulation or arousal that is too high will be avoided. Stimulation or arousal that is too low will also be avoided.

We have been referring to a preferred level of stimulation *or* arousal because some investigators have focused on the intensity, novelty, and complexity of external stimuli whereas others have focused, as we learned in Chapter 4, on internal states of arousal caused by the perception of those stimuli. Clearly, the two are closely related to one another.

2. Reinforcement. The second principle of optimal level theory states that any response that moves the organism into its preferred level or range of stimulation will be reinforced. If your overall level of stimulation is too low, then an increase in stimulation will be reinforcing. However, if you are overstimulted, then a reduction in stimulation can be reinforcing.

3. Stimulus Simplification. The third principle states that the longer we interact with a complex stimulus the more simple it seems to us. Thus if we stare at, and think about, a complex painting, or a gigantic chemical formula, we learn about it. Somehow it seems less complex as we interact with it.

The major implication of this principle for optimal level theory is that stimuli are not constant in their attractiveness and in their ability to arouse us. They lose some of their potency as we interact with them. The first time you hear a Mozart flute concerto you will probably be overwhelmed by, but attracted to, its complexity. But as you listen to it the complexity lessens. Finally, if you listen many, many times it becomes, although still beautiful, less attracting in terms of its complexity.

The impact of exposure on preference for complex stimuli is demonstrated nicely by a study done by Smith and Dorfman (1975). They constructed visual stimuli that were either somewhat complex, complex, or highly complex. Then they asked subjects how much they "liked" the various stimuli after one, five, ten, or twenty exposures to them. As can be seen in Figure 7.5, the somewhat complex stimuli were best liked and the highly complex stimuli were least liked, after one exposure. This suggests that the somewhat complex stimuli fell right in the preferred or optimal range of complexity whereas the other two types of stimuli were too complex to be appreciated immediately.

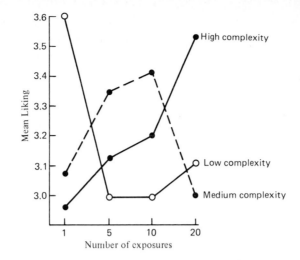

FIGURE 7.5
Liking as a function of complexity and number of exposures. (Adapted from Smith, G. F. & Dorfman, D. D. The effect of stimulus uncertainty on the relationship between frequency of exposure and liking. Journal of Personality and Social Psychology, 1975, 31, 150–155. Copyright 1975 by the American Psychological Association. Reprinted by permission.)

But now notice what happened to liking for the various stimuli as number of exposures increased. These changes can be accounted for by the principle that states that stimuli seem more simple as our exposure to them increases. Specifically, the least complex stimuli became even less complex as exposures increased. In fact, they became *too* simple to be enjoyed; they moved out of the optimal range. The most highly complex stimuli, on the other hand, became simpler as exposure increased, and moved *into* the preferred range. Hence, liking for these stimuli went up. The liking of the medium-complexity stimuli went up and then down. This suggests that these stimuli were too complex to enjoy when they were first perceived. As exposure increased they moved into the preferred level and were liked. However, as exposure continued people finally became bored with them, too.

White's Theory of Competence

We have seen that animals explore and show curiosity. We have learned that both drive theory and optimal level theory have been assumed by some to account for these phenomena. But there are still other explanations of these behaviors, and it is to one of them that we now turn. Robert White (1959) was well aware of the research from the 1950s which showed that animals and humans are motivated by more than basic biological drives. He interpreted exploratory behavior in terms of a more general motive system that can be called *competence motivation*. According to White, the reason we explore is because understanding our environment is rewarding. We explore the environment, not just because we enjoy novel and complex stimulation but because the comprehension, understanding, and sense of competence we obtain as a result of exploring is very rewarding to us. We like to be on top of things, and one way to become effective is to explore.

When we have completely explored a given situation, this form of motivation is assumed to subside. We will seek and explore only as long as the situation holds out the promise of new discovery or knowledge.

This form of motivation is assumed to operate only when more basic survival-related motives are satisfied. It is only when basic needs are satisfied that we have the time and leisure to fully explore our environment.

Although not worked out in any great detail, and perhaps a bit, shall we say, "fuzzy," White's approach does strike a positive cord. It does seem that, when we explore, we are driven at least partially by an interest in competence and mastery.

Maslow's Theory of Self-Actualization

As a fitting close to this chapter let us consider Maslow's (1970) theory of self-actualization. It is a fitting example because it draws upon, and contains elements of, most of the theories we have already discussed in this chapter.

Maslow's theory is based upon the assumption that we are innately driven toward the satisfaction of more and more elevated needs. Figure 7.6 contains Maslow's pyramid of human motives that can help you understand his position. Notice that the "baser" or more primitive needs are located at the bottom of the pyramid. Maslow argues that we are driven to move up the pyramid, satisfying more elevated needs as we go. But he also assumes that we must satisfy the needs at one level before we can move up to the next level. For example, if you are dying of thirst you will not be overly concerned with doing scientific research. You must satisfy your basic needs first. It is only once the more basic needs are satisfied that we can even consider moving up to the next level.

For Maslow, the height of achievement, and something we all strive for, is self-actualization. The characteristics of this state of self actualization are described in Table 7.2. Unfortunately, not many of us ever get that far. According to Maslow only a very small percentage of us manage to spend much time in the self-actualized state.

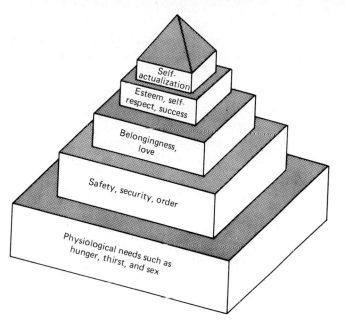

FIGURE 7.6
Maslow's pyramid of
motives. We must satisfy
lower needs before we
can move up the pyra-
mid to higher concerns.

**TABLE 7.2   Some Attributes of the Self-
Actualized Individual, as Seen by Maslow***

Accurately perceives what can be known about reality.
Accurately perceives what cannot be known.
Accepts reality.
Accepts her or himself.
Accepts others as they are.
Rejoices in the experience of living.
Acts spontaneously.
Is capable of creative action.
Has a sense of humor.
Is concerned for humanity.
Establishes a few deep, close personal relationships.
Can experience life as a child would experience it.
Works hard and accepts responsibility.
Is honest.
Explores the environment, and tries new things.
Is not defensive.

*From Houston, J. P., Bee, H., and Rimm, D. C. *Invitation to
Psychology*, New York: Academic Press, 1983. Table 5 on p.
511.

However, many of us can get at least a taste of self-actualization. According to Maslow we may be there briefly in what he calls a *peak experience.* The peak experience doesn't last long because we are dragged back down the pyramid by more mundane concerns such as income taxes being due. Life is seen as a struggle to move up the pyramid with occasional advances followed by retreats. We all do the best we can, because we are all striving for self-actualization, but few of us experience it for any sustained period of time.

Maslow's theory has not stimulated a great deal of empirical work. It serves more as a general scheme of things, and does seem to make sense when we try to comprehend what life is all about.

SUMMARY

1. Drive theory is based upon the common sense notion that our behavior is often *pushed* or driven from within by internal states of tension or arousal.

2. Incentive motivation refers to the fact that we are sometimes *pulled* into behavior by attractive aspects of the environment.

3. Freud's psychoanalytic theory is a drive theory. He believed that all behavior is caused by basic internal primitive drives which he called instincts.

4. The instincts act to satisfy bodily needs and demand immediate gratification.

5. The id, the ego, and the superego are, according to Freud, the main components of our personality.

6. These may be thought of as blind desire, reason, and conscience, respectively.

7. Id satisfaction can be attained through direct action or through wish fulfillment.

8. The ego tries to satisfy the id and mediate conflicts between the id and superego.

9. According to Freud most of our behavior is unconsciously determined.

10. The psychological problems we experience are the result of unresolved conflicts among the id, ego, and superego.

11. Defense mechanisms are techniques we unconsciously use to reduce anxiety. They involve a degree of self-deception.

12. Freud believed that we pass through several psychosexual stages on the way to adulthood. These include the oral, the anal, the phallic, the latency, and the genital periods.

13. If gratification at one of these stages is either frustrated or overindulged, fixation at that stage can occur. This means the person will continue to seek gratification in that mode at later stages of life.

14. The superego develops out of the resolution of the Oedipus and the Electra complexes.

15. Critics of Freud have noted that his theory is untestable, overly concerned with sex and aggression, based on observations of neurotics, and able to interpret any behavior as maladjusted.

16. Hull was a behaviorist who developed an influential drive theory that was supposed to account for all behavior of all organisms.

17. His theory argued that behavior was the result of an interaction between drive, habit, incentive, stimulus intensity, and inhibition.

18. Drive is a state of arousal determined by biological need and/or noxious stimulation.

19. Hull believed that drive operated in a general fashion, energizing all behavior equally.

20. Drive stimuli account for the directionality of behavior.

21. Habit is equivalent to learning and can be measured in terms of number of reinforced responses.

22. Reinforcement is equivalent to drive reduction.

23. Incentives affect level of motivation and not learning.

24. The r_g-s_g mechanism accounts for the operation of incentives.

25. Two kinds of inhibition, reactive and conditioned, subtract from the overall tendency to respond.

26. Drives may be acquired or learned. The two-factor theory of avoidance conditioning is an example of this kind of analysis.

27. Conflict refers to the simultaneous arousal of two or more incompatible motives.

28. Conflicts include the approach-avoidance, approach-approach, and avoidance-avoidance.

29. Conflicts have been experimentally analyzed by Brown and others.

30. Ethological interpretations of instinctive behavior also represent drive interpretations.

31. Sensation-seeking behaviors are common among animals and humans.

32. Many investigators believe that drive theory cannot account for sensation seeking.

33. However, sensory-deprivation studies and deprivation dwarfism suggest that the issue is not at all clear.

34. Opponents of the drive interpretation of sensation seeking mention arguments involving increased arousal, unknown drives, and too many drives.

35. Sensation-seeking behavior is closely related to, but distinguishable from, incentive motivation.

36. Optimal level theory states that there is some preferred level of stimulation, that any response that moves the organism into its preferred level will be reinforced, and that interaction with a stimulus simplifies it.

37. White's theory of competence is another alternative theory of sensation seeking.

38. Maslow's theory of self-actualization holds that we are innately driven to satisfy more and more elevated needs but that we must satisfy more basic needs before we can move upward.

Cognitive
Approaches

CHAPTER 8

⬇

Cognitive Consistency and Expectancy Value Theory

In Section II of this text we focused upon biological approaches to the understanding of motivation. We looked at such topics as innate behavior, regulatory mechanisms, and arousal, among others. In Section III we examined learning, drives, and incentives. In all of that theory and experimentation very little attention was paid to the role of what we *think* in determining motivation. We looked at the pushing and pulling of innate and acquired internal motive states. We examined the intricate relationship between motivation and learning. We looked at the impact of internal physiological states and external stimulus conditions upon motivation. We covered a lot of ground. But we never really focused on the "contents of our consciousness," and the role that thought plays in motivational events.

In the next three chapters we correct this deficit by focusing upon *cognitive approaches* to motivation. Cognition is difficult to define, even though it currently forms one of the major areas of psychological study. In general, cognition, or complex mental activity, may be thought of as knowing, remembering, thinking, judging, reasoning, imagining, and using language (Houston, 1981). The cognitive approaches described in this and the following chapters don't limit the study of motivation to such things as basic biological processes or to a behavioristic approach that denies access to complex mental activity. To the contrary, the cognitive approaches hold that motivation cannot be fully understood *unless* we attend to complex cognitive activity. The modern theories described in Chapters 8, 9, 10, and 11 were stimulated by the earlier work of James (1890), Tolman (1932), and Lewin (1938).

Essentially, the cognitive approach holds that *thought can affect and determine motivation and motivation can affect and determine thought.* It is the intricate interplay of thought and motivation that forms the basis of the following cognitive approaches to motivation.

COGNITIVE CONSISTENCY THEORY

The General Idea

The first of several cognitive approaches to motivation is usually referred to as *cognitive consistency theory.* This approach is based upon the straightforward and intuitively appealing idea that *inconsistencies among our cognitions (our thoughts, beliefs, and attitudes) can generate motivation.* Inconsistency leads to efforts to reduce or eliminate that inconsistency. We are motivated to achieve consistency, coherence, and meaninfulness among our cognitions.

Relationship to Drive

Although not tied to basic, known biological needs, consistency motivation does have something in common with the notion of drive that we discussed in Chapter 7. It is often felt that cognitive inconsistency leads to a state of tension that we seek to reduce. Just as a lack of food leads to a state of tension we seek to reduce so too does cognitive inconsistency lead to an unpleasant state of arousal or tension that we seek to eliminate. So as you read through the description of cognitive consistency theory, keep in mind that it is not entirely new and foreign; it does have characteristics that remind us of other conceptions of motivation.

BALANCE THEORY

Nature of the Theory

Heider (1946) and Newcomb (1968) developed and refined one example of cognitive consistency theory called *balance theory.* The basic idea behind this, and other consistency models, is that people prefer, and will seek to achieve, balance, harmony, and a "good fit" among their feelings about other people and objects.

Balance models consider the feelings in a simple situation involving one person (P), another person (O), and an object (X). Consider yourself as P, a teacher as O, and the course material as X. Assume that your feelings and those of the teacher are either positive or negative. Given these constraints, there is a limited number of different combinations of positive and negative feelings that can exist among the three elements. These combinations are shown in Figure 8.1. You, the teacher, and the course material are referred to as P, O, and X, respectively. The arrows indicate the direction of the feelings involved and the pluses and minuses indicate whether those feelings are positive or negative.

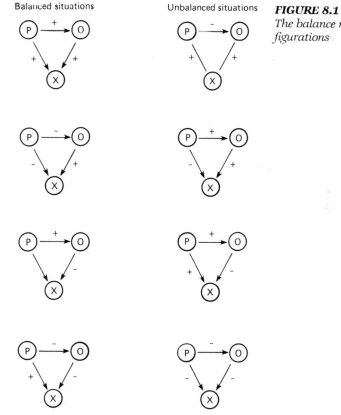

FIGURE 8.1
The balance model configurations

Let us begin by looking at the upper left-hand diagram, which refers to the situation in which you like the teacher and you both like the course material. This is a harmonious, balanced situation. The four patterns on the left side of the figure all represent balanced situations. The second diagram from the top on the left refers to the situation in which your teacher just loves his course material but you think both he and his course leave a lot to be desired. There is no inconsistency here; for you the situation is balanced. The third diagram from the top is the situation in which you like your teacher and you are both negative about the course material. This is also balanced. Finally, the bottom left diagram refers to the case in which you dislike the teacher and like the course material while he dislikes it. Although perhaps unlikely, this would be a balanced situation, too.

The four diagrams on the right side of Figure 8.1 all represent unbalanced situations. The unbalance in these situations stems from the fact that we expect people we like to have attitudes toward things that are similar to our own, and expect people we dislike to have attitudes toward things that are different from our own. The top right-hand diagram refers to the situation in which you don't like your teacher but you both like the course material. The diagram below refers to the situation in which you like the teacher but disagree with him about the course material, and so on. All four of the diagrams represent unbalanced conditions.

An easy way to remember whether a diagram is balanced or not is to count the minus signs. All the balanced diagrams on the left have even numbers of minus signs whereas all the unbalanced diagrams have odd numbers of minus signs.

The next crucial assumption in the balance model is that imbalance produces motivation to achieve balance. There is pressure to change unbalanced patterns into balanced patterns. We do not like, and find uncomfortable, unbalanced situations. We seek ways to change unbalanced conditions into more harmonious balance. We do this in many different ways. For example, if we like our teacher but don't like the course material that he adores, we may decide we like the material after all. Or we may conclude that he isn't such a great guy after all. If you don't like your teacher and you both dislike the course material, you can begin to like either the teacher or the material in order to achieve balance. Or you might even fool yourself and conclude that the teacher does like his material; then you can dislike him and his material in perfect balance.

Exactly which way balance is achieved is very complex. It depends upon the situation, what kind of a person you are, and the ease with which the various actions can and do change unbalanced situations into balanced ones.

Today, balance theory is not widely employed or explored. Part of the reason for this is that other, newer, more comprehensive theories have gripped the imagination of psychologists. But then there are some specific criticisms of balance theory, too. Most of these have to do with the fact that balance theory was never very precise; it was never worked out in great detail. For example, the theory is essentially restricted to three elements, *P*, *O*, and *X*. This is not necessarily a fatal flaw but it is obvious that there are many more complex interactions that a comprehensive theory would have to encompass. Furthermore, as mentioned, the theory is not particularly helpful in telling us exactly which way of reducing imbalance will be employed. And it is limited in that it restricts feelings to being either completely positive or negative. There are no gray areas allowed. Ambivalent feelings are beyond the scope of this model. In addition, some of our feelings can be more important than others. For example, your relationships with other people might be more important to you than your feelings toward objects or events; yet these subtle differences are not accounted for by the model.

Newcomb (1968) himself points out one limitation of the model. Specifically, the tendency to seek balance seems to be relatively strong when positive emotions are involved and relatively weak when negative feelings are involved. Consider the situation in which you dislike your teacher. In this case the tendency is to just withdraw from the whole situation; you are not particularly concerned about whether you and your teacher agree or disagree about the course material. You "couldn't care less." On the other hand, if you like your teacher then the passion to establish balance is substantial (see Crockett, 1974). In other words, the model, as originally formulated, represents an oversimplification of the situation. Research generally supports the predictions made by the model as far as they go. But thinking about three-element triads involving either-or feelings is not comprehensive enough to engage psychologists for long.

Problems with Balance Theory

COGNITIVE DISSONANCE

Although balance theory was interesting and stimulating, it was soon overshadowed by *cognitive dissonance theory* developed by Leon Festinger (1957).

Nature of the Theory

Dissonance theory is quite similar to balance theory in that it is another example of the general cognitive consistency approach. Just like balance theory, dissonance theory holds that inconsistencies among our cognitions lead to motivational states aimed at reducing those inconsistencies. We are motivated to maintain consistency or harmony among our various cognitions. For example, if we love salty food but know that salt is bad for us, then we have a problem because eating salt and knowing of its negative consequences leaves us uncomfortable and motivated to do something about the situation. As we shall see, there are many ways to eliminate the inconsistency.

Now let's look at some of the specific vocabulary of dissonance theory. According to this theory, two cognitions can be *consonant*, *dissonant*, or *irrelevant*. They are consonant if they are consistent with one another. Thus, if you know salt is bad but decide you don't like it very much then these two cognitions are consistent. Cognitions are called *dissonant* if they are inconsistent. If you love salt but know it is bad for you then these two cognitions are dissonant. Finally, two cognitions may be irrelevant to one another; they may imply nothing about one another such as would be the case if you loved salt but believed that skydiving was dangerous.

It is only the dissonant state that produces motivation. If two cognitions are consonant or irrelevant, no motivation is produced. Dissonance instigates pressure to achieve consonance. Once consonance is achieved, the motivational state subsides.

Relation to Drive Theory. All of this sounds somewhat familiar. In a sense, dissonance theory resembles drive theory. As Freedman, Sears, and Carlsmith (1981) put it:

Dissonance operates much like any other drive; if we are hungry, we do something to reduce our hunger; if we are afraid, we do something to reduce our fear; and if we feel dissonance, we do something to reduce it also. (pp. 406).

Thus, the work on dissonance is not entirely unrelated to earlier theories; it can be thought of as a drive theory. However, it does introduce a consideration of mental or cognitive events that, as we have seen, were pretty much ignored by many of the earlier behavioristic drive theoreticians.

Relation to Conflict.   In Chapter 7, we presented an analysis of conflict and discussed approach-approach, approach-avoidance, and avoidance-avoidance conflicts. If you think about it for a moment, you will realize that dissonance theory is related to conflict analysis. Think about the example in which the individual loves salt but knows it is bad for his health. This can be discussed as an example of dissonance or as an example of the approach-avoidance conflict. In either case something must be done to eliminate the problem. According to the language of dissonance theory, we might convince ourselves that we don't like salt so much after all. This would be equivalent, in the language of conflict analysis, to lowering the positive or approach gradient. Or we could conclude that salt is extremely dangerous and avoid it completely even though we like it. This would reduce dissonance. It could also be thought of as reducing conflict by raising the negative or avoidance gradient.

The point here is that dissonance theory has not developed in a vacuum. Although its vocabulary is different, it is related to other ways of thinking about motivation. Its true contribution may be not so much that it represents an entirely new way of thinking about motivation but rather that it has brought into better focus the fact that cognitions, and the relations among them, may be motivational factors. Dissonance yields motivation.

So far we have been talking as though two and only two cognitions are irrelevant, dissonant, or consonant. But that is an oversimplification. More often than not a given topic will be represented by more than two cognitions. For example, we love salt but know it is bad for us. But we also know that some salt is essential for life. And we know that some people seem to be genetically immune to the bad effects of salt. We also know that no matter how hard we try we cannot completely avoid the salt contained in prepared foods, and we might believe (incorrectly) that sea salt is less harmful than mined salt, and so on.

According to dissonance theory, dissonance is the result of the

The Number of Elements

interplay of *all* of these cognitions. If the sum of the dissonant elements outweighs the sum of the consonant elements, then dissonance exists. If the consonant elements outweigh the conflicting elements, then overall dissonance will be minimal. In other words, it is not an all-or-none situation; there are degrees of dissonance.

Not only do the relative numbers of consonant and dissonant elements contribute to overall dissonance, but the *importance* of the cognitions matters too. For example, if you love salt, and don't care too much about your health, then less dissonance will exist than if you also value your health highly.

Reducing Dissonance   The two principal ways of reducing dissonance are (1) adding additional consonant elements and (2) changing dissonant elements such that they are no longer dissonant. Let us look at each method in turn. Assume a young woman has been pressured into attending college by her parents. She believes that college is a waste of time in general and a double waste of time for her because she believes she will not do well. Going to college and her attitudes toward college are dissonant. How might she reduce the dissonance? First, she might add positive elements. She might decide that going to college would make her parents feel better, or she might obtain a student loan and conclude that either or both of these things are good reasons for going to college. The total amount or dissonance would be reduced. Second, she might change a dissonant element. For example, she might, after thinking about it, conclude that college is worthwhile after all, or she might conclude that she could do well at school.

In other words, we can reduce dissonance by either adding consonant elements or by changing dissonant cognitions.

Which way will a person choose to reduce dissonance? The theory suggests that people operate according to a "law of least effort." They will do whatever is easiest for them. For example, if our new college student has already mailed in a nonrefundable deposit and her parents have crowed about her acceptance into college to all their friends, then she might find it easier to think of some good reasons for attending college rather than backing out. However, if she has not yet been publicly committed to attending college then she might find it easier to defy her parents and not go than to alter her deeply felt ideas about college education. The easiest course of action will be followed whether it be (1) *changing existing cognitions*, (2) *changing* behavior, or (3) *adding new cognitions.* All three of these can reduce dissonance.

Whenever we choose between two or more alternatives, some degree of dissonance is bound to be generated. It seems inevitable. For example, suppose a high school senior has been accepted by a large state university and by a small private college. Suppose the student is torn between the two alternatives but finally decides to attend the state university. Once the decision is made dissonance exists because all of the good aspects of the private school (small classes, nice location, high prestige) and all of the bad aspects of the large school (too crowded, impersonal, too close to home) are all dissonant with the choice. It does not make any difference which decision is made; some dissonance will result. If the student had chosen the small school, then the positive aspects of the large school (inexpensive, lots of research opportunities, a variety of majors) and the bad aspects of the small school (expensive, isolated) would be dissonant with that decision.

Making Decisions Creates Dissonance

It is a little bit like the approach-approach conflict we discussed in Chapter 7. Faced with a choice between two positive alternatives, we are bound to be conflicted because choosing one alternative automatically means we are denied the other positive alternative. We can't win completely.

Dissonance theory states that, once a decision is made, we will reduce the inevitable dissonance by increasing our liking for the alternative we have chosen and by decreasing our liking for the alternative we have rejected. Once the student chooses the state university, he will increase his liking for that school while he decreases his liking for the small school.

This effect has been demonstrated experimentally. Lawler, Kuleck, Rhode, and Sorenson (1975) had accounting students rate the attractiveness of various job alternatives three times, once in the fall of the senior year before a job had been selected, once in the spring of the senior year after a job had been chosen, and once a year later. They found that jobs that were initially rated about equal before job selection occurred became differentially attractive as time went on. Jobs that were chosen became more attractive whereas unchosen jobs became less attractive. The effect increased through the first year on the job.

Brehm (1956) conducted a classic study in this area. He showed college women eight household products, such as toasters, and asked them to indicate how much they would like each item. Then one third of the women were shown two of the items they rated as equally attractive and were asked to choose one of the items as a gift. Then they rerated all objects for attractiveness. One third of the women were shown two of the items that they had initially rated very differently and were asked to choose one as a gift. Then they rerated all objects. Finally, the last third of the subjects was merely given one of the eight items (no choice was involved) and asked to rerate all of the items.

The results are contained in Table 8.1. Notice first that there was a strong tendency for the women to increase their evaluation of the item they had chosen and to decrease their evaluation of the item they had not selected.

Furthermore, notice that this effect was stronger when the initial ratings of the two items were similar. Apparently more dissonance is generated in this situation than in the situation in which the two objects were first evaluated differently. If you have to give up one thing that you like a lot in order to receive another thing that you also like, then high dissonance occurs. But if you can give up something

TABLE 8.1. Dissonance Reduction As Determined by Decision Making*

Condition	Rating of chosen object	Rating of unchosen object	Total reduction[a]
High dissonance (objects initially rated close)	+ .32	− .53	.85
Low dissonance (objects initially rated far apart)	+ .25	− .12	.37
No dissonance (gift—no choice)	.00	na	.00

[a]Figures are the increased evaluation of the chosen object plus the decrease in evaluation of the unchosen object.

*Adapted from Brehm, J. W. Post-decision changes in desirability of alternatives. *Journal of Abnormal and Social Psychology*, 1956, 52, 348–389, and from Freedman, J. C., Sears, D. O., and Carlsmith, J. M. *Social Psychology*. Englewood Cliffs, NJ: Prentice-Hall, 1981. Table 11.1, p. 408.

you didn't like very much anyway in order to get a much more attractive item, then little dissonance results.

Finally, notice that the control group members did not increase their rating of the item they were given. They rated all items, were given one item, and then rerated all items. No dissonance appears to have occurred here. Actively making a choice between objects seems to be a crucial element in creating dissonance.

Forced compliance is a phrase that is applied to situations in which an individual is pressured into publicly behaving in a manner that is inconsistent with that individual's beliefs. Inconsistency between behavior and attitude or belief is a strong source of dissonance. Thus the person who takes a despised job because the pay is so good will experience dissonance. An individual who informs on a friend while believing that to do so is despicable will experience dissonance.

Dissonance of this sort is usually reduced by altering attitudes or beliefs. Once the behavior has occurred in public, the individual cannot normally deny that it has occurred. So the only thing left to do is the change the attitude. For example, the informer can conclude that informing is, after all, a good thing to do. The individual taking the disliked job can conclude that it really isn't any worse than any other job.

The greatest amount of dissonance in these situations will be produced when the pressure to act contrary to one's belief is just strong enough to get the person to act. If the pressure is enormous, and the person acts contrary to his beliefs, then less dissonance will result. For example, if someone says, "I will be angry with you if you don't inform on so and so," and you do inform on them, you will experience considerable dissonance. However, if someone says to you, "I will kill you if you don't inform me," then to inform will produce less dissonance.

Many forms of pressure can produce the forced compliance effect. In this section we discuss threat as a significant pressure and in the next section we look at reward as a means of producing forced compliance.

Aronson and Carlsmith (1963) conducted an experiment that is widely noted as demonstrating that threat can produce forced compliance and dissonance. They showed children a group of toys and told them they could play with all the toys except one. This particular toy was just not to be played with. Half the children were threatened

Forced Compliance

with mild punishment if they played with the forbidden toy and half were threated with severe punishment. After the children were secretly watched to make sure that they did not play with the forbidden toy, they were asked to rate the attractiveness of all the toys. Dissonance theory would predict that the mild threat would produce more dissonance than the severe threat. The severe threat group felt justified in not playing with the forbidden toy ("I could get killed"). The mild threat children, on the other hand, would more likely experience dissonance in that there was only a mild threat to justify the discrepancy between what they believed (they liked they toy) and what they did (they did not play with the toy). Given that the mild threat group members experienced more dissonance they should, when asked to evaluate the toys, reduce that dissonance by devaluing the toy ("I don't like it anyway."). The high threat group, on the other hand, would not feel as great a need to devalue the forbidden toy because the severe threat was enough to jusify not playing with it.

This is just what Aronson and Carlsmith found. The children reduced their evaluation of the forbidden toy much more often in the mild threat condition than in the severe threat condition.

Forced Compliance: Rewards

Threatening people is not the only way to get people to act in a way that is contrary to their beliefs. It can be done with rewards, too. And, once again, the *more* we offer people to act contrary to their beliefs the *less* dissonance they will experience, and the *less* likely they are to change their attitudes to reduce dissonance.

For example, if someone offers you a fortune to rake leaves, then there is little pressure for you to change your beliefs that this is a dumb job; you know it's dumb but you are justified in doing it because of the wonderful pay. However, if you are working for less than minimum wages you will experience dissonance. So you will be more likely to reevaluate the job. "It's good work because its outside, and it gives me time to think."

Festinger and Carlsmith (1959) ran an experiment that demonstrates these ideas. First they had three groups of subjects do a very boring task, such as turning a peg in a keyboard for an hour. Then the experimenter asked two of the groups if they would be willing to help him because his regular assistant was absent that day. All the subjects had to do was to try to convince other new subjects that the experiment was interesting. In other words, these two groups were asked to lie about the boring task. One of the two groups was given twenty dollars to lie whereas the second group was offered one dollar. These two groups then went ahead and actually tried to convince new subjects that the experimental task was interesting. Then they were asked to rate how interesting the original task had been to them. The third group of subjects was not asked to convince anyone of anything and was not offered money. It merely rated the original task (it rated it as boring).

The most interesting comparison was between the task ratings of the twenty-dollar and one-dollar groups. As predicted by dissonance theory, the one-dollar group rated the task much more positively than did the twenty-dollar groups. The group members needed to change their attitude about the task (make it more positive) to justify the fact that they had told another person that it was interesting. The twenty-dollar subjects, on the other hand, already had their justification (they were doing it for money) and therefore did not have to change their attitude. So once again, the greater the pressure, the less was the dissonance, and the less was the attitude change.

Commitment.   Let us say two longtime Republicans vote for a Democrat in an important election. One of the two Republicans, himself a candidate for office, publicly announces that he voted for a Democrat whereas the other Republican keeps his voting behavior to himself. These two individuals will apparently not experience equal amounts of dissonance or feel equal pressure to bring their beliefs into line with their behavior. It seems that the pressure to readjust beliefs or to justify the voting behavior will only be strong in the case of the individual who has *publicly committed* himself to the voting behavior by announcing it to others. This individual will feel pressured to make certain readjustments such as concluding that that particular Democrat is "more like a Republican than like an ordinary Democrat." Or he might announce that he doesn't really support the Democrat's position on one particular issue that is crucial to the Republican's hometown folk.

On the other hand, the Republican who voted for the Democrat but did not admit to it publicly would feel little dissonance or little pressure to make any adjustment at all. Irreversible public commitment to a course of action leads to pressure to reduce dissonance. Merely *thinking* dissonant thoughts does not seem to be nearly as motivating as publicly committing to those thoughts.

Carlsmith, Collins, and Helmreich (1966) ran a study that demon-

The Importance of Commitment, Consequences, and Choice

strates this effect. They had subjects engage in the same boring task (peg turning) used by Festinger and Carlsmith (1959) in their study described previously. Following the boring task, half the subjects were required to publicly try to convince the next subject that the task was interesting and worth doing. The other half of the subjects merely had to write an *anonymous* statement to the same effect. Thus, all subjects had to respond in a way that was contrary to what they felt but only half of them had to do so publicly.

Then all subjects were required to rate the pleasantness of the boring task. The prediction was supported; the publicly committed subjects rated the task as more positive than did the anonymous statement writers.

Consequences.   Believing that you could have foreseen the negative consequences of a decision also seems to be important in producing dissonance. For example, if everyone tells you a particular movie is wonderful and you go see it and hate it, dissonance is not likely to be aroused if you believe there was no way you could have known ahead of time that you would dislike the film. "No one is perfect." On the other hand, if you believe you "should have known better" then dissonance may be aroused. Then you will have to reduce dissonance by concluding something like, "It was educational," or, "I would have wasted the time anyway."

Choice.   Dissonance is also much more likely to be aroused if we feel we make a choice of our own free will. If we are forced into a choice, or have no choice at all in the matter, then dissonance is less likely to be aroused. For example, suppose you are traveling and your car breaks down in the country. You look in the telephone book and there is only one towing service. You decide to use them and they charge you an arm and a leg. But what could you do? You had no choice. So you don't feel any dissonance. However, if there are several towing services in the telephone book and you impulsively call the first one that turns out to be expensive you may feel dissonance. There is an inconsistency between what you believe (always get three estimates ahead of time) and what you did (impulsively called the first towing service). In this case there will be pressure to reduce dissonance by deciding things like, "Well, *all* tow services rip you off in the country," or, "It would have wasted time to call other services."

Linder, Cooper, and Jones (1967) ran some experiments to demonstrate the importance of free choice in producing dissonance. All subjects wrote an essay that was in disagreement with their stated opinion about the Fifth Amendment. Half of the subjects were led to believe that they had no choice in the matter; they *had* to write that essay. The other subjects were led to believe that they had a choice in the matter; they could choose either to write or not to write. Then all subjects were again tested for their attitude toward the Fifth Amendment. In agreement with the prediction, people who believed they had no choice changed their attitude about the Fifth Amendment less than did those who believed they had a choice.

Self-Perception Theory

According to Bem (1967) we find out how we are *feeling* by looking at what we are doing. If we find we are at a football game, cheering along with the rest of the fans, then we conclude we must like football games. Why else would we be there? Bem argues that, to one degree or another, we act like independent observers of our own behavior. It is as though we "stand outside of ourselves" and look at, or watch, what we are doing and then make inferences about what we are feeling. Just as we might conclude, upon seeing someone drink a cup of tea, that that person likes tea so too would we conclude that we must like tea if we observe ourselves drinking it.

Obviously, this is not the only mechanism whereby we draw conclusions about what we are feeling. However, Bem believes that it is a significant mechanism and that we do draw conclusions about our internal states based upon our observations of our own overt behavior. If we belong to the Democratic party then we conclude that we must hold Democratic opinions. If we belong to the Sierra Club then we must be a conservationist.

Bem argues that this mechanism, termed *self-perception theory*, can serve as an alternative to dissonance theory. He does not merely argue that self-perception theory can act as a supplement to dissonance but rather as direct, complete substitute for it. He believes that self-perception theory can account for the so-called dissonance effects without ever having to refer to the arousal of any kind of drive-like discomfort as dissonance theory does.

As an example of how self-perception theory can make the same predictions as dissonance theory, recall the Festinger and Carlsmith (1959) study in which one group of subjects was paid twenty dollars to convince the next subject that a boring task was worth doing. Another group was paid one dollar for doing the same thing. Dissonance theory predicted, and it was found, that the one-dollar subjects would be more likely to rate the original task positively than were the twenty-dollar subjects. But self-perception theory can make the same prediction without having to refer to some internal dissonance-based motivational state. Specifically, when the one-dollar subjects are asked to evaluate the original task, they may say to themselves, "I told that new subject that the task was worthwhile. And I only got paid one dollar, which certainly isn't enough to make me lie about the task. Therefore I must have enjoyed the original task." The twenty-dollar subjects, on the other hand, say, "I told that new subject that the task was interesting. But they paid me twenty dollars to do so. Therefore I may well have been exaggerating the pleasantness of the task for that much money. I probably didn't like the original task."

Self-perception theory, although interesting and certainly capable of accounting for some of the dissonance data, has not replaced dissonance theory. Both theories seem logical, but no one has yet come up with an experiment that will conclusively establish one as correct and the other as incorrect (see Higgens, Rhodewalt, and Zanna, 1979; Olson and Zanna, 1979). The two theories may both be helpful some of the time but not all of the time. Specifically, dissonance theory is seen as being more appropriate when the issues involved are important and controversial and where the individual is likely to have strong, clear-cut opinions such as one might have toward war, abortion, and taxation. Self-perception theory, on the other hand, may be more appropriate in connection with minor issues about which the individual holds rather vague, poorly formed opinions. Self-perception analysis may be more appropriate for the kinds of minor issues that we use in laboratory experiments whereas dissonance theory does a better job of explaining the big "real life" issues.

Final Comments   Cognitive consistency theory, and dissonance theory in particular, has stimulated considerable thought and research. The appeal of the approach lies in the fact that it has tapped into the importance of cognitive activity in determining motivational effects while, at the same time, remaining in contact with earlier approaches such as drive theory. Prior to these theoretical efforts, the motivating properties of cognitive inconsistencies were, although perhaps intuitively suspected, relatively unexplored and unexplained.

On the other hand, cognitive consistency theory has fallen on hard times. Although the professional journals were at one time filled with consistency studies, this is no longer the case. There are at least two reasons for the demise of consistency theory. First, newer, more novel and exciting approaches have been developed. As we see in Chapters 9 and 10, the study of cognitive motivation has moved on to new areas of concern. Second, the shortcomings of cognitive consistency theory have become so apparent that not many researchers are willing to continue to use this approach. Some of these shortcomings, as proposed by many investigators, are described as follows.

Cognitive consistency is fairly vague and imprecise. It lacks rigor and has proven to be difficult to work out in any detail. For example, the theories are not particularly helpful in telling us when and in which individuals cognitions will conflict. The theories do not tell us much about how multiply related cognitions function in relation to inconsistency. They are not precise in terms of telling us which of many possible inconsistency-reducing changes will be made by a particular individual at a particular time. It is suggested that the *easiest* change is the one that will be made, which may be obvious in some cases but in others it is not, and the theories do little to help us decide which changes are easiest. Furthermore, cognitive consistency theory tells us that inconsistency is motivating but doesn't tell us *why* it is motivating. In this sense the theory is more descriptive than analytical. Claiming that the state of inconsistency is like a drive state poses as many questions as it answers. For instance, in the absence of any known biological basis for it, aren't we falling into the common trap (outlined in Chapter 7) of merely inventing new drives to account for new behaviors when we propose the existence of an "inconsistency drive?" Cognitive consistency theory argues that inconsistency is something we are always motivated to reduce. But life is not that simple. Sometimes we act as though we want to *increase* inconsistency. We think of ourselves as frugal and careful with our money and yet we go out on lovely, exciting spending binges. We ride roller coasters and go to horror films even though we claim to be timid. Perhaps we do some of these things because it "feels so good when we stop." Perhaps we are trying to hide or avoid other even less pleasant feelings. Perhaps we like arousal. In other words, consistency theory, by claiming to be a drive theory, inherits all of the problems of classical drive theory.

EXPECTANCY-VALUE THEORY

General Approach

Expectancy-value theory comprises another of the cognitive approaches to motivation. It emphasizes the idea that how we perceive ourselves and the world around us determines our state of motivation. Motivation, according to this approach, is determined by what we think.

This approach maintains that our level of motivation is determined by two factors, namely, our expectations about how likely it is that we will attain some goal and how much we value that goal. In its simplest form:

Value × Expectancy = Motivation

Let us consider some of the implications of this multiplicative relationship. If we value a goal, such as getting admitted to medical school, but don't think we have a chance, then motivation toward that goal will be low. If we thought we could easily be admitted to medical school, but did not want to go, then motivation would also be low. High value and high expectations would lead to maximum motivation.

According to this theory, our level of motivation or approach tendency is determined by complex mental events. We place a value on a particular goal and then we estimate our chances of attaining that goal. Sometimes we are not completely accurate in making these estimates. One individual might underestimate her chances of going to medical school and thus fail to pursue a goal that was within her grasp. Another person might overestimate his chances of going to medical school and waste time preparing only to face final disappointment.

This simple illustration reveals that the expectancy-value approach can involve some very intricate situations. We have moved far beyond simple conceptions of motivation, such as those that measure hunger in terms of time of deprivation, and now must consider complex human motivation that is shaped and controlled by our diverse cognitive activities.

Achievement Motivation

Expectancy-value theory is a very general approach to the problem of motivation. It has been applied to such diverse topics as the need for power and the need to affiliate with other people. However, by far and away the most widely discussed topic is that of achievement motivation, and it is to this topic that we now turn.

The Need to Achieve. It is obvious that people differ in terms of their interest in achievement. Some of us are driven from the moment we get up until late at night. Others are unconcerned with goals and ambition. It is not surprising, then, to learn that psychologists have been interested in, and studying, the need to achieve for over fifty years.

Work on achievement can be traced back to Murray (1938). He worked at a time when it was fashionable to try to identify the major human needs. One of a long list of needs that he and his colleagues at Harvard developed was the need to achieve. He defined this need as the urge to "overcome obstacles, to exercise power, to strive to do something difficult as well and as quickly as possible" (Murray, 1938, pp. 80–81). In other words, the need to achieve has to do with the desire to meet or exceed standards of excellence.

Measurement: The TAT. Given that we accept that people differ in terms of their need to achieve, how do we go about measuring achievement motivation? Murray developed the *Thematic Appreciation Test*, commonly called the TAT, to measure achievement motivation, as well as other forms of motivation.

The TAT is based upon the simple notion that if you tell a story about a general topic or situation you will reveal something of yourself in that story. You *project* some of your own needs, wants, wishes, and desires into the story you make up. For this reason the TAT and any other test designed to measure personality differences in this way are called *projective tests*.

Murray's procedure, which has been followed and expanded upon by more recent investigators, was to show a subject a series of ambiguous pictures and ask him to make up a story about each of them. The subject was asked to describe what was going on in the picture, what led up to the scene in the picture, what the people are thinking and feeling, and what the outcome of the situation will be.

It is easy to see how this technique might reveal important differences among people. For example, suppose we show a picture of a figure in a white coat standing next to a table upon which another human form is lying. One of our subjects says this depicts a young medical student about to perform a daring medical procedure that will save the patient's life and make the medical student famous, respected, and self-satisfied. Another of our subjects describes the standing figure as a mass murderer who is about to add another body to his collection. We get quite a different message from our two subjects. The implication behind the use of the TAT is that we can reliably make sense out of these different sorts of stories.

You can also see why many clinicians and psychotherapists use the TAT in their attempts to understand their patients' inner problems.

Whereas Murray developed the TAT to measure *all* human needs, McCelland (1958, 1961) and his associates focused upon its usefulness in measuring achievement motivation. You might ask how, exactly, do we *score* a story or decide exactly how much of a need to achieve it contains. You need training to be able to score a TAT story. McCelland trained his scorers to recognize eleven different achievement themes that can show up in a story. These themes include mention of unique accomplishments, success and failure, and a concern for long-term processes. A story is given a +1 for each of these themes it contains and a 0 if that particular theme does not appear. Thus, depending upon how much achievement imagery it contains, a story can receive a score from 0 to +11. The higher the score the higher is the assumed achievement motivation.

Reliability and Validity. Before any test can be accepted as a good test it must be shown to be *reliable* and *valid*. A test is reliable if it gives the same score for the same individual on two different occasions. If you score high on achievement on day 1 then, if the test is reliable, you will score high on day 2 as well.

Although the situation is complicated by the fact that achievement motivation seems to be differentially arousable by what is going on around us, TAT measurement does seem to be fairly reliable. People classified as high or low in their need to achieve tend to be classified in the same way each time they take the TAT (McCelland, Atkinson, Clark, and Lowell, 1953).

A test is valid if it measures what it is supposed to measure. The validity of the TAT in connection with achievement motivation seems to have been established to almost everyone's satisfaction. That is, the TAT, scored for achievement imagery, seems to differentiate among people who really do differ in terms of their need to achieve. The assumption is that there is a general motive to achieve and that by using the TAT we can predict a person's behavior in many different situations (see Atkinson, 1953; Lowell, 1952; Mischel, 1961). Validity is said to be shown if a test can predict or account for relevant behavior. For example, the validity of the TAT is supported by the fact that people who score high on it are more likely to go to college (Atkinson, Lens, and O'Malley, 1976) and to do better in their chosen field once they get there (Raynor, 1970).

Increasing Achievement Motivation.   Is there anything that has been done to increase levels of achievement motivation? Yes, at least to some extent, achievement motivation seems to be alterable. Mc-Celland and Winter (1969) devised training programs that ranged in length from three to six weeks. Essentially these programs were designed to train people to think and act like high achievers. For example, they encouraged people to work longer hours, to initiate new activities, and to think in terms of long-range goals. McCelland and Winter report significant gains in achievement-oriented behaviors as a result of their programs being used among businesspeople. Others, such as Kolb (1965), have been somewhat successful in improving the grades obtained by so-called underachieving students or students who seem to be achieving at a less than optimal level.

So, although achievement motivation is seen as a fairly stable factor, it can be altered by experience and learning. These training programs should be looked at as experimental efforts; they have not been used widely enough to be accepted as proven, practical techniques for increasing achievement activity.

There may be other ways to alter achievement motivation. For example, it has been observed that our *initial* experience with a new task can be crucial (Feldman and Bernstein, 1978). If we fail on that first experience then we will tend to conclude that we do not have what it takes to succeed in that area. Initial success leads us to conclude that we do have the ability to succeed. So if we can arrange the situation such that initial efforts are successful, then achievement-oriented activity may be more likely generated. It's kind of like "getting off on the right foot." If a third grader is overwhelmed by her first few arithmetic problems, she may conclude she "can't do math" and never really try again. On the other hand, if the situation is structured such that initial success is guaranteed (e.g., by careful selection of problems by the teacher), then achievement motivation may be fostered.

The Origins of Achievement Motivation. Closely related to the techniques discussed previously is the problem of the origin of achievement motivation. Why are some of us so high and some so low on this variable? A number of investigations have suggested that differences in childrearing practices may contribute to at least some of the observed natural differences in achievement motivtion. Some of the factors that are suspected of fostering high achievement motivation are listed here:

1. Early independence training by the mother.
2. High expectations about achievement by the parent.
3. High rewards for achievement.
4. Low domination of the child by the father.

Atkinson's Theory Atkinson's theory is an expectancy-value theory because it revolves around the idea that our level of motivation depends upon how much we value a goal and our estimate of how likely it is that we will attain that goal. But this theory is not that simple; he has gone beyond basic assumptions of expectancy value theory, as we shall now see.

1. Conflicting Motives. Atkinson believed that two conflicting motive systems operate in every individual. The first, the *hope of success*, motivates us to seek achievement. The second, the *fear of failure*, motivates us to avoid achievement situations. We are pushed toward achievement tasks by our hope of success but, at the same time, repelled by the same task because of our fear of failure. We want to go to medical school; we would feel pride if we succeeded at that difficult task. But, at the very same time, our fear of failure tends to make us want to avoid medical school. We are afraid we will fail, and feel shame and embarrassment.

Atkinson believes that our *overall* tendency to approach an achievement task is the result of the combination of these two conflicting factors. Very simply, if the hope of success exceeds the fear of failure, we will try to go to medical school. If the fear of failure exceeds the hope of success, then we will avoid medical school. According to Atkinson, people differ in terms of how strong these two factors are at any given moment.

2. Hope of Success. The best way to understand Atkinson's full-blown theory is to break it down into its components. We first look at hope of success, then fear of failure, and then at how they combine to produce net achievement motivation.

Atkinson has an equation for each of his two factors. The equation for the tendency to seek achievement is:

$$T_s = M_s \times P_s \times I_s$$

Let us look at each factor in this question. T_s is the tendency to seek achievement tasks, or the hope of success. The strength of T_s is determined by three factors (M_s, P_s, I_s). We are already familiar with two of these factors. P_s refers to our estimate of how likely we feel it is that we will succeed at the task. If P_s is 1, then we are completely convinced that we will succeed. If P_s is .5, we feel we have a "fifty-fifty" chance of succeeding. If P_s is 0, we are sure we will fail.

Our estimates of success (P_s) can obviously be affected by many factors. Some of the factors that have been mentioned include our past experience, our observation of the experiences of others, and the competition. If we have failed or succeeded on similar tasks in the past, then our estimate of success in the present situation will be adjusted accordingly. If we have seen other people succeed or fail, then we will take that information into consideration as we estimate our chances of success. And if we see that we are competing against mobs of people for the same goal, then we will be likely to reduce our subjective estimate of success. If we are the only person going after a prize, we will increase P_s.

I_s refers to the value we place on the goal. If we value the goal highly then we will be more motivated to achieve it. If we care not at all for the goal, then I_s will be zero (and T_s will then be zero too). Atkinson made the interesting assumption that I_s is equal to $1 - P_s$. What this says is that when the probability of success is low, then the value of the goal will be high. When the probability of success is extremely high, then I_s will be low; if *everyone* can do it, who cares? The goals that we really prize are those that are difficult to attain. Although perhaps an oversimplification, this assumption is an integral part of Atkinson's theory.

M_s refers to the individual's stable long-term interest in achieving success. Although P_s and I_s can vary from moment to moment and situation to situation, M_s is seen as an enduring aspect of the individual's personality. M_s is measured with the TAT, as outlined in preceding sections. In essence, this means that people who are high in general achievement motivation are the ones who have high M_s.

According to Atkinson's formula, T_s is determined by multiplying together M_s, P_s and I_s. If any one of these three factors is 0, then T_s will be 0. In other words, for an individual to approach achievement she must value the goal, feel she has a better than 0 chance of attaining the goal, and have at least a minimal amount of stable achievement motivation.

3. Fear of Failure.   Now let us turn to the second of the two conflicting motive systems described by Atkinson. The fear of failure, or the motivation to avoid achievement tasks, is also expressed by a simple equation:

$$T_F = M_F \times P_F \times I_F.$$

The tendency to avoid a given achievement task is a function of the stable personality disposition to avoid failure (M_F), the probability of failure (P_F), and the unpleasantness of failing (I_F).

Like M_s, M_F is seen as a stable enduring personality characteristic. Atkinson believed that M_F represented a person's tendency to feel shame and embarrassment when she fails at a task. On an intuitive level this seems like an important factor. We all know people who seem to be especially mortified if they fail. Others seem immune to failure; some laugh about their failures whereas others hardly seem to notice them.

How do we measure M_F? Although M_s is measured with the TAT, Atkinson proposed that M_F is best measured through the use of the *Test Anxiety Questionnaire* (TAQ). This test, designed by Mandler and Sarason (1952), is a paper and pencil test used to determine how nervous or anxious people are about taking tests. Questions on the TAQ consist of items such as, "How much do you worry while taking an intelligence test?" Although it was originally designed for other purposes, Atkinson reasoned that the TAQ could provide a good measure of M_F. People who score high on the TAQ are people who will tend to avoid achievement tasks. The assumption has been that the TAQ can be used as a valid measure for fear of failure.

P_F is our expectation of failing a given task. Once again, like P_s, P_F is determined by our past experience with similar tasks, by our perception of how others have done on the task, and by our estimation of the competition.

P_F is seen as being equal to $1 - P_s$. This makes sense. If we believe we have a 75 per cent chance of succeeding, then we also believe that we have a 25 per cent chance of failing.

I_F is the negative emotional response we have to the anticipation of failing a particular task. The greater I_F is the more likely we are to avoid that task. I_F is tied to P_F. If we fail a task that we perceive as being very difficult, then we don't feel so bad. But if we fail a task that a two-year-old could pass, then we truly feel bad. Thus, $I_F = 1 - P_F$.

4. Combining the Two.   Atkinson believes that to predict and understand achievement behavior, we must consider *both* T_s and T_F. The two opposing motive systems must be considered together. Atkinson *adds together* T_s and T_F to come up with the *net tendency* to approach or avoid a given achievement task. Table 8.2 contains some examples of how the addition of T_s and T_F leads to specific predictions.

TABLE 8.2.   Calculations of T_s, and T_{-f} for Five Levels of Task Difficulty when $M_S > M_F$, when $M_F > M_S$, and when $M_S = M_F$

	Task (P_s)	$(M_S \times P_s \times In_s)$	+	$(M_F \times P_f \times In_f)$	=	$T_s + T_{-f}$
$M_s > M_F$,	A (.9)	$(5 \times .9 \times .1)$	+	$(1 \times .1 \times -.9)$	=	.36
where $M_S = 5$	B (.7)	$(5 \times .7 \times .3)$	+	$(1 \times .3 \times -.7)$	=	.84
and $M_F = 1$	C (.5)	$(5 \times .5 \times .5)$	+	$(1 \times .5 \times -.5)$	=	1.00
	D (.3)	$(5 \times .3 \times .7)$	+	$(1 \times .7 \times -.3)$	=	.84
	E (.1)	$(5 \times .1 \times .9)$	+	$(1 \times .9 \times -.1)$	=	.36
$M_F > M_S$,	A (.9)	$(1 \times .9 \times .1)$	+	$(3 \times .1 \times -.9)$	=	$-.18$
where $M_F = 3$	B (.7)	$(1 \times .7 \times .3)$	+	$(3 \times .3 \times -.7)$	=	$-.42$
and $M_S = 1$	C (.5)	$(1 \times .5 \times .5)$	+	$(3 \times .5 \times -.5)$	=	$-.50$
	D (.3)	$(1 \times .3 \times .7)$	+	$(3 \times .7 \times -.3)$	=	$-.42$
	E (.1)	$(1 \times .1 \times .9)$	+	$(3 \times .9 \times -.1)$	=	$-.18$
$M_S = M_F$,	A (.9)	$(5 \times .9 \times .1)$	+	$(5 \times .1 \times -.9)$	=	0
where $M_S = 5$	B (.7)	$(5 \times .7 \times .3)$	+	$(5 \times .3 \times -.7)$	=	0
and $M_F = 5$	C (.5)	$(5 \times .5 \times .5)$	+	$(5 \times .5 \times -.5)$	=	0
	D (.3)	$(5 \times .3 \times .7)$	+	$(5 \times .7 \times -.3)$	=	0
	E (.1)	$(5 \times .1 \times .9)$	+	$(5 \times .9 \times -.1)$	=	0

From "Motivational Determinants of Risk-Taking Behavior," by J. W. Atkinson. In *Psychological Review*, 1957, *64*, 359–371. Copyright 1957 by the American Psychological Association. Reprinted by permission.

The upper third of Table 8.2 refers to the case of an individual whose M_s is stronger than her M_F. This is an individual whose personality is such that she is more interested in pursuing success than she is in avoiding failure. Assume that this individual is faced with five tasks (A through E) which vary in terms of how easy they seem to the individual. *Using only the M_s, M_F, and P_s values contained in Table 8-2 it is possible to calculate T_s and T_F, which is Atkinson's way of combining hope of success and fear of failure. Notice in the right-hand column of the upper third of Table 8.2 that the greatest net approach tendency is predicted for tasks with a .5 difficulty level. In other words, Atkinson predicts that people who are more highly motivated to approach achievement tasks than to avoid them will be most likely to go after a task where they have about a fifty–fifty chance of success. They will be less interested in tasks that have either very high or very low probabilities of success.

Now look at the middle section of Table 8.2. This section contains predictions about what an individual whose M_F is greater than his M_s will do when faced with the same five task difficulty levels. Notice here that it is predicted that these people will most strongly *avoid* the .5 difficulty level. This is just the opposite of what the high M_s, low M_F people will do.

Intuitively, this prediction makes sense. People who are primarily concerned with avoiding failure can approach a very easy task or a very difficult task without too much trepidation. If they fail the difficult task they don't feel bad because "almost everyone fails that task." If they approach the very easy task, they will also avoid feeling bad because they probably *will* succeed.

These predictions have received some support. For example, Isaacson (1964) found that men who were higher in M_s than M_F were more likely to choose college majors that were of an intermediate level of difficulty than were men who were higher in M_F than M_s. However, support for Atkinson's predictions has not been perfect. For example, Atkinson and Litwin (1960) looked at college men who were either of the $M_s < M_F$ or the $M_F < M_s$ type. The two groups took part in a ring toss game and were allowed to choose how far from the peg they stood when they threw the ring. In agreement with the prediction $M_F < M_s$ subjects preferred to throw from intermediate distances. But the $M_s < M_F$ subjects did not show a clear preference for very far or very close distances, as predicted by the theory. These and other studies (see Atkinson and Birch, 1978) offer some support for Atkinson's theory, but do not substantiate it unequivocally.

"She's really a bright girl but she hides it in class because she doesn't want to look too smart." "She could run the business better than her husband but she's afraid to."

Do Women Fear Success?

These and similar statements express the idea that women may shun success because to be female and to be successful in this country is to invite negative consequences. We have all run across this idea, in one form or another; but is there any truth to it? Do women really fear success? The study of achievement motivation has led to some information concerning this issue.

Early on in the study of achievement motivation, McCelland noticed differences between women and men. For example, when men are put into achievement-oriented conditions, their achievement imagery goes up significantly, relative to "relaxed" or nonachievement-oriented conditions. Women, however, do not show this increase. When put into achievement-oriented conditions they show either no increase or an actual decrease in achievement imagery. Why do the very conditions that increase achievement imagery in men do just the opposite in women? Although McCelland and Atkinson were aware of this sex difference, they could not explain it.

Horner (1969) offered the most controversial and best-known explanation of these results. She argued that women have *another* stable motive system, similar to M_s and M_F, which she called *fear of success*. The idea is that women fear success because success leads to negative consequences such as loss of friends, loss of popularity, and loss of a sense of femininity. The notion is that to be feminine, this culture says you must not be strong, independent, and competent.

Horner did a study that seemed to support her hypothesized fear of success. She had women complete stories when they were given statements like: "After first-term finals, Anne finds herself at the top of her medical school class." Men were given the same sentences except that the name "John" replaced the name "Anne." Horner then developed some scoring techniques that were supposed to pick up the fear of failure. The themes she looked for included anticipation of negative consequences and denial of responsibility, among others. Horner found that about 62 per cent of the women showed some fear of success imagery such as getting married or lowering Anne's standing in the class. Only about 9 per cent of the men displayed some fear of success imagery.

Horner's work quicky captured the imagination of a number of investigators and stimulated a good deal of research. Unfortunately, much of this research failed to find women displaying more fear of success imagery than men (see Condry and Dyer, 1976; Tresemer, 1974; Karabenick, 1977; Marshall and Karabenick, 1977). As a result, the fear of success hypothesis has been fairly widely rejected as an explanation of women's achievement behavior. Differences between the sexes in terms of fear of success are not presently apparent.

Peplau (1976) has proposed that sex-role attitudes are more important in determining women's achievement behavior than the fear of success concept. For example, she found that sex-role attitudes correlate better with life successes than does fear of success imagery.

Society and Achievement

Based upon his understanding of the early work of Max Weber and others, McCelland (1961) became intrigued with the idea that the productivity of *entire cultures* could be linked to early childrearing practices. Specifically, he argued that cultures that fostered high achievement motivation, through such mechanisms as early independence training and an emphasis upon the value of hard work, would be the cultures that would display high economic gains.

McCelland did a number of studies that support his hypothesis. In one study, he looked at the amount of achievement imagery contained in children's books in twenty-three different countries in the year 1929. Arguing that these differences would show up in actual economic activity in later years as these children grew up, McCelland looked at electrical production rates in those twenty-three countries during the years 1929 to 1950. In agreement with his ideas, McCelland found a significant positive correlation between amount of increase in electrical production and amount of achievement imagery in children's books. The idea is that the children were acquiring from books in 1929 the achievement motivation that would later be reflected in actual economic gains.

In another study, McCelland correlated economic success as reflected by coal imports in England during the years 1500 to 1800 with amount of achievement imagery contained in that country's literature. As you can see in Figure 8.2 the relationship is striking. Both increases and decreases in achievement imagery were followed, fifty

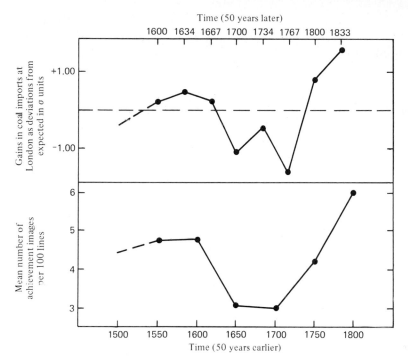

FIGURE 8.2
Achievement imagery in English literature (1550–1800) compared with gains in London coal imports 50 years later. (From McCelland, D. C. The achieving society, New York: D. Van Nostrand Co., 1961. Fig. 4.3 on p. 139. Copyright 1961 by D. Van Nostrand Co. Reprinted by permission of Litton Educational Publishing, Inc.)

years later, by corresponding increases and decreases in economic activity.

One interesting question that is sometimes asked is whether achievement imagery leads to economic activity or whether economic activity leads to greater achievement imagery. McCelland's work clearly indicates that the latter cannot be true. By looking at economic activity that occurs *after* the appearance of the achievement imagery, he has eliminated the possibility that the imagery is caused by the economic activity.

SUMMARY

1. The cognitive approach to motivation attempts to include a consideration of the role of thinking, feeling, and believing in motivated behavior.

2. Cognitive consistency theories are all based upon the idea that we prefer cognitive consistency and that inconsistencies among our thoughts, beliefs, opinions, and behaviors can generate motivation.

3. The motivational state aroused by cognitive inconsistency is often thought to resemble a drive state.

4. Balance theory holds that we will attempt to establish harmony among our feelings about people, objects, and events.

5. Balance theory involves an analysis of eight different triads each composed of a person, another person or object, and the feelings among them. Four of the triads are balanced and four are unbalanced. Imbalance produces motivation to achieve balance.

6. Balance theory is not popular now and has been criticized for its lack of precision.

7. Cognitive dissonance theory became more popular than balance theory, even though it is another example of cognitive consistency theory.

8. Cognitive dissonance theory also maintains that inconsistencies among our cognitions are motivating.

9. Two congitions can be consonant, dissonant, or irrelevant to one another.

10. Dissonance operates like a drive.

11. The dissonance analysis is also related to the analysis of conflict.

12. If the sum of dissonant elements outweighs the sum of consonant elements, then dissonance exists.

13. If consonant elements outweigh dissonance elements, in terms of both number and importance, then no dissonance exists.

14. Dissonance may be reduced by adding consonant elements or by changing dissonant elements.

15. Dissonance will be reduced by changing whatever is easiest to change, whether it involves the addition of consonant elements, the changing of existing cognition, the changing of behavior, or some combination of these.

16. Making decisions inevitably produces some dissonance.

17. Threats can be used to induce forced compliance, which creates dissonance.

18. The greatest amount of dissonance will be produced when the pressure to act contrary to one's beliefs is just barely enough to get the person to act.

19. Rewards can also produce forced compliance effects.

20. Commitment, consequences, and free choice are all crucial elements in the determination of dissonance.

21. Self-perception theory is an alternative to dissonance theory.

22. Dissonance theory has become less popular as competing theories took over and as its weaknesses became apparent.

23. In its most general form, expectancy-value theory maintains that our level of motivation is determined by our expectations about how likely it is that we will attain a goal and how much we value that goal.

24. The study of achievement motivation is the best-known example of expectancy-value theory.

25. Murray developed the Thematic Apperception Test (TAT), a projective test, to measure human motives, including achievement motivation.

26. McCelland extended the use of the TAT in measuring the need to achieve.

27. The validity and reliability of the TAT have been extensively investigated.

28. It may be possible to increase achievement motivation through certain training procedures.

29. Achievement motivation may be related to early independence training, high parental expectations about achievement, high rewards for achievement, and low domination of the child by the father.

30. Atkinson proposed that net achievement motivation is the result of the interaction between hope of success and fear of failure, which we all possess to varying degrees.

31. Hope of success, or the tendency to approach an achievement task, is a function of our estimate of achieving success, how much we value the goal, and our stable long-term interest in achieving success.

32. Fear of failure, or the tendency to avoid achievement tasks, is a result of our personality disposition to avoid failure (measured by the TAQ), by our estimate of how likely it is that we will fail, and by how unpleasant we feel failure will be.

33. Overall, or net, achievement motivation is a result of the combination of the two.

34. Atkinson's theory predicts that when we are more interested in avoiding failure than in trying for success, we will choose tasks that are either very easy or very difficult.

35. When we are more interested in pursuing success than in avoiding failure, then we will choose tasks that are of an intermediate level of difficulty.

36. The hypothesis that women in America fear success stimulated a great deal of research but is probably an inadequate explanation of female achievement behavior.

37. McCelland has shown that increases and decreases in the economic activity of entire countries are preceeded by corresponding increases and decreases in achievement motivation as reflected by achievement imagery found in that country's literature.

CHAPTER 9

Attribution Theory

THE ATTRIBUTION APPROACH

Suppose you own a restaurant that features home delivery. Your delivery person has just quit her job and you are trying to hire someone to replace her. You have two candidates. Both look good to you except that each of them has had one minor car accident in the last year. What do you do? Your impulse is to try to determine the causes of each of the accidents. To what can these two accidents be attributed? Suppose you find that one of them was the applicant's fault (he went through a red light and hit a bus) whereas the other resulted from bad luck (someone else ran a light and hit the job applicant). Clearly, once you have made these attributions, or assigned these causes, you will offer the job, all else being equal, to the second candidate.

In this example we see that we are motivated to find out the causes of things that go on around us. In turn, these inferences about causes can affect our future behavior. This process of inferring causes, and then basing our behavior upon those inferences, is at the very heart of attribution theory.

It is not a rare or unusual process. According to attribution theory, we do it all the time. Not only do we make inferences about other people, based upon their behavior, but we make inferences about *ourselves* as well. For example, suppose you yell at someone and hurt her feelings. Later you wonder why you did it. Was it because you are a nasty person? Was it just the result of a "bad day" and not likely to happen again? Was it because you, normally a very serene person, had been pushed to your limit by that obnoxious other person? Clearly your future behavior can be strongly affected by which of these alternative interpretations you choose. Depending upon your inferences, you may end up apologizing or snubbing the other individual.

When we make inferences about other people's ideas, wants, wishes, and desires, we do so on the basis of limited and sometimes ambiguous information. All we have is overt behavior; we can't crawl inside their heads and observe exactly what is going on in there. As a result, we make errors in this attribution process. As we shall see, some of these errors are systematic and predictable.

Attribution theory argues, first, that we are motivated to determine causes, second, that we base our behavior on those inferences, and, third, that there are general principles and rules that guide this overall process. This process is not random, chaotic, and unpredictable. It is lawful, ordered, and within our capacity to understand.

Although we do spend a lot of time and effort trying to determine the causes of events in the world, we don't *always* do so. We don't constantly walk about asking, "Why, why does my hair keep growing?" or, "Why do people love to watch football games?". Sometimes we seem very motivated to determine causes and sometimes we couldn't seem to care less. The reasons for this have not been heavily researched but some preliminary ideas have been forwarded. For example, when something unusual, or statistically improbable occurs, our motive to determine causes seems to be aroused. If an ordinary person walks across the street, we don't ask, "Why, why, why?" But if the same person walks across the same street completely unclothed, we immediately begin to try to determine the reason for the unexpected behavior. "Is the person mentally ill?" "Is this a prank?"

Unpleasant or negative events also seem to arouse our need to find causes. The individual stricken with cancer may spend hours in the library learning about the disease. A couple having marital problems may seek professional assistance in rooting out and defining the core issues. The child who does not make a Little League team may try to find out why.

Uncertainly about the future can lead to a search for causes, too. A student who is accepted by a college may seek to understand the characteristics of the school and how they may affect him in the future. In other words, when events have had, or can have, a personal effect on our state of well-being, then we seem motivated to understand causes.

HEIDER'S NAIVE PSYCHOLOGY

Heider (1958), whose name we have already encountered in connection with balance theory, began the process of theorizing about attributions.

Two Needs

According to Heider, much of our behavior is propelled by two needs. The first of these is the need to *understand* the world around us. Second we want to *control* the world around us. We want to be able to control our destiny and to arrange things such that our life will be as pleasant as possible.

Heider argues that we can't possibly satisfy these two motives unless we can *predict* behavior. We must be able to predict events around us. If we make a reservation for a hotel room and a car, then we must be able to count on a room and a car rather than excuses. If we turn in a term paper we need to be able to count on the instructor's being fair. We need to be sure she won't shift grading policies and criteria in the middle of the semester.

Internal versus External Forces

When we make attributions about ourselves or about others, we tend to attribute the behavior in question to *either internal or external forces.* When you see someone crash his car into a telephone pole you can attribute that unfortunate piece of behavior either to internal or external causes. You might conclude that the person is a terrible driver or emotionally upset (internal causes), or you might conclude that another car forced the driver off the road (external cause). If you fail an exam you can attribute it to internal causes such as stupidity or a failure to study, or you can attribute it to external causes such as an unfair test or an overheated room.

In general, internal causes include such things as moods, effort, ability, attitudes, and personality predispositions. External causes include just about everything else that is external to the person in question, whether that person be you or someone else. When we speak of internal versus external causation we are talking about *locus of control.*

Stable versus Unstable Causes

In addition to attributing causes to internal or external factors, we also tend to make judgments about whether those causes are *stable or unstable.* For example, suppose we conclude that the accident victim was a victim of his own poor driving (an internal attribution). We then have the choice of deciding whether this cause is stable (he is always a poor driver) or unstable (he is sometimes a good driver and sometimes a poor one).

Similarly, we can make stability judgments about our own behavior. If we fail an exam and attribute it internally to "test panic," then we can conclude either that we always panic or that we only panic some of the time. If we make an external attribution, such as the instructor being unfair, then we can conclude that he is always unfair (stable) or that he is only sometimes unfair (unstable).

Achievement and Attribution

Heider's distinctions among these various attributional factors have found their way into more recent work. For example, Weiner (1974, 1980), in his consideration of achievement motivation, has presented the analysis contained in Table 9.1. When we succeed or fail at some achievement task we tend to attribute that performance to one of four factors including *ability*, *effort*, *luck* or *task difficulty*. Weiner pointed out that these four factors actually represent the four combinations of stability and locus of control depicted in Table 9.1. Let us say we do well on an exam and attribute it to our ability. According

TABLE 9.1. Weiner's Conception of the Perceived Determinants of Behavior.

	Locus of control	
Stability	*Internal*	*External*
Stable	Ability	Task difficulty
Unstable	Effort	Luck

From Weiner, B. *Achievement Motivation and Attribution Theory.* Morristown, N.J.: General Learning Press, 1974, p. 6.

to Weiner, ability represents an internal stable determinant of behavior. If we attribute our success (or failure) to effort, then we are referring to an internal unstable determinant. Task difficulty is a stable external factor. And finally, luck is an unstable external factor.

Weiner and his associates have done a great deal of work that shows that how we account for our success or failure can have important implications for our future behavior. For example, people's expectations about success or failure can be heavily affected by the kinds of attributions that were made with regard to similar tasks in the past. If you fail a calculus test and attribute the failure to a lack of ability, then you may anticipate failure on upcoming tests. However, if you attribute that initial failure to bad luck then you will be less likely to anticipate failure on subsequent tests. These two different attributions could have important effects in your life. If you believe that your initial failure was caused by a lack of ability, you may give up trying. However, if you believe that the failure was just the result of bad luck, then you will continue to put forth effort and hope for better luck in the future.

Weiner has applied an attributional analysis to the problem of trying to understand achievement motivation. Recall from the last chapter that high-achievement people pursue, approach, and work hard at achievement tasks whereas low-achievement people are those who avoid achievement-related tasks. What accounts for these different behaviors? Weiner thinks it has to do with the fact that high- and low-achievement people attribute success and failure to different causes.

For example, among other things, Weiner believes that high-achievement people attribute past successes to ability. Thus, believing that they must have ability because they have succeeded in the past, they expect success in the future. Therefore they approach new achievement-related tasks. What about when they have *failed* in the past? Interestingly, this *also* leads to future approach toward achievement tasks. This is because, in addition to attributing success to ability, high-achievement people also attribute past success to effort. If they have failed in the past they believe that the failure was, at least in part, caused by a lack of effort. So they try harder in the future. After failure they increase, rather than decrease, their effort.

Weiner says that low-achievement people avoid achievement-related tasks because they attribute past failures to a lack of ability and past success to external elements. They believe they failed because they lack ability so they avoid achievement tasks in the future, expecting further failure. They believe that external factors, such as luck, account for past successes. So there is little motivation for them to put out a lot of effort to succeed in the future.

Weiner's work, and there is a great deal of it, represents an important bridge between the older conceptions of achievement described in Chapter 8 and the newer, currently very popular, attributional approach. In essence, Weiner is arguing that our tendencies to approach or avoid achievement tasks are determined by what we *think* about our past experiences and how we interpret them. Two people can have the very same experiences but interpret them quite differently. Weiner has extended Heider's naive psychology into the analysis of achievement motivation.

Invariance

Heider argued that we make causal attributions by using what he called the *principle of invariance* which is what forms the basis of the scientific method. The principle of invariance refers to the fact that we make attributions when a particular cause is associated with a particular effect *across a number of different conditions*. For example, suppose you get a better grade on a math test than your friend, but she gets better grades on all your other common tests. Do you conclude, on the basis of this one test, that your math ability is higher than hers? No, you don't come to that conclusion unless you get higher math grades on a whole series of tests. If you *always* get better math grades than she does, regardless of the course or instructor, then you finally attribute your success to high ability. If you *invariably* get better math grades, then you make a causal attribution.

If an employer always hires blacks for low-paying positions but always opposes efforts to hire them for better-paying jobs, then we conclude that he is a racist. If team A always beats team B but never beats team C then we conclude that team A has intermediate ability.

Fundamental Attribution Error

We have already mentioned that our ability to make attributions, or to identify causes, is not perfect. We do make errors. People who bet on horse races know only too well the extent to which they can be wrong. If horse A wins one race and the gambler assumes it was because of ability, then he may bet on it again only to discover, painfully and expensively, that luck, the competition, or some other external factors accounted for the first victory.

Investigators have discovered that there are regular, consistent errors that creep into our efforts to identify causes. The errors we make are not random and unpredictable. Rather, many of them are systematic and predictable. The term *fundamental attribution error* (Ross, 1977) refers to one of the pervasive mistakes we make. Simply put, we tend to *overestimate* the extent to which people's behavior is determined by their stable inner dispositions and *underestimate* the extent to which the external environment or situation determines behavior. If we observe a person being mean, we tend to attribute the behavior to a "mean disposition" and underestimate the impact of the environment. (The person may have been driven to meanness by conditions that would propel even the most saintly person to aggressive behavior.) If we observe cowardly behavior, we overestimate the cowardice of the person and underestimate the frightening impact of the situation.

The fundamental attribution error has been demonstrated experimentally. For example, Jones and Harris (1967) gave subjects essays that were supposedly written by other students. The essays were either pro-Castro or anti-Castro. (This experiment took place when most Americans were against Castro.) Furthermore, subjects were told that in some cases the writers were free to choose which position they wished to defend (pro- or anti-Castro) whereas other writers had no choice; they were assigned either the pro- or anti-position and had to support that position regardless of their true opinion. The subjects who read these essays then had to estimate the writer's true position. The results are contained in Table 9.2. Notice first that in the choice condition pro- and anti-essays were easily attributed, as

TABLE 9.2. Degree of Pro-Castro Attitudes Attributed to Writers

Condition	Speech direction	
	Pro-Castro	Anti-Castro
Choice	59.6	17.4
No choice	44.1	22.9

Jones, E. E., and Harris, V. A. The attribution of attitudes. *Journal of Experimental Social Psychology*, 1967, 3, 1–24, pp. 6, 10.

expected, to underlying pro- and anti-Castro attitudes, respectively. But notice what happened in the no-choice condition. Here, even though the subject *knew* that the writer had been forced to take a position, the subject *still* felt that the written essay expressed the writer's opinion. This is the fundamental attribution error. The subjects underestimated the impact of being forced to defend a particular position and overestimated the importance of the writer's internal disposition. "If he wrote a pro-Castro essay then he must be a pro-Castro person, regardless of the fact that he had no choice about which position he would defend." It is illogical, but there it is, the tendency to overestimate the importance of dispositional, or internal, factors.

Stimulus Prominence Error creeps into our attributions in another related way. We tend to overestimate the importance of *salient, prominent,* or *conspicuous* stimuli when we make attributions. If a classroom is getting behind in its work, we tend to attribute the slowdown to those children making the most noise when in fact the true cause may be that other quiet students are egging the loud ones on. Politicians who are the most prominent receive the blame or credit for events over which they have little control. The barking growling dog is the one that is blamed for biting the child. The most prominent stimulus is, in fact, often the true causal agent. But not always. Sometimes we overestimate its importance.

Taylor and Fiske (1975) did a clever experiment that demonstrates our tendency to attribute too much significance to prominent stimuli. "Observers" and "actors" were arranged on chairs as depicted in Figure 9.1.

Observers were true subjects whereas the actors were confederates of the experimenter. Actors A and B engaged in a five-minute conversation during which they both contributed equal amounts of direction and information. They discussed mundane topics that would be expected in the case of two people who had just met. After the discussion, the observers were asked to judge which of the two actors set the tone and direction of the conversation and which contributed the most information. In other words, observers were asked to estimate which actor "caused the conversation."

From where observers 1 and 2 sat, actor B faced them whereas actor A faced away from them. Actor A faced observers 5 and 6 whereas actor B faced away from them. The assumption made in

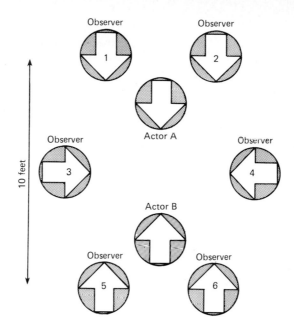

FIGURE 9.1
Seating arrangement of actors and observers. People looked in the direction the arrows are pointing. (Adapted from Taylor, S. E., & Fiske, S. T. Point of view and perception of causality. Journal of Personality and Social Psychology. 1975, 32, 439–445. Fig. on p. 441. Copyright 1975 by the American Psychological Association. Reprinted by permission.)

this experiment was that an actor who was faced would be more prominent and salient than an actor who was facing away from the observer. As predicted, it was found that observers 1 and 2 said that actor B was a stronger causal agent in the conversation whereas observers 5 and 6 said that actor A was more important. Remember, there actually was no difference between the two actors in terms of the amount they contributed to the conversation.

Finally, notice in Figure 9.1 that observers 3 and 4 were seated equally distant from both actors. Because neither actor was more salient than the other, it was predicted that observers 3 and 4 would attribute equal causal weight to the two actors. This prediction was supported.

KELLEY'S THEORY

So far we have discussed Heider's theory of attribution and looked at some of the extensions of his thinking, including Weiner's attributional analysis of achievement motivation and the concept of a fundamental attribution error. Harold Kelley (1967, 1973) has further refined and extended the concept of attribution and has developed what many consider to be the fullest system of this type.

Distinctiveness, Consensus, and Consistency

As we have seen, Heider proposed that we apply the principle of invariance when we make causal attributions; we look for a relationship between a cause and an effect across a number of different conditions. Kelley has accepted and expanded this idea. But Kelley also analyzes exactly how people go about determining causality. In a sense, we ask ourselves three different questions. Let us begin with an example. Suppose a friend of yours goes to a basketball game and comes home raving about the team. She says you *must* see them play. You want to decide whether or not to go to the next game. But you want to be sure the team is exceptional as you do not want to waste your time. So, according to Kelley, you ask yourself three different kinds of questions. First, you concern yourself with *distinctiveness* and ask, "Is this the only team your friend has raved about, or does she rave about every single team she watches?" Second, you concern yourself with *consistency*, and ask, "Does she always rave about this team or is she sometimes completely indifferent to it?" Third, you address the problem of *consensus* and ask, "Do other people think this is a good team, or is she the only one who does so?" For you to conclude that the team is good, all of these questions must be answered appropriately. Your friend must like this team consistently but not all other teams, and other people must also like this team.

For Kelley the overall process of making causal attributions consists of sorting through three different kinds of information. In this way his theory represents a refinement of Heider's theory, which, although including the idea of invariance, did not spell out the process by which invariance was established.

How Powerful Is Consensus? According to Kelley's theory the three factors we have been talking about (distinctiveness, consensus, consistency) should all be about equally important in determining attribution. But a number of experiments have suggested that Kelley was wrong in assuming that consensus was as important as the other two factors (see McArthur, 1976, Wells and Harvey, 1977). For instance, in the basketball example given, it turns out that what other people, the crowd, think about the team is of relatively little importance in determining causality. We tend to be relatively indifferent to consensus information.

Feldman, Higgins, Karlovac, and Ruble (1976) did a study, however, which suggests that consensus information is sometimes important and sometimes not. Specifically, it seems that consensus information is important when the subject makes an attribution in the absence of strong, clear information. A description of the Feldman et al. study will make this clear. Subjects watched videotapes containing five people, one of whom was shown picking the item he liked best from a group of objects. After this person made the choice, the other four people in the film were also asked if they liked that item selected by the first person best too. Half the time the four people said they did like it best too. This is the high-consensus condition. Half the time they said they did not like that item best (low consensus).

Then the real subject watching the film was asked the following question. Does the first person's choice of the selected object tell more about the actor or more about the object? According to Kelley, high consensus should lead subjects to conclude that the chosen object is best. Low consensus, on the other hand, should lead the subjects to conclude that the choice reveals something about the actor and not necessarily the object. Because only the first actor chose that object, and no one else did, then that object is probably not the best even though it was selected by the first actor.

The results that were obtained in the experiment as we have described it are depicted by the solid line in Figure 9.2. When consensus was high, subjects made an object attribution. When consensus was low, a person attribution was made. Consensus was important in determining attribution. But, so far, we have only described half the

FIGURE 9.2
Attribution as a function of consensus and information. (Adapted from Feldman, N. S., Higgens E. T., Karlovac, M., & Ruble, D. Use of consensus information in causal attributions as a function of temporal presentation and availability of direct information. Journal of Personality and Social Psychology, *1976, 34, 694–698. Fig. on p. 696. Copyright 1976 by the American Psychological Association. Reprinted by permission.*

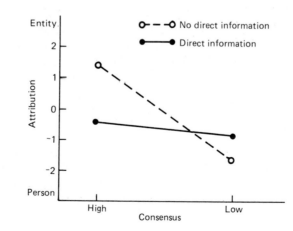

experiment. In this first half the subjects did *not see* the objects that the actors in the film were choosing among. Thus they had no direct concrete information about the objects in question. The second half of the study was just like the first half we have already described except for the fact that these subjects *were* shown in the film the objects from which the actors were choosing. In this case the results were quite different as shown by the dashed line in Figure 9.2. Here, where direct concrete information concerning the objects was available, consensus had no impact on attribution. Subjects were no more likely to make an object attribution in the high-consensus condition than they were in the low-consensus condition. Thus it seems that consensus information is used most heavily when there is an absence of other, more concrete sorts of information.

The Augmentation Principle

We are likely to attribute a behavior to a strong internal disposition if that behavior occurs even when external pressures *against* that behavior exist. For example, if someone speaks up as a lonely minority voice against a strong cohesive opposing majority, then we can conclude that that individual must feel exceptionally strong about the issue in question; otherwise he would keep quiet. Kelley calls this the *augmentation* principle. The occurrence of the behavior in the face of opposing external pressures augments the strength of the disposition that we attribute to the actor.

The Discounting Principle

Kelley introduces the *discounting principle* by saying, "The role of a given cause in producing a given effect is discounted if other plausible causes are also present" (Kelley, 1972).

Suppose you bump into an acquaintance on the street and he says, "Give me a call sometime. We'll get together and chew the fat." You say, "O.K.," and think, "What a nice guy. He must really like me." But at the same time you remember he is a member of a local charitable organization and may be thinking about trying to get a contribution out of you. So you discount your initial interpretation and say, "Well, maybe he doesn't like me all that much. Maybe he likes me but also wants some money."

Notice that the initial cause is discounted, but not counted out. We may still believe that the person likes us but may be less confident about that being the only reason for his wanting to get together with us.

The Jones and Harris (1967) study described earlier can serve as a good example of the discounting principle. If you will recall, subjects read essays written about Castro either by people who were free to choose an anti- or pro-Castro position or by people who were assigned a position. The fundamental attribution error was demonstrated by the fact that, even though the subjects *knew* that the topic position had been assigned, they still felt that essays in the assigned condition reflected the writer's true position. On the other hand, subjects did show a *reduced* confidence in their belief that the essays written in the assigned condition reflected the writer's true position relative to the essays written in the free-choice condition. This is the discounting principle in action. Subjects still believed that the essays reflected the writer's true position but they discounted this idea. They were less confident about this interpretation, because of the existence of the alternative possible cause (that the writers were merely taking a position to satisfy the requirements of the experiment.) This single study demonstrates *both* discounting and the fundamental attribution error.

Thibaut and Riecken (1955) also did some work that demonstrates the discounting principle. They had subjects get both a high- and a low-status person to go along with a suggestion made by the subject. Subjects were then asked why the high- and low-status people complied with their directive. What would the discounting principle predict here? The prediction is that the low-status people will be seen as complying in response to external pressure simply because they are of low status and subject to external pressure. This is what was found. However, the high-status people were perceived as being less susceptible to external pressure. Because they are high status they do not have to do what others ask of them. Hence, there must have been some other reason for their compliance. Subjects tended to conclude that the high-status people went along with their suggestion because they wanted to anyway. In the case of the high-status people the external pressure cause was discounted and supplemented by the internal cause. The results of the study supported these predictions. Low-status people were seen as complying because of external pressure alone. High-status people were seen as complying because of some mixture of external pressure and internal willingness.

ACTORS VERSUS OBSERVERS

Having looked at some of the theoretical formulations concerning the kinds of causal attributions people make, including the work of Heider and Kelley, we now turn to some of the interesting areas of research that developed out of, and revolve around, the concept of attribution.

The first of these has to do with the fact that the fundamental attribution error (overestimating internal or dispositional factors) seems to hold true for observers but not for actors. In fact, actors seem to lean in the other direction and overestimate the external causes of their own behavior. For example, suppose a teacher (the observer) catches a child cheating on a test. She will tend to attribute this behavior to internal causes; the child is dishonest, sneaky, unfair, and so on. The child, on the other hand, will tend to overestimate external courses; everyone else was cheating, the test was unfair, and so on. In other words, when we observe someone else doing something we attribute that behavior to internal or dispositional causes. But if we are the one that is doing the behavior then we tend to attribute our own behavior to external causes. The effect has been demonstrated experimentally many times. For example, Nisbett, Caputo, Legant, and Marecek (1973) had college students tell why they liked their girlfriend and why they had chosen their college major. They were also asked to tell why their best friend had made his choice with respect to girlfriend and college major. The results indicated that the subjects were more likely to make internal attributions with respect to their friend's behavior and more likely to make external attributions with respect to their own behavior. Thus they chose their own girlfriend because she was bright, interesting, and attractive whereas they believed their friend chose his girlfriend because he, the friend, needed a warm person and hated being alone. Similarly, the subject chose his major because it was likely to lead to a good job whereas the friend chose his major because he always loved animals so a biology major was perfect.

Given that the actor-observer difference can be easily demonstrated, we can ask the question, "Why?" Why do observers make internal attributions and actors make external attributions? Jones and Nisbett (1972) have proposed what seems to be a most reasonable explanation. They argue that the difference is the result of the different perspectives held by actors and observers. An observer is attending to and focusing on the actor. Therefore, the observer tends to attribute the observed behavior to the dispositional qualities of the actor. The actor, on the other hand, busily engaged in the behavior, is not focusing on himself. To the contrary, he is looking outward and is not the center of his own attentional processes. Hence, he tends to attribute his behavior to the external events he is attending to.

Here is an example of what Jones and Nisbett are talking about. Suppose you are watching a basketball game. One player skillfully passes the ball to another who then makes a spectacular shot. You (as an observer) might conclude that the shot was made because the shooter has tremendous ability (an internal attribution). The shooter, on the other hand, so busy out there on the court and not focusing on or watching himself, might make an external attribution. He might conclude that the shot was made because of the first player's great pass. "Hey, he was the one who got the ball to me. I just shot it like anyone would."

Storms (1973) argued that if the observer-actor difference really is caused by the different perspectives held by the observer and actor, then the difference should be reversed if the perspective is reversed. Accordingly, he set up an experimental situation in which perspectives were reversed. When actors were shown films of themselves interacting with another person, thereby making them into observers, they tended to increase their dispositional attributions. Similarly, when observers of an interaction were shown films of exactly what the actor saw, they tended to increase their situational attributions.

Although the "different perspectives" hypothesis seems to be a very popular interpretation of the actor-observer difference, there are other interpretations. Jones and Nisbett (1972), the authors of the "different perspectives" idea, also proposed what we can call the differential information hypothesis. According to this hypothesis, the actor-observer difference occurs because the actor has immediate information about her past history, her feelings, her desires, and her behavior in past similar situations. The observer, on the other hand, has none of this inside information and can assess internal states only indirectly. The argument is that the actor knows how variable she has been in the past and how inconsistent and complex her past behavior has been. Thus she is more likely to conclude that her present behavior is likely to be determined by external factors.

The two interpretations, different perspectives and different information, do not necessarily have to be mutually exclusive. To the contrary, both may play a complex role in the attributional process.

INTRINSIC VERSUS EXTRINSIC MOTIVATION

Another interesting area of research has to do with the distinction between intrinsic and extrinsic motivation. We are intrinsically motivated when we do something "for the fun of it," or for no other reason than to perform the behavior. We sing in the shower, not because we expect applause, or because we are trying to earn money, but merely because we like to do it. We do crossword puzzles, paint pictures, and look at the sunset because it is intrinsically rewarding to do so. We don't expect any external reward. Extrinsic motivation, on the other hand, refers to situations in which we do act because we expect some external reward. We may only show up at the office because we need the money. We may only go to school to please our parents. We may be exceptionally polite to a particular individual because we want something from her.

Obviously, this distinction has important implications for various segments of our society such as employers and teachers. If people do their jobs because they love the work (intrinsic motivation), then the employer will be sitting in the catbird seat. However, if work is extrinsically motivated, then the employer will constantly have to push, prod, promise, and reward the employees. Similarly, the teacher's dream is the student who learns for learning's sake, who exercises curiosity, and who pursues knowledge for its intrinsically rewarding qualities (see Rosenfield, Folger, and Adelman, 1980).

The Overjustification Effect

Behavior need not be solely the results of intrinsic motivation, or completely the result of extrinsic motivation. Clearly, any given behavior can be both intrinsically and extrinsically motivated. We may like our job and do it for money, too. A child may enjoy learning new words and also be rewarded by parental praise.

The interaction of intrinsic and extrinsic rewards is not a simple one. They do not just add together producing greater motivation. In fact, quite to the contrary, the introduction of external motivation appears to undermine or lessen intrinsic motivation. Suppose a two-year-old has been busy painting a picture, slopping paint around with great abandon, enjoying the intrinsically rewarding properties of the activity. Then, at some point, adults begin to praise and reward the child for painting (extrinsic reward). In the future it will be found, unfortunately, that the child will be less likely to paint for painting's sake and will be more likely only to paint when an external reward is expected. External reward "spoils the fun" of intrinsically motivated behavior. This is what we mean when we say extrinsic reward undermines intrinsic motivation, and it is referred to as the *overjustification effect* (Lepper, Greene, and Nisbett, 1973).

The following are some experimental demonstration of the overjustification effect. Deci (1971, 1972) ran a series of studies using puzzles. Three groups of subjects worked the puzzles that were assumed to be intrinsically motivating. One third of the subjects was told ahead of time that they would receive money for completing the puzzles. One third was told *after* they had completed the puzzles that they would receive money for doing so. The final third were told nothing and were given no money. Then, after the puzzle session, all three groups were left alone to wait for awhile. They were free to do whatever they wished during this wait. They believed that the experiment was over. Unknown to them the experimenters were interested in learning whether they would return to the puzzles on their own. The idea was that if they did work the puzzles it would have to be intrinsically motivated behavior because, as far as they knew, the experiment was over.

The overjustification effect was demonstrated by the fact that the subjects who had been told ahead of time that they would receive money were much less likely to do the puzzles than were the subjects who had been told nothing. The puzzles were still "fun" for this latter group whereas the money group's interest in the activity had been reduced.

Interestingly, the group that had been told about the money reward *after* completing the puzzles was as likely to return to the puzzles as the no-money group. Apparently, because they had not actually been working *for* money, intrinsic motivation was not undermined.

Although there are other interpretations of the overjustification effect (see Arkes, 1979), one of the most popular explanations revolves around the attributional concept of discounting described earlier. As previously noted, Kelley's discounting principle states that the importances of one cause will be discounted or lessened if other possible causes exist. This principle predicts the overjustification effect. If a

Overjustification and Discounting

person is not given an external reward, then he concludes, "I must be doing this because it is fun." However, if he is given a reward he may, to some degree, conclude, "I'm doing this because I'm being paid to do it, and not just for the fun of it." Believing that he does the activity for money, he will therefore be less likely to do it for nothing.

Behavior Modification and Overjustification   In Chapter 6 we discussed behavior modification in some detail. Essentially, behavior modification refers to attempts to modify behavior through the application of the principles of conditioning. One of the most common methods is the use of rewards. Desired behaviors are rewarded. One of the problems dicussed in Chapter 6 was that behavior modification effects are good and strong as long as the experimenter keeps supplying those rewards. But once the rewards are removed, the behavior often disappears. This is a serious problem for behavior modifiers because it means that modified behaviors will often fail to carry back into the subject's everyday life.

It has been suggested that part of the problem may relate to the overjustification effect (Friedman, Sears, and Carlsmith, 1981). For example, once we start giving mental patients tokens for desirable behaviors, any *intrinsic* interest the patient might of had in those behaviors is lessened. Then, when the tokens are removed, behavior may backslide seriously because not only have we removed extrinsic reward but we have managed, inadvertently, to reduce intrinsic motivation as well.

ATTRIBUTION AND EMOTION

The general attributional approach to the understanding of human behavior has been extended to a consideration of emotional experiences. Two areas of research are of particular interest. The first of these, learned helplessness, was introduced in Chapter 6. The second has to do with what is commonly called *misattribution*. Before looking at each of these research areas in detail a few comments about the study of emotion in general are in order.

Definitions of Emotion   What is an emotion? This is a difficult question. Obviously, emotions are very important in our lives. Emotions drive us here and there, and have an enormous motivational impact on us. Emotions serve as motivators. However, it is not so easy to define emotion. Emotions tend to be positive or negative; there aren't any neutral emotions. About the best anyone can do in trying to define emotions is to characterize them as strong, relatively uncontrollable feelings that affect our behavior. It is not an entirely satisfactory definition, because it really just introduces another difficult-to-define word (i.e., feelings). But it can give the reader a rough idea of what psychologists are pursuing when they study emotions. Young (1973) defines emotion as, "A strong visceralized, affective distrubance, originating within the psychological situation, and revealing itself in bodily changes, in behavior, and in conscious experience" (p. 440). Strongman (1973) defines it this way: "Emotion is feeling, it is a bodily state involving various physical structures, it is gross or fine-grained behavior, and it occurs in particular situations" (p. 1).

One problem that has plagued the study of emotion is that emotion can be viewed from at least three different perspectives. First, we can focus upon the *subjective experiences* of emotion. We have all *felt* emotions such as wonder, fear, anger, grief, and jealousy. Second, we can focus upon *external behavior*, such as fleeing, crying, laughing, or striking out when we study emotion. Third, we can focus upon *physiological events*. A number of significant physiological changes accompanies strong emotion. Some of these are included in Table 9.3.

You might say, "So what if there are three different ways of looking at emotion? They must all be equally valid." This is a good point, but the problem becomes apparent when we realize that changes in one

Three Perspectives

TABLE 9.3   *Some Physiological Changes Associated with Emotion**

1) The pupils of the eyes dilate.
2) Perspiration increases.
3) Breathing becomes more rapid.
4) Heart rate increases.
5) Blood pressure increases.
6) The level of sugar in the blood increases.
7) The gastrointestinal tract slows its actions.
8) Blood flows from the stomach to the brain and muscles.
9) The hairs on the skin become erect.

*Adapted from Houston, J. P., Bee, H., and Rimm, D. C. *Invitation to Psychology.* New York: Academic Press, 1983, Table 3 on p. 348.

of these three do not always correspond exactly with changes in the other dimensions. For example, suppose you become infuriated but effectively conceal your anger. If we focused exclusively on your external behavior, we would miss this internal turmoil completely. Or suppose you feign anger in order to "get your way." In this case external behavior would vary while internal physiological states and subjective feelings remained constant. The psychologist's efforts to understand emotion are complicated enormously by the lack of exact correspondence among these three aspects of the overall emotional event.

Classifying Emotions   It was once a common approach to try to list emotions (just as we saw it was once popular to try to list instincts). This strategy did not work out very well for a number of reasons. First, investigators could not agree about which were and which were not important emotions. Furthermore, there seem to be too many emotions, and too many shades of emotion, to allow efforts to classify them to be very helpful. Davitz (1970), for example, asked a large group of students to describe, in writings, their emotional states. He then looked over the responses and found no fewer than 556 different words and short phrases that described emotional conditions.

Efforts recently have been made in another direction. Rather than trying to list all possible shades of emotion, some investigations have attempted to identify some smaller set of crucial emotions, the numerous combinations of which can account for the many shades and varieties of emotional experience. For example, Plutchik (1980) suggests that there are only eight basic emotions (See Table 9.4). The complex interactions of these eight primary emotions are assumed to account for all of our rich and varied emotional life. However, the same problems remain; who is to say which small set of primary emotions is the correct set?

Thought Versus Emotion   We often, on an intuitive level, make a distinction between thought and emotion. We sometimes see the two elements as being in conflict with one another. For example, we say, "I know I have no *reason* to be angry with him but I can't help the way I feel." Or we say, "I really want to marry so-and-so but I know in my mind that it would be one of the decade's great errors." People refer to the heart ruling the head or vice versa. In other words, we tend to think of these two aspects of

TABLE 9.4. From Left to Right, the Sequence of Events Involved in Emotion According to Plutchik*

Stimulus Event	Inferred Cognition	Feeling	Behavior	Effect
Threat	"Danger"	Fear, terror	Running, or flying away	Protection
Obstacle	"Enemy"	Anger, rage	Biting, hitting	Destruction
Potential mate	"Possess"	Joy, ecstasy	Courting, mating	Reproduction
Loss of valued person	"Isolation"	Sadness, grief	Crying for help	Reintegration
Group member	"Friend"	Acceptance, trust	Grooming, sharing	Affiliation
Gruesome object	"Poison"	Disgust, loathing	Vomiting, pushing away	Rejection
New territory	"What's out there?"	Anticipation	Examining, mapping	Exploration
Sudden novel object	"What is it?"	Surprise	Stopping, alerting	Orientation

*Adapted from Plutchik, R. A general psychoevolutionary theory of emotion. In R. Plutchik and H. Kellerman (Eds.), *Emotion, theory, research, and experience*, Vol. I. New York: Academic Press, 1980, Tab. 1-2, p. 16.

our overall makeup as, if not actually at war with one another, at least distinct and separate facets of our personality.

However, no matter how appealing this distinction is, it is not as clear a distinction as we sometimes think it is. Quite simply, thought can influence emotion and emotion can determine thought. The two are closely intertwined. For example, thought can arouse emotion. If you learn that someone has said something nice about you, you will tend to develop similar feelings toward her. Similarly, if you buy a refrigerator, only to learn that it doesn't work, or was on sale down the block, these cognitions will lead to emotional states. Thought determines emotion.

It works the other way, too. Emotion can determine thought. If you are smitten by a beautiful young woman, and feel great positive regard for her, your cognitive evaluation of her will be affected. You will believe she is replete with positive qualities; she will, in your mind, be perfect.

The general idea that thought can affect emotional experience has intrigued attribution theoreticians. The two following topics (learned helplessness and misattribution) serve as expressions of this concern for the impact of thought and attributional processes upon the experience of emotion.

The Revised Theory of Learned Helplessness

Seligman's (1975) proposal that there is a correspondence between learned helplessness and depression is a prime example of the way that attributional processes become involved in emotional experiences. Refer, for a moment, back to the discussion of learned helplessness in Chapter 6. We learned that if a dog is subjected to a series of inescapable shocks it will, in the future, fail to learn a learnable avoidance response. The animal begins to act as though it had learned to be hopeless and helpless during the inescapable phase of the experiment.

Seligman and his associates (see Hiroto, 1974) were able to demonstrate similar effects using humans as subjects. Apparently we too will learn to give up and become helpless if we are subjected to inescapable noxious stimulation.

Seligman then went on to suggest that learned helplessness could serve as a model for some kinds of human depression. In particular, *reactive depression*, a common form of depression brought on by something unpleasant and uncontrollable in our environment, was thought to be best related to learned helplessness.

Widely acclaimed, Seligman's hypothesis also ran into a lot of trouble. A number of studies criticized Seligman's experimental work, whereas others presented results that do not support his hypothesis (see Costello, 1978; Willis and Blaney, 1978). The upshot of all of this was that it became apparent to all, including Seligman, that the original formulation was too simple. Specifically, the original formulation did not take into account important *cognitive* events that can influence and determine the nature of depression. To think of human depression in terms of dogs experiencing inescapable shock was a bold and useful step. But it was not enough. It did not explain why the nature of depression is heavily influenced by attributional processes. For example, the nature of our depression about a particular failure might vary depending upon whether we attribute that failure to a personal shortcoming or to some global inescapable factor. It began to be clear that depression is heavily affected by what we *think* about the causes, nature, and consequences of that depression.

One of Seligman's own studies underscored the importance of attribution in the determination of depression. Klein, Fencil-Morse, and Seligman (1976) had depressed and nondepressed subjects work on unsolvable tasks. One third of the subjects were told that most poeple could solve these tasks. This would lead these subjects to believe that their failure was caused by their own lack of ability. One third of the subjects were told that almost no one could solve these problems. These subjects would believe that their failure was the result of external factors and not "their fault." The final third of the subjects were told nothing.

Then, in a second phase of the experiment, all subjects were asked to work solvable anagrams. The times it took the various groups to solve the anagram problems are depicted in Figure 9.3. The crucial aspect of these results is the fact that depressed subjects who had been led to believe that their earlier failure was not their fault (it was externally caused) did just fine on the anagram task. In other words, their attribution about the cause of their earlier failure determined later performance.

As a result of the growing belief that attributions affect depression and performance, Abramson, Seligman, and Teasdale (1978) presented a sweeping reformulation of their model of depression. The revised model centers around three dimensions, including the *per-*

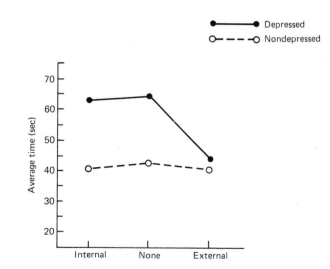

FIGURE 9.3
Time to solve anagrams as a function of attribution and depression.
(Adapted from Klein, D., Fencil-Morse, E., & Seligman, M. Learned helplessness, depression, and the attribution of failure. Journal of Personality and Social Psychology, *1976, 33, 508–516. Copyright 1976 by the American Psychological Association. Reprinted by permission.)*

sonal-universal, the *specific-global*, and *stable-unstable* dimensions, all of which we now consider.

1. Personal versus Universal Attributions. Seligman and his associates pointed out when people fail, or perceive that they lack control over a situation, they can attribute this lack of control to either personal or univesal causes. Suppose a student fails a test miserably. The student can attribute this failure either to personal causes, such as a lack of intelligence or effort on his own part, or to universal causes such as the extreme difficulty of the test. In the first case the student blames himself alone; he makes an internal attribution. In the second case the student makes an extenal attribution and blames his failure on the difficulty of the test.

Both personal and universal attributions can lead to poor performance in the future. But, according to Seligman, our sense of *self-esteem* or self-worth will only be affected when we make an internal or personal attribution. If we believe that everyone failed the test and that no one could possibly pass it then we don't feel so bad and don't "run ourselves down." However, if we make a personal or internal attribution, we blame ourselves. We believe we are no good and personally responsible for our failure. As a result, our self-esteem suffers. We feel less worthwhile.

Seligman was aware that depressed people tend to have a lowered sense of self-esteem and that they tend to blame themselves for their failures. By introducing the personal-universal dimension, he believed that some sense could be made of these well-known facts. It is only when a personal attribution is made that these conditions exist. If an external attribution is made a motivation deficit may exist but the low self-esteem so commonly associated with depression will not.

2. Specific versus Global Attributions. The second of Seligman's critical dimensions was introduced to account for the fact that helplessness sometimes seems to be quite general and sometimes quite specific. For example, one individual might feel helpless and hopeless in schoolwork but not nearly so helpless in the business world. Another individual might feel and display helplessness in *all* situations. Seligman's early formulation did not account for these striking differences in the generality of helplessness and depression.

By introducing his specific-global dimension, Seligman was able to shed light on these differences. He argues that people sometimes attribute their failures to specific circumstances (I never do well in school but I'm O.K. elsewhere) and sometimes to global factors (This just goes to show that I can't do anything right.)

People who make global attributions (I fail at everything) will show very little effort and will not attempt to overcome their perceived lack of control. People who make specific attributions may also show deficits in performance but not to the same extent.

3. Stable versus Unstable Attributions. Finally, Seligman's third dimension was introduced to account for the fact that some depressions seem to go on forever whereas others are quite short-lived. Again his early formulation could not account for these differences. People who make stable attributions (I flunked the exam because I am dumb) will tend to show longer-lasting depression than will individuals who make unstable attributions (I flunked that exam because I momentarily panicked).

In general the three dimensions of Seligman's new formulation provide much greater explanatory power than did the first version of the model. They go a long way toward encompassing some of the complexity that characterizes depression.

The following is an example of the kind of finding that is better explained by the reformulated model than by the original model. Douglas and Anisman (1975) advertised tasks as being either simple or difficult. One group of subjects experienced failure on the simple tasks and one group experienced failure on the difficult tasks. Then both groups were tested on additional tasks. The original model predicts that both groups should show poor performance on the second task because both had experienced unavoidable failure on the first tasks. But that is not what happened. Only the subjects who were told the original tasks were simple showed the subsequent poor performance. Subjects who believed the first tasks were difficult did just fine on the subsequent tasks. Clearly, the reformulated theory is better able to explain this result. Specifically, failure on the original simple task will lead to an internal attribution (I must be dumb if I can't do this) whereas failure on the difficult tasks would lead to an external attribution (I'm fine because no one could do these tasks successfully).

One of the most famous interpretations of emotion was developed independently and simultaneously by William James and Carl Lange (James, 1950; Lange; 1922). According to the James-Lange hypothesis, the emotions we feel are the result of physiological changes that occur

James-Lange Theory of Emotion

when we perceive emotion-producing stimuli. It goes like this: when you first see a rabid dog your body reacts strongly. Adrenalin would be pumped into your bloodstream, you would perspire, your heart would pound, and you would tremble. These physiological responses stimulate the experience of emotion. We feel afraid because we are sweating rather than sweating because we are afraid. We are sorrowful because we cry rather than cry because we are sad.

The theory, on an intuitive level, seems backwards. Most of us think of the physiological changes, such as perspiring, as being the *result* of emotion. But, according to the James and Lange hypothesis, it works the other way around; we first experience the physiological responses and then the emotion. Let us say you are crossing a rushing stream on a log. You slip, almost fall, but catch yourself at the last moment. What happens? As you stumble your physiological reactions go off as expected. But you don't actually feel fear until you catch yourself, have a moment to reflect on your escape, and feel the adrenalin rushing through your system.

But the James-Lange hypothesis has not faired well at all (see Bard, 1928; Cannon, 1927). The most difficult problem for the James-Lange position is that different emotions are *not* associated with clearly distinct physiological patterns. In fact, it is fair to say that most emotions are associated with the same, or roughly the same, overall general diffuse set of physiological changes. No one has been able to clearly differentiate emotions on the basis of their accompanying physiological response. Clearly, this flies in the face of the James-Lange hypothesis.

There are additional problems. For example, the physiological responses you display in connection with a given emotion may vary from one occasion to another. You might sweat one time you are angry but not every time you feel anger. In addition, people vary in terms of their physiological response; one person might always sweat when afraid whereas others might never sweat.

Schachter's Work   More recent thinking about emotion has emphasized the cognitive aspects of emotional experiences. Given that all emotions are associated with roughly the same physiological responses, why do we sometimes feel one emotion and somethimes another? According to this new way of thinking, we *interpret our internal state of arousal in terms of what is going on around us.* Emotion is determined by an undifferentiated state of physiological arousal plus a label (such as anger or happiness) that is determined by what we perceive to be happening in our environment.

For example, suppose you handle a snake for the first time. This event definitely arouses you. But how do you interpret this arousal? It could be fear or it could be pride and satisfaction. According to the cognitive interpretation of emotion, you will look around you for clues. If everyone else is screaming and yelling, you are likely to interpret your own internal state of arousal as, if not outright fear, at least uneasiness. On the other hand, if everyone around you is calmly supporting and encouraging you, you may interpret your physiological arousal as exhilaration and pride.

Schachter and his colleagues (Schachter, 1971; Schachter and Singer, 1962) have done some interesting experiments that, although controversial and not always supported by other data, do seem to provide evidence for the idea that we interpret undifferentiated internal arousal in terms of what is going on around us.

Subjects were first told that the experiment had to do with the effects of a new vitamin on vision. Then they were all given an injection (presumably of this new substance) and asked to fill out a questionnaire. Half of the subjects, called the experimental subjects, actually received an injection of adrenalin that causes an increase in breathing and heart rate and a feeling of edginess. One third of the adrenalin-injected subjects was told correctly how the drug would make them feel. One third was given no information about the effects of the drug. The final third of the adrenalin-injected experimental subjects was misinformed about the effects of the drug; they were told it would produce numbness, itching, and a headache. Control subjects were injected with a saline solution that has no perceptible physiological effects.

Then all subjects, both experimental and control, were asked to wait either with a happy, euphoric fellow subject (actually a confederate of the experimenter acting in a happy manner) or with an angry fellow subject (also a confederate of the experimenter).

Schachter predicted that groups experiencing unexplained internal arousal would interpret that arousal in terms of what was going on around them, and that is just what he found. The uninformed and misinformed experimental subjects were the ones with unexplained arousal. When the confederate acted in a euphoric manner, so did they. When the confederate was angry, they displayed anger too. Even though the internal arousal state was the *same* in these happy and angry conditions, the subjects interpreted that internal arousal quite differently.

Neither informed experimental nor control subjects were heavily affected by the confederates. Control subjects had no unexplained arousal to account for, and the correctly informed experimental subjects correctly attributed their feelings to the drug.

Misattribution   Schachter's work led to what are commonly called *misattribution studies.* These experiments demonstrate that it is possible to get people to misattribute their emotions to some environmental stimulus and thus to reduce their felt emotion. A few examples should suffice.

Nisbett and Schachter (1966) had a group of people take harmless sugar pills. Experimental subjects were told that the pill would produce marked physiological symptoms, such as trembling hands and heart palpitations. Control subjects were led to believe that the pill would produce no physiological symptoms. All subjects were then subjected to quite strong electric shocks. The dependent measure was how much the subjects felt the shock hurt. The idea was that the experimental subjects would attribute some of their reactions to the shock to the pill rather than to the shock. Control subjects, on the other hand, would attribute all of their discomfort to the shock. In agreement with this line of thinking, it was found that the control subjects found the shock to be more painful than did the experimental subjects.

Another study, by Storms and Nisbett (1970), also demonstrates how causal attributions can affect emotional experience. Storms and Nisbett gave two groups of insomniacs harmless sugar pills before they went to bed. One group was told that the pill would stir up and arouse the members. The other group was told that the pill would reduce arousal. The subjects who were told that the pill would be arousing got to sleep more quickly than normal because they attributed any feelings of arousal they had, not to the usual sorts of thoughts or feelings that normally kept them awake, but to the pill. The subjects who were told that the pill would calm them had even more than normal trouble getting to sleep. This was because they were thinking things like, "I must *really* be worried tonight because I just took a sedative and I still can't get to sleep."

These and other studies show the extent to which we interpret our inner states in terms of what goes on around us. But it would be an enormous mistake to conclude that all of our feelings are determined by the environment. Obviously, we do have inner resources, attitudes, beliefs, and feelings that persist regardless of the nature of the external environment.

SUMMARY

1. We are motivated to find the causes of events in the world around us and the causes of our own behavior.

2. In turn, these inferences about causality affect the way we behave.

3. We tend to seek the causes of events that are unusual and/or unpleasant and when we are uncertain about the future.

4. Heider's naive psychology, the first of the attribution theories, begins with the assumption that we all have two needs: 1) the need to understand the world around us and 2) the need to control the world around us.

5. Heider argues that to satisfy these two needs we must be able to predict events and to predict events we must know the causes of these events.

6. When we make attributional inferences, or make decisions about the causes of events, we tend to attribute events either to internal or external forces.

7. We also tend to attribute events to stable or unstable factors.

8. Achievement motivation has been analyzed in terms of attribution by Weiner and others.

9. According to Weiner, four factors contributing to success (ability, effort, luck, and task difficulty) can be understood in terms of the four possible combinations of the internal-external and stable-unstable dimensions.

10. High-achievement behavior can be seen as stemming from the fact that high-achievement people see past successes as being the result of ability and past failures as being the result of a lack of effort.

11. Low-achievement behavior may be caused by the fact that low achievers attribute past success to luck and past failure to lack of ability.

12. The principle of invariance refers to the fact that we make causal attributions when a particular cause is associated with a particular effect across a number of different conditions.

13. The fundamental attribution error refers to the fact that we tend to overestimate the importance of stable internal dispositions and underestimate the extent to which the environment determines behavior.

14. Stimuli that are salient or prominent tend to be assigned causal roles.

15. Kelley's theory holds that, when making attributions, we tend to ask questions about distinctiveness, consensus, and consistency.

16. The augmentation principle holds that we are likely to infer a strong internal disposition if an external pressure against the behavior in question exists.

17. The discounting principle holds that the role of a given causal agent is discounted if other plausible causes are present.

18. The fundamental attribution error holds true for observers but not for actors. Actors seem to overestimate external causes of their behavior.

19. Attempts to explain the actor-observer difference have centered around the different perspectives hypothesis and the differential information hypothesis.

20. We are intrinsically motivated when we do something "for the fun of it." Extrinsic motivation refers to motivated behavior controlled by external rewards.

21. Extrinsic reward appears to undermine or weaken intrinsic motivation. This is called the overjustification effect.

22. Overjustification is consistent with the discounting principle.

23. The overjustification effect underscores the problems presented by failures to generalize in behavior modification efforts.

23. Emotions are strong, relatively uncontrollable feelings that affect our behavior.

24. Emotions can be studied from three different viewpoints including subjective experiences, external behavior, and physiological events. Unfortunately, changes in these dimensions do not always correlate very well.

25. Emotions may eventually be classifiable into some small set of basic emotions whose multiple combinations account for the many shades of emotional experience.

26. The distinction between thought and emotion is intuitively appealing but difficult to maintain because thought determines emotion and vice versa.

27. Seligman's original model relating depression to learned helplessness has been expanded to include important attributional processes.

28. The new model involves three dimensions, including personal versus universal attributions, specific versus global attributions, and stable versus unstable attributions.

29. Early theories of emotion held that we first experience physiological reactions and then emotions.

30. These early theories have been discredited and replaced by cognitive theories.

31. Schachter's work has shown that we probably sometimes interpret our diffuse internal states of arousal in terms of what is going on around us.

32. Misattribution studies demonstrate this process.

CHAPTER 10

Social Motivation

SOCIAL MOTIVATION

The essence of the material in this chapter is that it is concerned with social motivation, *or the motivating effects that people have on one another.* In previous chapters we have examined such varied factors as hunger, instincts, incentives, and the id, among many other motivational variables. But in this chapter we change our focus a bit and attend to a more narrow band of the overall spectrum of motivational variables. Specifically, we look at some of the areas of research that primarily revolve around the ways that we, as people, affect one another's motivational state.

Clearly, such social motivation is extremely important in our lives. One need do nothing more than imagine standing up in front of a bored and negative mob of people to deliver a controversial speech in order to *feel* the enormous impact that people can have upon our motivational state. Depending upon who we are, we might be motivated to run, scream, faint, remain aloof, or verbally attack that unresponsive group of people.

The fact that we focus on social motivation in this chapter should not obscure the fact that we have already, in previous chapters, touched on and begun to explore this topic. For example, we discussed attribution theory in Chapter 9. Clearly, attributional processes sometimes, although not always, have a strong social motivation component. If you perceive someone's abusive behavior as merely defensive, rather than as truly aggressive, your behavior, in turn, will be affected. Individuals acting upon other individuals is the essence of all types of social motivation.

Social motivation appears in species other than humans even though humans are of paramount importance to us. For example, you can go back to the little stickleback fish discussed in Chapter 2 and argue that there is a social component (fish acting upon other fish) even in something as basic as instinctive behavior.

The point to remember is that social motivation, or the motivating effects of organisms upon one another, is intertwined with, and probably inseparable from, many of the topics we have already discussed in this text. The topics we have chosen to discuss in this chapter represent prime examples of social motivation, but they in no way represent an exhaustive list of all of the instances of social motivation addressed in the field of motivation.

The discussion takes the following form. In the rest of this section we briefly discuss two areas of social motivation (coaction-audience effects and modeling), which provide something of the flavor of this area. Then, in the rest of the chapter we discuss, in much greater detail, a number of the major areas of social motivation research.

Coaction-Audience Effects

Żajonc (1972) points out that it has long been known that the presence of other people has a strong impact on an individual's behavior. Two basic situations have been considered. In a *coaction* situation individuals compete against one another at the same task. This kind of competition seems to energize the individuals. Thus people will run faster if they are competing against other people than they will if they are just running alone. We often note that athletes do things in the "big game" that far exceed their ordinary practice behaviors. Other people seem to energize us when we compete against them.

The second basic situation is called the *audience* situation. Here other people merely watch a performer; they do not actively participate. Again, the effect seems to be one of energizing the performer. High school basketball players are much more energized or are "higher" during the actual game than they are during Thursday afternoon practice, not only because they are competing (coaction effect) but because they are being watched (audience effect) as well.

Coaction or audience situations sometimes help performance but at other times they hinder it. Imagine two children taking a vocabulary test. The teacher is walking around the classroom looking over everyone's shoulder. The children also know they are competing against one another for their grades. This represents a simultaneous coaction and audience effect. One of the two children does better than expected whereas the other does worse than expected. Why? Both were subjected to the same pressure, yet one's performance was facilitated whereas the other's suffered.

The answer seems to be that if a person's dominant responses are the correct ones, then they will be energized and revealed as facilitated performance. If a person's dominant responses are incorrect, then they will be energized and displayed as poor performance. In the case of our two students, the argument would be that an audience and competition would energize both children equally. But the student who showed improved performance would be the one who knew most of the answers, whereas the student who showed a performance deficit did so because his dominant or most salient responses were the incorrect ones.

Modeling

Modeling, or *observational learning* as it is sometimes called, can serve as another example of the importance of social motivation. As noted in Chapter 1, people will imitate the behavior of those around them. They seem to adopt these behaviors, which can range all the way from language use to violence, without going through the sort of trial-and-error response-then-reinforcement sequences that form the basis of conditioning (see Chapter 5). For example, a child may learn to do something she has never done before, not through a trial-and-error sequence but merely by watching someone *else* do it and receive a reward. A child might learn to eat a strange new food by watching her father eat it with obvious pleasure. A child might stop complaining on the playground after observing one of his playmates being punished for the same sort of complaining. A child, or an adult for that matter, may become aggressive and violent merely by seeing someone else being aggressive and getting away with it.

In other words, other people can determine our behavior and our motivational states. They influence us because we watch them and learn from these observations. We learn what we can and cannot "get away with." We learn, by observing, what will bring us reward without having to go through all the intermediate conditioning steps.

Motivational states, such as aggression, are often imitated. Chapter

11 reviews aggression in detail and contains a discussion of some of the details of modeled aggression. For now, it is sufficient to realize that we do imitate the behavior of others.

CONFORMITY

Definition   Conformity refers to *the performance of a behavior because others are performing it.* Because conformity has been one of the major areas of study that can be included under the heading of social motivation, we spend some time pursuing the ins and outs of this fascinating topic. As we see, conformity is related, but not identical, to the process of modeling or observational learning described in the previous section.

Examples   One of the best ways to understand what psychologists mean by conformity is to look at a couple of examples of the kinds of experiments they do.

1. Asch's Experiments.   Solomon Asch (1952, 1965) conducted a number of experiments that have become classic demonstrations of conformity. One experiment involved five subjects. The subjects sat at a table and were told that they would be judging the lengths of some lines. Specifically, they were shown one card that contained three lines of varying length and a second card that contained a single line (see Figure 10.1). The subject's task was to pick the line on the first card (A, B, or C) that most closely matched in length the single line on the second card. Actually, one of the lines on the first card was

FIGURE 10.1
The kinds of stimulus materials used in Asch's demonstrations of conformity.

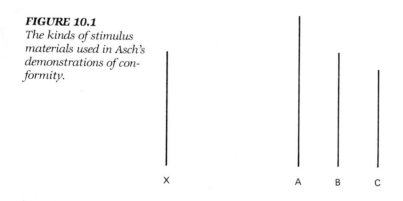

exactly the same length as the line on the second card, so the task was very easy.

The experimenter had the subjects give their answers one at a time. On the first two sets of cards everything went very smoothly; all five subjects picked the correct line. But then, on the third set of cards, something different happened. Let us say that the cards in Figure 10.1 were the ones used on this trial. The first subject chose line C as being equal to line X. The second subject also chose line C, as did the third and fourth subjects. Obviously these answers were incorrect. Unknown to that poor fifth subject, who now had to make a public choice, the first four subjects were confederates of the experimenter and had been coached to give the wrong answer. What would you do if you were that fifth subject? Would you give in and say that line C was correct, or would you stick to your guns and give the correct answer, line B?

In these conditions Asch found that about 35 per cent of the time subjects yielded to the pressure of the group and said that line C was the correct response. Now that's a lot of conforming when you think about it. Here we have perfectly normal healthy subjects and an answer that is obviously incorrect. Yet 35 per cent of the time that wrong answer was given by the fifth subjects. Some people yielded part of the time but not all of the time, some yielded all of the time, and some not at all.

After the experiments, Asch questioned the subjects about their behavior. A very small number of them seemed to suffer from what Asch called *perceptual distortion*. That is, they reported that they saw the group's choice as being accurate. But more often than not the subjects engaged in what Asch called *distortion of action*. They knew perfectly well what the correct answer was but they gave in to the pressure of the group anyway. The disparity between what they saw and what the group reported made them feel uneasy, inferior, and like an outsider. So they conformed knowing full well that the response they were making was incorrect. In other words, people don't always accept as true what others are saying. But they will, when asked to respond publicly, often act as though they do agree with the majority.

2. Autokinetic Phenomenon. When a single stationary point of light is seen in a dark room, that point of light seems to move about. When asked to describe the movement of the light, subjects who do not know that the light is really stationary will describe the apparent movement in many different ways. Some will say that it moves only a few inches, whereas others will say it moves many, many feet. This kind of apparent movement is referred to as the *autokinetic effect*. Almost everyone reports seeing some movement as long as the room is completely dark, which ensures that there will be nothing visible against which to judge movement. If the subject can see something in addition to the point of light, then the illusion disappears. Even when the illusion does appear, people are not certain about the movement they report.

Have you ever wondered why planes flying at night carry blinking rather than constant lights? If is because a blinking light breaks up the autokinetic effect. If a plane carries only unblinking lights, then other pilots observing that plane may suffer from a dangerous form of distortion. They will think that the plane they are watching is going where it is not really going.

Sherif (1935) used the autokinetic effect to demonstrate substantial conformity. He had a true subject and a confederate judge the movement of a spot of light. First, the true subject made a report. Then the experimenter's confederate made a response that differed substantially from that of the true subject and stuck with that estimate throughout a series of trials. For example, if the true subject first said that the light moved ten feet, then the confederate might say it moved twenty feet, or only one foot. It was observed over a series of trials that the estimates of the true subject began to resemble more and more closely those of the confederate. Conformity to the behavior of others was observed.

Types of Conformity

Obviously, in any given culture or society people behave in similar way. We all, or most of us, carry driver's licenses, eat with forks, and speak English. We vote, read the paper, and watch television. In a sense, all of this obvious commonality represents conformity. But it is not the kind that really fascinates the student of conformity. It represents learned behavior that is essential for the working of the group or culture. If some of us used money while others only bartered, life would be more complicated and probably less pleasant. These forms of conformity are useful, perhaps even necessary, but they are of less interest to some psychologists than conformity which is *not* necessary for the functioning of the group. The fascinating kind of conformity is the type that occurs when the individual is perfectly free to behave in two or more ways and chooses to behave the way others are behaving. People wear the latest fashions even though the culture would not disintegrate if they failed to keep up. People use the latest slang even though the culture would move along very nicely without the newest phrases. In other words, even though this distinction is somewhat murky, psychologists seem to be interested in conformity when that conformity occurs in the absence of any real cultural need to conform.

Psychologists draw an important distinction between *conformity* and *obedience.* Conformity refers to the situation in which we do something because everyone else is doing it. Obedience, or *compliance* as it is sometimes called, refers to the situation in which people do what they are requested to do even though they would prefer not to do it. If we look through a hole in a wall because everyone else is taking a peek, we call that conformity. However, if we look through the hole because someone asks us to do so, even though we don't especially want to, that's obedience.

Conformity and Obedience

The two are closely related; they both refer to giving in to group pressure. But they are usually addressed separately in the literature so we too will conform and follow that convention. Obedience is considered in the next major section after we look at some of the variables that affect the strength and nature of conformity.

VARIABLES AFFECTING CONFORMITY

Why do people give in to group pressure and conform? What kinds of variables affect the amount of conformity that is observed? In this section we discuss what psychologists have learned about the nature and causes of conformity. The discussion draws heavily and directly upon the analysis presented by Freedman, Sears, and Carlsmith (1981).

Sometimes we conform because we believe that the group knows something we don't know. If we go to a ballgame and find that everyone is sitting on one side of the stadium, we may figure that they must know something we are not aware of and we will sit with them. We might guess that it is shady there, or has a better view, or may

Information

simply assume that there is *some* legitimate reason for their behavior and go along with it.

If everyone around us looks up in the sky, we may also feel an urge to look upward. If everyone else looks up, we will assume they must be looking at something interesting; they must have information that we do not have.

Of course, if we believe that we have more information than the group, then we may refrain from conforming. If all of our friends are going to a certain movie, or eating at a particular restaurant, but we have read a negative review of the film or have been told firsthand that the restaurant's food is greasy and strangely colored, we may not conform. To conform for the reason being discussed here, we must believe that the group has significant information that we do not have.

Fear of Group Rejection   We often conform because we do not want to "stand out" in the group; we don't want to be different. Our desire to be like everyone else is not just some illogical weakness on our part. Groups really do make life difficult for members who deviate. They reject deviation and they reward conformity.

Rejection of Deviates.   Schachter (1951) had three confederates join a group and adopt either a deviant position, a position similar to that of the group, or a position that initially disagreed with the group but quickly "slid" over to the group position. At first, the group put real pressure on the deviate to change to the group's position. Continued deviation finally led to the "cold shoulder"; the group no longer communicated with the deviate. After the experiment was over, the group indicated that it liked the confederates who agreed with the group. It also liked the "convert," but it was much less positive about the consistent deviate.

Rejection of a deviate by a group can slip over into overt punishment. In fact, deviation can lead to the death of the deviate in extreme conditions, as in the cases of religious heresy and political purges.

Rewards for Conformity.   Rewarding conformity is just as strong a controlling factor as is rejection and/or punishment for deviation. If we go along with group standards of behavior, we reap the blessings of the group and are rewarded appropriately. We receive recognition, promotions, respect, and general all-around "good feelings" if we "go along with the program."

Unanimity Is Crucial.   If we find ourselves in a group that is unanimously opposed to us, then we will feel great pressure to conform to that group's behavior. But if just one member of that group breaks ranks and makes a response that differs from the other members of the group, then there will be a dramatic decrease in the pressure upon us to conform. If pressure to conform is to remain high, then group unanimity must be maintained. The loss of conformity that occurs when unanimity is lost is not trivial; up to 75 per cent of observed conformity can be lost when unanimity is broken (Morris and Miller, 1975).

The Nature of the Dissent.   One of the most striking aspects of this effect is the fact that the nature of the dissenter and the nature of the dissent is relatively unimportant in determining loss of conformity. As we have seen, even a single dissent can break the power of the majority. In addition, the dissenter can be of low status and prestige; the dissenter need not be a "big shot" to cause us to go against the majority. In fact, the dissenter does not even have to be correct in his dissent. He can give a wrong response and it will still help reduce conformity. The dissenter can give resonses that are even more incorrect than that of the majority and we will still reduce our conformity. For example, Allen and Levin (1971) set up a situation in which subjects were faced with either a unanimous incorrect four-person majority, a three-person majority and a fourth person who gave the correct response, or a three-person majority and a fourth person who gave a response that was more wrong than the response given by the majority. Among other results, they found that under some conditions conformity was reduced as much in the condition involving an even more incorrect dissenter as it was in the condition involving a correct dissenter. Apparently it does not make much difference what a dissent or a dissenter is like; as long as someone dissents in some way conformity will be reduced dramatically.

Causes of the Dissenter Effect.   Why is it that a single dissenter, no matter what the nature of his response, can have such a profound effect on conformity? Although no one knows for sure, some specu-

The Power of a Unanimous Majority

lations have been made. It may be that the existence of a dissenter reduces our fear of being deviant. We will not stand out and be so unusual in our stance if even just one other person will also make a response that disagrees with the majority. A dissenter will also reduce our confidence or trust in the majority opinion. Faced with unanimity, we tend to think, "Oh well, if they all agree they must be correct." But if even one person dissents, then we begin to think that the majority might, after all, be wrong.

The Size of the Group

Conformity seems to increase as the size of the group increases. But the relationship is not a simple one. Some studies suggest that conformity increases as the size of the group increases up to about three or four people, but beyond that further increases in group size do not produce further increases in conformity. For example, Asch (1951) found that conformity increased markedly as the unanimous majority grew from one to four people, but that further increases up to ten people did not further increase conformity.

On the other hand, some have reported further increases in conformity with additions to a majority beyond four. Milgram, Bickman, and Berkowitz (1969) had either one, two, three, five, ten, or fifteen confederates stand on a city street and look up at a particular window across the street. Then they counted the numbers of pedestrians who stopped and looked up too. In this simple test conformity continued to increase beyond the limit found in the Asch (1951) study. In fact, the further increases were substantial; when the majority was five, 16 per cent of the pedestrians stopped and looked. But when the majority had risen to fifteen, a full 40 per cent of the passing pedestrians stopped and looked up.

Some studies suggest that conformity levels off when group size increases, whereas others suggest that it does not. Presumably this means that some number of as yet unidentified variables affects the relationship between group size and conformity. So it is probably fair to conclude that there tends to be a positive relationship between conformity and group size but that the exact nature of this function depends upon the specific situation being examined.

Group Expertise

Conformity goes up as the perceived expertise of the group goes up. Suppose you are asked the height of Mount Whitney in the Sierra Nevada. Your tendency to go along with a group opinion will be much greater if that group is composed of experienced and well-known mountain climbers than it will be if the group is composed of dry cleaners.

The social status of the members of the group can influence conformity, too. Feshbach (1967) had four members of a college fraternity try to determine which of two cards contained the most dots. Two of the four subjects were high-status members of the fraternity (well liked) whereas the other two were low-status (less well liked). Correct responses were rewarded with money whereas incorrect responses took money away from the fraternity. It was observed that low-status subjects were much more likely to agree with the high-status people than the other way around. This effect appeared even when the low-status individuals were convinced that the high-status people were responding incorrectly.

Group Status

Conformity is strongly influenced by how confident we are in our own ability to respond correctly. Thus anything that increases our confidence will tend to decrease conformity.

Self-Confidence

At least two lines of research support this conclusion. The first is based on the idea that our confidence will be affected by the difficulty of the task. Coleman, Blake, and Mouton (1958) set up a conformity situation in which subjects were asked factual questions that varied in terms of difficulty. As predicted, the more difficult the questions the more conformity on the part of the subjects was noted.

A second line of research is based on the idea that if we give subjects relevant information, then their self-condifence should go up and conformity should go down. Snyder, Mischel, and Lott (1960) had subjects make artistic judgments in a conformity situation. Half the subjects were given a lecture on art before making the judgment and half were not. In accordance with the prediction, the former group showed less conformity than the latter.

OBEDIENCE

Having considered conformity, wherein people make certain responses because everyone else is making them, we now turn to the issue of obedience, which refers to situations in which we execute certain behaviors because we are asked to or pressured into making them, even though we may not want to. Although there are other important demonstrations of obedience, the work of Stanley Milgram provides the best known and perhaps most dramatic example of obedience research (Milgram, 1963, 1965, 1974).

Milgram's Experiments   Milgram placed advertisements in a newspaper circulated in a northeastern city in order to recruit subjects for the experiment. Subjects showed up for the experiment in pairs. The experimenter, wearing a white coat, explained that the experiment was concerned with the effects of punishment on learning. One subject was called the "learner" and the other was called the "teacher." The teacher read pairs of words out loud and the learner was supposed to memorize them. Each time the learner made a mistake the teacher punished the learner by administering shock. This was done by having the teacher sit in front of an imposing "shock machine" that had a row of thirty small levers or switches arranged along its front. The voltage of each of the levers was designated, and ranged from 15 volts to 450 volts (roughly four times ordinary household voltage). The strength of the shock was further indicted by labels placed above the levers that ranged from "slight," through "extreme intensity shock," to "danger: severe shock."

The teacher was given a sample shock. Actually this sample was quite intense and painful, but it was called mild by the experimenter. The learner said that he had a heart condition, but the experimenter said not to worry. With the teacher watching, the learner was seated in another room. His arm was strapped down and electrodes were attached. Then the experimenter and the teacher returned to the first room, from which the learner was not visible. The teacher heard the learner's responses over an intercom system. The teacher was instructed to administer the weakest shock when the learner made his first error but to increase the severity of the shock by one step each time subsequent errors were made, and to keep on increasing the severity of the shock as long as the learner continued to make errors.

As the experiment progressed, the learner made errors. Each time an error occurred the teacher's task was to tell him he was wrong and to deliver an ever stronger shock as punishment. In response to the first few shocks the learner merely grunted. But as shock strength increased the learner began to shout and beg the teacher to stop. The learner kicked and pounded the walls and furniture. Finally, as the shock became extreme the learner stopped responding all together. Total silence.

If the teacher appealed to the experimenter, the experimenter said things like, "The experiment must go on. It is necessary for you to continue," and, "You have no choice but to go on." No other pressure was applied to the teacher.

What do you think the teacher did? What would you do? Milgram asked students and colleagues how they thought that the teachers would behave. Most of them felt that all but a very few of the teachers would refuse to administer what they believed to be dangerous shock. We like to think of ourselves as strong, independent people but apparently we are not, at least under some circumstances. Well over half of the teachers went all the way to the end of the scale, supposedly administering 450 volts to the learner (see Table 10.1). And even the ones that quit early administered "intense shock" in spite of the yelling and screaming of the learners.

Unknown to the teachers, who were the only real subjects, the so-called learners were really confederates of the experimenter. No one ever actually received any shock. The responses of the so-called learners were all tape recorded ahead of time and played back to the teachers. But from the teacher's point of view the delivery of the shock was very real. The experiment represents a dramatic demonstration of obedience. People are apparently willing to deliver potentially fatal punishment to others merely because some person in a white coat says they must. Milgram's original work was done with male American adults. But later work (see Shanab and Yahya, 1977) showed that

TABLE 10.1. *The Numbers and Percentages of Subjects Who Stopped at the Various Shock Levels.*

Voltage indication	Number of subjects	Percentage of subjects
Slight shock	0	0
Moderate shock	0	0
Strong shock	0	0
Very strong shock	0	0
Intense shock	5	12.5
Extreme-intensity shock	8	20.0
Danger: severe shock	1	2.5
Switch 30, the final shock	26	65.0

Adapted from: Milgram, S. Behavioral study of obedience. *Journal of Abnormal and Social Psychology*, 1963, 67, 376. Copyright 1963 by the American Psychological Association. Reprinted by permission.

people of other ages, other nationalities, and the other sex will also display this remarkable and disturbing willingness to "electrocute a stranger."

There has been a good deal of discussion about Milgram's work in connection with the Nazi atrocities of World War II. Many of the guilty Germans justified their actions by claiming that they were merely following orders. Although horrifying, the action of the Nazis apparently was not an isolated thing. Milgram's and others' work suggests that there lie within each of us, regardless of sex, age, or nationality, the seeds of such cruel and destructive behavior. History, too, leads us to the same conclusion. Atrocities have been only too common through the pages of recorded history. The lesson to be learned is that the potential for such behavior remains ready to be translated into behavior by the next "man in a white coat."

Although Milgram's demonstration of obedience is dramatic and socially significant, other examples of obedience are also available. For example, Hofling, Brotzman, Dalrymple, Graves, and Pierce (1963) had a confederate pose as a doctor on duty and call nurses and tell them to give certain patients a drug. The so-called doctor was unknown to the nurses and the dose indicated by the doctor was abnormally high. And yet almost all of the nurses were willing to administer the drug.

Personal Responsibility

So much for the basic fact that we will sometimes obey. Now let us turn to a consideration of some of the factors that influence this tendency to obey. Sometimes we obey and sometimes we don't. Why?

The first element discussed is the fact that anything that makes us feel more personally responsible for our behavior will tend to *reduce* obedience. The Nazis, after World War II, often showed a lack of remorse; they did what they did because they were "good soldiers under orders." They were not responsible, and so suffered no remorse. Milgram's (1977) subjects sometimes showed a similar lack of remorse even though they believed they had hurt the other subject. "You told me to do it."

Proximity of the "Victim." There are several experimental demonstrations of the idea that personal responsibility reduces obedience. Milgram (1965) set up four conditions that varied the proximity of the learner to the teacher (see Figure 10.2).

In the "remote" condition the learner sat in another room with the

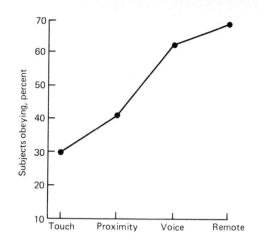

FIGURE 10.2
Obeying as a function of the distance between learner and teacher. (From Milgram, S. Some conditions of obedience and disobedience to authority. Human Relations, *1965, 18, 57–76. Fig. 1 on p. 63.)*

door closed. In the "voice" condition the adjoining door was left open. In the "proximity" condition the learner sat next to the teacher. In the "touch" condition the teacher held the learner's hand on a "shock plate." As Figure 10.2 shows, obedience dropped sharply as proximity, and presumably responsibility, increased. It is interesting to note, however, that some 30 per cent of the teachers still administered the highest shock in the proximity condition. This form of personal responsibility does not completely eliminate obedience.

Proximity of Authority. Milgram also showed that the closer the authority figure issuing the orders is to the teacher the greater will be the obedience. In one condition teachers received instructions from a tape recorder. This condition produced the least obedience. In an intermediate condition the experimenter left the room after initial instructions. In the condition producing the most obedience, the experimenter stayed in the room with the teacher throughout the experiment. It can be assumed that the presence of the authority figure relieved the teacher of some personal responsibility.

Choice. In a very direct demonstration of the power of personal responsibility, Mantrell (1971) set up two conditions. In the first, the subject was told to punish the confederate. Over 80 per cent of the subjects complied. In the other condition the subject was personally responsible for choosing not only whether or not to punish but how much punishment to deliver as well. In this high personal responsibility condition less than 10 per cent of the subjects administered maximum punishment.

The Principles of Conditioning: Behavior Modification

Behavior modifiers attempt to alter behavior through the application of the principles of conditioning. Essentially, behavior modification refers to the influencing of behavior through the use of rewards, punishers, and extinction. We discussed topics such as systematic desensitization, token economies, and aversion therapy in Chapter 4. There is a close relationship between some forms of behavior modification and obedience. *Obedience can be brought about through the use of behavior modification methods, or the use of rewards, punishment, and extinction.*

Take token economies, for example. It has been shown that compliance with certain rules, such as those requiring mental patients to care for and keep track of their personal belongings, can be brought about through the use of a token reward system. This is a form of obedience because people are doing things they would not necessarily choose to do. In other words, obedience can be effected through the use of rewards, punishment, and extinction. This is true not only in artificial experimental situations but in everyday life, too. Every time a parent gets her child to pick up his toys by rewarding him with some treat, she is bringing about obedience through the use of a reward system.

The Hawthorne Effect

People can be made to do what we want them to do if we convince them that we like them, care about them, and are paying attention to them. If we make someone feel "special" then he is likely to go along with our request. Contrary to the popular notion, flattery does seem to get us somewhere.

There is an interesting demonstration of this fact called the Hawthorne effect. Our discussion of it follows the one presented by Freedman, Sears and Carlsmith (1981). Homans (1965) was studying the effects of various work conditions on performance in the Hawthorne plant belonging to the Western Electric Company. Six women, whose job it was to assemble telephone equipment, were selected as subjects. The idea was to vary the conditions under which they worked over a number of months and to see which of these various conditions led to the best performance. The conditions that were varied included things such as type of rest period and length of work day.

The changes were quite complex. First, their performance under normal conditions was measured. Then they were put into a special room with no other changes being made and their performance was watched for five weeks. Then the method of paying them was changed for several weeks. Then five-minute rest periods in the morning and afternoon were introduced. In successive periods these rest periods were altered in length and number. At one point a light lunch was introduced. Then changes in the length of the work day and the work week were introduced. Finally, all of the original work conditions were reintroduced as if nothing had happened.

You would think that some of these changes would be more popular with the workers than others. Referring back to our knowledge of the principles of conditioning, we would expect performance to increase under preferred conditions and decrease under less preferred (less rewarding) conditions. But that is not what happened. What happened was that *each* change, no matter what it was, led to better performance. The nature of the change had no impact at all; performance increased with each and every change.

The main reason for this unexpected result was that the women felt that they were important, that they were being paid attention to, and that they were somehow special. They knew that their performance was being measured and they seemed happy to do what their employer wanted them to do.

Another way to get people to comply with a request is called the foot-in-the-door method. Essentially, this method involves getting someone to go along with some major request by first getting them to comply with some minor request. It is like the door-to-door salesperson who will try first to get you to listen, or look at something, or answer a few innocent sounding questions before they let on that they want to sell you a new roof.

Freedman and Fraser (1966) did an interesting experiment that demonstrated the foot-in-the-door effect. First they went around a neighborhood and asked housewives to sign a petition. The petition, which was to be sent to state legislators, urged those politicians to work toward safe-driving legislation. Most of the subjects signed the petition. Then, in a few weeks, the experimenters returned and asked if the subject would be willing to have a large "Drive Carefully" sign placed in his front yard. A control group of housewives were also

The Foot-in-the-Door Method

asked to accept the sign. These control women had *not* been approached with the petition.

The results indicated that, compared to the controls, many more of the women who had gone along with the small request (signing the petition) went along with the large request (accepted the sign).

Getting Off Easy Suppose some well-meaning person asks you to contribute a full weekend to work for some charitable organization. With horror and some guilt you refuse. Then the person says, "Well, will you contribute five dollars?" With relief you fork over the money. Now what would have happened if the person had only asked you for the money without first asking for your time? You would probably have been less willing to give the money.

This example represents an effect that seems to be the opposite of the foot-in-the-door method. Instead of first asking for something small and then something large, the opposite is done; something large is asked for first, followed by a request for something small.

Cialdini and his associates (1975) did a study that demonstrates this effect. Some of the subjects were asked to donate a large amount of time and then, when they refused, were asked to contribute a much smaller amount of time. About 50 per cent of these subjects agreed to donate the smaller amount of time. Other subjects were only asked to contribute the smaller amount of time without first being asked to give the larger amount. Only a little over 15 per cent of these subjects agreed to the request.

Low-Balling Low-balling is a sneaky way to get people to comply by getting them to agree to a small request and then immediately increasing the size of the request before the first request is complied with.

Suppose you decide to buy a used car. After some bargaining you settle on a price. Then, when you go into the office to fill out the papers you are told that, of course, "destination charges" and/or "dealer preparation charges" will be added to the price. Angry though you may be, you will probably go along with this request. You will end up spending more than you wanted to. In fact, you might have refused to pay the higher price had you known about it from the beginning. But, having committed yourself it is difficult for you to go back to square one. The thought of starting all over is too much for you.

Thus far we have been discussing ways in which compliance or obedience can be increased by increasing pressure upon the individual. However, sometimes added pressure will lead to less rather than more compliance. This effect has been called *reactance* by Brehm and Sensenig (1966).

Brehm and Sensenig did the following experiment. Subjects were given the choice of working on Problem A or Problem B. In one condition a note from another "subject" said, "I choose Problem A." In another condition the note from the other "subject" said, "I think that we should both do Problem A." The first of these conditions represents low pressure whereas the second represents high pressure. The investigators found that 70 per cent of the subjects in the low-pressure condition chose Problem A whereas only 40 per cent of the subjects in the high-pressure condition chose Problem A. High pressure led to low rather than high compliance.

The reactance effect is usually interpreted in terms of the subject's sense of loss of control. The idea is that if the subject feels she is losing control, then she will act in a way that restores personal control. When faced with the high-pressure note the subject may say to herself, "Who does that person think he is? I'm going to chose Problem B in spite of what he says!"

The point here is that compliance and obedience are quite often increased when pressure is applied to the subject. But under some conditions, especially those involving a sense of loss of control, just the opposite can occur; greater pressure can lead to less compliance.

AFFILIATION

People prefer to be with other people. We have all heard of hermits who live out in the desert surrounded by wrecked cars who swear up and down that they love it out there. However, these few individuals are the exception; if anything, they are looked upon as being rather odd, if not a little bit crazy. For the most part, people live with and among other people. This general tendency to stay with other people is referred to as the affiliation motive.

Clearly we are not the only species to affiliate. One need only look at films of the African plains, with their great herds of animals, to recognize the power of this motive system among many different species. The tendency to affiliate is not limited to herbivores. Predators, such as lions and wolves, also display affiliative tendencies.

Although all affiliation refers to the tendency to stay near members of one's own species, the reasons for this behavior are not at all clear. Some species, such as antelope and coyotes, display a great deal of affiliative behavior whereas others, such as tigers and moose, display much less. The reasons for affiliation probably vary from species to species. Thus, one species might affiliate because "togetherness" promotes effective hunting. African wild dogs prey upon large animals such as zebra. A solitary wild dog would never be able to bring down a zebra, but a pack of dogs does very well. Lions also profit from group membership because, even though they are large enough to kill a zebra by themselves, they have relatively poor speed and stamina. Hence they profit from group membership in that it allows the principles of encirclement and ambush to be used in hunting. Other species, such as baboons and gazelles, profit from affiliating because there is "safety in numbers" and because the group provides an effective alarm system that protects the individual.

Many species are rather solitary. Although they occasionally congregate near some special food supply, animals such as bears and bald eagles tend to be fairly solitary. Although the reasons for a *lack* of affiliation are not well understood, some possibilities come to mind. For example, the bear and the eagle have few natural enemies. When was the last time you heard of an animal other than the human hunting grizzlies? Hence these animals do not need the protection afforded by group membership. In addition, their diet is such that they do not need help in obtaining food. Bald eagles eat fish, either dead or alive. They swoop down and pick fish right out of the surface of the water, or they find dead fish on the banks. Neither method requires assistance. Bears, on the other hand, eat just about anything. Related to the pig, they eat like humans. Scavenging and eating berries and small animals, they too do not need a big crowd to help them out.

The point here is that, although affiliation is often discussed as a single concept, it may well be that there are many different kinds of affiliation in the sense that different species "stick together" for many different reasons. Because we are primarily interested in human behavior, we will focus on human affiliative tendencies.

Many of the experiments we discuss detect affiliative tendencies by giving people a choice as to whether they would rather be alone or with other people. The Thematic Apperception Test (TAT), discussed in connection with achievement motivation in Chapter 8, can also be helpful in measuring affiliative tendencies. People are given ambiguous pictures and asked to make up stories about them. The idea is that the individual will project some of her wants, wishes, and desires into the story. Although not nearly as widely investigated as achievement motivation, affiliative motivation has been of concern to psychologists for many years.

Boyatzis (1973) presents a good summary of the research on affiliation. He points out that affilative motivation has been broken down into "hope of affiliation" and "fear of separation" by some investigators (see Atkinson, Heyns, and Veroff, 1954; Shipley and Veroff, 1952). This split parallels the distinction made in the achievement motivation literature between hope of success and fear of failure. However, Boyatzis (1973) concludes that, although this distinction is clear on a theoretical level, the actual use of TAT scoring techniques does not distinguish between fear of separation and hope of affiliation. If anything, Boyatzis believes that more fear of separation is projected into TAT stories than hope of affiliation.

People who score high on TAT-measured affiliative motivation do differ from people who score low on affiliation. For example, Mc-Keachie, Lin, Milholland and Issacson (1966) found that students who were high in affiliative motivation got better grades when their teachers were warm and friendly. This was not true for students who were low in affiliative motivation. In another study, Atkinson and Walker (1956) presented four different stimulus patterns, only one of which was a face, for very brief periods of time. They found that people who were high in the need to affiliate picked out the faces more accurately than did people who were low in the need to affiliate.

1. Natural Selection. Although no one is quite sure why people affiliate, there are two major theories concerning this powerful motive system. The first of these argues that the tendency to affiliate is instinctive, innate, or prewired into our neutral system. This theory holds that we inherit the tendency to affiliate with others.

The argument is based upon the principle of natural selection. The human body is not particularly strong or fast or deadly; we really are somewhat puny when compared with the other major predators.

Many thousands of years ago there was probably a great advantage in gathering together in groups. Warning, defense, and attack would all be better done by a group of humans than by a single individual. Those individuals who gathered together would be more likely to survive long enough to reproduce. (Can you imagine facing the great beasts of the past alone?) And if the people who gathered together did survive and reproduce, then that genetically determined trait would be passed on to their offspring. "Loners" would be less likely to survive to reproduce and hence their genetic makeup would not be passed on. The idea is that the genetically based affiliative tendency would be naturally selected; it would persist because it allowed its carrier to survive and reproduce.

No one really knows whether or not this is what really happened. But it has an intuitively appealing ring to it. Humans who "stick together" have a better chance of surviving. Of course, there are unanswered questions. For example, if affiliation leads to a survival advantage, then why haven't all species evolved this way? Why, for example, are tigers relatively solitary? Can you imagine the effectiveness of a pack of twenty or thirty tigers? And why do some species, such as elephants, show definite affiliative tendencies when they have few natural enemies and do not need one another to procure their food?

2. Two Forms of Learning. By now you may have anticipated the second major theory of affiliation. This one argues that affiliative behavior is learned just like any other behavior.

There are at least two ways that affiliative behavior could be learned. First, affiliation motivation may involve classical conditioning and acquired drives as outlined in Chapters 5 and 7 (see Miller and Dollard, 1941). Essentially, it might work something like this. If, every time something good happens to you, you happen to be in the company of other people, then those positive feelings will be classically conditioned to people such that, in the future when you come upon additional people, they will evoke all those old classically conditioned positive feelings. When you are an infant most good things happen in the presence of your parents; they feed, love, clean, and comfort you. All of these good feelings become classically conditioned to the human stimulus elements that your parents hold in common with other humans. Thus, after conditioning with your parents has progressed, *any* other human will begin to evoke conditioned positive feelings.

The second way that affiliative behavior can be learned is more straightforward. It involves instrumental conditioning that is also discussed in earlier chapters. Instrumental conditioning refers to the fact that we will tend to do again what we have been rewarded for doing in the past. Coupled with the fact that affiliative behavior is rewarded in most cultures it is easy to see why we learn to affiliate. Each time we hug someone they hug back (reward us). Each time we act in a friendly social manner we are rewarded for doing so. Each time we act in an antisocial manner, punishment, or at least an absence of reward, occurs. Affiliative behaviors that we learn in one situation (e.g., the home) will then tend to occur in other situations (e.g., school or work) according to the principle of stimulus generalization outlined in Chapter 5.

Although we have discussed instinctive and learning interpretations of affiliative behavior separately, the situation need not be all-or-none. That is, affiliation need not be all instinctive or all learned. There are many different forms of affiliation. Probably some of them are instinctive, some learned, and some the result of intricate interplay between the two.

Although the instictive and the learning theories represent general views of the nature of affiliation, some detailed work has also been done on more specific determinants of affiliative behavior.

Fear and Affiliation

One of the factors that seems to lead people to want to be with others is fear. When we are afraid, our desire to be with others seems to increase. This was demonstrated by Schachter (1959) in the following way. Subjects were first brought into a laboratory containing imposing-looking electrical equipment. All subjects were led to believe that the experiment would involve electric shock. But some subjects were told that the experiment would involve extremely painful shock whereas others were told that the shock would be nothing more than a painless tingle. The idea was that the high-shock subjects would be much more frightened than the low-shock subjects. Then the experimenter said there would be a delay of about ten minutes while the equipment was readied. All subjects were given the choice of waiting in a room all alone or in a room with other people. In agreement with the hypothesis that fear leads to a tendency to affiliate something like 60 percent of the high-fear people chose to wait with others, whereas only about a third of the low-fear people chose to wait with others.

In another study, Schachter (1959) told some of the subjects that if they chose to wait with others they could not talk about the upcoming experiment. When this was done, these subjects were much less interested in waiting with others. Just being with others, and either not talking or talking about irrelevant matters, did not maximize affiliation. Apparently, when they are afraid, people want to get together and talk about what it is that is frightening them.

Affiliation and Social Comparison Theory

Leon Festinger (1954) presented another interpretation of affiliation. He argued that we all want to evaluate ourselves and that one of the important ways that we evaluate ourselves is by comparing ourselves with other people. When you get a 93 on an exam you want to know how well you did relative to the rest of the class. When you run a six-minute mile you want to know if that is "good, bad, or indifferent." You find out by comparing your performance with the performances of others.

Festinger argues that we use social comparison in making decisions about our feelings and emotions too. We "check in" with other people to see if our feelings are appropriate in a given situation. If we read in the newspaper that asbestos has been found in vinyl floor tiles we don't know quite how to feel. Should we be frightened or indifferent? We find out by making social comparisons. We find out how other people are feeling.

According to Festinger, the need to make social comparisons may be one factor that leads to affiliative behavior. We approach others because that is a natural consequence of making social comparisons.

In the preceding section we discussed how fear can lead to affiliation. Schachter's experiments demonstrating the fear effect can also be interpreted in terms of social comparison theory. According to this theory, the reason the "high-fear" subjects chose to wait with others is because they want to find out how other people are feeling and to evaluate their own feelings in the light of how others are feeling. "Am I being silly or should I be tearing the walls down to get out of here?"

The fact that people will reduce their tendency to affiliate when they can't talk about the situation seems consistent with social comparison theory.

The fear reduction interpretation of affiliation differs from the social comparison explanation in that the former claims that the sole aim of affiliation is fear reduction whereas the latter claims that the individual seeks clarification of what kind and what strength of feeling is appropriate.

Clearly, the determinants of affiliative behavior are complex. Just as there are probably many forms of affiliation so too are there probably many determinants of affiliation including innate and learned behaviors, fear reduction, and social comparison.

LIKING

Relationship to Affiliation

When psychologists talk about liking, they refer to something quite different from the kind of affiliative tendency we have been discussing. Affiliation refers to wanting or needing to be around people in general without special regard for who those people are as individuals. Liking, on the other hand, refers to a special relationship between particular individuals. We are affiliating when we join a crowd after an earthquake has struck. We may not like any specific member of that group. We are displaying liking, on the other hand, when we call up a close friend and suggest dinner together.

Loving, as we shall see in the next section, is difficult to define. In general, it refers to an even deeper and more intimate relationship than one involving liking. But it can be distinguished from affiliation in that it represents what goes on between specific individuals as distinct from the affiliative tendency to be near people in general.

The Determinants of Attraction

A good deal of the work on liking has revolved around the problem of what it is that determines attraction. Why do we like certain people but not others? A number of important variables have been identified and it is to them that we now turn.

1. Proximity. We are more likely to become friends with people who are physically close to us than we are with people who live in more distant locations. A whole series of studies (see Newcomb, 1961; Segal, 1974) have shown that we tend to become freindly with the people who live closest to us. We are more likely to be friends with the next-door neighbor than we are with people down the block. If a freshman college student is assigned a dormitory room, she is more likely to become friends with her roommate or the people in adjacent rooms than she is with people down the hall, on another floor, or in another dormitory.

2. Familiarity.   Closely related to the proximity variable is that of familiarity. The idea here is that "mere exposure" may increase liking. Zajonc (1968) did a series of studies that demonstrate the "mere exposure" idea. In one of them subjects were shown pictures of faces. The numbers of exposures of the faces varied from zero to twenty-five times. Then Zajonc asked the subjects how much they thought they would like the people in the pictures. As you can see in Figure 10.3 liking went up as the number of exposures increased.

It may be that familiarity accounts for at least part of the proximity effect described in the preceding section. That is, proximity may correlate with liking because those who live or work close to us are more familiar to us than people who live or work further away.

3. Similarity.   We tend to be drawn to people who are similar to us. When traveling in a foreign country we will feel drawn to other Americans, even if we feel strongly that we should "get to know the people" of the foreign country. People who are similar "stick together." Old people stick together, young people stick together, and so do people in the same professions, the same social classes, and the

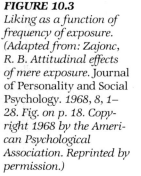

FIGURE 10.3
Liking as a function of frequency of exposure. (Adapted from: Zajonc, R. B. Attitudinal effects of mere exposure. Journal of Personality and Social Psychology. *1968, 8, 1–28. Fig. on p. 18. Copyright 1968 by the American Psychological Association. Reprinted by permission.)*

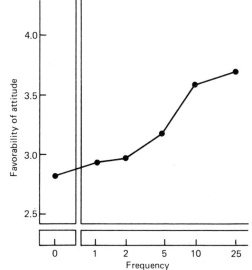

same religions. In fact, people even tend to select others with similar physical attributes (see Berscheid and Walster, 1969).

4. Reciprocity. We tend to like people who "like us back". This *reciprocity rule* can be demonstrated experimentally. Aronson and Linder (1965) first had subjects interact with a confederate of the experimenter. Then the subject overheard a conversation between the experimenter and the confederate during which the confederate talked about the subject. Unknown to the subject, these conversations were preplanned. In one condition the confederate praised the subject throughout a series of conversations with the experimenter. In a second condition the confederate's evaluation of the subject was uniformly negative. In a third condition the confederate started out being negative but shifted to being positive about the subject. In the fourth condition evaluation shifted from positive to negative. After these overheard conversations were completed, the subjects were asked whether or not they liked the confederate. The results are contained in Table 10.2. As you can see the reciprocity rule was upheld. Confederates who ended up "liking" the subjects were liked in return. Confederates who ended up "disliking" the subjects were disliked in return.

There are some other interesting aspects of these results. The positive-negative evaluation led to more disliking than negative evaluation throughout. Apparently we are particularly put off by people who first like us and then decide they don't like us.

TABLE 10.2. Approval As a Function of Interpersonal Attraction

Condition	Liking*
Positive evaluation throughout	6.42
Negative evaluation throughout	2.52
Negative-positive evaluation	7.67
Positive-negative evaluation	0.87

*Figures are ratings on a scale from -10 to $+10$. Adapted from: Aronson, E., and Linder, D. Gain and loss of esteem as determinants of interpersonal attractiveness. *Journal of Experimental Social Psychology*, 1965, *1*, 156–171.

On the other hand negative-positive evaluation tended to lead to greater liking than did positive evaluation throughout. It seems we are particularly impressed by people who start out not liking us but who soon discover and appreciate our sterling qualities.

5. Rewards and Punishment. The reciprocity effect is really nothing more than an example of the more general rule that states that we like people who are associated with the receipt of rewards and dislike people who are associated with the receipt of punishers. This principle is so obvious that we need not spend a lot of time discussing it. People who bring us pleasure are liked and those that bring us pain or discomfort are disliked.

However, a few wrinkles in the argument are interesting. For example, we may end up disliking someone who is associated with discomfort but is not personally responsible for that discomfort. Griffitt (1970) had people get acquainted in either a comfortable situation or in an uncomfortable one such as an overheated room. Even though no one was personally responsible for the discomfort, appropriate measures indicated that more liking developed in the comfortable than in the uncomfortable situation.

Another interesting fact is that if people are nice to us, but we suspect them of having ulterior motives, liking will be inhibited (see Jones, 1964). We must trust people and feel that they genuinely like us before we will reciprocate.

In general, though, liking can be, and has been, looked at as a piece of behavior, like any other behavior, which can be controlled through the application of the principles of conditioning explored in Chapters 5 and 6.

6. Physical Attractiveness: Matching. A further factor that determines liking is physical attractiveness. In general, people who are thought to be attractive are liked more than unattractive people. However, even though the most attractive people are liked the most we don't all rush about bumping into one another trying to get close to the most attractive people. We seem to be more realistic than that. The *matching principle* (see Berscheid, Dion, Walster, and Walster, 1971) maintains that we tend to seek the company of not the most attractive person but the most attractive person we can get. We do the best we can. This results in our seeking a partner whose attractiveness roughly matches our own. Attractive people pursue and

One of the determinants of attraction is physical attractiveness. The matching principle states that people tend to seek the company of others who are of about equal attractiveness. (Courtesy of J. D. Anker.)

match up with attractive people. Less attractive people, athough they might want to pursue the most attractive people, in fact pursue people more equal to themselves in attractiveness.

7. The Halo Effect.   The halo effect refers to the fact that if someone is physically attractive then we will tend to believe that he also possesses a cluster of additional positive characteristics even though he may not. Dion, Berscheid, and Walster (1972) drew a set of portraits from a college yearbook and divided them into highly attractive, average, and unattractive categories. Then they had subjects rate the people in the photographs along a number of dimensions. Table 10.3 contains the results of these ratings. As you can see, the attractive people were rated higher than the unattractive people on every dimension except parental competence.

LOVING

All of the Above Plus

The problem that psychologists have had in studying love is that they are not quite sure what it is that they are studying. They know that most people refer to a deeper, more intimate, longer-lasting relation-

TABLE 10.3.   The Impact of Attractiveness on Judgment*

Trait	Attractive Stimulus Person	Average Stimulus Person	Unattractive Stimulus Person
Social desirability of personality	65.39	62.42	56.31
Occupational status	2.25	2.02	1.70
Marital competence	1.70	.71	.37
Parental competence	3.54	4.55	3.91
Social and professional happiness	6.37	6.34	5.28
Total happiness	11.60	11.60	8.83
Likelihood of marriage	2.17	1.82	1.52

*Adapted from Dion, K., Berscheid, E., and Walster, E. What is beautiful is good. *Journal of Personality and Social Psychology*, 1972, 24, 285–290. Table 1, p. 288.

ship when they refer to love as distinct from mere liking. But love remains as much a mystery to psychologists as it always has been to artists, writers, and philosophers.

In a sense we can think of love as involving everything that we talked about in connection with liking *plus* some additional variables. Thus love involves proximity, familiarity, similarity, reciprocity, rewards, physical attractiveness, plus additional factors we discuss in this section.

Social Penetration

Freedman, Sears, and Carlsmith (1981) argue that *social penetration* and *self-disclosure* should both be considered in connecton with intimate relationships. When Freedman, Sears and Carlsmith speak of social penetration, they refer to the work of Altman and Taylor (1973). Social penetration moves from superficial levels to more intimate levels of exchange. It occurs along two dimensions: *breadth* and *depth*. Breadth refers to the number of different areas that people share in their relationship. Thus two people who are friends but not in love might know about each other's jobs and recreational activities. As they become more intimate and more toward love, they expand upon the number of areas of contact. Thus they extend their relationship into areas such as sex, family problems, wild dreams, and special forms of humor.

Depth refers to the degree of penetration that occurs within any given area of contact. Two friends might joke with one another in a standard social manner but as they move toward love they begin to share more idiosyncratic forms of humor. Similarly, two friends might share their hopes and dreams, but only lovers will share their most secret fantasies and anxieties.

Self-Disclosure

The second concept that helps us understand love is that of *self-disclosure*, which refers to the extent to which we reveal ourselves to others. Apparently the closer and more intimate our relationship, the more of our "inner selves" we are willing to reveal to our partner. Self-disclosure seems to increase as a relationship becomes more intimate. In a sense, self-disclosure can be looked at as a mechanism which increases social penetration.

The more we disclose of ourselves the more the other person will like us. However, the relationship between liking and self-disclosure is complicated by the fact that to be maximally effective self-disclosure must be done slowly, easily, and gently. If we disclose too much too rapidly, a negative reaction can set in. If someone rushes up to you and says, "Hi! I like to make love in trees. I'm fairly insecure. I like beets, and I just got a divorce, and I heard voices once," you're likely to recoil a bit. It's the old story of someone "coming on too strongly." We like disclosure, and respond postively to it, but only if it is done at a relatively slow and gentle pace.

Five Kinds of Love?

The problem of trying to understand love is complicated by the fact that there may well be no such thing as a single distinct form of love. Harlow (1958) argues that there are at least five different forms of love. Although we do not know very much about these different forms of love, they may well represent at least partially independent processes. The five forms of love Harlow identifies are:

1. Maternal love: The love of a mother for her offspring.
2. Infant love: An offspring's love of her mother.
3. Peer love: The strong social bonds between children and between adults.
4. Heterosexual love: The sexual passion between people.
5. Paternal love: A father's love for his offspring.

SUMMARY

1. Social motivation refers to the motivating effects that individuals have on one another.
2. Coaction effects refer to what happens to performance when we compete with others

at the same task. Audience effects refer to what happens to our performance when people watch us perform.

3. Whatever responses are dominant (either correct or incorrect) will be energized in coaction and audience situations.

4. Modeling, or observational learning, refers to situations in which we learn by observing others.

5. Conformity, as exemplified by Asch's experiments, refers to the performance of a behavior because everyone else is performing it.

6. Conformity can also be easily demonstrated using the autokinetic effect.

7. There are various overlapping types of conformity.

8. Obedience refers to people doing what is requested of them even if they might prefer not to do it.

9. Variables affecting conformity include information, fear of group rejection, rewards for compliance, the power of the majority, group size, group expertise, group status, and self-confidence.

10. Milgram's experiments demonstrate an extreme form of obedience. These experiments have been related to Nazi activity during World War II.

11. A greater sense of personal responsibility results in less obedience.

12. Variables affecting responsibility include proximity of victim, proximity of authority, and choice.

13. Obedience can be brought about through the operation of the principles of conditioning.

14. The Hawthorne effect demonstrates that we will do what people want us to do if we are made to feel we are special and important.

15. The foot-in-the-door technique involves getting people to comply with some major request by first getting them to comply with some minor request.

16. People can be made to comply with some minor request by first asking them to comply with some unacceptable major request.

17. In low-balling people are induced to agree to some small request and are then immediately subjected to an increase in the size of the request before the first request has been complied with.

18. Reactance refers to the fact that added pressure to comply will sometimes backfire and lead to resistance.

19. Affiliation refers to people's tendency to want to spend time with other people.

20. Affiliative motivation has been measured with the TAT.

21. Affiliation may involve both a hope of affiliation and a fear of separation.

22. Theories of affiliation are based upon the ideas that affiliation is instinctual and that it is learned.

23. The learning interpretation includes both classical and instrumental conditioning mechanisms.

24. Fear may be at the basis of some affiliation. Affiliation may reduce fear.

25. Social comparison theory has also been applied to the problem of affiliation.

26. Liking, affiliation, and loving are related concepts, but they do differ from one another.

27. Attraction is determined by proximity, familiarity, similarity, reciprocity, rewards, and physical attractiveness.

28. The matching hypothesis and the halo effect have been investigated in connection with attraction.

29. Loving may involve all of the facets involved in liking plus increases in social penetration and self-disclosure.

30. Social penetration involves the dimensions of breadh and depth.

31. Many different forms of love include, mother, infant, peer, heterosexual, and paternal love.

CHAPTER 11

↓

The Many Facets of Behavior: Aggression

THE IMPORTANCE OF COMPREHENSIVE UNDERSTANDING: ECLECTICISM

This book has been organized around three major approaches to the study of motivation including the *biological*, the *learning*, and the *cognitive* perspectives. Through the years many investigators have come to specialize in one of these three perspectives. Thus, a particular psychologist may spend his entire career doing social motivation experiments and never pay very much attention to advances made in the understanding of the biological mechanisms underlying motivated behavior.

But this does not mean that psychologists are so narrow-minded as to reject the importance of the information obtained by investigations embracing an alternative point of view. To the contrary, most psychologists are acutely aware of, and grateful for, the existence of alternative approaches. They know that the understanding of motivation can, and should, advance along a broad front. It is probably fair to say that psychologists specialize, not because they deny the importance of alternative approaches but because the field has become so large that to try to grasp it all would be to dilute one's creative energy. Some specialization may be necessary for significant strides to be taken.

An eclectic approach, in which one takes the best from many different points of view, may be the direction in which the study of motivation is moving. When you look back over this text you will see materials that have been drawn from a number of fields of study, including social, physiological, and learning psychology.

To be able to draw upon a number of different approaches can provide us with a fuller, more complete understanding of motivation phenomena. In turn, this broad-based eclectic orientation can have practical implications. For example, imagine a nine-year-old who, over the course of several months, begins to display very disruptive behavior in the classroom. He shouts, yells, and begins some fights. Obviously this situation is not ideal. The question is, "Why is he behaving this way?" We know that this behavior can be looked at in terms of biological, learning, or cognitive factors. To look at the behavior from one point of view, without considering the alternatives, might deprive us of the most beneficial perspective. It could be that the child has been rewarded for, and learned, the disruptive response. Or perhaps he is trying to bring into balance his feelings about a classroom full of children who don't like him. Or perhaps the disruptive behavior can be traced to some disorder within the child's limbic system. Without being aware of all of these possibilities, an improvement in the situation might be difficult to realize.

In this chapter we underscore the importance of looking at the many facets of a given piece of behavior. We have chosen *aggression* as an example because it is of obvious concern in all our lives. Although we focus on aggression, the reader should keep in mind that there is nothing sacred or unusual about aggression; *any* behavior can be looked at in terms of biological, learning, and cognitive factors. *Aggression is merely the example we have chosen to illustrate the many faceted nature of motivated behavior.*

AGGRESSION: DEFINITION, TYPES, AND DISTINCTIONS

Definition   Aggression may be defined as *any action that is intended to hurt others*. Although this definition sounds simple, it is a little more complex than we might first imagine. For example, if one person hurts another we cannot simply conclude that this was an act of aggression. To be aggressive, the act must have been *intended* to hurt. Accidental injury is not aggression. Once we are committed to considering the intent behind an act, our task of correctly identifying aggression is vastly complicated. Suppose a little child knocks down her friend's sand castle and says, "I didn't mean it." But did she? Determining intent is difficult, but it must be considered when we speak of aggression.

Here is another problem with our definition. Suppose the little girl *wants* to break down the other child's sand castle. Not only that, but she has a very clear and satisfying image of pouring sand in the other child's face. But she does nothing because of fear of punishment. Is this aggression? It does not hurt anyone. But it certainly seems like the girl wanted to hurt the other person. In this case we would probably conclude that this situation did involve aggression but that it remained latent because of the fear of punishment.

The picture of aggression is further complicated by the fact that there seem to be many different types of aggression that serve different purposes. There is not just one kind of aggression; we and other species inflict pain and hurt for a wide variety of reasons.

Lorenz (1966) thought of aggression as essentially innate instinctive behavior. He broke down the overall concept of aggression into six distinct varieties as follows:

Lorenz's Types

1. Predatory Aggression. This kind of aggression refers to the situation in which a predator attacks its prey. Snakes strike at frogs, mice, fish, or even other snakes. Cats "get the canary." Chickens hunt insects. Lions bring down zebra.

In a sense, this form of behavior, although labeled aggression by Lorenz, does not really fit our definition because the predator does not necessarily *want to hurt* the prey; it wants to *eat* it. Whether or not the prey suffers some form of hurt may be completely irrelevant to the predator. Still, it is difficult for us to think of a leopard pulling down a sweet-eyed little antelope as nothing more than the innocent action of a nice old pussycat.

2. Mobbing. If you have ever been even a casual bird-watcher you will at some time probably have noticed a group of crows harassing a slower moving hawk. And you will probably have seen crows, in turn, being chased by a group of speedy little song birds. This form of aggression is called *mobbing* by Lorenz and refers to the counter-attack launched by prey against predator. Another common example of mobbing is when a cat is dive-bombed and jeered by birds of various sorts.

3. The Critical Reaction.   When cornered or surprised, many animals will attack. When hiking in grizzly territory, you should make noise as you travel. Tying a bell to your ankle, singing, or talking will avoid the charge of a surprised bear who would, if forewarned, much prefer to avoid you. This is called the critical reaction by Lorenz and generally refers to aggression that occurs when the animal believes it cannot escape danger. Animals as small as the common garter snake and as large as the cape buffalo will attack when cornered.

4. Territoriality.   The three types of aggression mentioned usually occur between different species (and, we might add, can and do often involve humans). Lorenz also identifies three types of aggression that usually occur withing a given species. Territoriality is the first of these. Animals will defend their "turf." Birds will attack intruders in their territory. Hyenas will fight when other hyenas enter their range. Humans often aggress toward people invading their homes.

There often seems to be a "home court advantage" in connection with territoriality. When one cardinal enters the territory of another cardinal, it is usually the intruder that is vanquished. Although very eager to repel members of its own species, the animal in its territory may be very tolerant of members of other species, especially if there is no competition for food. For example, if one maps out the territories of birds living in a given locale, one will find many different species living in the area but sometimes only one of each species living in a given territory.

5. Rivalry.   This form of aggression is said to occur when animals of a given species compete with one another for a mate. Rivalry usually occurs between males. Once again we have the problem of deciding intent. Many rivalries seem fierce enough, but it is commonly recognized that these contests often result in very little actual damage. Bighorn sheep pound heads together but do little damage. Deer tangle up their antlers and do a lot of pushing and shoving, but no one seems to suffer very much damage. Even fighting house cats, who *sound* like bloody murder, seldom suffer much more than a chewed ear; they simply do not kill one another very often.

6. Defense of the Young.   In this situation intent to do bodily harm seems more clear-cut. Animals, particularly mothers, are often likely to fight in defense of their young. Perhaps the best-known case is that of the mother bear tearing into anything that comes between her and her cubs. But even animals as diminutive as the hummingbird will buzz you if you come to close to their nests.

Feshbach's Types

Although Lorenz's distinctions are interesting and probably valid, other investigators have broken aggression down in different ways. Feshbach (1971) has drawn a distinction between *instrumental aggression* and *hostile aggression*. Instrumental aggression is designed to *get* the aggressor something. For example, a cat catches a mouse, not to hurt it but to eat it. One child may hit another child, not to hurt the other child but to get a toy away from her. The goal here is not aggression, but the means of obtaining that goal are aggressive. In hostile aggression, on the other hand, the goal is to hurt someone. If the child merely wants to be mean to his playmate, and does not care about any other goal, then that is a form of hostile aggression.

In instrumental aggression you may merely be using habits and responses that you have found to be effective means of obtaining your goals. In hostile aggression you are really steamed up and out to hurt someone.

Although the distinction between these two forms of aggression is clear on a conceptual level, they may often be mixed in everyday life. Suppose a child has learned to hit other children when they try to take his toys away because this form of aggression usually allows the child to retain control of the toy. It sounds like instrumental aggression, doesn't it? But it is also clear that irritation and anger (hostile aggression) may be motivating the attack. In summary, an overt aggressive act may be multiply determined; a given bit of aggression may be both hostile and instrumental.

Anti- and Prosocial Aggression

We usually think of aggression as bad or undesirable. But sometimes it is not all bad. When a police officer shoots an attacking murderer, society generally condones the officer's extremely aggressive act. When a SWAT team aggresses toward a terrorist holding hostages, the aggression is usually seen as acceptable if not laudatory.

In other words, sometimes aggression is prosocial and sometimes it is antisocial. It is antisocial when it violates common social norms (such as laws and rules of right and wrong) and it is prosocial when it supports those same social norms.

However, we sometimes have trouble distinguishing between pro- and antisocial aggression. The problem stems from the fact that we don't always agree upon what is right and what is wrong. To the government in power, revolutionaries are bandits guilty of antisocial aggression who need to be wiped out through prosocial aggression. But to the revolutionaries, who see themselves as freedom fighters, the government in power is filled with bandits engaged in antisocial violence, who need to be wiped out with prosocial aggression.

So it depends upon which social standards you subscribe to. Young gangs believe that revenge killings are acceptable whereas the culture at large does not. Riots are seen a justifiable by the rioters and as antisocial by those being rioted against.

Moyer's Types   Moyer (1968) has proposed that there are a number of different kinds of aggression to which we should pay attention. Some of these are similar to those we have already discussed, especially Lorenz's, whereas others represent new types.

1. Predation.   This form of aggression, already identified by Lorenz, refers to the attack made by a predator upon its prey.

2. Intermale Aggression.   This is the same as Lorenz's concept of rivalry. It is aggression triggered by a strange male of the same species, and it may be genetically determined.

3. Fear-induced Aggression.   Lorenz's critical reaction is similar to the notion of fear-induced aggression. This is aggression that occurs when the animal experiences fear upon being surprised or trapped.

4. Territorial Aggression.   Again Moyer agrees with Lorenz in identifying this important form of aggression.

5. Irritable Aggression.   This form, not identified by Lorenz, refers to aggression that is not preceded by attempts to escape. Thus you may find that if you do nothing more than approach a strange dog in a friendly manner the animal may snap at you. Or someone in the office may be grouchy and critical when you are trying to be friendly.

Moyer thinks that stress, in any form, may increase this kind of aggression. When the trip to the beach begins, the whole family is cheerful. But by 5 P.M., when the family is tired, sunburned, and caught in traffic, tempers may flair.

If anything, irritable aggression may be similar to Feshbach's idea of hostile aggression. When the sunburned father yells at the sunburned child in the back seat because she says she feels carsick, the father's goal, at least temporarily, may be to inflict a little irritation-based pain upon the child.

6. Instrumental Aggression. This is similar to Feshbach's idea of instrumental aggression. It is aggression that has been learned, not because it is felt but because it has paid off, or been reinforced, in the past. A person may beat his dog, not because he wants to hurt the animal but because he has learned that he can control its behavior by hurting it. Hired killers may kill, not always for the thrill of it but because the pay is good.

7. Sex-related Aggression. Finally, Moyer identifies sex-related aggression in which sex objects are subjected to aggression such as beatings, rape, and other assorted nasty acts. Although Moyer acknowledges that little is known about this form of aggression, in spite of its social significance, he feels that it may well be a distinct form of hostility.

1. Provoked versus Unprovoked. Imagine a young boy who throws a rock through the window of a stranger's house. Imagine a person being shot by a total stranger driving by in a car. These are examples of unprovoked violence. The object of the attack did nothing to "deserve" the attack. Provoked aggression, on the other hand, refers to all cases in which the victim of the aggressive act did something to cause the aggressor to act.

Although unprovoked violence does occur, and is often widely publicized, provoked aggression is probably the more common of the two. Someone insults another person. Someone intrudes upon his "rights." Someone cuts him off in traffic. Someone aggresses toward him first. Many of the crimes committed in our culture are provoked.

Further Distinctions

A man shoots his neighbor because of a dispute over dogs, or fences, or loud parties. A woman kills her husband, not because he did nothing but because he did something.

Although many of us fear unprovoked violence, the chances of suffering this sort of attack are slim compared to one of provoked aggression.

2. *Direct versus Indirect Aggression.* Suppose a man is chewed out and almost fired, unfairly, by his boss. He feels angry. What can he do? He can't yell back at his boss because then he really will be fired. So he goes home all bottled up. His wife meets him at the door and says, "Hi, honey. How was your day?" He snaps back, "Why in the hell is the kid's bike on the sidewalk. All I need is a lawsuit when someone trips over it!" Stunned, she gets dinner on the table only to have him grouse about that, too. Now also feeling angry herself, she takes it out on the child, by shouting, "Be quiet and eat your spinach!" Being afraid to show hostility toward his mother what can the child do? Throwing a few toys around after supper or pinching the kitten may help.

This example demonstrates *displaced aggression.* When attack of the frustrating object is impossible, we pick out something else, something more defenseless, upon which to vent our anger. We find a scapegoat and really give it a smack.

The distinction between direct and indirect aggression relates back to the distinction between provoked and unprovoked aggression. Provoked aggression is direct aggression in that we directly attack the provoking element. Unprovoked aggression, on the other hand, may sometimes (although not necessarily always) be indirect aggression. A child may throw a rock through a stranger's window because he is really mad at his parents or some other aspect of his life. The drive-by killing of a total stranger may sometimes also be indirect aggression; the killer's real anger is toward something he cannot attack.

3. *Physical-Verbal.* Although it may seem that we are surrounded by violence, it is probably closer to the truth to say that most of our adult aggressive impulses are only expressed verbally and stop short of actual physical violence. Children are more likely to display physical violence than adults. Once we have reached adulthood, we have pretty much learned to control our impulses. We may yell and scream at other drivers but we seldom actually get out of our cars and fight.

This is not to say that physical violence does not occur. Clearly, we are not all under control of our emotions at all times. However, one should try to balance against the instances of violence reported in the newspapers all of the untold instances of nonviolence. "Flash. Jane didn't kill anyone today." It just doesn't make good news. Think about your own life; when was the last time you saw an actual example of physical violence? Probably not very recently. Although you would never know it from reading novels, watching television, and going to movies, a great percentage of police officers go through their entire thirty-year careers without firing their weapons in the line of duty.

4. *Adaptive-Maladaptive.* Sometimes, although probably fairly infrequently, aggression can be adaptive. A new kid on the block may have to have a few fights before he can establish his right to be left alone. A drugstore owner may thwart further robberies by shooting an intruder. But most aggression is not adaptive because most societies have established harsh penalties for aggressive acts.

BIOLOGICAL FACTORS

Having looked at some important distinctions that have been made in the study of aggression, we now turn to the main thrust of this chapter: the biological, learning, and cognitive factors in aggression. We begin by looking at the biology of aggression including a consideration of *genetic*, *neurological*, and *chemical* elements in that order.

Genetic Factors

Is the Human a Killer by Nature? One of the most intriguing controversies within the study of aggression has involved the question of whether aggression, and particularly human aggression, is learned or innate. Is the human being essentially, and in some very basic sense, an aggressive animal? Are we "killers by nature" or are we born nonaggressive only to learn how to be violent? These questions bear upon the very essence of what it means to be human.

Unfortunately, we do not have the answer to the riddle, and the controversy remains in full swing. Some investigators hold that aggression is essentially inherited whereas others argue, often just as persuasively, that aggressive behavior is acquired. The question is whether aggression is essentially an innate behavior as that concept was outlined in Chapter 2, or a behavior acquired according to the principles of learning as outlined in Chapter 5.

That genetics are at least involved in aggression seems unarguable. For example, it has been shown repeatedly (McLearn, 1969) that various species, such as white rats, dogs, and fighting chickens can be bred for violence. By mating only the most aggressive members of a given population, a strain of aggressive animals can be developed easily. In the case of the human being, we cannot go about breeding or trying to breed violent offspring. But some evidence suggests that there may be, at least some of the time, a genetic basis for human violence. Specifically, certain chromosomal abnormalities such as the XYY condition seem to be associated with heightened aggression. Normally the twenty-third chromosomal position of the human male contains an X and a Y chromosome (females have an XX configuration). But sometimes males are born with an extra Y chromosome in addition to the normal XY pair. Although controversial (see Owens, 1972), it has been suggested that these XYY males are larger, more aggressive, and a have a stronger sex drive than normal XY males (Jacobs, Price, Court, Braun, Brittain, and Whatmore, 1968)

But examples of the influence of learning upon aggression are just as common. So perhaps the best we can suggest is that both our genes and our experiences affect our aggressiveness. In the next section we look at more of what is known about the role of heredity in aggression. Then we look at what is known about the physiological underpinnings of aggressive action. Following that we examine what has been discovered about the role of learning in aggression.

Lorenz's Theory. Lorenz (1969) has argued that aggression has evolved according to the principle of natural selection. He believes that aggression is an instinctive behavior that persists because it facilitates survival and reproduction of the species. It is innate rather than learned. For example, birds that mob intruders will be more likely to drive off the intruder and be thus more likely to avoid potential damage to their species posed by that intruder. A mother bear that attacks an animal which comes between her and her cubs is more likely to ensure the survival of, and eventual reproduction of, those cubs. The cubs of nonaggressive mothers would be more likely to suffer at the hands of the interloper.

Lorenz thinks that aggression can be understood in terms of the hydraulic model outlined in Chapter 2. If you recall, this model assumes that an instinct builds up like water in a tank only to be released when an appropriate sign stimulus appears. Thus, we and all other animals are thought of as reservoirs of aggressive energy that is constantly on the increase. When the appropriate sign stimulus appears (such as an intruder in our territory), this energy is released as violent behavior.

The concept of a vacuum reaction refers to Lorenz's idea that if a sign stimulus does not appear, and instinctual energy builds up too much, the instinctive behavior may just burst out by itself. The little male stickleback fish will simply attack anything if too much energy builds up in the absence of normal sign stimuli. Lorenz believes that this kind of thing happens too often with humans. He believes that aggressive energy is not drained off appropriately. It builds up and up in the absence of releasing stimuli, and often bursts out inappropriately in such a way as to do harm to the individual and those around him.

One controversial implication of this theory is that if we could present releasing stimuli in a harmless way, this excess energy should be drained off. Thus watching violence on television, or reading about it, or participating in rough sports should release some of this potentially dangerous aggressive energy. But, unfortunately, there are many people, adhering to the idea that aggression is acquired, who feel that watching violence will lead to *more* rather than *less* violence.

What really does happen to that little child who sits for so many hours before the violence on our television? Instinct theory suggests that excess aggressive energy may be released. But others argue that the result will be even more violence in an already violent world. We look at some of the evidence bearing upon this issue in upcoming sections, particularly when we turn to the roles of learning and cognition in aggression.

Territoriality. We have already had occasion to mention territorial aggression. This refers to the tendency for animals to drive intruders out of their range. The "owner" of the territory is more likely to stand and fight than the intruder.

Territoriality at first glance might seem to be difficult to explain in terms of natural selection because it involves intraspecies aggression; for example, one robin attacking another. But in terms of survival of the entire species, territoriality may be very helpful because it tends to spread the animals out over the available range evenly. In this way food sources will be used with maximum efficiency. In agreement with this interpretation, territoriality seems to be strongest when young are being raised and food is most critical. Once the young are out on their own, robins will be much more likely to group together.

Although it is difficult to extend genetic concepts based upon observations of animal behavior to the human condition, it does seem, at least on an intuitive level, that we humans do display territoriality. Our living conditions most readily display the efect. If we live in an apartment, the walls of that enclosure are the limits of our territory. People cannot just walk into our apartment any time; they must be invited. If we own a house, our yard sets the limits. Certain people, such as the mailperson or small neighborhood children, may travel across our yard, but not others, especially strangers. "Keep off" and "No salespeople" signs are our way of "marking" the territory, just as other species mark their territory with scent. The richer and more powerful we are the bigger is our territory. Intruders will be the object of one form or another of aggression. We speak to or yell at them. The police may be called. Weapons may come into play. All of these effects are consistent with Lorenz's idea that territorial aggression has persisted as a genetic mechanism because it assisted in the survival of our ancestors.

Dominance.   Many, although not all species of animals, establish a dominance hierarchy within their ranks. This is usually accomplished through ritualized aggression. In a pack of baboons or a herd of deer, the males will fight one another until the most effective fighter wins the dominant position. Although serious injury does occur, sometimes many of these contests stop short of bodily damage.

The dominant male is often the one that mates with the females. In terms of natural selection this ensures that the genes of the dominant male will be passed on. Notice that we do not say that the genes of the strongest male will be passed on, although this is often the case. What are preserved are the genes of the most effective fighter. This may often represent some combination of cleverness and strength rather than brute strength alone.

The hierarchy of dominance runs all the way from top to bottom. It is similar to the idea of a "pecking order." Dominance within a group of litter mates can begin very early in life, even when the young animals are tumbling about in "play." A dominance hierarchy can change. For example, when a strange male joins a group, he must find his place in the hierarchy by facing the dominant male and others. The aggression associated with the struggle for dominance among many species of animals is often thought to be a biologically determined form of aggression. Whether this analysis can be extended to humans is another matter. But there do seem to be dominance hierarchies within the human realm. Status, social class, power, and influence all seem to involve a hierarchical structure. Although we don't usually go out on the street and punch one another to determine who will be "up' and who will be "down," there have clearly been many armed clashes throughout history where the prize has been dominance of one sort or another. And there are many more subtle forms of aggression that we use to establish dominance, including political maneuvering, economic competition, and religious proselytizing.

Although we do not really know if human competition in the pursuit of dominance is the same as animal dominance, the analogy is appealing. It may well be that these forms of stylized aggression have at least some basis in genetics.

Neurological Factors

Regardless of whether aggression is determined by genetic factors or by experience or both, it must have physiological correlates. The instigation, occurrence, and cessation of aggression must be traceable in terms of what is happening within the machine we call our body during these events.

The neurological basis of aggression has intrigued many investigators and it is to what they have learned that we now turn. Several neural structures have been identified as being involved in the expression and control of aggression. Although progress is being made, the relationships between these structures and aggression is turning out to be quite a bit more complicated than was first imagined.

1. The Hypothalamus. The hypothalamus, located between the thalamus and the pituitary gland, is only about the size of a grape. Yet it seems to be important in the control of many functions including eating, drinking, sleeping, waking, and the control of hormones (Stricker and Zigmond, 1976). In addition, the hypothalamus is involved in aggression. For example, Berntson, Hughes, and Beattie (1976) found that by electrically stimulating a portion of the hypothalamus of a resting cat, they were able to cause the animal to leap into a predatory attack. Defensive behavior and rage responses have also been shown to be influenced by the hypothalamus (Roberts and Kiess, 1964; Bard, 1928).

2. The Limbic System.   The limbic system is a system of connected neural structures surrounding the upper end of the brain stem (see Figure 11.1). The limbic system is usually thought to include the *cingulate gyrus*, *septum*, *amygdala*, and *hippocampus* (sometimes the hypothalamus is included too). This limbic system is heavily involved, in complicated ways, in the control of emotional behavior, including aggression. The amygdala seems to be deeply involved in aggression. Removing parts of the amygdala tends to produce marked calmness (Grossman, 1967). Stimulation of the amygdala can lead to attack as well as defensive behavior. The amygdala has proven to be quite a complicated region. Different types of aggression seem to be associated with different areas of the structure (Moyer, 1976).

It is best, at the present time, to avoid firm conclusions concerning the role of brain tissue in controlling aggression. We know that the hippocampus and the various limbic structures are involved, but we do not yet know the details.

The important point to remember here is that aggression can be legitimately investigated in many different ways, only one of which is the exploration of its neurological foundations.

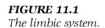
FIGURE 11.1
The limbic system.

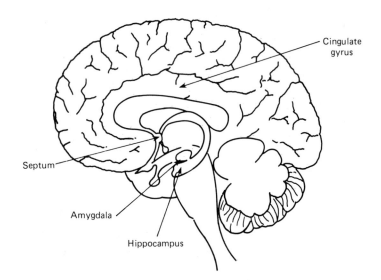

Just as there are neural factors controlling aggression, so too are there important chemical bases for aggressive activity. A few of these are discussed here. **Chemical Factors**

1. Norepinephrine. The neurotransmitter norepinephrine seems to be involved in aggression. This has been shown in at least two ways. First, levels of norepinephrine have been measured in psychiatric patients during periods of naturally occurring violence and during calm periods. The levels of norepinephrine are substantially higher during periods of violence. Second, injections of norephinephrine produce heart rate and blood pressure changes that resemble those occurring during anger.

2. Hypoglycemia. Hypoglycemia refers to a condition of low blood sugar. This condition can be brought about by a number of different causes. Whatever the cause, low blood sugar levels at least sometimes seem to be associated with aggressiveness (Wilder, 1947).

3. Sex Hormones. The male sex hormone testosterone seems to be involved with aggression. Castrated males (such as steers and geldings) tend to be much less aggressive than uncastrated males of the same species. One of the benefits of "fixing" a tom cat is that veterinarian bills for torn ears and infected bites go way down. That these calming effects result from testosterone is clearly shown by the fact that if a castrated male is given injections of testosterone, much of the aggressive behavior will return. Furthermore, during the mating season when testosterone levels are high many males will be extremely aggressive.

LEARNING AND AGGRESSION

We have seen that aggression can be fruitfully studied by looking for its genetic, neurological, and chemical bases. Now we want to turn to what is known about the role of learning and experience in the development and expression of aggression.

The approach to aggression that emphasizes conditioning principles holds that aggressive behavior is *learned* like any other behavior. Aggression is molded by the processes of *reinforcement*, *punishment*, and *extinction*. **Conditioning and Aggression**

Let us look at examples of each of these in action. Geen and Pigg (1970) rewarded subjects for administering shock to another person by saying things like, "good," and, "you are doing fine." Control subjects were asked to shock others but were not reinforced for doing so. The results showed that the reinforced subjects administered substantially stronger shocks than did the unrewarded subjects. In other words, aggressive behavior was increased through reward. The idea is that we learn to be aggressive if it pays off. If a child gets his way on the playground by being aggressive, then he will be aggressive in the future.

However, if aggressive behavior is punished rather than reinforced, then it will be eliminated. Punishment, or the presentation of noxious stimulation, is a powerful influence on all behavior, including aggressive behavior. If the child on the playground is punished rather than rewarded for his aggression, then that aggressive behavior will tend to drop out.

Some say, "All right, but why doesn't punishment seem to work sometimes? For example, why do so many criminals end up back in jail?" The learning theorist would argue that the principle of punishment is sound but that its application is not always perfect. For example, there are many reasons why a criminal might end up back in jail. He might actually prefer jail. Some criminals do in the sense that it is easier than trying to "make it on the outside." In other cases the punishing effect of jail might be outweighed by the rewarding qualities of criminal behavior. For these people "it is worth it" even though confinement may be unpleasant.

Finally, learning theorists argue that aggressive responses will extinguish if they are left unreinforced. If the child on the playground acts aggressively but doesn't gain control or get his way, aggressive behavior will slowly fade out even though it is not punished.

Although extinction should apply to aggressive behavior, it is probably likely that more aggressive behaviors are punished than are extinguished. Society simply can not wait around for aggressive responses to extinguish. Can you imagine us saying, "Oh, go ahead and let Jimmy punch the other children. As long as he doesn't get rewarded for it he'll stop sooner or later."

We should think about aggression as something that is in all probability heavily affected by learning but not necessarily completely governed by these principles. The principles of conditioning add to the depth of our understanding of aggression but do not totally account for its many diverse aspects.

Few would deny that reinforcements, punishers, and extinction play an important role in the development and expression of aggression; but the instrumental conditioning approach is limited in a very important way. Specifically, it implies that we always learn because of the consequences of our actions. The little boy learns to hit others because he gets his way when he aggresses. Chickens learn to run to the farmer when he calls them because food follows the running response.

Modeling

But acting and then waiting to see the results of our behavior must not be the only way we learn. If it were, we would be in a lot of deep trouble. We would stick our finger in an electric socket and wait to see what happens. We would jump off cliffs, eat pretty but deadly mushrooms, and put rattlesnakes in our lunchbags. But fortunately there is another, less dangerous, way that we can learn. We can *imitate* others, or *model* our behavior after others, without actually going through all the response-then-reinforcement steps we usually think of in connection with conditioning. We can learn how to open the new safety top on an over-the-counter medication by watching someone else do it. We can learn how to eat artichokes by watching others eat them. We can learn to avoid many of the pitfalls of life by modeling our behavior after the actions of others. In a sense, we don't have to go through all the usual trial-and-error steps. And we can also imitate aggressive behavior. If a child sees someone get what he wants through violence, then he too can behave violently in anticipation of the same reward.

The name most often associated with the ideal of learning through modeling is that of Albert Bandura (1969, 1977), who has identified three types of behavior that are acquired through modeling, as follows:

1. Learning Observed Behavior.   This refers to the learning of new behaviors that the individual has never done before. A child might learn to open a new lock, not by fooling around with the key in a trial-and-error fashion but merely by watching his parents open the lock a few times.

2. Inhibiting Behavior. It is possible to inhibit behavior that has already been learned through modeling. For example, suppose a child has learned to be rowdy and troublesome during gym class because his classmates laugh and reward him for being that way. Then a new gym teacher takes over the class and punishes one of the *other* children for being disruptive. It is quite likely, upon witnessing the fate of this other student, that our disruptive student will "cool it." He won't have to suffer punishment in order to inhibit his rowdy behavior; the "example" will have done the trick.

3. Disinhibiting Behavior. Bandura has also noted that, through modeling, behavior that was previously inhibited may become disinhibited. For example, a child who knows how to be disruptive in class may not do it because she is afraid. But if she observes someone else being disruptive and getting away with it, then she too may act in a similar fashion.

Four Conditions for Modeling   Bandura believes that four general conditions must exist for modeling to occur (see Figure 11.2). First, the subject must *attend* to the behavior in question. If you don't attend to a behavior, you can't imitate it. If a classmate is being snide to the teacher, but you don't realize it, then you can't imitate the behavior. Whether or not a given individual will be aware of a given behavior is a very complex issue. Attention depends upon many factors, including not only the salience and dis-

FIGURE 11.2.
Bandura's Four Components of modeling.
(From Bandura, A. *Social Learning Theory.* Englewood Cliffs, N.J.: Prentice-Hall, 1977. Fig. 1 on p.23.)

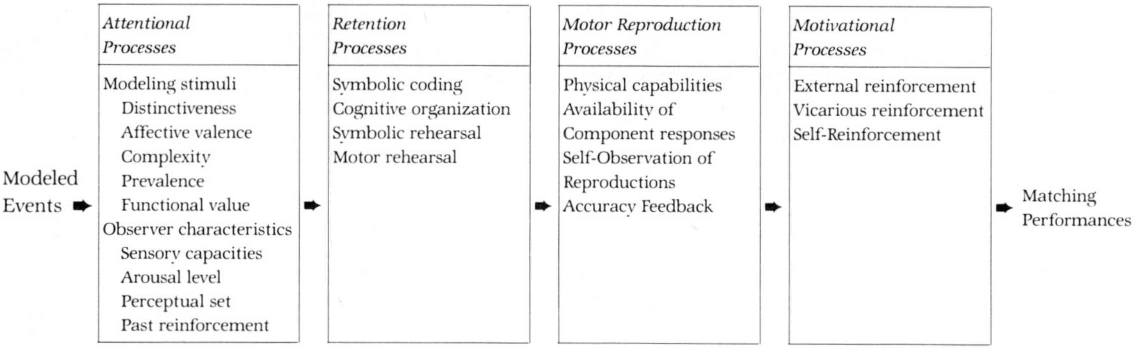

	Attentional Processes	Retention Processes	Motor Reproduction Processes	Motivational Processes	

Modeled Events ➡	Modeling stimuli
	  Distinctiveness
	  Affective valence
	  Complexity
	  Prevalence
	  Functional value
	Observer characteristics
	  Sensory capacities
	  Arousal level
	  Perceptual set
	  Past reinforcement
		Symbolic coding
		Cognitive organization
		Symbolic rehearsal
		Motor rehearsal
			Physical capabilities
			Availability of
			Component responses
			Self-Observation of
			Reproductions
			Accuracy Feedback
				External reinforcement
				Vicarious reinforcement
				Self-Reinforcement
					➡ Matching Performances

tinctiveness of the model behavior but upon various characteristics of the subject as well, as indicated in Figure 11.2. Second, the subject must *remember* what the model does. If we cannot remember what the model does, then we cannot imitate that behavior. Third, the subject must be *able to do* the behavior in question. Even if a student attends to a model saying sarcastic things to a teacher, and remembers the behavior, imitation will not occur unless the observer can make sarcastic remarks of his own. Fourth, the observer must be *motivated* to imitate the behavior. It doesn't make any difference how much the observer attends, remembers, or is able to do if he doesn't want to imitate. If the student doesn't want to be sarcastic, then he will not be so regardless of how strong the other three prerequisites are. Figure 11.2 provides some idea of the number of complex and interrelated factors that are subsumed by each of these four components of modeling.

Because our principal concern here is with aggression, let us look at one of Bandura's classical experimental demonstrations of modeled aggressive behavior. He had some nursery-school children watch films of other children attacking a large inflated plastic doll. Other children watched adults actually attack the doll in their classroom. Control subjects saw either no models at all, or passive nonaggressive models. Then all the children were allowed to interact with the very same doll, and numbers of aggressive acts were counted. As seen in Figure 11.3, much more aggression occurred after aggressive models had been observed than after either no model or a passive model had been observed. Children imitated the aggressive behavior of both other children and adults.

Modeling of Aggression

The implications here are profound. If people really do imitate aggressive acts we have a serious problem. Our culture is permeated with aggressive models. One need only turn on the television, at any time of the day, to realize that. What does all this media violence really do to us? As we have seen, some theoreticians, such as Lorenz, argue that viewing violence should lead to the discharge of pent-up aggressive energy and therefore to *less* aggression. Others, such as Bandura, argue that exposure to violence will lead to imitation and an *increase* in violence.

Media Violence

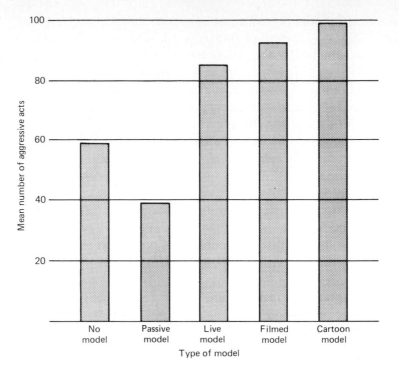

What is the answer to this issue? Well, it seems to depend upon who you listen to. After a review of the literature, Bee, writing in Houston, Bee, and Rimm (1983), states that people who watch a lot of violence on television "are more likely to use aggression in their own behavior" (p. 719). Freedman, Sears, and Carlsmith (1981), on the other hand, after an exhaustive review of the literature, conclude, "There is no good evidence yet that media violence contributes to violence and crime in our society" (p. 280).

So the jury is really still out on this issue. It may well be that media violence does increase the tendency to engage in violence. But the conditions under which it does and does not do so remain elusive.

Reducing Aggression: Catharsis

1. *Freud's Concept.* The idea of reducing aggression through the expression of that aggression is an old and intuitively appealing one. We often think that "letting off steam" and "getting it all out in the open" can help us reduce our aggression. Freud was the originator of the idea of catharsis. He felt that bottled-up internal aggression could be defused or reduced if we could somehow manage to express that aggressive energy.

2. *Frustration-Aggression Hypothesis.* Dollard, Doob, Miller, Mowrer, and Sears (1939) expanded Freud's ideas into what is known as the frustration-aggression hypothesis. This hypothesis states that frustration always leads to aggression and that aggression is always preceded by frustration. Frustration is defined as the blocking of a motivated organism in its attempts to reach some goal. Barker, Dembo, and Lewis (1941) demonstrated the frustration-aggression effect in this way. They first frustrated one group of children by showing them a room of very attractive toys but not letting them play with them. Then, after this frustrating delay, the children were finally allowed to play with the toys. Control children were allowed to play with the toys immediately without first having to wait. It was found that the frustrated children played with the toys much more aggressively than did the control children. The frustrated children bashed them about and threw them at the walls. The conclusion was that frustration led to aggression.

The original formulation of the frustration-aggression hypothesis fell on hard times. It soon became apparent that it is an oversimplification to state that frustration *always* leads to aggression and the aggression is *always* preceded by aggression. Still, the idea has persisted, and has led to a good deal of experimentation.

For our purposes it is important to note that the frustration-aggression hypothesis is usually thought to be consistent with the idea of catharsis originally formulated by Freud. The idea is that frustration-induced aggression can be reduced if that aggression can be expressed, and especially if it can be vented on the frustrating obstacle itself.

3. *Lorenz's Instinct.* Lorenz's thinking about aggression is also consistent with the catharsis idea. According to his hydraulic model, the pent-up aggression can be spewed out if the appropriate sign stimuli are present.

4. *Bandura's Opposition.* Three theoretical analyses (Frued, frustration-aggression, Lorenz) all support the idea of catharsis. Opposed to these interpretations is the thinking of Bandura who believes that watching or engaging in aggressive behavior will actually *increase* rather than decrease aggression.

5. Catharsis or No Catharsis?   Can aggression really be reduced through expression of that aggression? The following quotes will give you some idea of the only answers we have to this question:

Direct aggression against an attacker or frustrator can reduce aggressive feelings through the process of catharsis (Freedman, Sears, and Carlsmith, 1981, p. 280).

There does not seem to be much evidence to support the catharsis view (Beck, 1978, p. 307).

In other words, investigators have looked at the same body of literature and come to opposite conclusions. Obviously we need more and better data before a consensus concerning the validity of the catharsis notion can be established.

COGNITIVE AND SOCIAL FACTORS

We have looked at aggression on a biological level and in terms of learning theory. Now we want to round out the picture by discussing a few representative examples of the cognitive and social approaches to the study of this many faceted phenomenon.

In a sense, we have already begun the examination of social factors in aggression by looking at such things as Milgram's experiments that demonstrated the human's disquieting willingness to give dangerous shock to a complete stranger when told to do so by the experimenter. But there are some other interesting social and cognitive effects that bear mentioning.

Insults   Insults have a dual function in connection with aggression. First, they can be used to arouse aggression. In fact, psychologists themselves have often used insults to arouse aggression in their experiments. Second, insulting someone can reduce our own feelings of frustration and anger. If we are hot, tired, and caught in traffic we can yell out and call the driver in front of us an "air head," or whatever the newest insult is, and feel a lot better for having done it. In a sense, this use of

insults represents an example of aggression reduction through catharsis.

*Being Evaluated
Negatively*

Sometimes when others evaluate us negatively we become angry and
aggresive. But at other times we do not. For example, if we take an
important exam, and do very poorly, we may be disappointed and
anxious, but not necessarily angry and hostile. If we feel the exam
was fair we will tend not to be angry. However, if we feel the exam
was unfair or absurdly difficult, we will be more likely to show aggression (See Donnerstein and Wilson, 1976). If we perceive the intent
of the exam, and its contents, as honorable, legitimate, and above
board, then we tend not to be angry. But if we feel the exam is
capricious, unfair, or just plain out of line, then we will be much
more likely to become aggressive.

The important point here is that it is our *cognitive evaluation* of
what the tester is doing that is important in determining aggression.
What we *think* about the situation is crucial.

Crowding

A crowd is certainly a social factor. And we have all, at one time or
another, felt irritated by crowds, such as when we are trying to finish
up our Christmas shopping along with thousands of others. And
crowding appears to be a problem that is going to get worse before it
gets better (see Figure 11.4). So it is not surprising that psychologists
have studied the effects of crowding on human behavior, and on

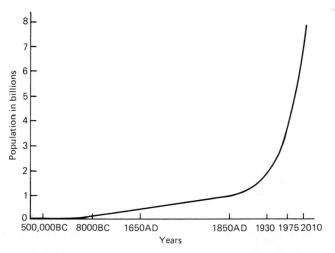

FIGURE 11.4
*Growth of world human
population. (Adapted
from Freedman, J. L.,
Sears, D.O., & Carlsmith,
J. M. Social psychology.
Englewood Cliffs, N. J.:
Prentice-HaLL, 1981. P.
617.)*

aggression in particular. As Freedman, Sears and Carlsmith (1981) note, some studies have suggested that crowding leads to increased aggression (Calhoun, 1962) whereas others have suggested that crowding probably has little or no effect on aggression (Freedman, 1975; Nogami, 1976). Freedman (1975) has made what seems to be the best guess about the relationship between crowding and behavior. He believes that crowding may intensify whatever is already going on. If you are already feeling cranky, then being thrown into a crowd will only make you feel more disagreeable. But if you are feeling good, such as when you are ready for a party, then arrival at the party and immersion in the crowd will make you feel even better. So the effects of crowding depend upon preexisting conditions. Crowding appears to intensify feelings, whatever they may happen to be.

Freedman, Levy, Buchanan, and Price (1972) did some work that further illustrates the complexity of the crowding-aggression relationship. Essentially, what they showed is that, at least under some circumstances, crowding may lead to more aggression in males but less aggression in females.

Groups of all women, all men, or of mixed sexes listened to tapes of what were presented as genuine criminal trials. The tapes were listened to either under crowded conditions (small room) or under uncrowded conditions (large room). The subjects were then asked to assign a penalty to the defendants. As you can see in Figure 11.5,

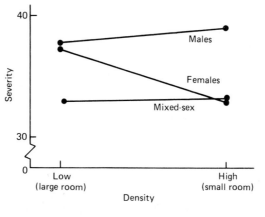

FIGURE 11.5

The relationship between density and aggression. (From Freedman, J. L., Sears, D. O., & Carlsmith, J. M. Social Psychology. Englewood Cliffs, N. J.: Prentice-Hall, 1981, p. 626. Based on original data from Freedman, J. L., Levy, A. S., Buchanan, R. W., & Price, J. Crowding and human aggressiveness. Journal of Experimental Social Psychology, 1972, 8, 528–548. Fig. 6, p. 541.)

crowding led to more severe (more aggressive) penalties being given by the males. Women, on the other hand, gave more lenient penalties under crowded conditions than they did under uncrowded conditions.

Whatever the final upshot of this sort of work (and it does not appear that there will be a simple solution), the work on crowding and aggression represents a social psychological approach to the problem of motivation.

Deindividuation can lead to aggression. Deindividuation refers to a condition in which our inner controls are weakened when we are no longer seen as or treated as individuals (Festinger, Pepitone, and Newcomb, 1952). One common form is when we give up our sense of personal, unique identity and identify heavily with some group. We become personally anonymous while, at the same time, adopting the goals of the group.

The less personal responsibility we feel the more we can give ourselves over to the goals of the group, whatever they may be. If the group goals happen to be irresponsible, then we too can be irresponsible. For example, which is easier to do, throwing a rock at a police officer while standing alone or throwing that rock while being a member of a mob?

Zimbardo (1969) ran an experiment in which girls were given an opportunity to electrically shock other people. Half the girls were impossible to identify because they wore hoods and were never identified by name. The girls in the other half were called by name, wore no hoods, and were identifiable by name tags. The subjects whose identity was hidden gave about twice as many shocks as did those who were identifiable.

The crucial variable here seems to be anonymity. If we can hide, if we can be a nameless hidden factor, if we can "get away with it," then we will tend to increase our antisocial behavior. Mere group membership, although it can sometimes *lead* to anonymity, seems to be less important than anonymity itself in stimulating aggression.

Deindividuation

CONCLUSION

In this text we have tried to provide a fair and broad picture of the complex and facinating field of motivation by covering what we believe are the three major approaches in the field. We discussed biological factors in Section II, learning approaches in Section III, and cognitive and social elements in Section IV.

Although these three approaches have been discussed sequentially, that is not the only way the text could have been organized. It is possible to break the field down into topics (such as aggression, depression, altruism) and look at what is known about each of these topics from the biological, learning, and cognitive points of view. This alternative approach, although not the main thrust of this text, was illustrated in Chapter 11. We have chosen an important topic, aggression, and looked at it from each of the three major point of views. The interested reader may wish to pursue this alternative way of organizing the field by looking at the other available sources (e.g., Franken, 1982).

SUMMARY

1. The eclectic approach takes the best from many different ways of studying the same topic.

2. Any topic in motivation can be studied from the eclectic point of view, as is aggression in this chapter.

3. Aggression is defined as any action intended to hurt others.

4. Lorenz identifies five types of aggression including predatory, mobbing, critical reaction, territoriality, and rivalry.

5. Feshbach distinguishes between instrumental and hostile aggression.

6. A distinction between antisocial and prosocial aggression may be made.

7. Moyer identifies seven types of aggression including predation, intermale, fear-induced, territoriality, maternal, irritable, instrumental, and sex-related aggression.

8. Aggression may be provoked or unprovoked, direct or indirect, physical or verbal, and adaptive or maladaptive.

9. Although the extent to which aggression is innate is unknown, genetic factors certainly play a part.

10. Lorenz argues that aggression is an innate mechanism which has been naturally selected. He thinks it can be understood in terms of his hydraulic model.

11. Territoriality and dominance can be used to support the idea that aggression is innate.

12. On a neurological level the hypothalamus and the limbic system have been implicated in the control and occurrence of aggression.

13. Chemical factors, such as norepinephrine, hypoglycemia, and sex hormones have been shown to be involved in aggression.

14. Some forms of aggression may be subject to the principles of conditioning including reinforcement, punishment, and extinction.

15. Aggression may be the result of modeling or imitation.

16. Bandura believes that behavior may be learned, inhibited, or disinhibited through modeling.

17. For modeling to occur the observer must attend, remember, be capable, and be motivated.

18. Modeling of aggression in the laboratory has been observed. But whether or not exposure to media violence leads to increased crime and violence remains an open question.

19. Catharsis refers to the reduction of aggression through the expression of that aggression.

20. Freud, Lorenz, and the frustration-aggression hypothesis all hold that catharsis should work. Bandura's social learning theory says that it should not.

21. No firm conclusion concerning the effectiveness of catharsis can be drawn at the present time.

22. Insults can cause aggression.

23. Negative evaluation can cause aggression but probably only when that evaluation is perceived as being unfair.

24. Crowding probably enhances whatever is already going on. Both positive and negative feelings can be heightened by crowding.

25. Deindividuation, or the process of losing inner controls when we are no longer seen or treated as indentifiable individuals, can lead to aggression.

References

Abramson, L. Y., Seligman, M. E. P., & Teasdale, J. D. Learned helplessness in humans: Critique and reformulation. *Journal of Abnormal Psychology*, 1978, *87*, 49–74.

Adams, D. B., Gold, A. R., & Burt, A. D. Rise in female-initiated sexual activity at ovulation and its suppression by oral contraceptives. *New England Journal of Medicine*, 1978, 299, *21*, 1145–1150.

Alcock, J. *Animal behavior: An evolutionary approach.* Sunderland, Mass.: Sinauer, 1975.

Allen, V. L. & Levin, J. M. Social support and conformity: The independent assessment of reality. *Journal of Experimental Social Psychology*, 1971, *7*, 48–58.

Altman, I., & Taylor, D. A. *Social penetration: The development of interpersonal relationships.* New York: Holt, Rinehart and Winston, 1973.

Anand, B. K., & Brobeck, J. R. Hypothalamic control of food intake in rats and cats. *Yale Journal of Biology and Medicine*, 1951, *24*, 123–140.

Andersson, B. Thirst and brain control of water balance. *American Scientist*, 1971, *59*, 408–415.

Anderson, D. C., Crowell, C. R., Cunningham, C. L., & Lupo, J. V. Behavior during shock exposure as a determinant of subsequent interference with shuttle box escape-avoidance learning in the rat. *Journal of Experimental Psychology: Animal Behavior Processes*, 1979, *5*, 243–257.

Anrep, G. V. Pitch discrimination in the dog. *Journal of Physiology*, 1920, *53*, 367–385.

Ardrey, R. *The territorial imperative.* New York: Atheneum, 1966.

Arkes, H. R. Competence and the overjustification effect. *Motivation and Emotion*, 1979, *3*, 143–150.

Aronson, E., & Carlsmith, J. M. The effect of the severity of threat on the devaluation of forbidden behavior. *Journal of Abnormal and Social Psychology*, 1963, *66*, 584–588.

Aronson, E., & Linder, D. Gain and loss of esteem as determinants of interpersonal attractiveness. *Journal of Experimental Social Psychology*, 1965, *1*, 156–171.

Asch, S. E. Effects of group pressure upon the modification and distortion of judgments. In H. Guetzkow (Ed.), *Groups, leadership and men.* Pittsburgh: Carnegie Press, 1951.

Asch, S. E. *Social psychology.* Englewood Cliffs, N. J.: Prentice-Hall, 1952.

Asch, S. E. Interpersonal influence. In H. Proshansky, & B. Seidenberg (Eds.), *Basic studies in social psychology.* New York: Holt, Rinehart and Winston, 1965.

Aserinsky, E., & Kleitman, N. Regularly occurring periods of eye mobility and concomitant phenomena during sleep. *Science*, 1953, *118*, 273–274.

Atkinson, J. W. The achievement motive and recall of interrupted and completed tasks. *Journal of Experimental Psychology*, 1953, *46*, 381–390.

Atkinson, J. W. Motivational determinants of risk–taking behavior. *Psychological Review*, 1957, *64*, 359–372.

Atkinson, J. W. *An introduction to motivation.* New York: Van Nostrand Reinhold, 1964.

Atkinson, J. W., & Birch, D. *Introduction to motivation.* New York: Van Nostrand, 1978.

Atkinson, J. W., Heyns, R. W., & Veroff, J. The effect of experimental arousal of the affiliation motive on thematic apperception. *Journal of Abnormal and Social Psychology*, 1954, *49*, 405–410.

Atkinson, J. W., Lens, W., & O'Malley, P. M. Motivation and ability: Interactive psychological determinants of intellectual performance, educational achievement, and each other. In W. H. Sewell, R. H. Hanser, & D. L. Featherman (Eds.), *Schooling and achievement in American society.* New York: Academic Press, 1976.

Atkinson, J. W., & Litwin, G. A. Achievement motive and text anxiety conceived as motive to approach success and motive to avoid failure. *Journal of Abnormal and Social Psychology*, 1960, *60*, 52–63.

Atkinson, J. W., & Walker, E. L. The affiliation motive and perceptual sensitivity to faces. *Journal of Abnormal and Social Psychology*, 1956, *53*, 38–41.

Ayres, C. E. Instinct and capacity: I. The instinct of belief in instincts. *Journal of Philosophy*, 1921, *18*, 561–566.

Azrin, N., Hontos, P. T., & Besalel-Azrin, V. Elimination of enuresis without a conditioning apparatus: An extension of office instruction of the child and parents. *Behavior Therapy*, 1979, *10*, 14–15.

Bandura, A. *Principles of behavior modification.* New York: Holt, 1969.

Bandura, A. *Social learning theory.* Englewood Cliffs, N.J.: Prentice-Hall, 1977.

Bandura, A., Ross, D., & Ross, S. Transmission of aggression through imitation of aggressive models. *Journal of Abnormal and Social Psychology*, 1961, *63*, 575–582.

Barash, D. P. *Sociobiology and behavior.* New York: Elsevier, 1977.

Bard, P. A. A. A diencephalic mechanism for the expression of rage with special reference to the sympathetic nervous system. *American Journal of Physiology*, 1928, *84*, 490–515.

Barker, R. G., Dembo, T., & Lewis, K. Frustration and regression: An experiment with young children. *University of Iowa Studies in Child Welfare*, 1941, *18 (1)*.

Barrett, J. E., Hoffman, H. S., Stratton, J. W., & Newby, V. Aversive control following imprinting in ducklings. *Learning and Motivation*, 1971, *2*, 202–213.

Bateson, P. Brief exposure to a novel stimulus during imprinting in chicks, and its influence on subsequent preferences. *Animal Learning and Behavior*, 1979, *7*, 259–262.

Beach, F. A. The decent of instinct. *Psychological Review*, 1955, *62*, 401–410.

Beck, R. C. *Motivation: Theories and principles.* Englewood Cliffs, N.J.: Prentice-Hall, 1978.

Bem, D. J. Self-perception: An alternative interpretation of cognitive dissonance phenomena. *Psychological Review*, 1967, *74*, 183–200.

Bemis, K. M. Current approaches to the etiology and treatment of anorexia nervosa. *Psychological Bulletin*, 1978, *85*, 593–617.

Benson, H., & Wallace, R. K. Decreased blood pressure in hypertensive subjects who practice meditation. *Circulation*, 1972, *2*, 516.

Berlyne, D. E. The influence of complexity and novelty in visual figures on orienting responses. *Journal of Experimental Psychology*, 1958, *55*, 289–296.

Berlyne, D. E. *Conflict, arousal and curiosity.* New York: McGraw-Hill, 1960.

Berlyne, D. E. Curiosity and exploration. *Science*, 1966, 25–33.

Berlyne, D. E. The reward value of indifferent stimulation. In J. T. Tapp (Ed.), *Reinforcement and behavior*, New York: Academic Press, 1969.

Berlyne, D. E. Novelty, complexity and hedonic value. *Perception and Psychophysics*, 1970, *8*, 279–286.

Berlyne, D. E. *Aesthetics and psychobiology*. New York: Appleton-Century-Crofts, 1971.

Berntson, G. G., Hughes, H. C., & Beattie, M. S. A comparison of hypothalamically induced biting attack with natural predatory behavior in the cat. *Journal of Comparative and Physiological Psychology*, 1976, *90*, 167–178.

Berscheid, E., & Walster, E. H. *Interpersonal attraction*. Reading, Mass.: Addison-Wesley, 1969.

Berscheid, E., Dion, K., Walster, E., & Walster, G. W. Physical attractiveness and dating choice: A test of the matching hypothesis. *Journal of Experimental Social Psychology*, 1971, *7*, 173–189.

Bertini, M. REM sleep as a psychophysiological "agency" of memory organization. In W. P. Koella, & P. Levin (Eds.), *Sleep: Physiology, biochemistry, psychology, pharmacology, clinical applications*. New York: Karger, 1973.

Bexton, W. H., Heron, W., & Scott, T. H. Effects of decreased variation in the sensory environment. *Canadian Journal of Psychology*, 1954, *8*, 70–76.

Blass, E. M., & Epstein, A. N. A lateral preoptic osmosensitive zone for thirst in the rat. *Journal of Comparative and Physiological Psychology*, 1971, *76*, 378–394.

Bolles, R. C. Species-specific defense reactions and avoidance learning. *Psychological Review*, 1970, *77*, 32–48.

Bolles, R. C. *Theory of motivation*, New York: Harper & Row, 1975.

Bowlby, J. *Attachment and loss* (Vol. 1). *Attachment*. New York: Basic Books, 1969.

Boyatzis, R. E. Affiliation motivation. In D. C. McCelland, & R. S. Steel (Eds.), *Human motivation: A book of readings*. Morristown, N.J.: General Learning Press, 1973.

Bracewell, R. J., & Black, A. H. The effects of restraint and noncontingent preshock on subsequent escape learning in the rat. *Learning and Motivation*, 1974, *5*, 53–69.

Bracker, B. S. *Learned voluntary control of systolic blood pressure by spinal cord injury patients*. Doctoral dissertation, New York University, 1977.

Brackner, J., Pressman, B., Cabitt, J., & Moran, P. Nonverbal intimacy, sex, and compliance: A field study. *Journal of Nonverbal Behavior*, 1982, *6*, 253–258.

Brehm, J. W. Post-decisional changes in desirability of alternatives. *Journal of Abnormal and Social Psychology*, 1956, *52*, 348–289.

Brehm, J. W., & Sensenig, J. Social influence as a function of attempted and implied usurpation of a choice. *Journal of Personality and Social Psychology*, 1966, *4*, 703–707.

Breland, K., & Breland, M. The misbehavior of organisms. *American Psychologist*, 1961, *16*, 681–684.

Broadhurst, P. L. Emotionality and the Yerkes-Dodson Law. *Journal of Experimental Psychology*, 1957, *54*, 345–352.

Broughton, R., & Gastaut, H. Memory and sleep. In W. P. Koella, & P. Levin (Eds.), *Sleep: Physiology, biochemistry, psychology, pharmacology, clinical applications*. New York: Karger, 1973.

Brown, J. S. Gradients of approach and avoidance responses and their relation to level of motivation. *Journal of Comparative and Physiological Psychology*, 1948, *41*, 450–465.

Brown, J. S., & Farber, I. E. Emotions conceptualized as intervening variables—with suggestions toward a theory of frustration. *Psychological Bulletin*, 1951, *48*, 465–495.

Bruch, H. *Eating disorders: Obesity, anorexia nervosa, and the person within.* New York: Basic Books, 1973.

Burish, T. G., Maisto, S. A., & Shirley, M. C. Effect of alcohol and stress on emotion and physiological arousal. *Motivation and Emotion*, 1982, *6*, 149–159.

Butler, R. A. Discrimination learning by rhesus monkeys to visual-exploration motivation. *Journal of Comparative and Physiological Psychology*, 1953, *46*, 95–98.

Butler, R. A. Incentive conditions which influence visual exploration. *Journal of Experimental Psychology*, 1954, *48*, 19–23.

Butler, R. A., & Harlow, H. F. Persistence of visual exploration in monkeys. *Journal of Comparative and Physiological Psychology*, 1954, 47, 258–263.

Calhoun, J. B. Population density and social pathology. *Scientific American*, 1962, *206*, 139–148.

Cannon, W. B. The James-Lange theory of emotions: A critical examination and an alternative theory. *American Journal of Psychology*, 1927, *39*, 106–124.

Cannon, W. B., & Washburn, A. L. An explanation of hunger. *American Journal of Physiology*, 1912, *29*, 444–454.

Cantor, J. R., Zillmann, D., & Bryant, J. Enhancement of experienced sexual arousal in response to erotic stimuli through misattribution of unrelated residual excitation. *Journal of Personality and Social Psychology*, 1975, *32*, 69–75.

Carlsmith, J. M., Collins, B. E., & Helmreich, R. L. Studies of forced compliance: I. The effect of pressure for compliance on attitude change produced by face-to-face role playing and anonymous essay writing. *Journal of Personality and Social Psychology*, 1966, *4*, 1–13.

Chapman, C., & Risley, T. R. Anti-litter procedures in an urban high-density area. *Journal of Applied Behavior Analysis*, 1974, *7*, 377–383.

Cialdini, R. B., Vincent, J. E., Lewis, S. K., Catalan, J., Wheeler, D., & Darby, B. L. Reciprocal consessions procedure for inducing compliance: The door-in-the-face technique. *Journal of Personality and Social psychology*, 1975, *31*, 206–215.

Cofer, C. N., & Appley, M. H. *Motivation: Theory and research.* New York: Wiley, 1964.

Coleman, J. F., Blake, R. R., & Mouton, J. S. Task difficulty and conformity pressure. *Journal of Abnormal and Social Psychology*, 1958, *57*, 120–122.

Condry, J., & Dyer, S. Fear of success: Attribution of cause to the victim. *Journal of Social Issues*, 1976, *32*, 63–83.

Costello, C. G. A critical review of Seligman's laboratory experiments on learned helplessness and depression in humans. *Journal of Abnormal Psychology*, 1978, *87*, 21–31.

Cotman, C. W., & McGaugh, J. L. *Behavioral neuroscience: An introduction.* New York: Academic Press, 1980.

Crespi, L. P. Quantitative variation of incentive and performance in the white rat. *American Journal of Psychology*, 1942, *55*, 467–517.

Crockett, W. H. Balance, agreement, and subjective evaluations of the P-O-X triads. *Journal of Personality and Social Psychology*, 1974, *29*, 102–110.

Cuniberti, B. Masters, Johnson defend sex therapy success rates. *Los Angeles Times*, May 27, 1983, Part 1, p. 7.

Dapcich-Miuri, E., & Hovell, M. F. Contingency management of adherence to a complex medical regimen in an elderly heart patient. *Behavior Therapy*, 1979, *10*, 193–201.

Davitz, J.P.A. A dictionary and grammar of emotion. In M. Arnold (Ed.), *Feelings and emotions: The Loyola symposium.* New York: Academic Press, 1970.

Deci, E. L. Effects of externally mediated rewards on intrinsic motivation. *Journal of Personality and Social Psychology*, 1971, *18*, 105–115.

Deci, E. L. Effects of contingent and non-contingent rewards and controls on intrinsic motivation. *Organizational Behavior and Human Performance*, 1972, *8*, 217–229.

Decke, E. Effects of taste on the eating behavior of normal and obese persons. Cited in S. Schachter, *Emotion, obesity, and crime.* New York: Academic Press, 1971.

Dember, W. N., & Earl, R. W. Analysis of exploratory, manipulatory, and curiosity behaviors. *Psychological Review*, 1957, *64*, 91–96.

Dement, W. C. *Some must watch while some must sleep.* Stanford, CA: Stanford Alumni Association, 1972.

Dement, W. The effect of dream deprivation. *Science*, 1960, *131*, 1705–1707.

Dement, W., & Villablanca, J. Clinical disorders in man and animal model experiments. In O. Petre-Ouadens, & J. Schlag (Eds.), *Basic sleep mechanisms.* New York: Academic Press, 1974.

Dickinson, A., & Mackintosh, N. J. Classical conditioning in animals. In M. R. Rosensweig, & L. W. Porter (Eds.), *Annual Review of Psychology* (Vol. 29). Palo Alto, Calif.: Annual Reviews, 1978.

Dion, K, Berscheid, E., & Waslter, E. What is beautiful is good. *Journal of Personality and Social Psychology*, 1972, *24*, 285–290.

Dollard, J., Doob, L., Miller, N. E., Mowrer, O. H., & Sears, R. *Frustration and aggression.* New Haven: Yale University Press, 1939.

Donahoe, J. W., & Wessells, M. G. *Learning, language, and memory.* New York: Harper & Row, 1980.

Donnerstein, E., & Wilson, D. Effects of noise and perceived control on ongoing and subsequent aggressive behavior. *Journal of Personality and Social Psychology*, 1976, *34*, 774–781.

Douglas, D., & Anisman, H. Helplessness or expectation incongruency: Effects of aversive stimulation on subsequent performance. *Journal of Experimental Psychology: Human Perception and Performance*, 1975, *1*, 411–417.

Duffy, E. *Activation and behavior.* New York: Wiley, 1962.

Eibl-Eibesfeldt, I. *Love and hate: The natural history of behavior patterns.* New York: Holt, Rinehart and Winston, 1972.

Ekman, P., & Friesen, W. V. Felt, false and miserable smiles. *Journal of Nonverbal Behavior*, 1982, 6, 238–252.

Elmadjian, F., Hope, J. M., & Lamson, E. T. Excretion of epinephrine and norepinephrine in various emotional states. *Journal of Clinical Endocrinology*, 1957, *17*, 608–620.

Epstein, A. N., Fitzsimmons, J. T., & Rolls, B. J. Drinking induced by injection of angiotensin into the brain of the rat. *Journal of Physiology*, 1970, *210*, 457–474.

Erdmann, G., & Janke, W. Interaction between physiological and cognitive determinants of emotion: Experimental studies on Schachter's theory of emotions. *Biological Psychology*, 1978, *6*, 61–74.

Fantino, E., & Logan, C. A. *The experimental analysis of behavior: A biological perspective.* San Francisco: Freeman, 1979.

Faust, I. M., Johnson, P. R., & Hirsch, J. Surgical removal of adipose tissue alters feeding behavior and the development of obesity in rats. *Science*, 1977, *197*, 393–396.

Feldman, N. S., Higgins, E. T., Karlovac, M., & Ruble, D. N. Use of consensus information in causal attributions as a function of temporal presentation and availability of direct information. *Journal of Personality and Social Psychology*, 1976, *34*, 694–698.

Feldman, R. S., & Bernstein, A. G. Primacy effects in self-attribution of ability. *Journal of Personality*, 1978, *46*, 732–742.

Feshbach, N. D. Nonconformity to experimentally induced group norms of high-status versus low-status members. *Journal of Personality and Social Psychology*, 1967, *6*, 55–63.

Feshbach, S. Dynamics of morality of violence and aggression: Some psychological considerations. *American Psychologist*, 1971, *26*, 281–291.

Festinger, L. A theory of social comparison processes. *Human Relations*, 1954, *7*, 117–140.

Festinger, L. *A theory of cognitive dissonance.* Stanford: Stanford University Press, 1957.

Festinger, L., & Carlsmith, J. Cognitive consequences of forced compliance. *Journal of Abnormal and Social Psychology*, 1959, *58*, 203–210.

Festinger, L., Pepitone, A., & Newcomb, T. Some consequences of de-individuation in a group. *Journal of Abnormal and Social Psychology*, 1952, *47*, 382–389.

Fiske, D. W., & Maddi, S. R. (Eds.). *Functions of varied experience.* Homewood, Ill: Dorsey, 1961.

Franken, R. E. *Human motivation.* Monterey, Calif.: Brooks/Cole, 1982.

Franken, R. E., & Strain, A. Effect of increased arousal on response to stimulus change in a complex maze. *Perceptual and Motor Skills*, 1974, *39*, 1076–1078.

Freedman, J. L. *Crowding and behavior.* San Francisco: Freeman, 1975.

Freedman, J. L., & Fraser, S. C. Compliance without pressure: The foot-in-the-door technique. *Journal of Personality and Social Psychology*, 1966, *4*, 195–202.

Freedman, J. L., Levy, A. S., Buchanan, R. W., & Price, J. Crowding and human aggressiveness. *Journal of Experimental Social Psychology*, 1972, *8*, 528–548.

Freedman, J. L., Sears, D. O., & Carlsmith, J. M. *Social Psychology*. Englewood Cliffs, N.J.: Prentice-Hall, 1981.

Freud, S. *New introductory lectures on psychoanalysis*. New York: Norton, 1933.

Friedman, M., & Rosenman, R. H. *Type A behavior and your heart*. New York: Knopf, 1974.

Gaioni, S. J., Hoffman, H. S., DePaulo, P., & Stratton, V. N. Imprinting in older ducklings: Some tests of a reinforcement model. *Animal Learning and Behavior*, 1978, *6*, 19–26.

Garcia, J., Ervin, F., & Koelling, R. Learning with prolonged delay of reinforcement. *Psychonomic Science*, 1966, *5*, 121–122.

Garcia, J., Hankins, W. G., & Rusiniak, K. W. Behavioral regulation of the milieu interne in man and rat. *Science*, 1974, *185*, 824–831.

Garcia, J., & Koelling, R. Relation of cue to consequence in avoidance learning. *Psychomic Science*, 1966, *4*, 123–124.

Garcia, J., & Rusiniak, K. W. What the nose learns from the mouth. Paper presented at the Symposium on Chemical Signals in Vertebrate and Aquatic Mammals, Syracuse University, 1979.

Garcia, J., Rusiniak, K. W., & Brett, L. P. Conditioning food-illness aversions in wild animals: Caveant Cononici. In H. Davis, & H. M. B. Hurwitz (Eds.), *Operant-Pavlovian interactions*. Hillsdale, N.J.: Erlbaum, 1977.

Gardner, L. I. Deprivation dwarfism. *Scientific American*, 1972, *227*, 76–82.

Garfinkel, P. E., Kline, S. A., & Stancer, H. C. Treatment of anorexia nervosa using operant conditioning techniques. *Journal of Nervous and Mental Disease*, 1973, *157*, 428–433.

Geen, R. G., & Pigg, R. Acquisition of an aggressive response and its generalization to verbal behavior. *Journal of Personality and Social Psychology*, 1970, *15*, 165–170.

Geiselman, P. J. The role of hexoses in hunger motivation. (Doctoral dissertation, University of California, Los Angeles, 1983).

Ginsberg, A. A reconstructive analysis of the concept of "instinct." *Journal of Psychology*, 1952, *33*, 235–277.

Gjerde, P. F. Attentional capacity dysfunction and arousal in schizophrenia. *Psychological Bulletin*, 1983, *93*, 57–72.

Glass, D. C. Stress, behavior patterns, and coronary disease. *American Scientist*, 1977, *65*, 177–187.

Glickman, S. E., & Schiff, B. B. A biological theory of reinforcement. *Psychological Review*, 1967, *74*, 81–109.

Goldiamond, I. Stuttering and fluency as manipulatable operant response classes. In L. Krasner, & L. P. Ullman (Eds.), *Research in behavior modification*. New York: Holt, 1965.

Goldwater, B. C. Psychological significance of pupillary movement. *Psychological Bulletin*, 1972, *77*, 340–355.

Gould, J. L. *Ethology: The mechanisms and evolution of behavior*. New York: Norton, 1982.

Green, E. Biofeedback for mind-body self-regulation: Healing and creativity. In D. Shapiro, T. X. Barber, L. V. DiCara, J. Kamiya, N. E. Miller, & J. Stoyva (Eds.), *Biofeedback and self-control 1972*. Chicago: Aldine, 1973.

Griffitt, W. Environmental effect of interpersonal affective behavior: Ambient effective temperature and attraction. *Journal of Personality and Social Psychology*, 1970, *15*, 240–244.

Grossman, M. I., & Stein, I. F. Vagotomy and the hunger producing action of insulin in man. *Journal of Applied Physiology*, 1948, *1*, 263–269.

Grossman, S. P. *A textbook of physiological psychology*. New York: Wiley, 1967.

Grossman, S. P., & Grossman, L. Food and water intake following lesions or electrical stimulation of the amygdala. *American Journal of Physiology*, 1963, *205*, 761–765.

Gustavson, C. R., Garcia, J., Hankins, W. G., & Rusiniack, K. W. Coyote predation control by aversive conditioning. *Science*, 1974, *184*, 581–583.

Haith, M. M., Bergman, T., & Moore, M. J. Eye contact and face scanning in early infancy. *Science*, 1977, *198*, 853–855.

Hall, J. F. *Classical conditioning and instrumental learning: A contemporary approach*. Philadelphia: Lippincott, 1976.

Harlow, H. F. The nature of love. *American Psychologist*, 1958, *13*, 673–685.

Harlow, H. F. *Learning to love*. San Francisco: Albion, 1971.

Harlow, H. F., Harlow, M. K., & Meyer, D. R. Learning motivated by a manipulation drive. *Journal of Experimental Psychology*, 1950, *40*, 228–234.

Hartmann, E. L. *The functions of sleep*. New Haven: Yale University Press, 1973.

Hatch, J. P., & Gatchel, R. J. Development of physiological response patterns concomitant with the learning of voluntary heart rate control. *Journal of Comparative and Physiological Psychology*, 1979, *93*, 306–313.

Hauri, P. *The sleep disorders*. Kalamazoo, Mich.: The Upjohn Co., 1977.

Heider, F. Attitudes and cognitive organization. *Journal of Psychology*, 1946, *21*, 107–112.

Heider, F. *The psychology of interpersonal relations.* New York: Wiley, 1958.

Hellenthal, L., & Marcucella, H. Stimulus control in multiple variable-ratio schedules of reinforcement. *Animal Learning and Behavior*, 1978, *6*, 198–204.

Hensley, W. E. The effects of attire, location, and sex on aiding behavior: A similarity explanation. *Journal of Nonverbal Behavior*, 1982, *6*, 3–11.

Heron, W., Doane, B. K., & Scott, T. H. Visual disturbances after prolonged perceptual isolation. *Canadian Journal of Psychology*, 1956, *10*, 13–16.

Hess, E. H. Imprinting. *Science*, 1959, *130*, 133–141.

Hess, E. H. "Imprinting" in a natural laboratory. *Scientific American*, 1972, *227*, 24–31.

Hess, E. H. *Imprinting.* Princeton, N.J.: Van Nostrand-Reinhold, 1973.

Hess, W. R. *Functional organization of the diencephalon.* New York: Grune & Stratton, 1957.

Hetherington, A. W., & Ranson, S. W. Hypothalamic leisions and adiposity in the rat. *Anatomical Record*, 1940, *78*, 149–172.

Higgens, E. T., Rhodewalt, F., & Zanna, M. P. Dissonance motivation: Its nature, persistence, and reinstatement. *Journal of Experimental Social Psychology*, 1979, *15*, 16–34.

Hineline, P. N. Negative reinforcement without shock reduction. *Journal of the Experimental Analysis of Behavior*, 1970, *14*, 259–268.

Hiroto, D. S. Locus of control and learned helplessness. *Journal of Experimental Psychology*, 1974, *102*, 187–193.

Hoffman, H. S., & Ratner, A. M. A reinforcement model of imprinting: Implications for socialization in monkeys and men. *Psychological Review*, 1973, *80*, 527–544.

Hofling, C. K., Brotzman, E., Dalrymple, S., Graves, N., & Pierce, C. M. An experimental study on nurse-physician relationships. *The Journal of Nervous and Mental Disease*, 1963, *67*, 214–218.

Holmes, T. H., & Masuda, M. Life change and illness susceptibility. In B. S. Dohrenwend, & B. P. Dohrenwend (Eds.), *Stressful life events: Their nature and effects.* New York: Wiley, 1974.

Holmes, T. H., & Rahe, R. H. The social readjustment rating scale. *Journal of Psychosomatic Research*, 1967, *11*, 213–218.

Homans, G. C. Group factors in worker productivity. In H. Proshansky, & L. Seidenberg (Eds.), *Basic studies in social Psychology.* New York: Holt, 1965.

Horner, M. S. Woman's will to fail. *Psychology Today*, Nov. 1969, 36–38.

Houston, J. P., Bee, H., & Rimm, D. C. *Invitation to psychology*, 2 E. New York: Academic Press, 1983.

Houston, J. P. *Fundamentals of learning and memory* (2nd ed.). New York: Academic Press, 1981.

Howe, M. J. *The psychology of human learning.* New York: Harper & Row, 1980.

Hull, C. L. *Principles of behavior.* New York: Appleton, 1943.

Hull, C. L. *Essentials of behavior.* New Haven: Yale University Press, 1951.

Hull, C. L. *A behavior system.* New Haven: Yale University Press, 1952.

Hulse, S. H., Egeth, H., & Deese, J. *The psychology of learning.* New York: McGraw-Hill, 1980.

Hunt, E. L. Establishment of conditioned responses in chick embryos. *Journal of Comparative and Physiological Psychology*, 1949, 42, 107–117.

Isaacson, R. L. Relation between achievement, test anxiety, and curricular choices. *Journal of Abnormal and Social Psychology*, 1964, 68, 447–452.

Jacobs, P. A., Price, W. H., Court, A., Brown, W. M., Brittain, R. P., & Whatmore, P. B. Chromosome studies of men in a maximum security hospital. *Annals of Human Genetics*, 1968, 31, 339–358.

James, W. *Principles of psychology.* New York: Holt, 1890.

Jones, E. E. *Ingratiation.* New York: Appleton-Century-Crofts, 1964.

Jones, E. E., & Harris, V. A. The attribution of attitudes. *Journal of Experimental Social Psychology*, 1967, 3, 1–24.

Jones, E. E., & Nisbett, R. E. The actor and the observer: Divergent perceptions of the causes of behavior. In E. E. Jones, & R. E. Nisbett (Eds.), *Attribution: Perceiving the causes of behavior.* Morristown, N. J.: General Learning Press, 1972.

Jouvet, M. The states of sleep. *Scientific American*, Feb. 1967, 62–72.

Karabenick, S. A. Fear of success, achievement and affiliation dispositions, and the performance of men and women under individual and competitive conditions. *Journal of Personality*, 1977, 45, 117–149.

Keesey, R. E., Boyle, P. C., Kemnitz, J. W., & Mitchell, J. S. The role of the lateral hypothalamus in determining the body weight set point. In D. Novin, W. Wyrwicka, G. Bray (Eds.), *Hunger: Basic mechanisms and clinical implications.* New York: Raven, 1976.

Keesey, R. E., & Powley, T. L. Hypothalamic regulation of body weight, *American Scientist*, 1975, 63, 558–565.

Kelley, H. H. Attribution theory in social psychology. In D. Levine (Ed.),

Nebraska symposium on motivation (Vol. 15). Lincoln: University of Nebraska Press, 1967.

Kelley, H. H. Attribution in social interaction. In E. E. Jones, & R. E. Nisbett (Eds.), *Attribution: Perceiving the causes of behavior.* Morristown, N. J.: General Learning Press, 1972.

Kelley, H. H. The processes of causal attribution. *American Psychologist*, 1973, *28*, 107–128.

Kimble, G. *Foundations of conditioning and learning.* New York: Appleton, 1967.

Kinsey, A. C., Pomeroy, W. B., & Martin, C. E. *Sexual behavior in the human male.* Philadelphia: Saunders, 1948.

Kish, G. B. Learning when the offset of illumination is used as reinforcing stimulus. *Journal of Comparative and Physiological Psychology*, 1955, *48*, 261–264.

Klein, D. C., Fencil-Morse, E., & Seligman, M. E. P. Learned helplessness, depression, and the attribution of failure. *Journal of Personality and Social Psychology*, 1976, *33*, 508–516.

Klein, K. Discomfort expectancies and imagined distress in a role-play of a visit to the dentist. *Motivation and Emotion*, 1982, *6*, 181–192.

Klein, R. D. Modifying academic performance in the grade school classroom. In M. Hersen, R. M. Eisler, & P. M. Miller (Eds.), *Progress in behavior modification* (Vol. 8). New York: Academic Press, 1979.

Knight, M. F., & McKenzie, H. S. Elimination of bedtime thumbsucking in home settings through contingent reading. *Journal of Applied Behavior Analysis*, 1974, *7*, 33–38.

Kolb, D. Achievement motivation training for underachieving high school boys. *Journal of Personality and Social Psychology*, 1965, *2*, 783–792.

Konorski, J. *Integrative activity of the brain.* Chicago: University of Chicago Press, 1967.

Kovach, J. K., & Hess, E. H. Imprinting: Effects of painful stimulation upon the following response. *Journal of Comparative and Physiological Psychology*, 1963, *56*, 461–464.

Krieckhaus, E. E. Innate recognition aids rats in sodium regulation. *Journal of Comparative and Physiological Psychology*, 1970, *73*, 117–122.

Kubie, J. L., & Halpern, M. Chemical senses involved in garter snake prey training. *Journal of Comparative and Physiological Psychology*, 1979, *93*, 648–667.

Kulik, J. A., & Brown, R. Frustration, attribution of blame, and aggression. *Journal of Experimental Social Psychology*, 1979, *15*, 183–194.

Kuo, Z. Y. The genesis of the cat's response to the rat. *Journal of Comparative Pscyhology*, 1930, *11*, 1–30.

Lacey, J. I. Somatic response patterning and stress: Some revisions of activation theory. In M. H. Appley, & R. Trumbull (Eds.), *Psychological stress*. New York: Appleton-Century-Crofts 1967.

Lagerspetz, K. Studies on the aggressive behavior of mice. *Annales Academiae Scientiarum Fennicae*, Series B., 1964, *131*, 1–131.

Lange, C. G. *The emotions*. Baltimore: Williams & Wilkins, 1922.

Lawler, E. E., Kuleck, W. J., Rhodes, J. S., & Sorenson, S. E. Job choice and post decision dissonance. *Organizational Behavior and Human Performance*, 1975, *13*, 133–145.

Lepper, M. R., Greene, D., & Nisbett, R. E. Undermining children's intrinsic interest with extrinsic rewards: A test of the "overjustification" hypothesis. *Journal of Personality and Social Psychology*, 1973, *28*, 129–137.

Levine, S. Stimulation in infancy. *Scientific American*, 1960, 80–86.

Levine, S. Stress and behavior. *Scientific American*, Jan. 1971, 26–31.

Levis, D. J., Smith, J. E., & Epstein, W. Is fear present to the CS following short-latency avoidance responding? Paper presented at the 19th annual meeting of the Psychonomic Society, San Antonio, 1978.

Lewin, K. *The conceptual representation and the measurement of psychological forces*. Durham, N.C.: Duke University Press, 1938.

Linder, D. E., Cooper, J., & Jones, E. E. Decision freedom as a determinant of the role of incentive magnitude in attitude change. *Journal of Personality and Social Psychology*, 1967, *6*, 245–54.

Lindsley, D. B. Emotion. In S. S. Stevens (Ed.), *Handbook of experimental psychology*. New York: Wiley, 1951.

Lorenz, K. The companion in the bird's world. *Auk*, 1937, *54*, 245–273.

Lorenz, K. The comparative method of studying innate behavior patterns. *Symposia of the Society of Experimental Biology*. Cambridge: At the University Press, 1950.

Lorenz, K. *On aggression*. New York: Harcourt, Brace, & World, 1966.

Lorenz, K. Innate basis of learning. In K. H. Pribram (Ed.), *On the biology of learning*. New York: Harcourt, Brace, & World, 1969.

Lowell, E. L. The effect of need for achievement on learning and spread of performance. *Journal of Psychology*, 1952, *33*, 31–40.

Lundberg, O., & Walinder, J. Anorexia nervosa and signs of brain damage. *International Journal of Neuropsychiatry*, 1967, *3*, 167–173.

Lundberg, U. Urban commuting: Crowdedness and catecholamine excretion. *Journal of Human Stress*, 1976, *2*, 26–32.

Mahoney, M. J., & Kazdin, A. E. Cognitive behavior modification: Misconceptions and premature evaluation. *Psychological Bulletin*, 1979, *86*, 1044–1049.

Maier, S. F., & Seligman, M. E. P. Learned helplessness: Theory and evidence. *Journal of Experimental Psychology: General*, 1976, *105*, 3–46.

Maltzman, I. Orienting in classical conditioning and generalization of the galvanic skin response to words: An overview. *Journal of Experimental Psychology*, 1977, *106*, 111–119.

Mandel, P., Mack, G., & Goridis, C. Function of the central catecholaminergic neuron: Synthesis, release, and inactivation of transmitter. In A. J. Friedhoff (Ed.), *Catecholamines and behavior* Vol. I: Basic neurology. New York: Plenum, 1975.

Mandler, G., & Sarason, S. B. A study of anxiety and learning. *Journal of Abnormal and Social Psychology*, 1952, *47*, 166–173.

Mantrell, D. M. The potential for violence in Germany. *Journal of Social Issues*, 1971, *27*, 101–112.

Marshall, G. D., & Zimbardo, P. G. Affective consequences of inadequately explaining physiological arousal. *Journal of Personality and Social Psychology*, 1979, *37*, 970–988.

Marshall, J. M., & Karabenick, S. A. Validity of an empirically derived projective measure of fear of success. *Journal of Consulting and Clinical Psychology*, 1977, *45*, 564–574.

Maslach, C. Negative emotional biasing of unexplained arousal. *Journal of Personality and Social Psychology*, 1979, *37*, 953–969.

Maslow, A. H. *Motivation and personality.* New York: Harper, 1970.

Masters, W. H., & Johnson, V. E. *Human sexual response.* Boston: Little, Brown, 1966.

Matthews, K. A. Psychological perspectives on the Type A behavior pattern. *Psychological Bulletin*, 1982, *91*, 293–323.

Mayer, J. Regulation of energy intake and the body weight: The glucostatic theory and the lipostatic hypothesis. *Annals of the New York Academy of Science*, 1955, *63*, 15–43.

McArthur, L. A. The lesser influence of consensus than distinctiveness information on causal attributions: A test of the person-thing hypothesis. *Journal of Personality and Social Psychology*, 1976, *33*, 733–742.

McCall, R. B. Initial-consequent-change surface in light contingent bar pressing. *Journal of Comparative and Physiological Psychology*, 1966, *62*, 35–42.

McCelland, D. C. Risk taking in children with high and low need for achievement. In J. W. Atkinson (Ed.), *Motives in fantasy, action, and society.* Princeton, N. J.: Van Nostrand, 1958.

McCelland, D. C. *The achieving society.* Princeton, N. J.: Van Nostrand: 1961.

McCelland, D. C. The need for power, sympathetic activation, and illness. *Motivation and Emotion*, 1982, *6*, 31–41.

McCelland, D. C., Atkinson, J. W., Clark, R. A., & Lowell, E. L. *The Achievement motive.* New York: Appleton-Century-Crofts, 1953.

McCelland, D. C., & Winter, D. G. *Motivating economic achievement.* New York: Free Press, 1969.

McDougall, W. *An introduction to social psychology.* London: Methueen, 1908.

McKeachie, W. J., Lin, Y., Milholland, J., & Issacson, R. Student affiliation motives, teacher warmth, and academic achievement. *Journal of Personality and Social Psychology*, 1966, *4*, 457–461.

McLearn, G. E. Biological bases of social behavior with particular reference to violent behavior. In D. J. Mulvihill, M. M. Tumin, & L. A. Curtis (Eds.), *Crimes of violence.* Washington, D.C.: Government Printing Office, 1969.

Meichenbaum, D. Cognitive behavior modification: The need for a fairer assessment. *Cognitive Therapy and Research*, 1979, *3*, 127–132.

Merriam-Webster Dictionary. New York: Pocket Books, 1974.

Milgram, S. Behavioral study of obedience. *Journal of Abnormal and Social Psychology*, 1963, *67*, 371–378.

Milgram, S. Liberating effects of group pressure. *Journal of Personality and Social Psychology*, 1965, *1*, 127–134.

Milgram, S. *Obedience to authority: An experimental view.* New York: Harper & Row, 1974.

Milgram, S. Subject reaction: The neglected factor in the ethics of experimentation. *Hastings Center Report*, 1977, 19–23.

Milgram, S., Bickman, L., & Berkowitz, L. Note on the drawing power of crowds of different size. *Journal of Personality and Social Psychology*, 1967, *13*, 79–82.

Miller, N. E. Experimental studies in conflict. In J. McV. Hunt (Ed.), *Personality and the behavioral disorders* (Vol. 1). New York: Ronald Press, 1944.

Miller, N. E. Studies of fear as an acquirable drive: I. Fear as motivation and fear-reduction as reinforcement in the learning of new responses. *Journal of Experimental Psychology*, 1948, *38*, 89–101.

Miller, N. E. Interactions between learned and physiological factors in mental illness. In D. Shapiro, T. X. Barber, L. V. DiCara, J. Kamiya, N. E. Miller, & J. Stoyva (Eds.), *Biofeedback and self-control: 1972.* Chicago: Aldine, 1973.

Miller, N. E. Biofeedback and visceral learning. In M. R. Rosensweig, & L.

W. Porter (Eds.), *Annual Review of Psychology* (Vol. 29). Palo Alto, Calif.: Annual Reviews, 1978.

Miller, N. E., & Dollard, J. *Social learning and imitation.* New Haven: Yale University Press, 1941.

Miller, R. E., Caul, W. F., & Mirsky, I. A. Communications of affects between feral and socially isolated monkeys. *Journal of Personality and Social Psychology*, 1967, *7*, 231–239.

Mineka, S., & Gino, A. Dissociative effects of different types and amounts of nonreinforced CS exposure on avoidance extinction and the CER. *Learning and Motivation*, 1979, *10*, 141–160.

Mineka, S., & Kihlstrom, J. F. Unpredictable and uncontrollable events: A new perspective on experimental neurosis. *Journal of Abnormal Psychology*, 1978, *87*, 256–271.

Minor, T., & LoLordo, V. M. Escape deficits following inescapable shock: The role of contextual shock. *Journal of Experimental Psychology*, in press.

Mischel, W. Delay of gratification, need for achievement, and acquiescence in another culture. *Journal of Abnormal and Social Psychology*, 1961, *62*, 543–552.

Moltz, H. Imprinting: Empirical basis and theoretical significance. *Psychological Bulletin*, 1960, *57*, 291–314.

Money, J. The syndrome of abuse dwarfism (psychosocial dwarfism or reversible hyposomatotropinism). *American Journal of Disabled Children*, 1977, *131*, 508–513.

Morgan, C. T., & Morgan, J. T. Studies in hunger. II: The relation of gastric denervation and dietary sugar to the effect of insulin upon food-intake in the rat. *Journal of Genetic Psychology*, 1940, *57*, 153–163.

Morosko, T. E., & Baer, P. E. Avoidance conditioning of alcoholics. In R. Ulrich, T. Stachnik, & J. Mabry (Eds.), *Control of human behavior.* Glenview, Ill.: Scott, Foresman, 1970.

Morris, W. N., & Miller, R. S. The effects of consensus-breaking and consensus-preempting partners on reduction in conformity. *Journal of Experimental Social Psychology*, 1975, *11*, 215–223.

Moruzzi, G., & Magoun, H. Brainstem reticular formation and activation of the EEG. *Electroencephalography and Clinical Neurophysiology*, 1949, *1*, 455–473.

Mowrer, O. H., & Lamoreaux, R. R. Avoidance conditioning and signal duration—a study of secondary motivation and reward. *Psychological Monograph*, 1942, *54*, (Whole No. 247).

Mowrer, O. H., & Lamoreaux, R. R. Fear as an intervening variable in avoidance conditioning. *Journal of Comparative Psychology*, 1946, *39*, 29–50.

Moyer, K. E. Kinds of aggression and their physiological bases. *Communications in Behavioral Biology*, 1968, *2*, 65–87.

Moyer, K. E. *The psychobiology of aggression*. New York: Harper & Row, 1976.

Murray, H. A. *Explorations in personality*. New York: Oxford University Press, 1938.

Newcomb, T. M. *The acquaintance process*. New York: Holt, Rinehart and Winston, 1961.

Newcomb, T. M. Interpersonal balance. In R. E. Abelson (Ed.), *Theories of Cognitive consistency: A source book*. Chicago: Rand McNally, 1968.

Nisbett, R. E., Tase, deprivation, and weight determinants of eating behavior. *Journal of Personality and Social Psychology*, 1968, *10*, 107–116.

Nisbett, R. E. Hunger, obesity, and the ventromedial hypothalamus. *Psychological Review*, 1972, *79*, 433–453.

Nisbett, R. E., Caputo, C., Legant, P., & Marecek, J. Behavior as seen by the actor and as seen by the observer. *Journal of Personality and Social Psychology*, 1973, *27*, 154–164.

Nisbett, R. E., & Schachter, S. Cognitive manipulation of pain. *Journal of Experimental Social Psychology*, 1966, *2*, 227–236.

Nogami, G. Y. Crowding: Effects of group size, room size, or density? *Journal of Applied Social Psychology*, 1976, *6*, 105–125.

Novin, D. Visceral mechanisms in the control of food intake. In D. Novin, W. Wyrwicka, & G. Bray (Eds.), *Hunger: Basic mechanisms and clinical implications*. New York: Raven, 1976.

Olson, J. M., & Zanna, M. P. A new look at selective exposure. *Journal of Experimental Social Psychology*, 1979, *15*, 1–15.

Oomara, Y. Significance of glucose insulin and free fatty acid on the hypothalamic feeding and satiety neurons. In D. Novin, W. Wyrwicka, & G. Bray (Eds.), *Hunger: Basic mechanisms and clinical implications*. New York: Raven, 1976.

Orne, M. T., & Scheibe, K. E. The contribution of nondeprivation factors in the production of sensory deprivation effects: The psychology of the panic button. *Journal of Abnormal and Social Psychology*, 1964, *68*, 3–12.

Owen, D. R. The 47, XYY male: A review. *Psychological Review*, 1972, *78*, 209–233.

Peck, J. W., & Novin, D. Evidence that osmoreceptors mediating drinking in rabbits are in the lateral preoptic area. *Journal of Comparative and Physiological Psychology*, 1971, *74*, 134–147.

Peplau, L. A. Impact of fear of success and sex-role attitudes on women's competitive achievement. *Journal of Personality and Social Psychology*, 1976, *34*, 561–580.

Perin, C. T. Behavior potentiality as a joint function of amount of training and the degree of hunger at the time of extinction. *Journal of Experimental Psychology*, 1942, *30*, 93–113.

Pfaffman, C. Taste preference and reinforcement. In J. T. Tapp (Ed.), *Reinforcement and behavior*. New York: Academic Press, 1969.

Plutchik, R. A. A general psychoevolutionary theory of emotion. In R. Plutchik, & H. Kellerman (Eds.), *Emotion: Theory, research and experience*. (Vol. I). New York: Academic Press, 1980.

Powell, L., Felce, D., Jenkins, J., & Lunt, B. Increasing engagement in a home for the elderly by providing an indoor gardening activity. *Behavior Research and Therapy*, 1979, *17*, 127–135.

Premack, D. Toward empirical behavioral laws: I. Positive reinforcement. *Psychological Review*, 1959, *66*, 219–233.

Premack, D. Reinforcement theory. In D. Levine (Ed.), *Nebraska symposium on motivation*. Lincoln: University of Nebraska Press, 1965.

Rajecki, D. W. Imprinting in precocial birds: Interpretation, evidence, and evaluation. *Psychological Review*, 1973, *79*, 48–58.

Raymond, M. J. Case of fetishism treated by aversion therapy. *British Medical Journal*, 1956, *2*, 854–857.

Raynor, J. O. Relationships between achievement-related motives, future orientation, and academic performance. *Journal of Personality and Social Psychology*, 1970, *15*, 28–33.

Razran, G. The observable unconscious and the inferable conscious in current Soviet psychophysiology. *Psychological Review*, 1961, *68*, 81–147.

Rescorla, R. A., & Wagner, A. R. A theory of Pavlovian conditioning: Variations in the effectiveness of reinforcement and nonreinforcement. In A. Black, & W. F. Prokasy (Eds.), *Classical conditioning (II): Current research and theory*. New York: Appleton, 1972.

Richter, C. P., Holt, L. E., Barelace, B., & Hawkes, C. D. Changes in fat, carbohydrate and protein appetite in vitamin B deficiency. *American Journal of Physiology*, 1938, *124*, 596–602.

Rimm, D. C., & Masters, J. C. *Behavior therapy: Techniques and empirical findings*. New York: Academic Press, 1979.

Riskind, J. H., & Gotay, C. C. Physical posture: Could it have regulatory or feedback effects on motivation and emotion? *Motivation and Emotion*, 1982, *6*, 273–298.

Roberts, W. W., & Kiess, H. O. Motivational properties of hypothalamic aggression in cats. *Journal of Comparative and Physiological Psychology*, 1964, *58*, 187–193.

Rodin, J. Has the distinction between internal versus external control of feeding outlived its usefulness? In G. A. Bray (Ed.), *Recent advances in obesity research: II.* London: Newman, 1978.

Roffwarg, H. P., Muzio, J. N., & Dement, W. C. Ontogenetic development of the human sleep-dream cycle. *Science*, 1966, *152*, 604–619.

Rosenfield, D., Folger, R., & Adelman, H. F. When rewards reflect competence: A qualification of the overjustification effect. *Journal of Personality and Social Psychology*, 1980, *39*, 368–376.

Rosensweig, M. R. The mechanisms of hunger and thirst. In L. Postman (Ed.), *Psychology in the making.* New York: Knopf, 1962.

Ross, L. The intuitive psychologist and his shortcomings: Distortions in the attribution process. In L. Berkowitz (Ed.), *Advances in experimental social psychology.* New York: Academic Press, 1977.

Roth, S., & Kubal, L. The effects of noncontingent reinforcement on tasks of differing importance: Facilitation and learned helplessness effects. *Journal of Personality and Social Psychology*, 1975, *32*, 680–691.

Routtenberg, A. The two-arousal hypothesis: Reticular formation and limbic system, *Psychological Review*, 1968, *75*, 51–80.

Rozin, P. Thiamine specific hunger. In C. F. Code (Ed.), *Handbook of physiology.* Baltimore: Williams & Wilkins, 1967.

Ruch, L. O., & Holmes, T. H. Scaling of life change: Comparison of direct and indirect methods. *Journal of Psychosomatic Research*, 1971, *15*, 221–227.

Russek, M. Participation of hepatic glucoreceptors in the control of food. *Nature*, 1963, *197*, 79–80.

Salzen, E. A. Imprinting and environmental learning. In L. R. Aronson, T. Tobach, D. S. Lehrman, & J. S. Rosenblatt (Eds.), *Development and evolution of behavior.* San Francisco: W. H. Freeman, 1970.

Scaramella, T. J., & Brown, W. A. Serum testosterone and aggressiveness in hockey players. *Psychosomatic Medicine*, 1978, *40*, 262–265.

Schachter, S. Deviation, rejection, and communication. *Journal of Abnormal and Social Psychology*, 1951, *46*, 190–208.

Schachter, S. *The psychology of affiliation.* Stanford: Stanford University Press, 1959.

Schachter, S. Some extraordinary facts about obese humans and rats. *American Psychologist*, 1971, *26*, 129–144. (a)

Schachter, S. *Emotion, obesity, and crime*. New York: Academic Press, 1971. (b)

Schachter, S., & Singer, J. E. Cognitive, social, and physiological determinants of emotional states. *Psychological Review*, 1962, *69*, 379–399.

Schaefer, H. H., & Martin, P. L. Behavioral therapy for "apathy" of hospitalized schizophrenics. *Psychological Reports*, 1966, *19*, 1147–1158.

Schiff, M. *Leçons sur la physiologie de la digestion*. Florence: Loescher, 1867.

Segal, M. W. Alphabet and attraction: An unobtrusive measure of the effect of propinquity in a field setting. *Journal of Personality and Social Psychology*, 1974, *30*, 654–657.

Seligman, M. E. P. On the generality of the laws of learning. *Psychological Review*, 1970, 77, 406–418.

Seligman, M. E. P. *Helplessness: On depression, development, and death*. San Francisco: Freeman, 1975.

Seligman, M. E. P., & Maier, S. F. Failure to escape traumatic shock. *Journal of Experimental Psychology*, 1967, 74, 1–9.

Selye, H. *The stress of life*. New York: McGraw-Hill, 1956.

Selye, H. The evolution of the stress concept. *American Scientist*, 1973, *61*, 692–699.

Shanab, M. E., & Yahya, K. A. A behavioral study of obedience in children. *Journal of Personality and Social Psychology*, 1977, *35*, 530–536.

Sheffield, F. D. A drive induction theory of reinforcement. In R. N. Haber (Ed.), *Current research in motivation*. New York: Holt, 1966.

Sheffield, F. D., & Roby, T. B. Reward value of a non-nutritive sweet taste. *Journal of Comparative and Physiological Psychology*, 1950, *43*, 471–481.

Sherif, M. A study of some factors in perception. *Archives of Psychology*, 1935, (187).

Shettleworth, S. J. Reinforcement and the organization of behavior in Golden Hamsters: Punishment of three action patterns. *Learning and Motivation*, 1978, *9*, 99–123.

Shipley, T. E., & Veroff, J. A. A projective measure of need for affiliation. *Journal of Experimental Psychology*, 1952, *43*, 349–356.

Smith, G. F., & Dorfman, D. D. The effect of stimulus uncertainty on the relationship between frequency of exposure and liking. *Journal of Personality and Social Psychology*, 1975, *31*, 150–155.

Smith, G. P., & Gibbs, J. Cholecystokinin and satiety: Theoretic and therapeutic implications. In D. Novin, W. Wyrwicka, and G. Bray (Eds.), *Hunger: Basic mechanisms and clinical implications*. Raven: New York, 1976.

Snyder, A., Mischel, W., & Lott, B. Value, information, and conformity behavior. *Journal of Personality*, 1960, *28*, 333–342.

Solomon, R. L., & Corbit, J. D. An opponent-process theory of motivation: I. Temporal dynamics of affect. *Psychological Review*, 1974, *81*, 119–145.

Solomon, R. L., & Wynne, L. C. Traumatic avoidance learning: The principles of anxiety conservation and partial irreversibility. *Psychological Review*, 1954, *62*, 353–385.

Spelt, D. K. The conditioning of the human fetus *in utero*. *Journal of Experimental Psychology*, 1948, *38*, 338–346.

Spence, K. W. *Behavior theory and conditioning*. New Haven: Yale University Press, 1956.

Spielberger, C. D., & Ying, L. Stress: An overview of theory and research. *Psi Chi Newsletter*, 1982, *8*, 1–5.

Storms, M. D. Videotape and the attribution process: Reversing actors' and observers' points of view. *Journal of Personality and Social Psychology*, 1973, *27*, 165–175.

Storms, M. D., & Nisbett, R. E. Insomnia and the attribution process. *Journal of Personality and Social Psychology*, 1970, *16*, 319–328.

Strassman, H. D., Thaler, M. B., & Schein, E. H. A prisoner of war syndrome: Apathy as a reaction to severe stress. *American Journal of Psychiatry*, 1956, *112*, 998–1003.

Straus, E., & Yalow, R. S. Cholecystokinin in the brains of obese and non-obese mice. *Science*, 1979, *203*, 68–69.

Stricker, E. M. Drinking by rats after lateral hypothalamic lesions: A new look at the lateral hypothalamic syndrome. *Journal of Comparative and Physiological Psychology*, 1976, *90*, 127–143.

Stricker, E. M., Brodshaw, W. G., & McDonald, R. N. The reninoangiotensin system and thirst: A reevaluation. *Science*, *1976*, *194*, 1169–1171.

Stricker, E. M., Friedman, M. I., & Zigmond, M. J. Glucoregulatory feeding by rats after intraventricular 6-hydroxydopamine or lateral hypothalamic lesions. *Science*, 1975, *189*, 895–897.

Stricker, E. M., & Zigmond, M. J. Brain catecholamines and the lateral hypothalamic syndrome. In D. Novin, W. Wyrwicka, and G. Bray (Eds.), *Hunger: Basic mechanisms and clinical implications*. New York: Raven, 1976.

Strongman, K. T. *The psychology of emotion*. New York: Wiley, 1973.

Taylor, S. E., & Fiske, S. T. Point of view and perception of causality. *Journal of Personality and Social Psychology*, 1975, *32*, 439–445.

Teitelbaum, P. Disturbances in feeding and drinking behavior after hypothalamic lesions. In M. R. Jones (Ed.), *Nebraska symposium on motivation* (Vol. 9). Lincoln: University of Nebraska Press, 1961.

Templer, D. I. Anorexic humans and rats. *American Psychologist*, 1971, *26*, 935.

Thibaut, J. W., & Riecken, H. W. Some determinants and consequences of the perception of social causality. *Journal of Personality*, 1955, *24*, 113–133.

Thompson, R., & McConnell, J. Classical conditioning in the planaria, *Dugesia dorotocephala*. *Journal of Comparative and Physiological Psychology*, 1955, *48*, 65–68.

Tinbergen, N. *The study of instinct*. New York: Oxford University Press, 1951.

Tolman, E. C. *Purposive behavior in animals and men*. New York: Appleton-Century, 1932.

Tresemer, D. Fear of success: Popular but uproven. *Psychology Today*, March 1974, pp. 82–85.

Vanderwecle, D. A., & Sanderson, J. D. Peripheral glucosensitive satiety in the rabbit and the rat. In D. Novin. W. Wyricka, & G. Bray (Eds.), *Hunger: Basic mechanisms and clinical implications*. New York: Raven, 1976.

Vogel, G. W. Sleep-onset mentation. In A. M. Arkin, J. S. Antrobus, & S. J. Ellman (Eds.), *The mind in sleep: Psychology and psychophysiology*. Hillsdale, N. J.: Erlbaum, 1978.

Walker, E. L. *Psychological complexity and preference: A hedgehog theory of behavior*. Monterey, Calif.: Brooks/Cole, 1980.

Wallace, R. K., & Benson, H. The physiology of meditation. *Scientific American*, Feb. 1972, 84–90.

Walters, J., Apter, M. J., & Svebak, S. Color preference, arousal, and the theory of psychological reversals. *Motivation and Emotion*, 1982, *6*, 193–215.

Wangensteen, O. H., & Carlson, A. J. Hunger sensation after total gastrectomy. *Proceedings of the Society for Experimental Biology*, 1931, *28*, 545–547.

Watson, J. B., & Raynor, R. Conditioned emotional reactions. *Journal of Experimental Psychology*, 1920, *3*, 1–14.

Webb, W. B. Sleep behavior as a biorhythm. In P. Coloquohon (Ed.), *Biological rhythms and human performance*. New York: Academic Press, 1971.

Webb, W. B., & Agnew, H. W. Analysis of the sleep stages in sleep–wakefulness regimens of varied length. *Psychophysiology*, 1977, *14*, 445–450.

Weiner, B. *Achievement motivation and attribution theory*. Morristown, N. J.: General Learning Press, 1974.

Weiner, B. *Human motivation*. New York: Holt, 1980.

Weisfeld, G. E., & Beresford, J. M. Erectness of posture as an indicator of dominance or success in humans. *Motivation and Emotion*, 1982, *6*, 113–131

Wells, G. L., & Harvey, J. H. Do people use consensus information in making causal attributions? *Journal of Personality and Social Psychology*, 1977, *35*, 279–293.

Wenger, M. A., Bagchi, B. K., & Anand, B. K. Experiments in India on "voluntary" control of the heart and pulse. *Circulation*, 1969, *24*, 1319–1325.

White, R. W. Motivation reconsidered: The concept of competence. *Psychological Review*, 1959, *66*, 297–333.

Wilder, J. Sugar metabolism in its relation to criminology. In S. Linduer, & B. J. Seliger (Eds.), *Handbook of correctional psychology*. New York: Philosophical Library, 1947.

Williams, C. D. The elimination of tantrum behavior by extinction procedures. *Journal of Abnormal and Social Psychology*, 1959, *59*, 269.

Williams, H. L., Holloway, F. A., & Griffiths, W. J. Physiological psychology: Sleep. In P. H. Mursen, & M. R. Rosenzweig (Eds.), *Annual Review of Psychology*, 1973, *24*, 279–307.

Williams, J. L. Effects of the duration of a secondary reinforcer on subsequent instrumental responses. *Journal of Experimental Psychology*, 1970, *83*, 348–351.

Williams, J. L. *Operant learning: Procedures for changing behavior*. Monterey, Calif.: Brooks/Cole, 1973.

Willis, M. H., & Blaney, P. H. Three tests of the learned helplessness model of depression. *Journal of Abnormal Psychology*, 1978, *87*, 131–136.

Wilson, E. O. *Sociobiology, the new synthesis*. Cambridge, Mass.: Harvard University Press, 1975.

Wilson, G. T. Behavioral treatment of obesity: Maintenance strategies and long-term efficacy. In P. Sjödén, S. Bates, & W. S. Dockens (Eds.), *Trends in behavior therapy*. New York: Academic Press, 1979.

Wilson, G. T., Leaf, R. C., & Nathan, P. E. The aversive control of excessive alcohol consumption by chronic alcoholics in the laboratory setting. *Journal of Applied Behavior Analysis*, 1975, *8*, 13–16.

Winett, R. A., Neale, M. S., & Grier, H. C. Effects of self-monitoring and feedback on residential electricity consumption. *Journal of Applied Behavior Analysis*, 1979, *12*, 173–184.

Wirtshafer, D., & Davis, J. D. Body weight: Reduction by long-term glycerol treatment. *Science*, 1977, *198*, 1271–1274.

Wolpe, J. *The practice of behavior therapy*. Elmsford, N.Y.: Pergamon, 1973.

Worchel, P. The effect of three types of arbitrary thwarting on the instigation to aggression. *Journal of Personality*, 1974, *42*, 301–318.

Wynne, L. C., & Soloman, R. L. Traumatic avoidance learning: Acquisition and extinction in dogs deprived of normal peripheral autonomic functioning. *Genetic Psychological Monographs*, 1955, *52*, 241–284.

Wyrwicka, W. The problem of motivation in feeding behavior. In D. Novin, W. Wyrwicka, & G. Bray (Eds.), *Hunger: Basic mechanisms and clinical implications*. New York: Raven, 1976.

Yerkes, R. M., & Dodson, J. D. The relation of strength of stimulus to rapidity of habit formation. *Journal of Comparative Neurology and Psychology*, 1908, *18*, 459–482.

Young, P. T. Hedonic organization and regulation of behavior. *Psychological Review*, 1966, *73*, 59–86.

Young, P. T. *Emotion in man and animal*. Huntington, N.Y.: Krieger, 1973.

Zajonc, R. B. Attitudinal effects of mere exposure. *Journal of Personality and Social Psychology*, 1968, Monograph Supplement, 1–29.

Zajonc, R. B. *Animal social behavior*. Morristown, N. J.: General Learning Press, 1972.

Zastrow, C. How to become more assertive. In C. Zastrow, & D. H. Chang (Eds.), *The personal problem solver*. Englewood Cliffs, N. J.: Prentice-Hall, 1977.

Zimbardo, P. G. The human choice: Individuation, reason and order versus deindividuation, impulse and chaos. In N. J. Arnold, & D. Levine (Eds.), *Nebraska Symposium on Motivation*. Lincoln: University of Nebraska Press, 1969.

Zubek, J. P. (Ed.), *Sensory deprivation*. New York: Appleton–Century–Crofts, 1969.

Name Index

Abramson, L. Y., 176, 275
Adams, D. B., 76
Adelman, H. F., 268
Agnew, H. W., 105
Alcock, J., 30
Allen, V. L., 291
Altman, I., 312
Anand, B. K., 54, 172
Anderson, B., 72
Anderson, D. C., 178
Anisman, H., 277
Anrep, G. V., 133
Appley, M. H., 21, 207
Apter, M. J., 90, 211
Ardrey, R., 46
Arkes, H. R., 269
Aronson, E., 231, 232, 309
Asch, Solomon, 286–287, 292
Aserinsky, E., 96
Atkinson, J. W., 23, 240–247, 303
Ayres, C. E., 22
Azrin, N., 160

Baer, P. E., 162
Bagchi, B. K., 172
Bandura, Albert, 14, 332–338
Barash, D. P., 47
Bard, P. A. A., 278, 330
Barelace, B., 60
Barker, R. G., 337

Barrett, J. E., 36
Beach, F. A., 22
Beattie, M. S., 329
Beck, R. C., 338
Bee, H., 187, 336
Bem, D. J., 235
Bemis, K. M., 68
Benson, H., 117, 172
Beresford, J. M., 44
Bergman, T., 44
Berkowitz, L., 292
Berlyne, D. E., 86, 152, 153, 211
Bernstein, A. G., 241
Bernston, G. G., 329
Berscheid, E., 309, 310, 311
Bertini, M., 101
Besalel-Azrin, V., 160
Bexton, W. H., 85, 86, 208
Bickman, L., 292
Birch, D., 247
Black, A. H., 178
Blake, R. R., 293
Blaney, P. H., 274
Blass, E. M., 73
Bolles, R. C., 30, 180, 201, 202
Bowlby, J., 45
Boyatzis, R. E., 303
Boyle, P. C., 56
Bracewell, R. J., 178
Bracker, B. S., 171

Brackner, J., 44
Braun, W. M., 326
Brehm, J. W., 230, 301
Breland, K., 179
Breland, M., 179
Brett, L. P., 61
Brittain, R. P., 326
Broadhurst, P. L., 85
Brodshaw, W. G., 73
Brokbeck, J. R., 54
Brotzman, E., 296
Broughton, R., 101
Brown, J. S., 203, 204, 205
Brown, R., 13
Brown, W. A., 9
Bruch, H., 68, 69
Bryant, J., 89
Buchanan, R. W., 340
Burish, T. G., 115
Burt, A. D., 76
Butler, R. A., 87, 207

Cabitt, J., 44
Calhoun, J. B., 340
Cannon, W. B., 53, 278
Cantor, J. R., 89
Caputo, C., 266
Carlsmith, J. M., 15, 226, 231–235, 270, 289, 298, 312, 336, 338, 340
Carlson, A. J., 53
Caul, W. F., 41
Chang, D. H., 168
Chapman, C., 168
Cialdini, R. B., 300
Clark, R. A., 240
Cofer, C. N., 21, 207
Coleman, J. F., 293
Collins, B. E., 233
Condry, J., 248
Cooper, J., 234
Corbit, J. D., 121
Costello, C. G., 274
Cotman, C. W., 56, 60, 70, 72
Court, A., 326
Crespi, L. P., 199
Crockett, W. H., 225
Crowell, C. R., 178
Cuniberti, B., 78
Cunningham, C. L., 178

Dalrymple, S., 296
Dapcich-Miuri, E., 158–159
Darwin, Charles, 22
Davis, J. D., 57
Davitz, J. P. A., 272
De Paulo, P., 32, 35, 37
Deci, E. L., 269
Deese, J., 135, 201
Dember, W. N., 153, 211

Dembo, T., 337
Dement, W. C., 97, 100, 106
Dickinson, A., 140
Dion, K., 310, 311
Doane, B. K., 85
Dodson, J. D., 84
Dollard, J., 305, 337
Donahoe, J. W., 129
Donnerstein, E., 339
Doob, L., 337
Dorfman, D. D., 212
Douglas, D., 277
Duffy, E., 85
Dyer, S., 248

Earl, R. W., 153, 211
Egeth, H., 135, 201
Eibl-Eibesfeldt, I., 41, 43
Ekman, P., 42
Epstein, A. N., 73
Epstein, W., 203
Erdmann, G., 90
Ervin, F., 61

Fantino, E., 32
Farber, I. E., 203
Felce, D., 159
Feldman, N. S., 263
Feldman, R. S., 241
Fencil-Morse, E., 275
Feshbach, S., 293, 321
Festinger, Leon, 226, 232, 234, 235, 306, 341
Fiske, D. W., 153, 260
Fitzsimmons, J. T., 73
Folger, R., 268
Franken, R. E., 16, 87, 342
Fraser, S. C., 299
Freedman, J. L., 15, 112, 226, 289, 298, 299, 312, 336, 338, 340
Freud, Sigmund, 37, 102–104, 184–192, 336–337
Friedman, M. I., 56, 114, 270
Friesen, W. V., 42

Gaioni, S. J., 32, 35, 37
Garcia, John, 61, 62, 64
Gardner, L. I., 209
Garfinkel, P. E., 70
Gastaut, H., 101
Gatchel, R. J., 171
Geen, R. G., 332
Geiselman, P. J., 59
Gibbs, J., 58, 59
Gino, A., 144
Ginsberg, A., 31
Glass, D. C., 114
Glickman, S. E., 153
Gold, A. R., 76
Goldiamond, I., 163

Goldwater, B. C., 135
Goridis, C., 94
Gotay, C. C., 42
Gould, J. L., 39
Graves, N., 296
Green, E., 172
Greene, D., 269
Grier, H. C., 160
Griffiths, W. J., 98
Griffitt, W., 310
Grossman, L., 56
Grossman, M. I., 53
Grossman, S. P., 56, 330
Gustavson, C. R., 64

Haith, M. M., 44
Hall, J. F., 135
Halpern, M., 143
Hankins, W. G., 62, 64
Harlow, H. F., 77, 87, 207, 313
Harlow, M. K., 87, 207
Harris, V. A., 259, 265
Hartmann, E. L., 101
Harvey, J. H., 262
Hatch, J. P., 171
Hauri, P., 104, 106
Hawkes, C. D., 60
Heider, F., 222, 255–256, 258, 262
Hellenthal, L., 150
Helmreich, R. L., 233
Heron, W., 85, 86, 208
Hess, E. H., 32, 33–34, 36, 37
Hess, W. R., 55
Hetherington, A. W., 54
Heyns, R. W., 303
Higgins, E. T., 236,. 263
Hineline, P. N., 203
Hiroto, D. S., 173, 274
Hoffman, H. S., 32, 35, 36, 37
Hofling, C. K., 296
Holloway, F. A., 98
Holmes, Thomas, 109, 111
Holt, L. E., 60
Homans, G. C., 298
Hontos, P. T., 160
Horner, M. S., 247–248
Houston, J. P., 12, 135, 172, 178, 187, 221, 336
Hovell, M. F., 159
Hughes, H. C., 329
Hull, Clark, 151, 192–203
Hulse, S. H., 135, 201
Hunt, E. L., 135

Issacson, R., 303

Jacobs, P. A., 326
James, William, 22, 23t, 222, 227–278
Janke, W., 90

Jenkins, J., 159
Johnson, V. E., 78
Jones, E. E., 234, 259, 265, 266, 267, 311
Jouvet, M., 98

Karabenick, S. A., 248
Karlovac, M., 263
Kazdin, A. E., 164
Keesey, R. E., 56–57
Kelley, Harold, 261–265
Kemnitz, J. W., 56
Kiess, H. O., 330
Kihlstrom, J. F., 137
Kimble, Gregory, 129–132
Kinsey, A. C., 78
Kish, G. B., 87, 207
Klein, D., 275
Klein, K., 116
Klein, R. D., 158
Kleitman, N., 96
Kline, S. A., 70
Knight, M. F., 160
Koelling, R., 61, 64
Kolb, D., 241
Konorski, J., 178
Kovach, J. K., 36
Krieckhaus, E. E., 60
Kubal, L., 175
Kubie, J. L., 143
Kuleck, W. J., 229
Kulik, J. A., 13
Kuo, Z. Y., 23

Lacy, J. I., 93
Lagerspetz, K., 9
Lamoreaux, R. R., 144, 203
Lange, James, 277–278
Lawler, E. E., 229
Leaf, R. C., 162
Lefrancois, G. R., 189t
Legant, P., 266
Lens, W., 241
Lepper, M. R., 269
Levin, J. M., 291
Levine, S., 113
Levis, D. J., 203
Levy, A. S., 340
Lewin, K., 222
Lewis, K., 337
Lin, Y., 303
Linder, D. E., 234, 309
Lindsley, D. B., 91
Litwin, G. A., 246
Logan, C. A., 32
LoLordo, V. M., 177
Lorenz, Konrad, 24, 27, 31, 32, 152, 319–321, 326–328, 337
Lott, B., 293
Lowell, E. L., 240, 241

Lundberg, U., 112
Lunt, B., 159
Lupo, J. V., 178

McArthur, L. A., 262
McClelland, D. C., 115, 240, 241, 247, 248, 249
McConnell, J., 135
McDonald, R. N., 73
McDougall, William, 22
McGaugh, J. L., 56, 60, 70, 72
Mack, G., 94
McKeachie, W. J., 303
McKenzie, H. S., 160
Mackintosh, N. J., 140
McLearn, G. E., 326
Maddi, S. R., 153
Magoun, H., 91, 92
Mahoney, M. J., 164
Maier, S. F., 173
Maisto, S. A., 115
Maltzman, I., 135
Mandel, P., 94
Mandler, G., 244
Mantrell, D. M., 297
Marcucella, H., 150
Marecek, J., 266
Marshall, G. D., 90
Marshall, J. M., 248
Martin, P. L., 158
Maslach, C., 90
Maslow, Abraham, 51, 214–216
Masters, J. C., 162
Masters, W. H., 78
Masuda, M., 109
Matthews, K. A., 114
Mayer, J., 55
Meichenbaum, D., 164
Meyer, D. R., 87, 207
Milgram, Stanley, 292, 294–296, 297
Milholland, J., 303
Miller, N. E., 169–171, 203, 204, 305, 337
Miller, R. E., 41
Miller, R. S., 291
Mineka, S., 137, 144
Minor, T., 177
Mirsky, I. A., 41
Mischel, W., 241, 293
Mitchell, J. S., 56
Moltz, H., 38
Money, J., 209
Moore, M. J., 44
Moran, P., 44
Morgan, C. T., 53
Morgan, J. T., 53
Morosko, T. E., 162
Morris, W. N., 291
Moruzzi, G., 91, 92
Mouton, J. S., 293
Mowrer, O. H., 144, 203, 337

Moyer, K. E., 9, 322, 330
Murray, H. A., 239–240

Nathan, P. E., 162
Neale, M. S., 160
Newby, V., 36
Newcomb, T. M., 222, 225, 307, 341
Nisbett, R. E., 67, 68, 266, 267, 269, 280
Nogami, G. Y., 340
Novin, D., 56, 58, 73

Olson, J. M., 236
O'Malley, P. M., 241
Oomura, Y., 55
Orne, M. T., 85
Owens, D. R., 326

Pavlov, Ivan, 133–134, 136, 137, 139
Peck, J. W., 73
Pepitone, A., 341
Peplau, L. A., 248
Pfaffman, C., 153
Pierce, C. M., 296
Pigg, R., 332
Plutchik, R. A., 90, 272
Powell, L., 159
Powley, T. L., 56, 57
Premack, D., 153–154
Pressman, B., 44
Price, J., 340
Price, W. H., 326

Rahe, R. H., 109
Rajecki, D. W., 32
Ranson, S. W., 54
Ratner, A. M., 32, 36, 39
Raymond, M. J., 160
Raynor, J. O., 241
Raynor, R., 137, 138
Razran, G., 140
Rescorla, R. A., 141
Rhode, J. S., 229
Rhodewalt, F., 236
Richter, C. P., 60
Riecken, H. W., 265
Rimm, D. C., 162, 187, 336
Riskind, J. H., 42
Risley, T. R., 168
Robbins, Thomas, 305, 316
Roberts, W. W., 330
Roby, T. B., 197
Rodin, J., 68
Rolls, B. J., 73
Rosenfield, D., 268
Rosenman, R. H., 114
Rosenzweig, M. R., 53
Ross, D., 14
Ross, L., 259
Ross, S., 14
Roth, S., 175

Subject Index

reinforcement and, 153–154
sensation-seeking behavior and, 209, 211–212
sexual, 76
sleep and, 94–95
states of, 83
stress and, 107
two curves of, 90–93
Assertion training, 164–165
procedures, 166t–168t
Attack behavior, 25–28, 30
Attraction, determinants of, 307–311
Attribution theory, 253–281
achievement motivation and, 256–258
actors vs. observers, 266–268
emotion and, 270–281
fundamental attribution error, 258–260
Heider's naive psychology, 255–256
intrinsic vs. extrinsic motivation, 268–270
invariance, 258
Kelley's theory, 261–265
nature of, 253–255
stimulus prominence, 260–261
Audience effect, 284–285
Augmentation principle, 264
Autokinetic effect, 288
Autonomic nervous system, arousal and, 93–94
Aversion training, 65, 162–163
Aversions, taste, 60–65
Avoidance-avoidance conflict, 204, 206
Avoidance conditioning, 143–144, 176, 203
species-specific defense reactions (SSDR) and, 180

Balance theory, 222–225
nature of, 222–224
problems with, 225
similarity to cognitive dissonance theory, 226
Barbiturates, insomnia and, 105–106
Behavior modification, 157–168
assertion training, 164–168
aversion training, 162–163
cognitive, 164–168
definition, 157–158
obedience and, 298
overjustification and, 270
problem of generalization, 165, 168
reinforcers and behaviors, 159–160
relation to clinical approaches, 158
systematic desensitization, 160–162
token economies, 158–159
Behavior System, A (Hull), 193
Behavior therapy, 157
See also Behavior modification
Behaviorism, 12
Behaviorists, 193
Beta waves, 92

Biofeedback, 169–172
applications, 171–172
Miller's work, 169–170
physical and mental mediation, 171
Biological approach to motivation, 8–10, 21–49, 51–81, 83–125
aggression, 325–331
arousal, 83–94
basic physiological needs, 51–52
drug addiction, 118–123
ethology, 24–32
hunger and eating, 53–70
imprinting, 32–40
innate human behavior, 40–48
instincts, 21–24
regulation, 52–53
sexual motivation, 74–79
sleep, 94–107
stress, 107–118
thirst, 70–74
Biological constraints to learning, 178–180
Body weight, long-term control of, 56–57
Brain
arousal and, 91–93
hunger and, 54–59
sleep and, 95, 98
thirst control and, 72, 73

Catecholamines, 94
Catharsis, aggression and, 336–339
Childrearing practices, achievement motivation and, 248–249
Choice, cognitive dissonance and, 234–235
Cholecystokinin (CCK), 58–59
Cingulate gyrus, 330
Classical conditioning, 133–141, 169, 170
elements, 134–135
examples, 135
extinction, 146
information and, 140–141
motivation and, 135–140
Pavlov's experiments, 133–134
reinforcement, 148–149
See also Conditioning; Reinforcement
Coaction effect, 284–285
Cognition
depression and, 176
emotion and, 278–280
stress and, 116
Cognitive approach to motivation, 12–13, 221–251, 253–282
aggression, 338–341
arousal and, 88–90
attribution theory, 253–281
cognitive consistency theory, 222–237
expectancy-value theory, 238–249
Cognitive behavior modification (CBM), 164–168

Electroencephalograph (EEG), 92, 93
  patterns during sleep, 92–93, 95–97
Emotions, 7
  arousal and, 85–88
  classical conditioning and, 137
  classifying, 272
  definitions, 270–271
  facial expression and, 42–43
  interaction between cognitive appraisal
    and arousal and, 88–90
  James-Lange theory, 277–278
  learned helplessness and, 75, 274–277
  limbic system and, 330
  misattribution of, 280–281
  Schacter's theory, 279–280
  thought vs., 272–273
  three perspectives on, 271–272
Endocrine system, stress and, 107
Epilepsy, sleep disorders and, 106
Epinephrine, 89, 94
Escape training, 145
Essentials of Behavior (Hull), 193
Estrogen, 75
Estrus, 76
Ethology, 24–32
  concepts, 25–27
  criticisms, 30–31
  defined, 24
  hierarchical model (Tinbergen), 29–30
  hydraulic model (Lorenz), 27–28
Evolution, 22
Exhaustion stage, 108–109
Expectancy-value theory, 238–249
  achievement motivation, 238–242
  Atkinson's theory, 242–247
  general approach, 238
Expectations, 13
  stress and, 116
Experience
  learning and (Hull's theory), 197–198
  stress and, 113–114
  See also Learned behavior
Experimental neurosis, 136–137
Extero-interoceptive conditioning, 140
Extinction, 145–147
  aggression, 331, 332
  in systematic desensitization, 160, 162
Extracellular fluid, 71, 72
Extrinsic motivation, 268–270
Eye fixation, 44–45

Facial expressions, 41–43
Failure, fear of, 242, 244–246
Familiarity, liking and, 308
Fantasy, 189t
Fat cells, 57
Fear
  acquired: two-factor theory, 144

affiliation and, 305–306
aggression and, 322
classical conditioning and, 137–138
conditioned, 203
Female sexuality, 75, 76, 78–79
Fixation, 190–191
Fixed action pattern, 26, 28
Fixed interval reinforcement schedule,
    150–151
Fixed ratio reinforcement schedule, 150
Foot-in-the-door method, 299–300
Forced compliance, 231–233
Fractional anticipatory goal, 200
Freudian dream theory, 102–104
Frustration-aggression hypothesis, 337
Fundamental attribution error, 258–260, 266

General adaptation syndrome (GAS),
    108–109
Generalization in conditioning, 147
  problem with, 165, 168
Genetics, 9
  aggression and, 325–329
  personality type and, 115
  stress and, 113
  See also Innate behavior; Instincts
Genital period, 190
Glucoreceptors, 55–58
Glucose, 108
  hunger control and, 55–59
Glucostatic theory, 55–56, 57, 59
Glycerol, 57
Gonadal hormones, 75

Habit (H), 197–198
Habits, aversion training and, 162–163
Halo effect, 311
Hawthorne effect, 298–299
Heart attacks, personality types and,
    114–115
Helplessness. See Learned helplessness
Hepatic portal vein, 58
Hierarchical model of instinctive behavior,
    29–30
Hierarchies of anxieties, 160, 161t–162t
Hippocampus, 330
Hormones, 9
  animal sexuality and, 76
  sexual motivation and, 75, 76
  stress and, 107
Hostile aggression, 321
Hunger and eating, 53–70
  anorexia nervosa, 68–70
  CCK, 58–59
  differences from sexual motivation, 74–75
  dual hypothalamic control, 53–55
  glucostatic control, 55–56
  lipostatic control, 56–57

objections and reformulation, 176
relationship to depression, 175–176, 177*t*
revised theory, 274–277
Learning
  defined, 129–132
  imprinting and, 32, 34–39
  vs. motivation, Hull's theory, 199–200
Learning approach to motivation, 10–12,
    129–155, 157–218
  aggression, 331–338
  behavior modification, 157–168
  biofeedback, 169–172
  biological constraints, 178–180
  classical conditioning, 133–141
  drives and incentives, 183–206
  instrumental conditioning, 141–145
  learned helplessness, 173–178
  learning perspective, 129–133
  principles of conditioning, 145–154
  sensation-seeking behavior, 206–216
Levels of analysis, 8
  vs. topics, 16
LH, anorexia nervosa and, 68
Life changes, stress and, 109–111
Liking, 307–311
  determinants of attraction, 307–311
  relation to affiliation, 307
Limbic system
  aggression and, 330
  arousal and, 93
  sleep and, 98
Lipostatic theory, 56–57
Liver, hunger control and, 58, 59
Locus coerulus nuclei, 98
Loving, 307, 311–313
  forms of, 313
  nature of, 311–312
  self-disclosure, 313
  social penetration, 312–313
Low-balling, 300

Male sexuality, 75, 79
Masochism, 139–140
Matching principle, 310–311
Mediation, 171
Medicine preference effect, 60, 61*f*
Meditation, 116–117, 172
Methamphetamine, 88
Misattribution, 280–281
Mobbing, 319–430
Modeling, 14–15, 285–286
  aggression and, 335–336
  behaviors acquired through, 333–334
  conditions for, 334–335
Motivation
  biological approach, 8–10, 21–49, 51–81,
    83–125
  characteristics, 5–7

cognitive approach, 12–13, 221–251,
    253–282
defining, 5
eclectic approach, 15, 317–343
learning approach, 10–12, 129–155,
    157–218
levels of analysis in research, 8
social approach, 14–15, 283–315
topics vs. levels of analysis, 16
See also Biological approach to motivation;
    Cognitive approach to motivation;
    Eclectic approach to motivation;
    Learning approach to motivation;
    Social approach to motivation
Myoclonus, 106

Narcolepsy, 104–105
Natural selection theory, 22, 47
  affiliation and, 303–304
  aggression and, 326, 328
Net approach tendency, 245, 246
Neural factors, 9
Neurosis, 187
  experimental, 136–137
  sleep and, 106
Nonrestorative sleep, 106
Nonverbal communication, 40–44
  facial expressions, 41–43
  other, 43–44
Norepinephrine, 94, 114
  aggression and, 331
NREM (nonrapid eye movement) sleep, 96,
    98, 101

Obedience, 293–301
  behavior modification and, 298
  conformity and, 289
  foot-in-the-door method, 299–300
  getting off easy, 300
  Hawthorne effect, 298–299
  low-balling, 300
  Milgram's experiments, 294–296
  personal responsibility and, 296–298
  reactance, 301
Obesity, 65–68
  biological bases, 68
  CCK and, 59
  differences in eating habits and, 65–67
  hyperphagia, 54, 55
Observational learning, 285
Oedipus complex, 191
Opponent-process theory, 121–123
Optimal-arousal-level theories, 152–153,
    211–213
Oral stage, 190
Orgasm, 78, 79
Osmoreceptors, 72, 73
Osmotic thirst, 71–72, 74

Ovaries, 75, 76
Overjustification effect, 268–270
    behavior modification and, 270
    discounting and, 269–270

Pavlovian conditioning, 134
    See also Classical conditioning
Peak experience, 216
Perceptual distortion, 287
Performance
    arousal and, 83–85
    attribution and, 275–277, 276
    coaction-audience effects and, 284–285
    Hawthorne effect, 298–299
    relation between learning, motivation, and, 133
Persistence of behavior, 6–7
Personal space, 46–47
Phallic stage, 190
Phobias, 132
    interpretations of, 138–139
    systematic desensitization, 139, 160–162
Physical attractiveness, 310–311
Physiological needs, 51–52
    See also Hunger and eating; Sexual motivation; Thirst Pituitary gland, 209
    gonadal hormones and, 75
    stress and, 107
Pleasure principle, 186
Postures, as nonverbal communication, 43–44
Power, need for, 115
Practice, learning and, 130, 131
Predation, 322
Predatory aggression, 319
Preferences in taste, learned and innate, 60
Preparedness for learning, 178–179
Principles of Behavior (Hull), 193
Progesterone, 75
Projection, 189t
Projective tests, 239
Prosocial aggression, 322
Prospective studies, 111
Proximity, 307–308
Psychiatric problems, sleep and, 106
Psychoanalytic theory, 184–192
    criticisms, 191–192
    defense mechanisms, 188–189
    development of superego, 191
    fixation, 191–192
    Freudian instincts, 185
    id, ego, and superego, 185–187
    psychosexual stages, 190
Psychotics, sleep and, 106
Punishment, aggression and, 331, 332
Punishment training, 145, 163

Raphe nuclei, 98
Rationalization, 188, 189t
Reactance, 301
Reaction formation, 189t
Reaction-specific energy, 25, 27, 28
Reactive depression, 176, 274
Reactive inhibition, 202
Reality principle, 187
Reciprocity rule, 309–310
Regulation, 52–53
    voluntary and involuntary, 52–53
Regulatory mechanisms, 51–81
    basic physiological needs, 51–52
    hunger and eating, 53–70
    regulation, 52–53
    sexual motivation, 74–79
    thirst, 70–74
Reinforcement, 147–154, 212
    aggression and, 332, 333
    amount of, 149
    in classical conditioning, 148–149
    delay of, 149
    Hull's theory, 197–198
    learning and, 131, 132
    schedules of, 149–151
    secondary, 154
    theories of, 151–154
Rejection, fear of, conformity and, 290–291
Relaxation, 117
Reliability, 240
REM rebound, 101
REM (rapid eye movement) sleep, 95–101, 104, 106
Renin, 73
Repression, 189t, 102
Reproduction, Tinbergen's hierarchical conception of, 29–30
Resistance stage, 108
Respondent conditioning, 134
    See also Classical conditioning
Response theory of reinforcement, 153–154
Reticular activating system (RAS), 91–93
    sleep and, 98
Retrospective studies, 111
Reward training, 141–143
r_g, 200–201
r_g-s_g mechanism, 200–201
Rivalry, 320–321

Salt, innate preference for, 60
Scalloping pattern in fixed interval reinforcement schedules, 150, 151f
Schizophrenics, sleep and, 106
Secondary reinforcement, 154
Self-actualization theory, 214–216
Self-confidence, conformity and, 293
Self-disclosure, 313
Self-esteem, attribution and, 276

Self-perception theory, 235–236
Sensation-seeking behavior, 206–216
  anti-drive theory interpretation, 209–210
  drive theory interpretation, 207–209
  examples, 207
  Maslow's theory of self-actualization, 214–216
  optimal level theory, 211–213
  relation to incentive motivation, 210–211
  White's theory of competence, 213–214
Sensory deprivation, 86, 87, 208
Septum, 330
Set-point theory, 56–57
Sex hormones, aggression and, 331
Sex-related aggression, 323
Sex-role attitudes, women's achievement behavior and, 248
Sexual motivation, 74–79
  animals vs. humans, 76–77
  differences from hunger and thirst, 74–75
  dreams and, 102, 103
  female sexual response, 78–79
  Freudian view, 185, 190, 191, 192
  interacting neural and hormonal factors, 75
  male sexual response, 79
s_g, 201
Sign stimulus, 25–30
Similarity, liking and, 308–309
Skinner box, 141
Sleep, 94–107
  as active process, 94–95
  age and, 98–100
  disorders, 104–107
  EEG patterns during, 92–93, 95–97
  nightly patterns of dreaming and, 97–98
  purpose, 100–104
  REM (rapid eye movement), 95–97
Sleep apnea, 105
Sleepwalking, 95
Smiling, 41, 42
Social approach to motivation, 14–15, 283–315
  affiliation, 301–307
  aggression, 338–341
  coaction-audience effects, 284–285
  conformity, 286–293
  liking, 307–311
  loving, 311–313
  modeling, 285–286
  nature of, 283–284
  obedience, 293–301
Social behavior, genetic basis of, 47–48
Social comparison theory, affiliation and, 306–307
Social penetration, 312–313
Social Readjustment Rating Scale, 111
Society, achievement and, 248–249

Sociobiologists, 47
Soviet Union, interoceptive conditioning studies, 140
Species-specific defense reactions (SSDR), 180
Species-specificity of instinctive behavior, 21–22, 24
Specific hungers, 60
Stimulus intensity dynamism (V), 201
Stimulus prominence, 260–261
Stimulus properties, 201
Stimulus simplification, 212–213
Stimulus theories of reinforcement, 153
Stomach, hunger and, 53, 58
Stress, 107–118
  aggression and, 323
  alcohol and, 115
  arousal and, 107
  causes, 109
  coping with, 116–118, 157–172
  crowding and, 112–113
  disease and life changes and, 109–111
  endocrine system and, 107
  expectations and, 116
  experience and, 113–114
  general adaptation syndrome (GAS), 108–109
  genetics and, 113
  positive effects, 114
  sleep and, 101
  Type A, Type B, heart attacks and, 114–115
Stuttering, 163
Success
  fear of, 247–248
  hope of, 242–244
Sugar, innate preference for, 60
Superego, 187, 191
Supernormal stimuli, 26–27, 28
Symbols, in dreams, 103
Systematic desensitization, 139, 160–162

Taste, 60–65
  aversions, 60–65
  innate preference, 60
  learned preference, 60
Television, violence on, 14–15, 335–336
Territoriality, 320, 322, 327–328
  in humans, 46–47
Test Anxiety Questionnaire (TAQ), 244
Testes, 75
Testosterone, 9, 75
  aggression and, 331
Thematic Apperception Test (TAT), 239–240, 243, 303
Thirst, 70–74
  bodily distribution of water, 71
  differences from sexual motivation, 74–75
  dry mouth and, 73–74